CW01080655

The North through its Names

A Phenomenology of Medieval and Early-modern Northern England

Dave Postles

Marc Fitch Research Fellow,
University of Leicester

English Surnames Survey
Volume 8

Oxbow Books

Published by
Oxbow Books, Oxford, UK

© Oxbow Books and the author 2007

ISBN 978 1 84217 176 9

A CIP record for this book is available from The British Library

This book is available direct from
Oxbow Books, Oxford, UK
(Phone: 01865-241249; Fax: 01865-794449)

and

The David Brown Book Company
PO Box 511, Oakville, CT 06779, USA
(Phone: 860-945-9329; Fax: 860-945-9468)

or from our website

www.oxbowbooks.com

Printed in Great Britain by
CPI Antony Rowe, Chippenham

Blessed are your north parts, for all this long time
    My sun is with you, cold and dark is our clime;
Heaven's sun, which stayed so long from us this year,
    Stayed in your north (I think) for she was there,
And hither by kind nature drawn from thence,
    Here rages, chafes and threatens pestilence;
Yet I, as long as she from hence doth stay,
    Think this no south, no summer, nor no day.

[John Donne, 'To Mr I. L.'
A. J. Smith, ed., *John Donne. The Complete English Poems*
(Harmondsworth, 1996 edn), p. 203]

CONTENTS

ACKNOWLEDGEMENTS
AND COMMENT

With this volume the English Surnames Survey embarks upon both a new departure and a move to its dissolution. When the ESS was inaugurated in the middle of the 1960s, the objective was optimistically established of proceeding county by county towards a conglomerate picture of English surname patterns. By the late 1980s it became evident that that ambition could not be realized. It was determined then to move at some future stage to a higher level of organization – through a regional approach. In fact, it had long been realized that the county provided no more than an artificial administrative structure for research into surnames – it had been selected as a heuristic device because so much of the data had been collected at that level of administration, principally records of taxation (however exclusive those might be). Attempting a regional approach allows the data to define the zones, sub-regions, localities and boundaries in a less predetermined manner. Without the previous research into Lancashire and the West Riding of Yorkshire, however, the project would not have been as inviting. To a large degree, the selection of a 'northern' region was influenced by those prior elucidations of two large areas within a northern onomastic zone.[1] Although this consideration of the 'North' has been informed by this previous literature from the English Surnames Survey, to a large extent the discussion here starts *ab initio* for two reasons: to avoid too much repetition; and to allow a more cohesive and holistic account rather than commencing with the two regions explored and building from them.

Nor, however, would the 'North' have been so comprehensible without the creative interpretations of Charles Phythian-Adams.[2] An even wider intellectual debt is owed to him and is genuinely acknowledged here. An acknowledgement of similar magnitude belongs to Harold Fox who has been an invariably stimulating colleague. My obligations extend beyond the Centre for English Local History to those who have, through their friendship, sustained me over the years. From some of these friends much academic support has also been gratefully received: Professor Elaine Treharne, Professor Greg Walker, Dr Julie Coleman, and Dr Anne Marie Darcy have all responded to my questions about medieval literature and (socio)linguistics with sureness, warmth and encouragement. In particular, I have benefited immensely from the programme of activity arranged by the Centre for Medieval Research under the auspices of Professors Treharne and Walker and Dr Jo Story. Through those events my horizons have been considerably widened, to the benefit – I hope – of this present volume. I would, too, have been a poorer medievalist without the acquaintance of Paul Hyams and Steve White, but I do not hold them responsible for my remaining, considerable shortcomings, although in many ways have I tried to emulate them.

In the context of expanding my understanding of the medieval and early-modern contexts of naming, I have incurred another immense debt to Drs David Gentilcore, Ian Harris and Michael Davies, for their stimulating Early Modern Seminar series, enlivened by so many fabulous speakers. For the impact of ideas about social history, I am delighted to acknowledge the stimulus of Paul Griffiths and Andy Wood – if from afar. In that same context, I am much indebted to Professor Eric Dunning for conversations about social interactionism and interdependency index as well as other sociological notions.

My work for the Marc Fitch Fund would have collapsed many years ago had it not been for the motivation and encouragement of Roy Stephens, erstwhile Executive Secretary to the Fund who also gently directed me through the processes of book publication. My acknowledgement to him is sincere. When Richard Smith was closely involved with the work of the English Surnames Survey, he was not only supportive, but a researcher whom one could (vainly) aspire to imitate. That responsibility has been assumed in more recent years by Jenny Kermode.

For the maintenance of spiritual wellbeing, a large debt of gratitude is owed to Audrey, Catherine, Charlotte, Jackie, Jean, Odette, Peter, Rose and Sue in the SCR for their kindness. Audrey Larrivé continues to be a star.

This book is dedicated, nonetheless, emotionally to Suella, Fred and Mercury.

Dave Postles
July 2004

'Place, then, as a social site related to other positions and social localities and known as a locality in which experience, memory and feeling are constituted, is critical to understanding being-in-the-world. And Merleau-Ponty's phenomenology of the lived-body allows us to understand how place is experienced through the founding of sense by human communities.'

(Simon Charlesworth, *A Phenomenology of Working Class Experience* (Cambridge, 2000), p. 19. Thank you, Simon, for the understanding – and a lovely book).

Notes

1 G. Redmonds, *Yorkshire, West Riding* (English Surnames Survey 1, Chichester, 1973); R. A. McKinley, *The Surnames of Lancashire* (ESS 4, Oxford, 1981).

2 More particularly, but not exclusively, *Land of the Cumbrians: a Study in British Provincial Origins, A.D. 400–1120* (Aldershot, 1996).

Editorial Conventions

Before 1350 – simply and only as a rule of thumb – and in other cases where it is probable that the second qualifying name had not become hereditary (a surname) – bynames (*cognomina*) are given in italic. For the most part, the terms established by the English Surnames Survey have been used here; where the text deviates from that usage, it is to adopt some more precise terms propagated by continental researchers.[1] Dates are given in New Style.

Notes

1   M. Bourin, ed., *Genèse Médiévale de L'Anthroponymie Moderne: Études d'Anthroponymie Médiévale* (Tours, 1989) and subsequent volumes.

ABBREVIATIONS

Bedfordshire 1297	A. T. Gaydon, ed., *The Taxation of 1297: a Translation of the Local Rolls of Assessment for Barford, Biggleswade, and Flitt Hundreds, and for Bedford, Dunstable, Leighton Buzzard and Luton* (Bedfordshire Historical Record Society 39, 1959)
Bishop Hatfield's Survey	W. Greenwell, ed., *Bishop Hatfield's Survey: a Record of the Possessions of the See of Durham, Made by Order of Thomas de Hatfield, Bishop of Durham, with an Appendix of Original Documents and a Glossary* (Surtees Society 32, 1857)
BL	British Library, London
Bodl.	Bodleian Library, Oxford
Buckinghamshire	A. C. Chibnall, ed., *Early Taxation Returns: Taxation of Personal Property in 1332 and Later* (Buckinghamshire Record Society 14, 1966)
Cat. Ancient Deeds	*A Descriptive Catalogue of Ancient Deeds in the Public Record Office* (6 volumes, London, 1890–1915)
Cumberland	J. P. Steel, ed., *Cumberland Lay Subsidy ... 6th Edward III* (Kendal, 1912)
'Derbyshire'	J. C. Cox, 'Derbyshire in 1327: being a lay subsidy roll', *Journal of the Derbyshire Archaeological and Natural History Society* 30 (1908), pp. 23–96.
Devon	A. M. Erskine, ed., *The Devonshire Lay Subsidy of 1332* (Devon & Cornwall Record Society 14, 1969)
Dorset1332	A. D. Mills, ed., *The Dorset Lay Subsidy Roll of 1332* (Dorset Record Society 4, 1971)
'East Riding Poll Tax'	E. Lloyd, 'Poll Tax returns for the East Riding 4 Ric. II', *Yorkshire Archaeological Journal* 20 (1909), pp. 318–52
Essex	J. C. Ward, ed., *The Medieval Essex Community. The Lay Subsidy of 1327* (Chelmsford, 1983).
Farrer, *Early Yorkshire Charters*	W. Farrer, ed., *Early Yorkshire Charters* (3 volumes, Edinburgh, 1914–16)
Fenwick, *Poll Taxes* 1	C. C. Fenwick, *The Poll Taxes of 1377, 1379 and 1381. Part 1, Bedfordshire-Leicestershire* (British Academy Records of Social and Economic History new series 27, 1998)
Fenwick, *Poll Taxes* 2	C. C. Fenwick, ed., *The Poll Taxes of 1377, 1379 and 1381. Part 2: Lincolnshire-Westmorland* (British Academy Records of Social and Economic History new series 29, 2001)
Gloucestershire	P. Franklin, ed., *The Taxpayers of Medieval Gloucestershire: an*

	Analysis of the 1327 Lay Subsidy Roll with a New Edition of its Text (Stroud, 1993)
Halmota Prioratus Dunelmensis	W. H. D. Longstaffe & J. Booth, eds, *Halmota Prioratus Dunelmensis, Containing Extracts from the Halmote Court or Manor Rolls of the Prior and Convent of Durham, A.D. 1296–A.D. 1384* (Surtees Society 82, 1889)
Hertfordshire	J. Brooker & S. Flood, eds, *Hertfordshire Lay Subsidy Rolls 1307 and 1334* (Hertfordshire Record Society 14, 1998)
Hoghton Deeds	J. H. Lumby, ed., *A Calendar of the Deeds and Papers in the Possession of Sir James De Hoghton, Bart.* (LCRS 88, 1936)
Huntingdonshire (followed by a date of a subsidy)	J. A. Raftis & M. P. Hogan, eds, *Early Huntingdonshire Lay Subsidy Rolls* (Toronto, 1976)
Jönsjö, *Studies*	J. Jönsjö, *Studies on Middle English Nicknames. 1, Compounds* (Lund Studies in English 55, 1979)
'Kent'	H. A. Hanley & C. W. Chalklin, 'The Kent lay subsidy of 1334/5' in F. R. H. DuBoulay, ed., *Documents Illustrative of Medieval Kentish Society* (Kent Records 18, 1964)
'Lancashire'	J. P. Rylands, 'The Exchequer lay subsidy roll of Robert de Shireburn and John de Radcliffe, taxors and collectors in the county of Lancaster', *Miscellany Relating to Lancashire and Cheshire* volume ii (LCRS 31, 1896)
Lancashire Court Rolls	W. Farrer, ed., *Some Court Rolls of the Lordships, Wapentakes and Demesne Manors of Thomas, Earl of Lancaster, in the County of Lancaster, for the 17th and 18th Years of Edward II, A.D., 1323–24* (LCRS 41, 1899–1900)
Lancs. P. R. Soc	Lancashire Parish Registers Society
LCRS	Lancashire and Cheshire Record Society
'Leicestershire'	W. G. D. Fletcher, 'The earliest Leicestershire lay subsidy roll, 1327', *Associated Architectural Societies Reports* 19 (1888–9), pp. 130–78, 209–312
Norris Deeds	J. H. Lumby, ed., *A Calendar of the Norris Deeds (Lancashire), 12th to 15th Century* (LCRS 93, 1939)
Northumberland	C. M. Fraser, ed., *The Northumberland Lay Subsidy Roll of 1296* (Society of Antiquaries of Newcastle upon Tyne Record Series 1, 1968)
n.s.	new series
P. R. Soc.	Parish Register(s) Society
Pudsay Deeds	R. P. Littledale, ed., *The Pudsay Deeds: the Pudsays of Bolton and Barforth and their Predecessors in those Manors* (YASRS 56, 1916)
'Shropshire'	W. G. D. Fletcher, 'The Shropshire lay subsidy of 1 Edward III', *Shropshire Archaeological and Natural History Society* 1907
'Staffordshire 1332'	G. Wrottesley, 'The subsidy roll of 6 Edward III A.D. 1332–33', *Collections for a History of Staffordshire* William Salt Archaeological Society X (1889), pp. 79–132.
Suffolk	*Suffolk in 1327: Being a Subsidy Return* (Woodbridge, 1906)
Surrey	*Surrey Taxation Returns* (Surrey Record Society 33, 1933)
Sussex 1327	W. Hudson, ed., *The Three Earliest Lay Subsidies for the County of Sussex in the Years 1296, 1327, 1332* (Sussex Record Society 10, 1910)

T.N.A. (P.R.O.)	The National Archives (Public Record Office)
Wakefield Court Rolls I	W. P. Baildon, ed., *Court Rolls of the Manor of Wakefield* [volume 1] *1274–1297* (YASRS 29, 1901)
Wakefield Court Rolls II	W. P. Baildon, ed., *Court Rolls of the Manor of Wakefield. Vol.2, 1297–1309* (YASRS 36, 1906)
Wakefield Court Rolls IV	J. Lister, ed., *Court Rolls of the Manor of Wakefield. Vol.4, 1315 to 1317* (YASRS 78, 1930)
Wakefield Court Rolls V	J. W. Walker, ed., *Wakefield Court Rolls* volume V *1322–1331* (YASRS cix, 1945 for 1944)
Wakefield Court Rolls 1331–1333	S. S. Walker, ed., *Court Rolls of the Manor of Wakefield from October 1331 to September 1333* (Wakefield Court Rolls Series of the Yorkshire Archaeological Society III, 1983 for 1982)
Wakefield Court Rolls 1338–1340	K. Troup, *The Court Rolls of the Manor of Wakefield from October 1338 to September 1340* (Wakefield Court Rolls Series of the Yorkshire Archaeological Society xii, 1999)
Wakefield Court Rolls 1348–1350	H. M. Jewell, ed., *The Court Rolls of the Manor of Wakefield, from September 1348 to September 1350* (Wakefield Court Rolls Series of the Yorkshire Archaeological Society 2, 1981)
Warwickshire	W. F. Carter, ed., *The Lay Subsidy Roll for Warwickshire of 6 Edward III (1332)* (Dugdale Society Publications 6, 1926)
'West Riding Poll Tax'	'Rolls of the collectors in the West Riding of the Lay Subsidy (Poll Tax) 2 Richard II', *Yorkshire Archaeological Journal* 5–7 (1879–84), 5: pp. 1–51, 241–66, 417–32; 6: pp. 1–44, 129–71, 287–342; 7: pp. 6–31, 145–86.
Wiltshire	D. A. Crowley, ed., *The Wiltshire Tax List of 1332* (Wiltshire Record Society 45, 1989)
'Worcs.' (followed by a date of a subsidy)	J. W. Willis Bund & J. Amphlett, eds, *Lay Subsidy Roll for the County of Worcester, circ. 1280* (Worcester Historical Society, 1893) (bound in the same volume is the subsidy of 1332)
Yorkshire Assize Rolls	C. T. Clay, ed., *Three Yorkshire Assize Rolls for the Reigns of King John and King Henry III* (YASRS 44, 1911).
YASRS	Yorkshire Archaeological Society Record Series
Yorks. P. R. Soc.	Yorkshire Parish Registers Society
Yorkshire 1297	W. Brown, ed., *Yorkshire Lay Subsidy ... 25 Edward I (1297)* (YASRS 21, 1894)
Yorkshire 1301	W. Brown, ed., *Yorkshire Lay Subsidy ... 30 Edward I (1301)* (YASRS 21, 1897)

1

Introduction:
northen-ness and names

Of o toun were they born, that highte Strother,
Fer in the north; I kan nat telle where.[1]

Oure hors is lorn, Alayn, for Goddes banes,
Step on thy feet! Com of, man, al stanes![2]

In the middle of the fifteenth century, John Bouchere *alias* Northerenbouchour, a butcher, was indicted for homicide at Tewkesbury in Gloucestershire.[3] The import of his attributed *alias* probably involved a rhetorical depiction of not just an outsider, but of perceptible alien character. Implicit in his *alias* is a consciousness of difference. No indication, however, is given of what constituted the 'northernness' of Bouchere in the perception of those making the presentment in Tewkesbury. Their under-standing of this 'North' is not defined. Over two centuries earlier, one of the compurgators for a criminous clerk before the Bishop of Carlisle in his cathedral in 1309 was Adam Northman, who also acted again in this capacity in 1312.[4] Carlisle, of course, is almost as far north in England as it is possible to venture. Assuming that there is no other etymology, where in the north qualified Adam to be conceived in Carlisle as from the north?[5] Perhaps less ambiguously, the incumbent of Garstang in 1629 registered the baptism of Grace, daughter of 'a poore woman called commonlye by the name of Northerne Jane'.[6] Located in the northern reaches of Lancashire, Garstang would, in some perceptions, qualify as northern, but the inference from the incumbent's intervention is that the real north was further north. The conundrum of defining the 'North' has remained a perennial problem into the twenty-first century, compounded by relative perceptions of insiders and outsiders.[7]

The 'North' has remained, then, a mutable concept, informed by a multitude of variables – social, political, cultural, geographical and linguistic.[8] The last type of evidence is important, but discussion of linguistic variation was once predicated merely on the evidence of literary texts, with all their rhetorical vigour – William of Malmesbury, Higden and Trevisa, all of whom suggested the difficulty of com-munication between northerners and southerners.[9] On the other hand, it has recently been contended that the dialect speech of the northern students – possibly from Northumberland – in the Reeve's Tale in *The Canterbury Tales* is not marked and demonstrates a 'fine example of dialect democracy'.[10]

Earlier delineation of Middle English (ME) dialect variation started heuristically from a premise of broad regional entities: Northern; West Midland; East Midland; Southern; and Kentish.[11] Initially, research deploying non-literary evidence – such as lay subsidies (tax lists) – retained this framework, considering presumed region after presumed region, commencing with the 'North' constituted as the six northern counties with Lincolnshire.[12] For some linguists, that framework has continued to be the point of conception.[13]

That point of departure has not been without criticism, however, from two perspectives. One suggests rather adamantly that this particular non-literary evidence – lay subsidies – is not a substantially localized text, especially if Exchequer redactions are involved.[14] Another response to this tradition has contested the notion of bundles of isoglosses forming consolidated dialect boundaries and rather asserts a dialect continuum as much as clear regional differences.[15] We have to consider too how dialectologists of more recent sociolinguistic material have concentrated more on intensely localized dialect differences rather than broad regional comparisons.[16]

Now, all those considerations complicate how to undertake an analysis of names as an indicator of northern-ness. The explanation of the extreme localism of dialect areas can be associated with the idea of *l'espace vécu* – the intensely localized space within which life in the past was experienced, the 'life experience of space'.[17] Spatial perception of dialect difference depends also, however, on whether the viewpoint is internal or external; viewed from the inside, the differences are exaggerated, but from the outside they are somewhat dissolved with an emphasis on similarities and convergences. Such perceptions are not mutually exclusive or incompatible – they are simply differences of position and experience. For the purposes of approaching the significance of names, furthermore, it is impossible to attempt to configure a mosaic without some appreciation of wider geographical patterns.

Acceptance of the 'North' as a broad Middle English linguistic or dialect region, however, remains problematic. To a certain extent, a dialect continuum did exist. Differences in the 'North' were sometimes comparative or relative, matters of intensity rather than absolute dichotomy. Nor does this suggest simply a substitution of a zone for a definite boundary, for the gradation was finer and not just a matter of an intermediate area or porosity. A successful investigation thus will depend on a careful consideration of spatial methodology and that approach is illuminated further below and constitutes the dialogue between chapters two and four below.

Place-ness

The principal question at issue with any investigation of the North concerns the extent to which there was a consciousness of the North both inside and outside its parameters. Traditionally and philosophically (since Hegel), territorial consciousness has been associated with the nation state. Can that concept of territorial consciousness be translated to the notion of the region, 'the evocative concept of locale, a bounded region which concentrates action and brings together in social life the unique and particular as well as the general and nomothetic'?[18] In pursuing the notion of the locale – apparently here treated synonymously with region – it has been asserted that '[t]erritoriality, almost by definition, is present in every locale at least at the outer boundary' (where the absence of interaction begins).[19] In the same vein, the contention has been advanced that '[l]ocalities ... can be defined as particular types of enduring locales stabilized socially and spacially ...'[20]

A similar differentiation has been proposed by Jiménez who asserts that places remain 'territorially demarcated, culturally bounded and neatly enclosed societies' by contrast with space which provides 'a field of social relations', 'the shifting constellation of social relationships through which "places" are activated as they are practised and brought to life.'[21] Refining this notion, Jiménez proceeds, 'Put somewhat differently, social relationships are inherently spatial, and space an instrument and dimension of people's sociality. Social life is no longer to be seen as unfolding through space but with space, that is, spatially ... It is what people do, not where they are ... In other words, people relate to and engage with landscape in various ways because social relationships are inherently spatial.'[22] Although throughout the following discussion about northern-ness and naming, place and space will occasionally be confused, even confounded, there remains a mindfulness that the 'North' for some purposes continued to be ambiguous, changing and reconfigured, sometimes amorphous, other times more precise – that is, a space where social relationships were enacted rather than a bounded place or locality.

The anomalies in the context of northernness and northern consciousness, however, are contained in permeable or soft and shifting 'boundaries' and boundaries that are merely perceptions. The consequent question then arises as to whether 'boundaries' of regions are fixed and permanent or whether they shift over time. In attempting to address these questions, the principal material analysed here is names and the language of names. The formation and distribution of names do not permit absolute 'bounded-ness', but rather produce zones of transition.

Until recently, place-ness was considered from the perspective of cultural integrity or integration, with an emphasis on homogeneity ('assumed isomorphism') as a positive influence – that is, of identity-production. More recently, perhaps, another perception has engaged with the effects – intended or otherwise – of the representation of space and place, so that visions of places are informed by authority and notions of alterity. How a space or place is considered – represented – as having a singular and particular characteristic is itself a discourse of authority against an other. This metonymy of place – defining it by singular characteristics – privileges one perspective – an external one imbued with authority – over others, usually the internal experience of the space or place. Whilst it will be impossible to ignore completely external representations of the North as place – since, indeed, that exterior ordering is one reason for selecting the north as an area of incredible onomastic as well as other interest – the focus here is on the lived experience in the north, both northern-ness as a generality and on localities within the north.[23]

Recovering the language of speech communities in the past is a hazardous affair. Inherent in the production of written records are issues of the rhetorical purposes of the written material, its authorial intention and its reception. Localization of writers presents further problems. In contending that the recording of personal names allows a perception of the language use of the speech community, all these issues must be encountered and must be addressed for each type of record.[24] Each form of record presents its own issues of production.

In further depending on personal name elements, moreover, the problems are magnified. Unlike place-name elements, personal names are not static in location, but are portable. Migration of persons might account for some locations of personal name elements. Occasionally, therefore, we are concerned with critical masses of data distribution rather than every dot distribution. Nevertheless, that aggregative approach also raises concerns, for the material of personal names, although apparently an extensive quantitative source, actually produces rather insubstantial datasets for key variables, whether phonemes [sounds] (necessarily through written representation as graphemes) or lexis [specific vocabulary].

These data, however, constitute the most quantifiable source that is available, a corpus linguistics of a special kind. Different forms of record should, even so, be approached in a sensitive manner, for data in charters or manorial records, cannot be exploited in the same quantifiable manner as taxation records. Taxation records (lay subsidies and Poll Taxes) consist of uniform data with a uniformity of rationale for inclusion – those who are taxable (regardless of the significant caveats discussed below). The reasons for appearances in charters and manorial records are more variable and so in that respect are less inclusive than taxation records.

The exclusiveness of lay subsidies is, however, well attested. At best, lay subsidies comprehend some 40 percent of heads of households and, at worst, a much lower proportion.[25] They exclude from our view therefore the poorest of society. On the other hand, their geographical coverage is much more comprehensive than any other form of record. In contrast, of course, the Poll Taxes of 1377–81 comprehended a fuller representation of independent taxpayers.

How we can deploy the evidence of these records then is to make crude quantification from the taxation records, bearing in mind the deficiencies of the lay subsidies, supplemented by the information particularly in manorial court records which penetrate even further down the social scale. The latter then supplement, complement and occasionally correct the former.

Although the lay subsidies were produced in a series, particularly between c.1290 and c.1332, thus theoretically allowing a sequential section through any local society, the sequence is complicated by the register used in the documents. It is only the later subsidies which permitted an intrusion of vernacular forms of personal names, whilst the earlier ones preferred a representation of name forms in the Latin register. That difference is important for the evolution and appearance of some vernacular forms in the lay subsidies, particularly the engendering of vernacular kinship suffixes (-son, -doghter, -wife) or occupational terms and suffixes (not least, -maker). Whilst the 1327 lay subsidy might thus have been more comprehensive with less evasion that that of 1332, there are some grounds for considering the later of the two to capture vernacular forms.

Now, in contrast to literary texts which have hitherto been employed as the principal source for exposing geographical differences in Middle English language use, records of taxation and manorial records penetrate beyond the culture of the literary text. Whatever the relationship between orality and literacy, between redactor and audience, literary texts do not permit as deep an excavation of the everyday language of the local speech community. The reporting of personal name forms was informed by the speech community itself, even if mediated by a literate redactor (in the sense of both literate and *literatus*).[26]

Finally, it should be emphasised that what these records allow, penetrating through their faux-Latin register, is (an admittedly imperfect) visibility of a northern speech community. Personal names in this context are linguistic phenomena, incorporating speech acts which defined a northern consciousness, both internal to the 'region' and externally to it. Language use engaged with 'territorial consciousness'. Differences of language use allowed those on the outside to mark off, even stigmatise, 'northern' language, whilst internally to the north it allowed a social cohesion.

What is attempted here then is a reconstruction of the language of the speech community and communities of northern England through the reporting and recording of personal name elements, a process by which it may be possible to identify a northern consciousness.

Northern-ness and other identities

One point of departure to capture some glimpse of contemporary perceptions is to consider the vocabulary of northern-ness and its alterity. Terms are complicated by code and register: variants of *le norreis* (Anglo-Norman), *norrensis* (Latin), and *le northerne* (Middle English); and similarly, *surreys*, *surrensis*, and *le sotheron*. How precisely those codes applied may perhaps be illustrated by how they obtained in the borough of Leicester. In 1225, Peter *filius Herberti Norrensis* entered the gild merchant, but he was preceded in his admission by Alexander *le Noreys* in 1196. The same status – the freedom – was conferred on William *filius Willelmi le Norreis* in 1242. Burgesses assessed to tallages in the borough in 1253, 1271, and 1286 included Peter *le Norreys*, William *le Norreys* (also admitted to the gild merchant in 1260), and Nicholas *le Norreys*. In subsequent tallages in 1307 and 1311, however, assessment was made on Nicholas *le Northerne*. Tallages in 1336 and 1354 were collected respectively from John *le Northerne* and Margaret *le Northerne* and in 1357 mention was made in the gild merchant rolls of William *de le North*. In 1337 admission to the gild merchant was allowed to Robert *othe North*, who, by that designation, was involved in a case of trespass in 1342. In the later middle ages, however, the surname which stabilized in the borough – not necessarily the descendant of the earlier northerners – was Norres, borne by Giles Norreys who died by 1372 and by John and Simon Nores (1441x1509).

Now, of course, what the distribution of these bynames reveals is ambiguous. Such bynames would be expected in the south of England. It is consequently not unusual to discover in the lay subsidy for Essex in 1327 John *Noreys* at Fange, Peter *Norays* at Hengham Sybil, Richard *Noreys* in Colchester, another Richard *Norays* in Stifford, or John *Northman* in Havering, or, in 1337, Nicholas *le Northern'* in Colchester.[27] Nor is it surprising to locate in the taxation of Devon in 1332 William *Noreys* at Loventor, Adam *Noreys* at Warcombe, John *Noreys* at North Huish, a *Noreys* at Sampford Peverel, North Tawton, Heanton Punchard, and Dodbrooke, a *Noricz* at Crediton and Philip *le Northern*

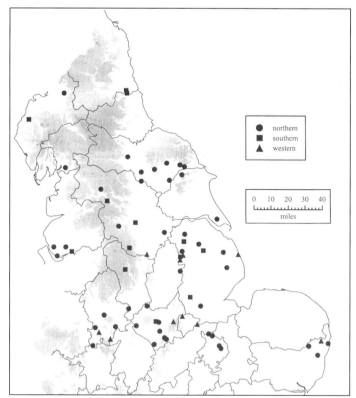

Figure 1 Bynames of generic origin, late thirteenth and early fourteenth centuries

at Bradninch.[28] *Noreys* was distributed in Wiltshire in the same taxation at Milford, Brinkworth, Great Sherston, Surrendell and Henset.[29] In Bedfordshire, therefore, nothing extraordinary is connoted by Hamo *le Norþerne* subjected to taxation in Wilden in 1297, or, indeed, Hugh *le Norreis* at Staploe in Eaton Socon or another *le Noreys* in the same parish.[30] Since northern-ness also connoted then – as perhaps now – a relative geographical location of origin, northern-ness in those cases in the south might have constituted little more than origins just further north rather than from a far north.

It might therefore prove more beneficial to concentrate on the distribution of these terms from the north Midlands northwards and for this purpose can be considered not only northern-ness but also southern-ness. Figure 1 therefore displays the location of terms for northern, southern and western accordingly. Ambiguity still tangentially complicates any analysis. Simply from the place-name Heaton Norris in Lancashire, it is evident that *le Noreys* existed as a localized, hereditary gentry surname in southern Lancashire. Of minor complication is the very occasional use of *Norreys* as a forename, exhibited by Norreys *le Venur* who was involved in an action of *novel disseisin* in Thornborough in 1218–19.[31]

Immediately of interest are the taxpayers *Northman* at Dyrah, *del North* at Walton and *del North* at Farleton in Cumberland and north Lancashire in 1327 and 1332.[32]

Throughout the Ridings of Yorkshire, taxpayers called *le Noreys* and its variants were widely distributed as well as those designated *del North* at Huddersfield, *Northeman* at Kirkbymoorside, *Northman* at Breckenborough and *Northen* at Byland.[33]

Directing attention further to the north, Hugh *le Surreis* was appealed in the Yorkshire Crown Pleas for battery committed in the wapentake of Dickering in the early thirteenth century.[34] About the same time, Ralph *le Surreys* sought local sanctuary in a parish church in Yorkshire on the death of Emma.[35] Then too, on the death of Ralph *Druery* of Tinsley, Geoffrey *le Surreys* was suspected.[36] Since Hugh could not be discovered to be brought to answer and neither Ralph nor Geoffrey reportedly had any chattels, it seems likely that both were itinerant. On the other hand, as William *Surrensis* extended a pledge before the justices in eyre, it is likely that he had permanent settlement.[37] In the 1327 lay subsidy for the North Riding, Thomas *Sorays* was assessed at 2s. 8d. at Ebberston, but at Ravenswath merely 1s. was expected from Robert *Norrays*, the same amount as exacted from Adam *Norrays* at Welbourn[38] Richard *Sorrays* also contributed at a higher level – 2s. – at Alverton.[39] It is not, however, issues of longer-distance migration or integration which are of concern here, but the consciousness of difference – of northern-ness, southern-ness and western-ness.

By the early sixteenth century, that memorialization of difference through second names might have become attenuated, not least as such names became hereditary. In 1509, the chamberlains of Newcastle-upon-Tyne purchased wine for £6 from Lewis Sothorn and he received regular payments for supervising unlading.[40] Previously, Robert Sothorn had received a payment from them.[41] In May 1510, another disbursement was made by them to William Sothorn, mason, for three and a half days of work.[42] The muster of 1539 in the borough enlisted a Stephen Sotheren and two Williams with this surname.[43] When Elizabeth, daughter of William, was baptised in 1662 at Winston, the surname had transmuted to Sudderen.[44]

Consciousness of trans-Pennine disparity is more obtuse, but perhaps it is indicated to the east of the Pennines by the byname *le Westreys* and variants. In 1252, John *le Westreys* agreed to compromise a plea of land.[45] A generation or more earlier, in 1219, Richard *le Westreys* had brought an appeal on a murder in Yorkshire.[46] At about this time, Thomas *le Westreys* was the first finder of a body of a boy who had drowned at Bickerton in Yorkshire.[47]

Phenomenology of naming

Interesting as it might superficially appear, the classification of types of byname and surname has tended to artifice. Emphasis on types of byname and surname – toponymic (or 'locative'), topographical, nickname, occupational and so on – has induced some degree of artificiality into the conceptualization of naming. Perhaps it was more likely that those attributing names had no classificatory scheme in their minds in labelling individuals. Naming emanated from everyday, lived experience, so that naming was phenomenological rather than classificatory. Phenomenology involves, through the employment of hermeneutics, deciphering the meanings encountered in quotidian experience – how the everyday gives meaning to lives.[48] Naming in its creative stages was informed by that quotidian experience and in its later, fixed stages contributed to that lived experience, these notions addressed in more detail below.

More straightforwardly, classification continues to be an imprecise heuristic. For a proportion of bynames the etymology will remain uncertain. For others, ambiguity will be inherent. Again, some bynames might have multiple origins. Other combinations or periphrases will present internal ambivalence: how should we classify affixes as in William *Elyson del Hough*, a grantor of land in Newham, Northumberland, in the early fourteenth century?[49] Occasionally, periphrases become explanatory, as in the case of the letter of attorney for John *atte Mylle alias dictus Mylleward clericus*.[50] Through this epithet we are reminded that some apparently topographical bynames were effectively occupational.

Nor is it difficult to elicit some epithets employed as the *nomen* to compound the problem further. The occasional deployment of Norreys has been observed above. In the early thirteenth century, *Bonhom fullo* of one of the Carltons in Yorkshire was killed.[51] That same eyre roll referred to *Mauvaisin de Hersin*.[52]

Despite those technical reasons for reducing the hardness and fastness of categorization of bynames and surnames, however, the most compelling reason for a less fastidious approach is that contemporaries probably never engaged in those sorts of mental processes of classifying. Bynames were integral to wider social experience and quotidian ways of life. If, therefore, in the discussion below, particular categories of byname and surname are addressed in separate chapters, that approach is simply heuristic whilst realising its artifice.

Returning to the influence of and contribution to everyday experience, in their formative stages – before bynames became stable and hereditary – *cognomina* (second names) were influenced by everyday experience. To a large extent names were taken from lived experience, from the immediate world around and how that world was understood and practised. Furthermore, bynames – particularly nickname bynames, but also others – were embroiled in common fame: how a person was perceived within daily, lived experience.[53] Bynaming consisted thus of all of social, communal and phenomenological motivations. Classification was in no sense important or significant to the social process.

How common fame influenced the process is most conclusively illustrated by any form (not merely derogatory) of nickname bynames. Their influence was not confined to northern-ness: in 1297, in Bedfordshire, taxpayers were recognised locally by their bynames *Makehait*, *Slingebotere*, and *Peckebene* (although, again, here we encounter in some of these nomenclatures the immense difficulty in some cases of segregating nickname from 'occupational' origins).[54] Nevertheless, common fame was a vital (in all its senses) influence on the northern-ness of northern naming.

A northern spirit in bynaming emanated from the lived experience in the north. Sometimes, the demonstrative aspects of the everyday appear only marginal. Again, in Bedfordshire in 1297, a contributor to the lay subsidy was identified as Simon *Bullocherde* (at Billington).[55] In Huntingdonshire, contemporaneously, *le Cuerde* or *Le Couherd* appeared in the lists of taxpayers in Upwood and Wistow.[56] Nevertheless, these *cognomina* appear unusual to the extent that they are not replicated to any degree in that local society. In contrast, although marginal in quantitative terms,

-herd names in the north profoundly reflected the quotidian experience of a local society embedded in an existence closer to livestock husbandry.[57]

How bynames emanated out of the environment in the north can be depicted through those associated with grain products, elaborated further below. Here, we might just pause to consider that these bynames became attached to knightly or gentry families during the middle ages.[58] The metonym *Graindorge* familiarly recurred in documents in the West Riding in the late twelfth and early thirteenth centuries, especially in the area around Rimington and Horton in the form of William *Graindorge*, distinguished in his later appearances by the seignorial title *dominus*.[59]

Assuming then that bynaming proceeded from everyday existence – uncomplicated by classification and unconscious of such artifice – how then did it feed into quotidian experience? After bynames became stabilized into hereditary surnames, the forms of these surnames produced an environment which was distinctive either generally or in specific aspects. In northern upland regions, as expressed in chapter 9 below, the environment was characterized by the high proportion of patronymic and metronymic surnames with –*son*. A characteristic cultural milieu was thus informed by naming.

In attempting to recover the experience of the attribution of names as a phenomenological process, however, we should not forget that the names – both first and second – which appear in written records are not necessarily the colloquial identification of the individual. For that reason, some considerable discussion is dedicated below to the employment – even in written records – of hypocorisms in the north. That consideration of pet forms might be pre-empted here by attestation of informal naming within the speech community. In the early fourteenth century, *Prester John* was outlawed for offences against the venison in the Forest of Pickering. It seems very probable that this outlaw was synonymous with the John *Prest* arrested with his mastiff on suspicion of poaching.[60] What of *Proud Adam* who, like John, was accused of hunting, this time in Ellerbeck, in 1305 – Adam with a posse of miscreants? That same Adam – Adam *dictus Proud Adam* – was again accused for poaching.[61] Whenever we assume that we have recovered the naming of an individual within a speech community, we must, nevertheless, recognise that we have only received a formal, written enunciation of that person's identity. One of the positive aspects of documentary evidence of northern naming is that it helps that appreciation and more readily reveals what is normally concealed by written records.

Characterization of northern naming

Attention has already been directed to several characteristic aspects of northern naming.[62] Principal amongst these features is the continued instability of northern bynames, extending much later than in more southerly areas of the country. Such flexibility is easily illustrated amongst the free peasantry of the north in the middle and late thirteenth century. For example, a quitclaim of a bovate in Rokesby was effected by Reginald *ad spinam filius H. de Rokesby*, as indeed was another implemented by William *barn filius Ade de Rokesby*.[63] In 1261, land in the same vill was alienated by Robert *carpentarius filius Johannis de Sunthorp'*, identified earlier in a quitclaim of his right in four selions in Sunthorpe in 1258 as Roger *Carpentarius de Pikal filius J. de Sienthorp'*.[64] It is not surprising, therefore, when the tourn jury of the manor of Wakefield in the late thirteenth century reported:

> *Item dicunt quod Ricardus del Rodes est clericus, et est villanus Comitis, eo quod pater suus, nomine Serlo de Ossete, erat nativus Comitis, et tenet se pro libero quia cepit in maritagium cum uxore sua…*

> [Item they say that Richard *del Rodes* is a *clericus* and the earl's villain since his father, called Serlo *de Ossete*, was the earl's villein, and he takes himself to be free since he took in dowry with his wife …][65]

Although some of the bynames on the manor of Wakefield were developing in the early fourteenth century into hereditary surnames, instability still pertained there. At Alverthorpe in 1307, Adam *Gerbot* impleaded Alice daughter of Alice for one acre of land because his father had purchased this land and been accepted into it in open court.[66] At this point, the formation of a byname derived from a predecessor's forename is visible. How this case developed in 1316, nevertheless, reveals how that newly-formed byname became an hereditary surname about 1316 (see below).

Although an hereditary surname was introduced in one branch of a kinship, it did not imply that that certainty applied in another branch. When William de *Ketelisthorpe* died at Sandall some time before 1307, he left issue two sons, William and Robert. William received the land as heir, as the senior line, leaving a son and heir, John *de Ketelisthorpe*, so that in the elder and inheriting line the byname continued into a hereditary surname. On the cadet side, however, Robert died leaving a son and heir Robert *le Plogwricht*, so that in the junior line instability of byname ensued.[67]

How that instability was prolonged in some instances in the far north is illustrated by the succession to lands in Penrith in the late 1370s, received by Alan *de Penruddok* son of John *Henrison*.[68] At Barton in Westmorland just about twenty years previously, William *del Stable* was described as the son of John *Cok*.[69]

Instability was not, however, the complete situation, for some succession to bynames did occur, at least amongst the free peasantry. Producing a writ of right in the honorial court of Knaresborough in the middle of the thirteenth century, the plaintiff was described as Richard *de Bosco filius Roberti de Bosco de Staynl'*.[70] A quitclaim to Fountains Abbey relating to Catton in Yorkshire was implemented by Simon *de Munketon' filius Roberti de Munketon'* in 1255.[71]

At a higher level of freedom, impermanence of bynames existed, reflected in a confirmation by Adam *de Ingletorp' filius Petri Camerarii* of land alienated from his fee in Markinfield.[72] At least of the status of substantial free peasantry, since he was involved in a dispute with Lanercost Priory about two messuages, thirty acres of land, and thirty acres of meadow in Great Farlam in 1292 (although suspiciously rounded numbers), Adam de Farlam *filius Walteri de Wyndesouer'* also illustrates the persistence of instability of bynames at not insignificant social levels.[73] A change of byname was allowed in 1349 in Alnwick to William *dictus Hanner filius et heres Johannis Cissoris de Alnewyk* (William called Hanner son and heir of John *Cissor* of Alnwick).[74]

During the thirteenth century, persistent instability of bynames across generations of free peasantry was normative. To Bridlington Priory Robert *Anceps filius Henrici de boningtoun'* granted a bovate in Bonnington.[75] When the son of Thomas *de Melsa* confirmed to the same priory his father's grant some time after 1225–6, the son styled himself John *de Drenghon filius Thome de Melsa*.[76] Consent to another charter was provided by William *Scaldhare filius Roberti de Beuerlaco*, relating to two bovates in Fraistingthorpe.[77] Other charters mentioned Thomas *de Bristhil filius Thome de Molscroft*.[78] A single acre was received by the priory from Robert *de Carby filius Roberti de Norfok*.[79] The more substantial donation of two bovates in Nafferton derived from William *de Nafferton' filius Rogeri dispensatoris* and when confirmed by his son, he fashioned himself as Ralph *de Nafferton' filius Willelmi filii Rogeri dispensatoris*.[80]

Instability affected burgesses too, as, for example, in the borough of Drax. Here one of the continuous benefactors of Drax priory assumed a wide range of styles: Adam *Marescallus filius Willelmi filii Achardi de Drax*; Adam *filius Willelmi filii Achardi de Drax*; Adam *Marescallus filius Willelmi Marescallus* (sic); Adam *filius Willelmi filii Achardi de Drax*; William *Marescallus filius quondam Ade Marescalli de Drax*; and William *Marescallus de Drax*.[81] The content of William's transfers reflect his local status: three acres; two acres; a toft, buildings and one acre; a rent; and one acre. Whilst the last constituted a sale (*pro quadam summa pecunie*), the other grants purport to be genuine benefactions for they were assigned to the fabric fund (*et precipue operi eiusdem ecclesie; ad fabricam eiusdem sancti Nicholai*).

At an even higher social level, when the advowson of the parish church of Sprotley was acquired by the priory, the grantor described himself as Walter *de Ver filius Ade de Gousle*.[82] That instability can be further perceived even in knightly families, exemplified, perhaps, in the varying styles of a particular knightly benefactor of Drax Priory: Peter *de Camelesford' filius domini Gerardi de Fontibus*; Peter *de Fontibus filius Gerardi*; Peter *de Fontibus*; Peter *filius Gerardi de Fontibus*; Peter *de Fontibus filius Gerardi de Fontibus*; and Peter *de Camellesford' domini Gerardi de Fontibus filius*.[83]

Despite the development of hereditary and family surnames within some knightly families and some of the free peasantry, considerable instability persisted at this social level through the thirteenth century. The extent of that instability was marginal, but characterized the far north. Without being in a position to make any categorical statements about the normative nature of hereditary surnames during the late middle ages, it is possible at the least to maintain that by the end of the fifteenth century, it was expected that surnames be hereditary within kinships. About that time, Arche Nykson, Davy Nykson, Clement Nykson and Quinton Nykson were bound to the bishop of Carlisle, the lord Dacre, Randolph Dacre and John Musgrave, knight, in twenty marks to restore stolen goods, more precisely that they 'or any of ther surname of clannes' restore the goods. It was thus anticipated that surnames had developed and by now normatively represented kinship groups.[84]

Although that general expectation pertained, in Lancashire at least instability continued in a special circumstance: patronymic and metronymic surnames in the vernacular, especially for daughters. It seems that *-son* surnames stabilized earlier for sons than for daughters. Whilst, therefore, Richard Sanderson son of Thomas Sanderson was baptised in Farnworth chapelry in 1539, almost concurrently Jane *Thomasdaughter*, Margaret *Williamsdaughter*, Margaret *Henrisdaughter*, Joan *Henriesdaughter* and Margery *Johnsdaughter* were also christened (1538–1545).[85] Marriages at Aughton illustrate how

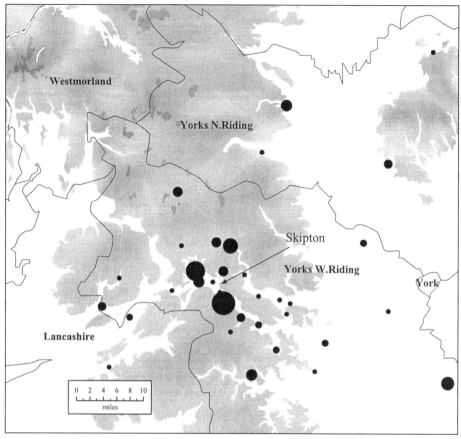

Figure 2 Marriage horizons: Skipton (Yorks. W. R.), 1603–26

long this patterning persisted, for, although there was a decline about mid-century in the conferral of unstable patronyms and metronyms on baptised daughters, those already baptised with -*daughter* names continued to bear them to their marriage. From mid-century, therefore, daughters received their father's patronym or metronym with the suffix -*son*, reflecting stabilization of this form of surnames for daughters. Even in the late sixteenth century, however, daughters baptised with -*daughter* names were still marrying with those names, the marriages thus recorded at Aughton of Blanche *Adamsdoghter* in 1542, Helen *Ricardoughter* in 1577, Elizabeth *Willyamsdoughter* and Alice *Johnsdaughter* in 1583, Elizabeth *Adamesdaughter* in 1594, Anne *Raffedaughter* in 1595, and even in 1606 and 1609 Margaret *Johnsdaughter* and Margery *Johnsdaughter*.[86] A transition is intimated at Aughton by the records of the marriages of Elizabeth *Robinson* alias *Johnsdaughter* in 1601 and Margery *Johnsdaughter* alias *Bryanson* in 1619, for these aliases suggest that existing -*daughter* names were regarded as erratic.[87]

More profuse illustration of this continuing instability of patronyms and metronyms obtained at Prescot. That flexibility affected both sons and daughters in the mid sixteenth century. For example, in 1541, Agnes *Johanisdowter* daughter of John Rogerson

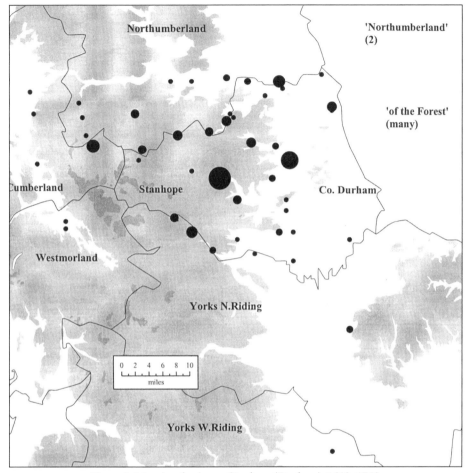

Figure 3 Marriage horizons: Stanhope (Durham), 1613–1740

of Sutton was baptised.[88] In the same year, John *Ricarson* son of Richard Robertson of Sutton was also christened.[89] Just to elucidate the formula, a few more baptisms can be recited: in 1544 Elizabeth *Rogersdowter* daughter of Roger Thomasson and in 1545 Roger *Johnson* son of John Roggerson.[90] For both sons and daughters this protocol continued until *c.*1549. Fourteen daughters received their second name in this manner with a *-dowter* suffix.[91] The number of sons affected was lower, at six.[92] By the 1540s, some intimation of stability was being introduced, attested by the entries for Anne *Wyllesedoghter* daughter of John Wylleson in 1544 and Richard Hareson son of Baldwin Hareson in 1548.[93] After 1560, it became increasingly the custom to assign to the offspring the father's surname rather than a newly-created form.[94] Whilst conformity to this new approach to patronyms and metronyms was observed for baptisms after 1560, however, marriages continued to resurrect the existing *-dowter* names. As late as 1595, Jane *Johnsdaughter*'s marriage was celebrated at Prescot.[95] From 1541 to 1595,

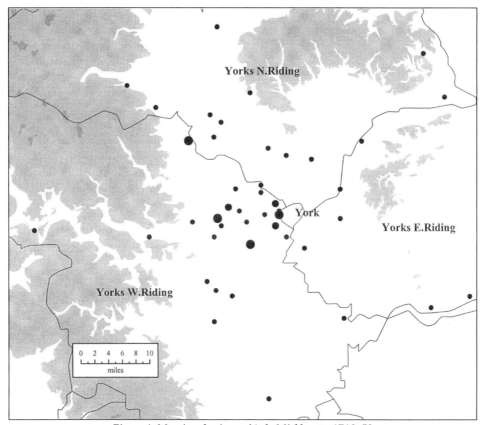

Figure 4 Marriage horizons: York, Micklegate, 1718–53

twenty-two brides disported *-dowter* names in the register.[96] Whilst those remaining names were worked through marriage registration, signs of stabilization also occurred in the marriage register: Catherine Rychardson in 1552, Isabel Rogerson and Isabel Thomasson in 1560, and Joan Rycarson and Jane Richerdson in 1562.[97]

To substantiate this residual instability connected with the element *-doghter*, the registers of Walton-on-the-Hill (Lancs.) furnish further material. Following the marriage of Margaret *Henryesdoughter* in 1590, sixteen other brides disported a *-doughter* second name in the dozen years between 1595 and 1617, finishing with the marriage of Jane *Rogersdaughter* in that final year.[98] Nevertheless, the transition was prolonged and varied between parishes. In Whalley, for example, unstable *-doughter* names *appear* to have been relinquished at an earlier time, for the register of baptisms recorded the celebration of that sacrament in 1538 for Joan Wilkingson daughter of John Wilkingson, Isabel Dobson daughter of Robert Dobson, Elizabeth Dobson daughter of Richard Dobson, and Joan Richardson daughter of John Richardson.[99]

Confirmation of this particular late instability can be replicated from several other parishes in Lancashire. At Huyton, the marriage of Elizabeth *Jamesdaughter* was celebrated in 1588, but the instability did not conclude there for she was succeeded

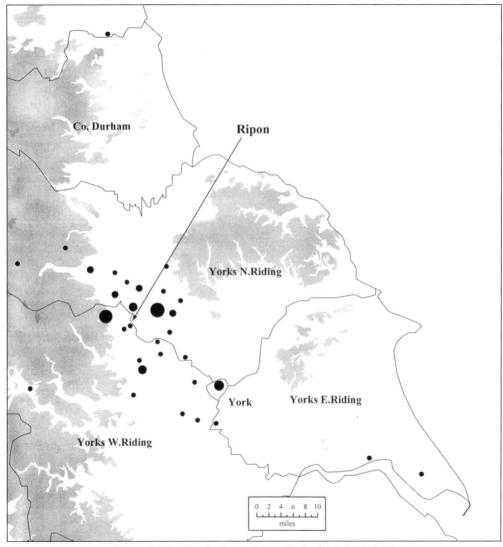

Figure 5 Marriage horizons: Ripon (Yorks. W. R.), 1619–29

by Jane and Margaret *Johnsdaughter*, both espoused in 1590. Between 1593 and 1614, a dozen more brides with -*daughter* names were registered in the registers of Huyton, with Elizabeth *Johnsdaughter* the final of this succession before a hiatus in the registers after 1617. Contemporary with all these weddings, however, was a tendency towards stabilization as other brides disported -*son* surnames. Our brides with -*daughter* surnames were, by the late sixteenth century, the remainder of a time and naming culture passing. The complexity of that transition is illustrated at Huyton by Helen *Johnsdaughter* alias Nickson in 1604.[100]

The process can be delineated too at Farnworth chapelry as it persisted into the

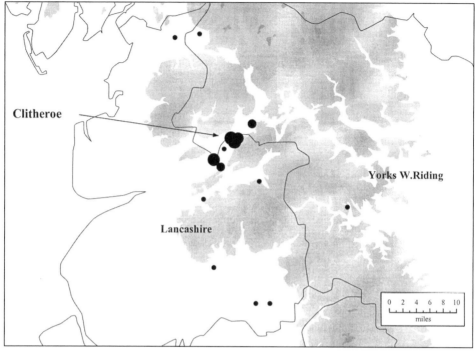

Figure 6 Marriage horizons: Clitheroe (Lancs.), 1570–87

late sixteenth and early seventeenth century. In 1546, Margery *Johnsdaughter* was buried at the time that Margery *Henrysdaughter*, Isabel *Robertsdaughter*, and Catherine *Thomasdaughter* were baptised.[101] Before then, the sacrament of baptism had been conferred on Jane *Thomsdaughter*, Margaret *Williamsdaughter*, and Margaret *Henris-daughter* in 1538 and Joan *Henriesdaughter* in 1541.[102] More christenings of female children with *-daughter* names were celebrated in 1553, 1562 (two), and 1564 (two), with the naming of Elizabeth *Thomasdaughter* daughter of Thomas Nicolas demon-strative of the formation.[103] Indeed, Margaret *Simonsdaughter* constituted a late successor, baptised in 1576.[104] As a consequence of these baptisms, *-daughter* names continued to be inscribed in the registers throughout their life-courses as they retained these *-daughter* names despite the general transition to more stable naming of females. Marriages were thus concluded with brides with *–daughter* names in 1569, 1573, 1575, 1579, 1583, 1597–9, and 1603 (some of the brides might have been exogamous).[105] The introduction of some aliases again reveals how these *-daughter* designations remained from an earlier process as a general transition was being perfected: Jane *Johnsdaughter* alias Harison, married in 1583, and Helen Thomasson alias *Johns-daughter*, buried in 1599.[106]

Finally, this particular onomastic process – prevalent in, but peculiar to, southern Lancashire – is attested also in the registers of Childwall. Here, between 1565 and 1609, twenty-five brides were registered with *–daughter* bynames, culminating as late as 1637 with Jane *Richardsdaughter*.[107] Moreover, between 1560 and 1586, the baptisms

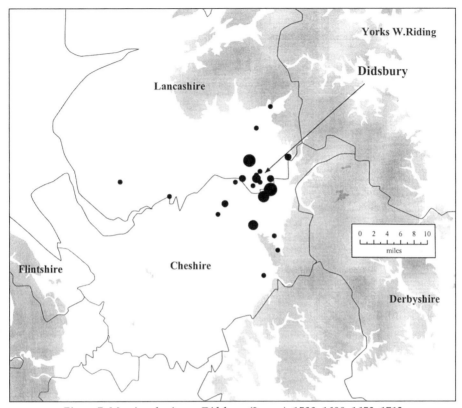

Figure 7 Marriage horizons: Didsbury (Lancs.), 1599–1600, 1653–1712

of fourteen female children were certified in this way in the register.[108] It should also be noted that another onomastic element circumscribed to southern Lancashire – the suffix *-mough* or *-maugh* – also appeared in the Childwall baptismal registers through Margery Huchmogh, William Huchmough, Robert Highmoughe, and Margery Huchmough, between 1568 and 1581.[109] As will be explained further below, then, although having an overall coherence, the 'North' yet contained a mosaic of distinctive localities, one of which, illustrated by these processes here, was southern Lancashire.[110]

Now a comparison by gender can be elicited here, for, although two sons were assigned unstable name forms at baptism – Richard *Robertsone* son of Robert Thomasson in 1540 and William *Robertsone* son of Robert Thomasone in 1543 – after the death of William in 1544, this form of naming was abandoned for male children, so that the instability of naming became associated with females in particular, perhaps to emphasise their relationship to a male, patriarchal authority.[111]

From previous investigation of Lancashire, it has also been demonstrated that toponymic bynames, especially those related to minor place-names – of hamlets – continued to be circumscribed around and within the hamlet of their origin. This characteristic was firmly associated with dispersed settlement in certain areas, such

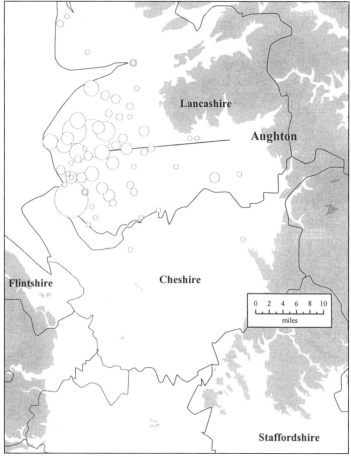

Figure 8 Marriage horizons: Aughton (Lancs.), 1697–1748

topographies and settlement patterns distributed throughout the northern zone, in upland and woodland areas where parishes remained enormous and comprised a multitude of hamlets.[112] So in 1316, Alice widow of Gerbode *de Alverthorp'* impleaded Robert *Gerbode* for dower in Alverthorpe within the manor of Wakefield.[113] At issue in this proceeding were twenty-one acres of land of which her husband had died seised (in possession). In defence, the defendant insisted that her husband had been entitled merely to a life interest from the defendant's father, Richard *Gerbode*. The jury of inquisition delivered its verdict in favour of the defendant on the following facts: Gerbode *de Alverthorp* had surrendered the land to his son, Richard *Gerbode*, father of the defendant, Robert *Gerbode*, before Gerbode *de Alverthorp*'s marriage to Alice. Now what is observed here is the connection of a toponymic byname associated with a minor placename with that place, but also the instability of bynames as the subsequent generations assumed as their byname the forename of their immediate predecessor.

The persistence into the early fourteenth century was more definitive in Richard *de*

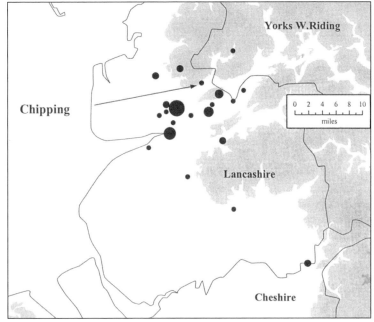

Figure 9 Marriage horizons: Chipping (Lancs.), 1653–92

Cartworth who alienated twelve and a half acres in Cartworth in Holne within the manor of Wakefield in 1316.[114] Just a year earlier, Robert *Gerbot*, upon payment of 2s. for a licence, received a third of four acres in Flansawe held by Amabel *de Flansawe* in dower.[115] Contemporaneously, it was presented at Holne that the township of Holne had concealed that four years previously Helen wife of Adam *de Holne* had stolen 9s. in silver coin and half a stone of wool.[116] At Ossett, Nalle *de Ossete*, wife of John *Certe*, initiated proceedings in trespass against two men in 1286.[117]

Further substance is provided by an unusual entry in the manor court of Wakefield at Holne in 1316 – idiosyncratic because it concerned moral regulation and the policing of local sexual mores which constituted more usually the business of the ecclesiastical courts. In this instance, however, the steward instituted the proceedings by summoning John *Kenward* of Hepworth to explain why he entertained in adultery Alice daughter of Simon *de Hepworth* for whom he had forsaken his wife.[118]

Approaches to bastardy and surnames

It might be suspected that illegitimacy complicated the attribution of surnames. Usually, the extent and nature of that problem is difficult to assess. That concealment is unfortunate because bastardy existed within English society not merely as a consequence of illicit sexual relationships, but for both structured and contingent reasons.[119] The late age of marriage and the relationship between customary and official attitudes to the *formation* of marriage induced some level of pre-marital

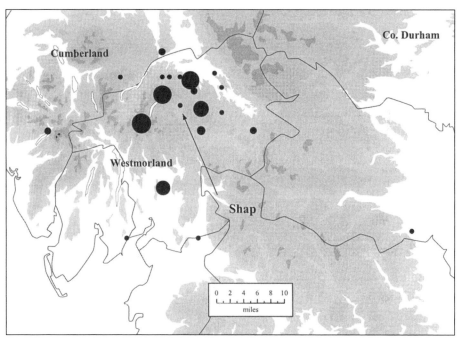

Figure 10 Marriage horizons: Shap (Westmorland), 1576–1616

sexual congress.[120] Furthermore, periods of economic and social disruption resulted in unfulfilled marriage agreements and illegitimacy.

Exceptionally, some insight into these issues is provided by the incumbents of at least two Lancashire parishes in the sixteenth century and so it constitutes an issue which can and should be explored in a northern context.[121] The registers of St Mary Magdalene at Clitheroe record in 1570 and between 1573 and 1606 whether children were regarded as legitimately conceived or not. Here, 4.85 percent of children baptised were remarked as illegitimate. It should be clarified that it is not only illegitimate children that are marked, but also legitimate children, so that the baptism of every child has a comment whether legitimate or illegitimate. The figures therefore are firm and unambiguous. Now, importantly, up to 1594, the incumbent made a rhetorical effort to ascribe to each illegitimate child not only a putative father, but the father's surname: thus, for example, John Preestley *filius putatus Johannis Preestley et Margarete Thorpe … illegitime procreatus* in 1573. For all twenty-four illegitimate children up to 1594 this protocol was enforced, so that each bastard child received its supposed father's surname.[122]

Remaining within Lancashire, but retreating to earlier in the sixteenth century, the registers for Prescot allow the same analysis, since each child baptised was categorised by the clergyman as either legitimate (lawfully begotten) or illegitimate (unlawfully begotten). Prescot comprised an immense parish, consisting of fifteen townships extending over fifty-eight square miles. From 1540 to *c.*1550, 14.2 percent of children baptized were stigmatized by the clergyman as unlawfully begotten.[123] Until 1548, the

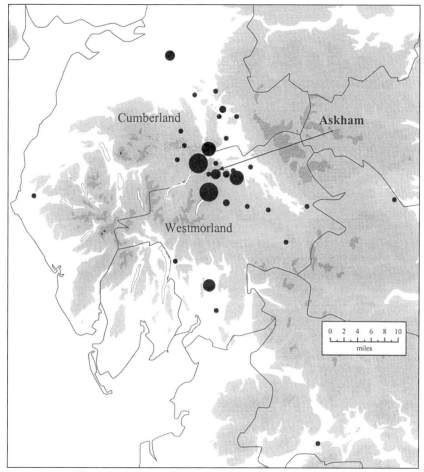

Figure 11 Marriage horizons: Askham (Lancs.), 1604–1722

entries were rhetorically inscribed so that the child was not only affiliated to a presumed father but also received that father's surname: thus Thomas Eccleston whose putative father was Peter Eccleston. That practice was abandoned *c*.1548.

Further north, in Shap, the incumbents persisted in attributing to illegitimate offspring the surnames of their reputed fathers, from at least 1569 to 1602, but occasionally revived as a practice in 1606, 1616, and 1619.[124] At Crosthwaite, the practice of registration between 1571 and 1651 was even more emphatic, for the inscription of bastards omitted the mother completely and indicated only the paternal relationship, allocating the father's surname to the child.[125]

Other incumbents signified a more circumspect position, describing bastards by an alias to incorporate both parents' surname. Such an approach was adopted in the register of baptisms for Ripon between 1600 and 1606. In 1600 were registered the christenings of Jane Dybb alias Raughton bastard and Richard Hewit alias Cravan

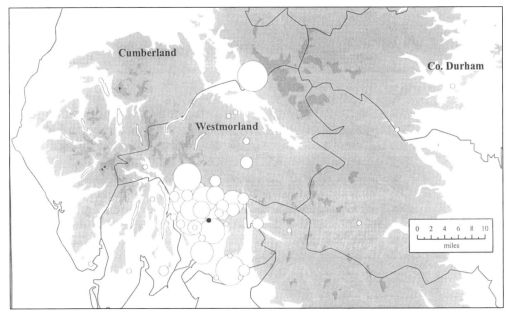

Figure 12 Marriage horizons: Kendal (Westmorland), 1557–61, 1575–1610

bastard. Almost every illegitimate child was recorded in this fashion, some eighteen altogether. [126]

To the extent that bastardy complicated the persistence, continuity and transfer of surnames in early-modern England, at whatever level of significance, its implications can be addressed in a northern context. That clarification is important for the environment of northern surnames in particular where there was at least a written attempt to confront the complication. The supposition that the clergy reflected a wider local social concern carries some weight.

Local horizons and persistence of local populations in northern localities

Whilst the persistence of toponymic bynames in their eponymous places reveals something of localized social organization in northern territories, more concrete evidence should be adduced to confirm the underlying processes. How local countries were delineated can to a certain measure be elucidated through marriage horizons and the extent of endogamous and exogamous marriages. To clarify, endogamous marriages were constituted where both parties were *specifically* defined as of this parish, whilst exogamous ones were constituted when one party belonged to another parish.

Fortunately, some incumbents of several northern parishes, if only for short periods, diligently recorded the origins of both parties. Between 1603 and 1626, seventy percent of marriages at Skipton parish church were endogamous, less than a third involving one party from another parish. [127] Within Yorkshire there are comparative data for

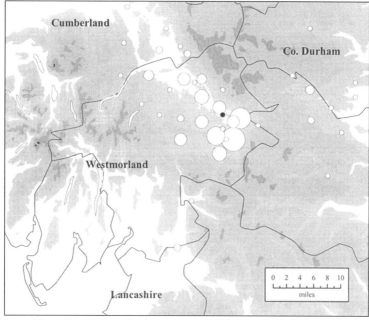

Figure 13 Marriage horizons: Warcop (Westmorland), 1597–1744

Ripon between 1619 and 1629, where seventy-nine percent of over three hundred marriages were endogamous, only twenty-one percent involving a party from another parish.[128]

The marriage horizons concerned in the exogamous marriages in Skipton are illustrated in Figure 2, which reflects how, even for a significant market town of the seventeenth century, these social arrangements were intensely localized. Similar exercises can be achieved for the parishes of Stanhope and York (Micklegate), the former between 1613 and 1740 and the latter from 1718 to 1753, presented in Figures 3 and 4. Divulged by all these figures is the intensely localized social network, contained within fairly defined countries and localities. Although exogamous partners in marriages at Ripon had their origin in over thirty other parishes, the radius of distance of marriage horizons was circumscribed (Figure 5). Indeed, the parishes of origin form a narrow, elongated transect along the Ouse valley.

Moving into different territory, in the north-west, similar exercises about marital endogamy and exogamy can be prosecuted for Shap between 1604 and 1616, unambiguously because during that period all marriage registration stated the origins of the parties including the fully descriptive statement: 'both of this parish' (or parishing as local vernacular required).[129] In those dozen years, seventy-five marriages were endogamous – both bride and groom resident in Shap – compared with merely nineteen exogamous liaisons. In a southerly direction, in Lancashire, although the numbers are small, forty-eight percent of marriages at Chipping between 1653 and 1692 were endogamous (N= 56), with a slightly higher number, sixty-one, involving a partner from another parish.[130]

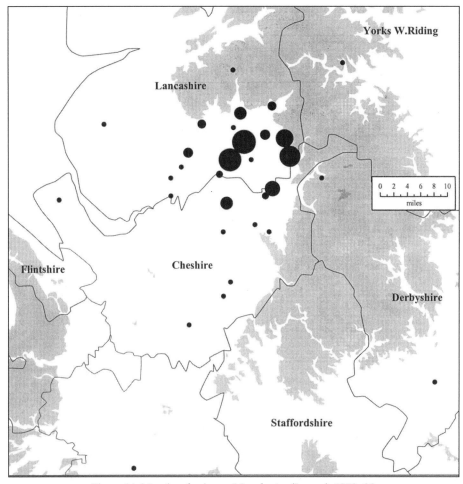

Figure 14　Marriage horizons: Manchester (Lancs.), 1573–99

For comparison against these data, marriage horizons can be reconstructed for some Lancashire parishes. Those for Clitheroe between 1570 and 1587 are illustrated in Figure 6. Although the data are not extensive, the localization is visible, with concentrations from Chatburn, Worston, Downham and Mitton.[131] Similarly circumscribed are the data for Didsbury, 1599–1600 and 1653–1712 (Figure 7).[132] For Aughton, the data for 1697 to 1748 (Figure 8) are considerably more significant, although the context should be explained. Aughton was one of the smaller parishes in Lancashire and, moreover, the larger proportion of marriages celebrated there involved exogamy. Both parties belonged to the parish in perhaps only about twenty-five percent of marriages. The seventy-five percent involving a partner from outside the parish still reveal, however, a highly concentrated marriage horizon: fifty-four involved parties from Ormskirk; forty-six from Liverpool; twenty-four from Halsall; fifteen

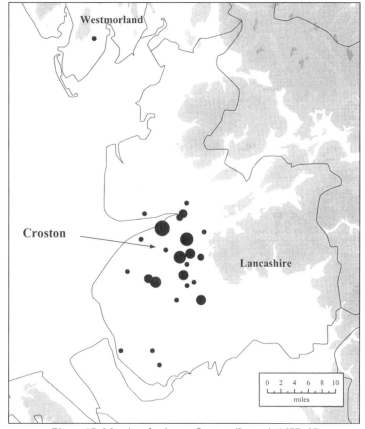

Figure 15 Marriage horizons: Croston (Lancs.), 1657–85

from Lathom; twelve from Lydiate; and ten from Scarisbrick.[133] The character of marriage horizons at Chipping exhibits the same intensity of localization (Figure 9).

For a timescale of just little more than a generation, from 1576 until 1616, the marriage horizons at Shap can be reconstructed, as Figure 10.[134] The exogamous marriage partners were concentrated in four parishes: Mardale; Morland; Bampton; and Crosby Ravenstone. Between 1604 and 1722, those horizons can be demonstrated for Askham too, revealing an association with Bampton and Barton (Figure 11).[135] With, as might be expected, more voluminous data, the configuration of marriage horizons for Kendal between 1557 and 1561 and from 1575 into the early seventeenth century, is particularly informative (Figure 12). Immense relationships are demonstrated with Crook, Greyrigg, Hutton, Kentmere, Natland, Over Staveley, Skelsmergh, Strickland Roger and Underbarrow.[136] Now, with all these parishes, the interest lies not only in the intensely localized character of the horizons, but also the barrier formed by the Pennine chain. Few certified liaisons were established across to the east of the Pennines.

A very slight contrast is presented by marriage horizons at Warcop between 1597

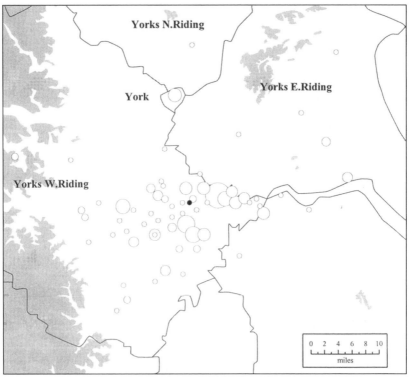

Figure 16 Marriage horizons: Snaith (Yorks. W. R.), 1538–1647

and 1744, for here trans-Pennine liaisons were consummated by marriage, although in limited numbers. Here too most marriage partners belonged to a severely localized area, the concentration of relationships being associated with Kirkby Stephen, Brough and Crosby Garrett (Figure 13).[137]

Confirmatory patterns of marriage horizons can be constructed for a few other parishes on either side of the Pennines. Although Manchester was already a developing urban location, and marriage partners originated from thirty-three external places between 1573 and 1599, all were concentrated in south Lancashire and north Cheshire; indeed, the highest numbers – twelve from Oldham, twenty from Chorley, and twenty-two from Prestwich – were from the immediate vicinity (Figure 14).[138] Also in south Lancashire, Croston in the seventeenth century comprised an immense parish containing Hook, Rufford, Tarleton, Hesketh, Becconsall and Bispham, as well as the eponymous Croston (Figure 15). Although between 1657 and 1685 the vast preponderance of marriages were endogamous to these townships, exogamous marriages existed but were confined to the immediately neighbouring parishes.[139] Transferring across the Pennines to the Fenlands of Yorkshire, marriage partners at Snaith between 1538 and 1647 derived from thirty-six external locations, but the concentration was localized, not least the twenty-four partners from Airmyn and ten from Fishlake (Figure 16).[140]

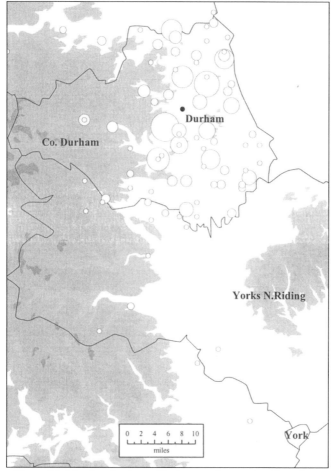

Figure 17 Marriage horizons: Durham, early seventeenth century

Onomastics, northern-ness and the politics of places

What has been attempted above has involved introducing two distinct, but inter-related, elements: to consider place-ness of the north – in the context of ideas of place and space and in terms of superficial, in the sense of overall, cohesion; and place as lived experience – *l'espace vécu* – which patterned the north into a mosaic of localities, which (ultimately) induced a politics of places of local difference and rivalries under an umbrella of northern-ness.

What follows will be an effort to define with more precision how those two concepts co-existed, were inter-related and defined each other, through the medium of onomastic material – one of the cultural media of the speech community and communities. Despite protestations from some onomasticians that names are not exclusively linguistic, not purely lexical elements, and thus perhaps not language *per se*, the perception argued here is that names did have linguistic value and thus were embedded in the language and language use of the speech community.

If it is apposite to emphasize 'the significance of local placenames, and how it is that toponyms, when employed in certain contexts, contribute to the creation of senses of place rich in moral, cosmological, and biographical texture', perhaps something similar might be accredited to bynames and surnames, through which the speech community at least formally addressed its individual parts.[141] That statement, however, is not unambiguous, for we do have to consider how frequently and in what manner bynames and surnames were actually encountered in speech communities. It must be recognized that surnames in particular came simply to constitute a formal mechanism of identification, perhaps experienced most frequently in written form or in formal exchanges of information. Surnames did not perhaps as frequently contribute to the quotidian, informal, verbal interchanges in the local speech community. Their position was backstage, memorialized in certain, perhaps limited, means, but still contributing to a consciousness, a politics of identity.[142]

Ideally a discussion of the two concepts of northern-ness and locality (delineated above) would proceed in a dialogic fashion, but for the most part such an approach proves to be elusive. Unfolding, therefore, in a more sequential manner, the next two chapters are directed to elucidating the isomorphism of the north (what onomastic usage contributed to a perception of cohesion), whilst the following section then estimates how far particular language usage through names reaffirmed a mosaic of localities. In that way, it is hoped, the context will be firmly established before exploring in more detail onomastic practices and processes.

Notes

1   *The Riverside Chaucer* (3rd edn, Oxford, 1987) p. 80 ('The Reeve's Tale', ll. 4014–15).
2   *Riverside Chaucer*, p. 80 ('The Reeve's Tale', ll. 4073–4.
3   T.N.A. (P. R. O.) Chancery Miscellanea 59/4/147.
4   W. N. Thompson, ed., *The Register of John de Halton Bishop of Carlisle* (2 volumes, Canterbury and York Society xii–xiii, 1913), ii, pp. 10, 68.
5   Because of the date, it may perhaps be legitimate to discount other etymologies such as Scandinavian or Norman-Scandinavian descent.
6   H. Brierley, ed., *The Parish Registers of Garstang Church* (Lancs. P. R. Soc. 63, 1925), p. 69.
7   R. Shields, *Places on the Margin. Alternative Geographies of Modernity* (London, 1991), ch. 5: 'The North-south divide in England' (pp. 207–51) attributes the 'divide' to the industrialization of the North, so that a social spatialization has ensued with the North – an imprecise geographical concept – synonymous with working class existence in a dialogic relationship with the South. His Figure 5.1 (p. 209) presents a fairly expansive and amorphous 'North' of England.
8   H. M. Jewell, *The North-South Divide. The Origins of Northern Consciousness in England* (Manchester, 1994).
9   Jewell, *North-South Divide*, pp. 198–201; M. F. Wakelin, *English Dialects. An Introduction* (repr. 1981), p. 34; D. Burnley, 'Lexis and semantics' in N. Blake, ed., *The Cambridge History of the English Language Volume II 1066–1476* (Cambridge, 1992), p. 411.
10   D. Crystal, *The Stories of English* (London, 2004), pp. 161–68 (quotation at p. 168); but compare

D. R. Howard, *The Idea of the Canterbury Tales* (Berkeley, 1976), pp. 106–9. For further comment, see chapter 10 below.

11 A. C. Baugh and T. Cable, *A History of the English Language* (repr. London, 1987), pp. 188–91; T. Pyles and J. Algeo, *The Origins and Development of the English Language* (Fort Worth, repr. 1993), p. 141; the legacy here is received from S. Moore, S. B. Beech and H. Whitehall, *Middle English Dialect Characteristics and Dialect Boundaries* (Ann Arbor, 1935).

12 G. Kristensson, *A Survey of Middle English Dialects 1290–1350: the Six Northern Counties and Lincolnshire* (Lund Studies in English 35, 1967); Kristensson, *A Survey of Middle English Dialects 1290–1350: the West Midland Counties* (Publications of the New Society of Letters in Lund 78, 1987); Kristensson, *A Survey of Middle English Dialects 1290–1350: the East Midland Counties* (Lund University Press, 1995).

13 Jönsjö, *Studies*, thus accepts *ab initio* the six northern counties with Lincolnshire; I. Hjertstedt, *Middle English Nicknames in the Lay Subsidy Rolls for Warwickshire* (Acta Universitatis Upsaliensis, Studia Anglistica Upsaliensia 63, 1987) assumes a broad differentiation between East Midland and West Midland dialects.

14 P. McClure, 'Lay subsidy rolls and dialect phonology' in F. Sandgren, ed., *Otium et Negotium: Studies in Onomatology and Library Science Presented to Olof von Feilitzen* (Acta Bibliothecae Regiae Stockholmiensis 16, 1973), pp. 188–94.

15 A. McIntosh, M. L. Samuels and M. Benskin, *A Linguistic Atlas of Late Mediaeval English* (4 volumes, Aberdeen, 1986); M. Benskin, 'Description of dialect and areal distributions' in *Speaking in Our Tongues. Medieval Dialectology and Related Disciplines* ed. M. Lang and K. Williamson (Cambridge, 1994), pp. 169–92; subsequently this approach is recognized by B. M. H. Strang, *A History of English* (repr. London, 1986), pp. 224–7 and J. Milroy, 'Middle English dialectology' in Blake, *Cambridge History … Volume II*, pp. 182–91.

16 P. Trudgill, *Dialects in Contact* (Oxford, 1986) and, originally, H. Orton *et al.*, *The Survey of English Dialects* (5 volumes, Leeds, 1962–71) and Orton, *The Linguistic Atlas of England* (London, 1978).

17 P. Claval, *An Introduction to Regional Geography* trans. I. Thompson (Oxford, 1998), pp. 45–6, 126–30 ('Speech and spatial differentiation') and p. 138 (quotation); for the physical experience of this *genius loci*, Norberg-Schulz, *Genius Loci. Towards a Phenomenology of Architecture* (New York, 1984).

18 E. Soja, *Postmodern Geographies. The Reassertion of Space in Critical Social Theory* (London, 1999 edn), p. 148.

19 Soja, *Postmodern Geographies*, p. 150.

20 Soja, *Postmodern Geographies*, p. 151.

21 A. C. Jiménez, 'On space as a capacity', *Journal of the Royal Anthropological Institute* 9 (2003), p. 139.

22 Jiménez, 'On space as a capacity', pp. 140, 148.

23 The most cogent discussion of these attitudes to place is now S. Feld and K. H. Basso, eds, *Senses of Place* (Santa Fe, 1996), pp. 3–11.

24 See further below, pp. 5, 19, 79.

25 For the background: J. F. Willard, *Parliamentary Taxes on Personal Property 1290–1334. A Study in Mediaeval English Administration* (Cambridge, Mass., 1934), pp. 81–5; for calculations of levels of 'capture': C. Dyer, *Lords and Peasants in a Changing Society. The Estates of the Bishopric of Worcester 680–1540* (Cambridge, 1980), p. 109; B. F. Harvey, 'The population trend in England between 1300 and 1348', *Transactions of the Royal Historical Society* 5th series xvi (1966), p. 28; A. Jones, 'Caddington, Kensworth, and Dunstable in 1297', *Economic History Review* 2nd series xxxii (1979), p. 324.

26 Throughout the discussion is informed by sociolinguistic concepts through the intermediary

of, for example, R. Wardhaugh, *An Introduction to Sociolinguistics* (Oxford, 1986), J. Holmes, *An Introduction to Sociolinguistics* (Harlow, 1992), and R. A. Hudson, *Sociolinguistics* (Cambridge, 1980, 2nd edn 1996); and in an historical context, P. Burke & R. Porter, eds, *The Social History of Language* (Cambridge, 1978).

27 *Essex*, pp. 4, 17, 32, 64, 97, 104; I. H. Jeayes, ed., *Court Rolls of the Borough of Colchester* volume 1 *(1310–1352)* (Colchester, 1921), p. 158.

28 *Devon*, pp. 3, 8, 9, 32, 40, 73, 86, 112, 120.

29 *Wiltshire*, pp. 32, 59–60, 103–4, 125.

30 *Bedfordshire 1297*, pp. 12, 25, 26.

31 D. M. Stenton, ed., *Rolls of the Justices in Eyre … Yorkshire in 3 Henry III (1218–19)* (Selden Society 56, 1937), p. 15.

32 *Cumberland*, pp. 14, 34; 'Lancashire', p. 100.

33 *Yorkshire1297*, p. 95; *Yorkshire 1301*, pp. 48, 88, 116.

34 *Yorkshire Assize Rolls*, p. 26.

35 Stenton, *Rolls of the Justices in Eyre … Yorkshire*, p. 202.

36 Stenton, *Rolls of the Justices in Eyre … Yorkshire*, p. 206.

37 Stenton, *Rolls of the Justices in Eyre … Yorkshire*, p. 356 (relating to Heslerton).

38 Colonel Parker, 'Lay subsidy rolls 1 Edward III N. R. & City of York' in *Miscellanea II* (YASRS lxxiv, 1929), pp. 111, 133, 142.

39 Parker, 'Lay subsidy rolls 1 Edward III N. R. …', p. 152.

40 C. M. Fraser, *The Accounts of the Chamberlains of Newcastle upon Tyne 1508–11* (Society of Antiquaries of Newcastle upon Tyne, Record Series 3, 1987), p. 102; for unlading, pp. 201, 202, 203, 205, 207, 208, 213, 214, 216, 224. It is possible that a contraction for -*er*- would convert these names into Sotherorn or similar.

41 Fraser, *Accounts of the Chamberlains*, pp. 77–8.

42 Fraser, *Accounts of the Chamberlains*, p. 155.

43 G. B. Richardson, 'A muster of the fencible inhabitants of Newcastle-upon-Tyne in the year 1539…' *Archaeologia Aeliana* IV (1855), pp. 126, 130, 135.

44 A. Edleston, *The Registers of Winston* (Durham & Northumberland P. R. Soc. xxxv, 1918), p. 13.

45 *Yorkshire Assize Rolls*, p. 45.

46 Stenton, *Rolls of the Justices in Eyre … Yorkshire*, p. 204.

47 Stenton, *Rolls of the Justices in Eyre … Yorkshire*, p. 289.

48 M. Merleau-Ponty, *Phénoménologie de la Perception* (Paris, 1945).

49 *Cat. Ancient Deeds* II, p. 330 (B2729).

50 *Cat. Ancient Deeds* V, p. 8 (A10478).

51 Stenton, *Rolls of the Justices in Eyre … Yorkshire*, p. 211.

52 Stenton, *Rolls of the Justices in Eyre … Yorkshire*, p. 17.

53 For the various implications of common fame, T. Fenster & D. L. Smail, eds, *Fama. The Politics of Talk & Reputation in Medieval Europe* (Ithaca, 2003).

54 *Bedfordshire 1297*, pp. 65, 99, 100.

55 *Bedfordshire 1297*, p. 85.

56 *Huntingdonshire*, pp. 35, 39, 41, 63 (see also William *Vaccarius* at Upwood: p. 40).

57 See below, pp. 91–4.

58 For an argument for a (proto-)gentry in Yorkshire by the early thirteenth century, H. Thomas, *Vassals, Heiresses, Crusaders, and Thugs. The Gentry of Angevin Yorkshire, 1154–1216* (Philadelphia, 1993).

59 *Pudsay Deeds* , pp. 94–5 (8), 98 (12), 100 (16), 106 (23), 124 (24).

60 R. B. Turton, ed., *The Honor and Forest of Pickering* (2 volumes, North Riding Record Society new series II and IV, 1895 and 1897), I, p. 34; II, p. 29.

61 Turton, *Honor and Forest of Pickering*, I, p. 81, II, p. 67.

62 G. Redmonds, *Yorkshire: West Riding* (English Surnames Survey 1, Chichester, 1978); R. McKinley, *The Surnames of Lancashire* (English Surnames Survey 4, Oxford, 1981).

63 Bodl. Rawl MS B 449, fos 66v, 67r.

64 Bodl. Rawl MS B 449, fos 67v, 75r.

65 *Wakefield Court Rolls* I, p. 42.

66 *Wakefield Court Rolls* II, p. 74 (1307).

67 *Wakefield Court Rolls* II, pp. 77–8 (1307).

68 *Cat. Ancient Deeds* VI, p. 25 (C3975) (6 Ric II).

69 *Cat. Ancient Deeds* VI, p. 233 (C5522).

70 Bodl. Rawl MS 449, fo. 101v.

71 Bodl. Rawl MS 449, fo. 102r.

72 Bodl. Rawl MS B 449, fo. 132v.

73 J. M. Todd, ed., *The Lanercost Cartulary* (Surtees Society 203, 1997), p. 337 (290).

74 *Northumberland Charters*, p. 332 (dcccx).

75 BL Add MS 40008, fo. 137r.

76 BL Add MS 40008, fo. 152v.

77 BL Add MS 40008, fo. 152r–v.

78 BL Add MS 40008, fo. 229v.

79 BL Add MS 40008, fo. 282r: but he also styled himself Robert *filius Roberti de Norfok de Careby*.

80 BL Add MS 40008, fo. 111r.

81 Bodl. MS Top Yorks c 72, fos 7v–9r.

82 BL Add MS 40008, fo. 232r.

83 Bodl. MS Top Yorks c 72, fos. 22v–25r.

84 *Cat. Ancient Deeds* III, pp. 497–8 (D790): 15 October 22 Henry VII (1506).

85 F. A. Bailey, ed., *The Registers of Farnworth Chapel in the Parish of Prescot, 1538–1612* (Lancs. P. R. Soc. 80, 1941). For Prescot, see further below.

86 F. Taylor, ed., *The Parish Registers for Aughton, 1541–1764* (Lancs. P. R. Soc. 81, 1942), pp. 1, 5, 6, 7, 8.

87 Taylor, *Parish Registers of Aughton*, pp. 7, 10.

88 J. Perkins, *The Register of the Parish of Prescot* (Lancs. P. R. Soc. 137, 1995), p. 2.

89 Perkins, *Register of the Parish of Prescot*, p. 5.

90 Perkins, *Register of the Parish of Prescot*, pp. 18, 21.

91 Perkins, *Register of the Parish of Prescot*, pp. 2, 6, 13, 18, 19, 21, 22, 27, 34, 36, 37.

92 Perkins, *Register of the Parish of Prescot*, pp. 5, 21, 23, 24, 31, 35.

93 Perkins, *Register of the Parish of Prescot*, pp. 21, 31.

94 Perkins, *Register of the Parish of Prescot*, pp. 66 (Peresson), 69 (Jackeson, Haryson), 72 (Heryson).

95 Perkins, *Register of the Parish of Prescot*, p. 185.

96 Perkins, *Register of the Parish of Prescot*, pp. 152, 155, 156, 162, 165, 168, 169, 170, 175, 177, 178, 179, 182, 183, 184, 185.

97 Perkins, *Register of the Parish of Prescot*, pp. 156, 157, 158, 159.

98 A. Smith, ed., *The Registers of the Parish Church of Walton-on-the-Hill* (Lancs. P. R. Soc. 5, 1900), pp. 155, 157–61, 164–7.

99 T. B. Ecroyd, *The Registers of the Parish Church of Whalley* (Lancs. P. R. Soc. 7, 1900), pp. 2–4.

100 F. A. Bailey, ed., *The Parish Registers of Huyton* (Lancs. P. R. Soc. 85, 1946), pp. 97, 100–4.

101 Bailey, *Registers of Farnworth Chapel*, pp. 18–19.

102 Bailey, *Registers of Farnworth Chapel*, pp. 1–2, 8.

103 Bailey, *Registers of Farnworth Chapel*, pp. 36, 38–9, 41, 43.

104 Bailey, *Registers of Farnworth Chapel*, p. 71.

105 Bailey, *Registers of Farnworth Chapel*, pp. 53, 64, 69, 71, 130, 133, 135, 159,

106 Bailey, *Registers of Farnworth Chapel*, pp. 91, 135.

107 R. Dickinson, ed., *The Registers of the Parish of Childwall. Part 1, 1557–1680* (LCRS 106, 1967), pp. 3–12 and 15.

108 Dickinson, *The Registers of the Parish of Childwall*, pp. 25–6, 28, 30, 32–3, 35–6, 38, 40.

109 Dickinson, *The Registers of the Parish of Childwall*, pp. 30, 32, 35–6.

110 For these aspects, see, of course, R. McKinley, *The Surnames of Lancashire* (English Surnames Survey 4, 1981).

111 Bailey, *Registers of Farnworth Chapel*, pp. 5, 12, 14.

112 McKinley, *Surnames of Lancashire*; see also O. Padel, 'Cornish surnames in 1327', *Nomina* 9 (1985), pp. 81–8.

113 *Wakefield Court Rolls* III, pp. 149, 152. Incidentally, one entry in 1316 describes a related case as Nalle *Gerbode* impleading Robert and John *Gerbode* for dower, which would suggest that Nalle is a hypocorism of Alice.

114 *Wakefield Court Rolls* III, p. 157.

115 *Wakefield Court Rolls* III, p. 83.

116 *Wakefield Court Rolls* III, p. 81.

117 *Wakefield Court Rolls* III, p. 179.

118 *Wakefield Court Rolls* III, p. 108.

119 The most comprehensive assessment of levels of bastardy in early-modern England is still contained within P. Laslett, K. Oosterveen, and R. M. Smith, eds, *Bastardy and its Comparative History. Studies in the History of Illegitimacy and Marital Nonconformity in Britain, Germany, Sweden, North America, Jamaica and Japan* (London, 1980), which reveals the peak of early-modern bastardy in England in the late sixteenth and early seventeenth centuries, declining through the seventeenth century and raises the question of whether there existed a 'bastardy-prone sub-society'.

120 R. M. Smith, 'Marriage processes in the English past: some continuities' in L. Bonfield, R. Smith and K. Wrightson, eds, *The World We Have Gained. Histories of Population and Social Structure* (Oxford, 1986), pp. 43–99.

121 The mechanism for extracting the putative father's surname is explained by L. Gowing, *Common Bodies: Women, Touch and Power in Seventeenth-Century England* (New Haven, 2003), pp. 159–64, in which the role of the midwife was critical.

122 J. Perkins, ed., *The Registers of St Mary Magdalene, Clitheroe, 1570–1680* (Lancs. P. R. Soc. 144, 1998), at p. 2 for Preestley.

123 Perkins, *Register of the Parish of Prescot*.

124 M. E. Noble, *The Registers of the Parish of Shap* (Kendal, 1912), pp. 18, 19, 20, 22, 36, 37, 39, 40, 45, 46, 53, 143, 144, 148.

125 J. F. Haswell, *Registers of Crosthwaite-cum-Lyth* (Penrith, 1935), pp. 6, 7, 9, 11, 14, 15, 16, 19, 27, 30.

126 W. J. Kaye, ed., *The Parish Register of Ripon* I (Yorks. P. R. Soc. 80, 1926), pp. 51–3, 57, 62, 64, 67–9, 119, 122, 124.

127 W. J. Stavert, ed., *The Parish Registers of Skipton-in-Craven, 1592–1680* (Skipton, 1894).

128 W. J. Kaye, ed., *The Parish Registers of Ripon* I (Yorks. P. R. Soc. 80, 1926), pp. 128–38.

129 Noble, *Register of the Parish of Shap*.

130 A. Brierley, ed., *The Registers of the Parish Church of Chipping* (Lancs. P. R. Soc. 14, 1903), pp. 122–30.

131 Perkins, *Registers of St Mary Magdalene, Clitheroe*.

132 H. T. Crofton & E. A. Tindall, eds, *The Register of the Church of St James, Didsbury* I (Lancs. P. R. Soc. 8, 1900).

133 F. Taylor, ed., *The Parish Registers of Aughton, 1541–1764* (Lancs P. R. Soc. 81, 1942).

134 Noble, *Register of the Parish of Shap*, pp. 71–87.

135 M. E. Noble, *The Registers of the Parish of Askham* (London, 1904), pp. 40–137.

136 H. Brierley, ed., *The Registers of Kendal* (Kendal, 1921–2), pp. 101–7 and 114 et seqq.

137 J. Abercrombie, *The Registers of Warcop* (Cumberland and Westmorland P. R. Soc., 1914), pp. 103–22.

138 H. Brierley, ed., *The Registers of the Cathedral Church of Manchester* I (Lancs. P. R. Soc. 31, 1908), pp. 424–51.

139 H. Fishwick, ed., *The Registers of the Parish Church of Croston* I (Lancs. P. R. Soc. 6, 1900).

140 W. Brigg, ed., *The Parish Registers of Snaith* I (Yorks. P. R. Soc. 57, 1917), pp. 140–86.

141 Feld and Basso, *A Sense of Place*, p. 9.

142 The term 'backstage' is borrowed from E. Goffman, *The Presentation of Self in Everyday Life* (New York, 1959); it has an importance here because colloquial forms of address by others and self-reference allowed the opportunity for self-presentation or fashioning 'front-stage', whilst more formal expressions as surnames remained backstage.

2

AN EXPANSIVE 'NORTH':

PATRONYMS AND METRONYMS WITH -*SON*

Johan de Warenne Counte de Surr' a toutz notz Seneschaux Resceuours Foresters Baillifs Prouotstz et autres Ministres et a toutz les bones gentz de la vile de Wakefeud salutz Sachez nous auoir grauntee de nostre grace especiale et par cestes notz letters confermee a Johan Hobbesone de la dite vile de Wakefeud que nul Tastour de ceruoise ny entre sa meson pur sa ceruoise taster la quele il ad auendre solom les usages et custumes de meismes la vile Par quei vous maundoms que ceste chose eiez ferme et estable et le dit Johan suffrez bien et peiseblement ceo nostre garaunt ioyr En tesmoignaunce de queu chose a cestes notz letters ouertes auoms mys nostre seal Don' a nostre Chastellion le vendredi prochein après les utaux de Pasque Lan du Regne nostre seignur le Roi Edward septisme.[1]

John de Warenne, earl of Surrey, to all our stewards, receivers, foresters, bailiffs, reeves and other ministers and to all law-worthy men of the vill of Wakefield greetings. May you know that we have granted by our special grace and by these our letters confirmed to John Hobbesone of the said vill of Wakefield that no ale-taster may enter his house to taste his ale which he has for sale according to the usages and customs of the same vill. About which we order you that this matter be firm and stable and the said John shall enjoy well and peaceably this our grant. In witness of which matter we have set our seal to these our letters. Given at our castle on the Friday before the *utaux* of Easter in the seventh year of our lord King Edward's reign.

One of the distinctive features of a 'northern onomastic zone' of England was the proliferation in the later middle ages of the patronymic and metronymic forms of byname and surname with the suffix -*son*.[2] The influences on this profusion have been variously considered, principally associated with both the persistent infusion of Middle English into personal naming and the use of Middle English vernacular and the circumlocutory contribution of Scandinavian name-forms in particular regions.[3] Those issues will not be addressed in detail here, but there is consistent evidence that two zones existed: a 'northern' one where patronyms and metronyms were constructed with the element -*son* contrasted with a southern area where appositional patronyms and metronyms largely obtained – defining appositional patronyms and metronyms as those names formed from personal names without any addition (William) or with the genitival inflection (Williams).[4] Although that broad difference obtained, the -*son* forms were not absent entirely from 'southern' areas, although the appositional forms were rare in the 'northern' zone. In terms of approaching the 'northern' area as a cohesive and discretely different zone, therefore, this contrast in personal-name formation is immediately illustrative. None the less,

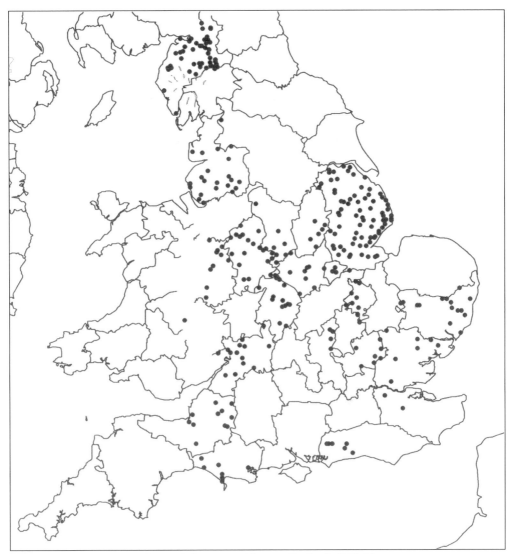

Figure 18 Bynames with -son: England, 1327–32

despite this depiction of broadly different and apparently coherent zones, it should also be remembered that within this 'northern' zone co-existed innumerable localised and distinctive sub-regions, constituted as small areas exhibiting very particular lexical and dialectal variations.

This zonal patterning is best illustrated by the geographical distribution of *-son* names in the Poll Taxes of 1377–81, the most comprehensive taxation records of the middle ages and, furthermore, compiled at a particularly apposite time – when the visibility of *-son* names was less impeded by Latin synonyms in the written records.

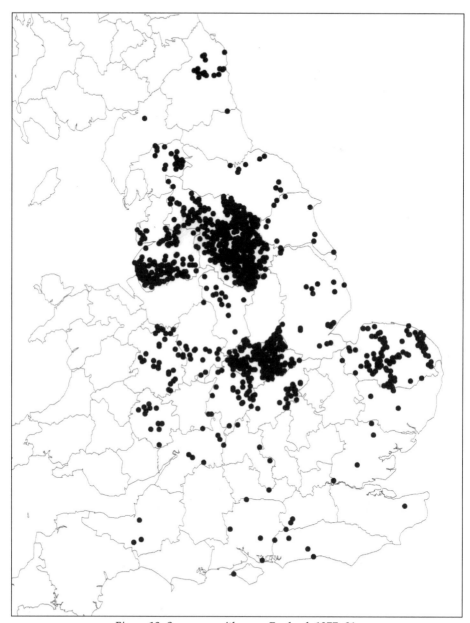

Figure 19 Surnames with -son: England, 1377–81

Figures 19 to 20 reflect this differentiation of naming of taxpayers in those lists of 1377–81. In Figure 19, the dot distributions represent the places where at least one taxpayer bore a patronym or metronym with the suffix *-son*. In Figure 20, the dots represent the number of taxpayers in each place with the same formation. Problematically, the particular assessments for some counties or parts of some counties do

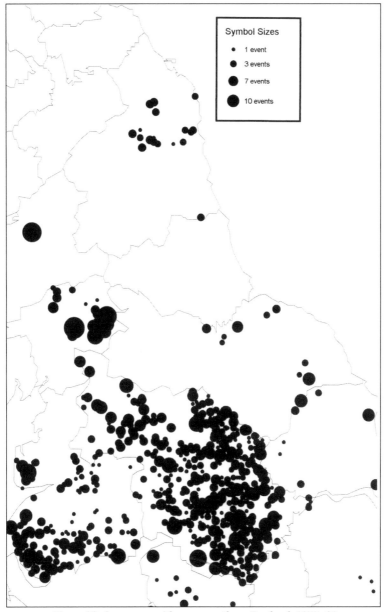

*Figure 20 Surnames with -*son: *northern England, 1377–81*

not survive – that is, there are no lists with taxpayers' names. That defect explains the lack of dots in several counties. Palatinate counties are also not represented. Moreover, although these lists survive for some urban centres in some counties, the remainder of the county is unrepresented by lists: thus Dartmouth with a list and the rest of Devon without lists and similarly for Carlisle and Cumberland.

Subject to those deficiencies, the zonal division is apparent. It is equally clear that the concentration of -son was not confined to the six northern counties, but extended into counties further south, in the Midlands and East Anglia, some of which pertained to areas of Scandinavian influence. In the 'northern' zone, consideration should perhaps be allowed for more extreme depopulation in some areas in the later middle ages, which might explain the thinner occurrence of these formations in parts of Lincolnshire, the East Riding and the North Riding.[5]

The intensity of the concentration of these vernacular forms of patronym and metronym in the northern counties is perhaps best illuminated by some aggregate statistics from the Poll Taxes of 1377–81. In the Lancashire Poll Tax, 5,322 male taxpayers were enumerated, 810 of whom were identified by bynames or surnames with the suffix -son – that is, fifteen per cent of male taxpayers had -son formations.[6] Amongst a total of 2,377 male taxpayers in the East Riding of Yorkshire, 252 (eleven per cent) were identified by -son bynames or surnames.[7] Although the tax list for Cumberland has not survived, Carlisle is represented by an extant listing in which twenty-five (four per cent) of a total of more than 600 male taxpayers, but it is probable that -son formations were more prevalent in rural than urban contexts.[8] In the West Riding of Yorkshire, the 1,850 male contributors to the Poll Tax who had -son bynames constituted seven per cent of the taxable male population.[9] Finally, although no Poll Tax listing exists for county Durham because of its Palatinate status, some impression of the extent of -son bynames and surnames in that area can be acquired from Bishop Hatfield's rentals of the Durham episcopal manors in 1382.[10] The difficulty which is presented by this source is that there is replication of the names of those tenants who held different categories of land. Nevertheless, some seventeen per cent of male tenants (507 from a total of 2,938) disported -son bynames or surnames.

To provide a firmer context, the contemporary extent of -son bynames or surnames in other counties can be contrasted. In the Poll Tax for part of Staffordshire, on the periphery of the 'North', the thirty-eight taxpayers with -son descriptors comprised 2.1 per cent of the taxable population.[11] In parts of Suffolk in 1381, only nine taxpayers of the total of 1,893 bore -son names.[12] In the small county of Rutland, merely six of the 917 taxpayers accounted for -son naming.[13]

A global assessment of the development of patronyms and metronyms with the suffix -son can be derived from comparing Figures 18 and 19, representing the incidence of bynames with -son in the lay subsidies of 1327–32 and in the Poll Taxes of 1377–81. Both distributions are affected by defects of data, each of the taxation lists being deficient for some counties. Now, for the earlier assessments to taxation, the formation of bynames with vernacular -son was incipient and so the distribution is ambiguous or incomplete. What is noticeable, however, is the intensity of the concentration in the far north-west – in Cumberland – and the extensive distribution in Lincolnshire.[14] On the other hand, a scattering of incidences existed outside the North. That scattering persisted in 1377–81, but what is more visible is, taking into account defects of survival of data, the concentration in the North, and also the strong presence across the north Midlands, on the periphery of the North, but also in Norfolk.[15] The diminution in the East Riding and Lincolnshire might be attributed to late-fourteenth-century demographic contraction in the upland parts of these counties. So illustrated by both figures – for the early and the late fourteenth centuries – is the concentration in the North, but an expansive North which extended down to Leicestershire and even spilled over that county's boundary into Warwickshire, and including substantial parts of Staffordshire and the north Midlands. The inclusion of Norfolk at such a profuse level complicates the question of influences. Whilst the extension into the north Midlands might have resulted merely from a continuum in Middle English vernacular usage, the inclusion of Norfolk would suggest a contributory Scandinavian effect. Moreover, in the case of the central Midland counties, the density of -son bynames and surnames implies a Scandinavian contribution, particularly the distribution in Leicestershire. Most demonstrably illustrated by the figures, nevertheless, is first a prior density of -son bynames in the far north-west in the early fourteenth century, and, in the late fourteenth century, an expansive north defined by the distribution of vernacular -son.

To a large extent, however, the earlier written taxation records conceal more than they reveal, for the formal register of Latin before the mid fourteenth century tended to exclude vernacular and colloquial naming. Although in 1327–32 some vernacular forms were inserted in the records, Latin renditions (*filius x*) were more profuse. Undoubtedly those Latin patronyms and metronyms were renderings of vernacular -son forms in the northern area.[16]

Visibly, these formations did appear in southern counties, but as isolated and sparse occurrences. Some comprehension of this geographical patterning can be acquired through examining the genealogy of the formations in -son. Old English -sunu formations had been more widespread in the south and south-west than anywhere else in pre-Conquest England – predominantly in Devon, Hampshire, Somerset and Kent, especially in comparison with the low recorded numbers in Yorkshire and Durham.[17] The preponderance of these bynames was constructed on Old English personal names and only twenty-four on Scandinavian ones. Thereafter, however, the occurrence of -son bynames in written records declined, with merely a few instances in the twelfth century. Reaney cited a small number of examples, including *Sareson* in London in 1286 and *Grimmesone* and *Fornessune* in twelfth-century Yorkshire.[18]

It is important here to re-examine the discontinuity of -son bynames in the twelfth and thirteenth centuries to illustrate their survival in areas other than the 'North'. In Norfolk in 1138x1147 occurred a reference to Aluric *Carlessone*'s land, unlikely to refer to a pre-Conquest tenant.[19] Pertinently in this present context, Arne *Grimsune* attested a charter to Whitby Abbey in the middle of the twelfth century.[20] About 1180 a small payment was made to the widow of God' [Godwin or Godric] *Clutessune* in Canterbury.[21] Sometime toward the middle of the twelfth century – perhaps before 1155 – a rent derived from the land of Lewin *Chetingessune* in Canterbury.[22] Two important conclusions can be elicited from this evidence. First, it confirms that the -sun element was not confined to the north in the twelfth century. Second, the suffix did continue in the twelfth century to be associated with insular personal names, not new forms of name.[23]

During the thirteenth century, in Yorkshire, Richard *Adamessone* alienated land in Calthorpe.[24] Much later, in the second decade of the fourteenth century, Geoffrey

Sallissone was involved in a plea of trespass in King's Lynn.[25] In Suffolk, William *Saressone* was recorded in a rental of 1328 as a free tenant holding a messuage and nine acres.[26] William son of Peter *Russessone* acted as a grantor at Emneth in 1309, so that this byname probably existed in this part of East Anglia before the end of the thirteenth century.[27]

In the central regions of the country, *-son* names were sporadic, but not unrecognised. In Oxfordshire in 1308, William *Moricessone* was outlawed on an appeal for robbery and abduction of his wife made by Thomas *Morice* of Sandford.[28] In Watlington, Roger *Swetesone* had died by *c*.1273.[29]

Just to the north, in Northamptonshire, Robert *Geffreysone* brought an arraignment for a robbery at Grafton in 1285.[30] Four men were accused of dragging a Welshman, John le *Greyuesone* of Swaton, from the church of St Michael, Northampton, and murdering him outside the cemetery. That heinous crime occurred in 1329–30, the same year in which Roger *Deyessone* of Little Billing in the same county was killed.[31] In that year too, William *Wydewesone* was arrested at Wellingborough in the same county for burglary at Harrowden. Convicted, he was hung, his chattels appraised at just over 1s. In this case, it can be presumed that the metronymic byname was associated with lowly status.[32]

What thus becomes noticeable in the thirteenth-century corpus of *-son* names is a continuing, but sporadic, occurrence throughout many areas of England, and secondly the transformation by which the suffix became attached to new forms of 'forename' replacing the association in the twelfth century with insular personal names.[33] These later features can be illustrated in considerable detail.

In 1308, Robert le *Revesone* was killed in Buckinghamshire.[34] In that county too, Walter *Ivottesone* acted on a jury of inquisition on the manor of Newton Longville in 1293.[35] In Coventry in 1315 Stephen *Modersone* acquired property and by 1356 both Thomas *Jeuesone* and Jordan *Julianessone* were tenants in the city.[36] In the small town of Solihull in Warwickshire, the *Dawesone* kinship became important inhabitants during the early fourteenth century. John *Dawesone* the elder had already established the family there before 1343, although he had died by 1350. In 1345, he alienated a burgage tenement in the town and in 1348 a croft and land there.[37] Witcham (Cambridgeshire) was the location for a plea of land in which John le *Revesone* was defendant in 1346.[38] On the Crowland Abbey manors in Cambridgeshire, John *Revessone*, John *Kynessone* and William *Revessone* all acted on a jury of inquisition in 1334.[39] In 1334 also, Hugh *Kynneson'* was summoned to appear before the assizes in Cambridgeshire, his mainpernor being Robert *Kynneson'*. In the same forum, John *Notessone* was arraigned.[40] In adjacent Huntingdonshire, Geoffrey *Edessone* of Coten made a grant in 1328, but long before then, in 1301, Nicholas *Thommesone* of King's Ripton had acquired part of a messuage in Ramsey.[41] Le *Revissone* was a byname to be found also at Little Dunmow in Essex in 1337.[42]

By the early sixteenth century, 557 inhabitants of Cambridge over the age of fifteen were assessed in two wards – Market Ward and Preachers' Ward – to the 'poll tax' of 1513, amongst whom ten percent were identified by surnames with the suffix *-son*.[43] Although a small number of the bearers of *-son* surnames here had Dutch or Flemish origins, nonetheless many such surnames were indigenous formations, for in the lay subsidy of 1327, twenty-two taxpayers already exhibited this form of byname.[44]

As far south as the county of Surrey, a grant of land was made by John *Jonesone* of Ashead in 1322.[45] In the south-west, Wiltshire was the location where Thomas *le Reveson*, with colleagues, was accused of theft in Nettleton in 1305.[46] About sixteen years earlier, John *le Swonherdesone* suffered capital punishment for multiple thefts, including sheep and pigs.[47] In the meantime, in 1305, Robert *Moldeson* was slain in the county.[48] In the far south of the country, in Pernstead in Sussex, John *Gofesone* was a tenant of a messuage and half a virgate.[49]

As early as the taxation of 1307 in Hertfordshire, -*son* bynames existed in that county. William *le Revesone* was assessed at a low level at Eastwick, Adam *le Revesone* at a higher rate (18d.) at Ware, and Adam *Revesone* at a higher level at Marston. Taxed at 12d., Walter *Brunesone* was assessed at Little Hadham, where also Margery *Emmeson* contributed 16d.; Henry and Hugh *Hobbesone* were assessed at Pirton at modest levels, but John *le Clerkessonne* at King's Walden at a high amount, whilst Sigar *Leveson* accounted for a low marginal rate at North Mimms.[50]

Of particular interest is the occurrence of -*son* bynames in the West Midlands, especially Worcestershire, Warwickshire and Gloucestershire. The significance is heightened here because these counties were located firmly within the wider area where appositional patronyms (William, Williams) dominated. Nevertheless, the lay subsidies enumerated here taxpayers reputedly named *Emmesone, Lucesone, Huwesone* or *Hughesone, Perisson* or *Peresson, Mallesone, Pennesone, Jonson, Mariesone, Wideweson* (Gloucestershire), *Moldesone, Fillesone, Eleynesone, Eddesone, Dyesone, Revesone, Wattesone, Hobbesone, Kayeson, Huggesone, Geffesone* and *Dobbesone* (Worcestershire).[51] In Gloucestershire, patronymic and metronymic formations in the vernacular were occurring in the early fourteenth century. In 1336, Thomas *Clerkessone* acted as a juror in Stanley, whilst Richard *le Clerkessone* performed the same office at Fairford in 1337, at Saperton in 1346, Gloucester in 1349, and in 1356.[52] Another juror, at an inquest at Micheldevere in 1338, was William *Maiotesone* and a year later Gilbert *Hanysone* of Staunton was enrolled in that capacity.[53]

By the late fourteenth century, patronyms and metronyms, although not frequent, can be observed amongst the population of Buckinghamshire. In the superior eyre of 1389, a not inconsiderable number of jurors had been accorded patronymic or metronymic bynames in -*son*: Gybbesone, Harrysone (Haversham); Gleveson (Thornborough); Maggesone, Doucesone (Waddesdon); Rychardussone (Walton); Revesone (Tingwick, Whaddon); Richardessone (Walton); Fysshernssone (Newport); Wyllyamsone (Warrington); Geffessone (Broughton); Tybbessone (Moreton); Elyottessone (Weston); Douceson (Quainton); and Iboteson (Weedon).[54] About the same time, the horse drawing Simon Sareson's cart knocked over and killed a child and John Moldessone died from a stab wound to the chest.[55] In default of a listing for more than a minor part of Buckinghamshire, the lists of jurors at the coroners' inquests can be used as an impressionistic substitute for this county. The 226 jury lists produced 2,712 male jurors, only twenty-three of whom bore -*son* names.[56]

In Bedfordshire in 1269 an inquest determined accidental death in the case of Alexander *Sweynissone* of Dunstable who had excavated a pit which collapsed on him.[57] Two years later a fine was exacted from Robert *Modersone* of Melchbourne.[58] The coroners' rolls for the same county recorded Ralph *Fellesson* in the early fourteenth century.[59] In 1303, an entry fine of 4s. was exacted from Roger *Notesone* for a messuage and croft in Wingfield in Bedfordshire and this Roger *Notesone* brewed in 1304.[60] In 1355, William Maggeson of Dunton, accused of battery, produced as one of his pledges Richard Maggeson.[61] In the same year and county, Richard Chommessone appeared before the sessions of the peace for nightwalking and disturbing the peace.[62] In that county also, Robert Doucessone acted as a pledge and William Simondessone as a bailiff in the 1350s.[63] About the same time, Richard Maggesone was assaulted at Dunton and Robert Dannessone at Clifton.[64] Contemporaneously, Robert Mariotessone was described as a fisherman of Turvey.[65]

During the late fourteenth century, some individuals in these counties continued to bear bynames and surnames with -*son*: William Moldessone outlawed in Bedfordshire; William Mathewesson exacted for a debt in the same county; John Maggesone of Wentworth in Cambridgeshire who was killed; Ralph Eleynesson also killed, at Buswell in Cambridgeshire; and Martin Bettesson outlawed under the Statute of Labourers.[66]

A focus on the counties of the north Midlands, however, illustrates more acutely the existence of patronyms and metronyms with -*son* in penumbra outside the North. In the northern extremity of Nottinghamshire, just below the boundary with the West Riding of Yorkshire, Peter *filius Willelmi Dynnesone* of Blyth gave one acre and one rood of land in Blyth to his sister, Cecily, in 1315, and in 1345 John *filius Hugonis Geressone* leased two selions and a garden in Carlton in Lindrick.[67] In the south of the county, taxpayers in 1332 included William *Gibson* at Langar who contributed 3s., Adam *Pelleson*, assessed at 1s. 8d. at Shelford, Hugh *Betoson* at Newark (1s.), John *le Personesson* at Elston (2s. 1d.), Thomas *Bateson* at Kersall (a higher level of 5s. 4d.) and Robert *Beteson* (merely 10d.) at Langford.[68]

In Chester in 1318, a case of trespass involved Richard *Dawesone* as plaintiff and John *le Wrightessone* as defendant and in another similar case Richard *Batesone* appeared as defendant in the same year.[69] The sequence of -*son* bynames in Cheshire can be more clearly illustrated for Middlewich. In 1326–7 half a wich house was leased to Gilbert *Welleson*, the transfer attested by Thomas *Hulleson*.[70] One of the tenants of Middlewich between 1315 and 1326 was Richard *Bateson*.[71] Gilbert *Weelesone* was remembered as the previous grantor in a subsequent charter of 1340 when the property passed to William *filius Ricardi Bateson*.[72] In 1332, John *filius Willelmi Kittesone de Teuerton'* acquired a burgage, whilst Thomas *Hulleson* attested a charter of 1336.[73] In another charter of 1343, the grantor was described as Robert *Margeriesson capellanus* and one of the witnesses named as Thomas *Hondeson*.[74]

In Staffordshire, in the first decade of the fourteenth century, John *le Poghwebbesone* of Shifnal was accused of theft and had a reputation as a common thief.[75] Perhaps in the late thirteenth century, Richard *le Webbesone* had attested a charter relating to Burton on Trent.[76] More precisely, in 1316, John *le Prestesone* held land in Wombourne in that county.[77] In 1344, it was recorded in a charter relating to the same place that William *le Wreytsone* had held land there.[78] By the first two decades of the fourteenth century, -*son* bynames were not uncommon in Staffordshire, for pleas in the royal courts concerned Richard *Milleson* for breaking fences in Walsall, William son of William *Ormessone* for trespass at Burnaston, Adam *le Smythessone* for theft, Robert *Personesune* who fled for homicide at Easington, Roger *Lutesone* for trespass, and Richard *Bateson* for rape.[79] In a specific context in Staffordshire – the urban location of Burton on Trent – the *Knyhtessone* kinship had developed by 1319: Richard *le Knyhtessone* holding a moiety of a tenement; Adam *Knyhtessone* a former tenant of a burgage; John *le Knyhtessone*; and reference to one and a half bovates formerly held by Robert *le Knittesone*.[80] In 1304, Adam *Paynessone* of Preston was prosecuted in a plea of trespass.[81]

In the inquests of the Audley estates in the same county, a sprinkling of the tenants were identified by patronymic or metronymic bynames in *-son* in 1298–9 and 1307–8: Hugh *Lovetsone* who held a burgage; William *le* (sic) *Dobbesone* a messuage, as did Peter *Dobbeson*; Henry *Jondeson* a messuage and six acres; John *Hobbesone* merely an acre; John son of *Mayotesone* the more substantial holding of one and a half virgates; and Adam *Idonsone* even more substantially a messuage and two bovates.[82]

A generation earlier, in 1291, Robert *filius Willelmi Smithysune* of Bradwell (Derbyshire) received from Rufford Abbey a lease of six acres of arable in Abney for a term of twenty years.[83] In north Derbyshire the appearance of patronyms and metronyms with *-son* occurred from the late thirteenth century and these name forms were not unusual.[84] So a charter for land in Chesterfield in 1285 was attested by Robert *Felleson*.[85] In that borough, Robert *Pelleson* acted as an attorney to deliver seisin of land in 1331; John Hanneson attested a charter there in 1390; and between those dates, in 1372 and 1383, Chesterfield charters referred to Matilda widow of Roger Dandeson and Margery widow of Roger Michelson.[86] Most of the locations of these forms of byname were confined to the north of the county, in the High Peak, an example of which was the attestation of a charter relating to Chapel en le Frith by John *Luckesone* in 1332.[87] Consequently, John le Vikerson acquired five acres in Hope in 1361, which he, by the same name, alienated in 1376.[88] A cottage in Longford was received into the hands of John Amysson in 1380.[89] In Matlock, Nicholas *Tybbesone* attested a charter in 1349.[90] Before 1394, tenants at Walton by Chesterfield included William Edison and Robert Saunderson.[91]

In the distribution of 1377–81, Lincolnshire reveals no strong association with patronymic and metronymic bynames with *-son*. Nevertheless, this formation had existed earlier, both in the lay subsidy of 1332 (see below) and casually (because of the nature of the source) in the royal inquest held in the county in 1341.[92] That inquest revealed that William *Carleson* of Somercotes had been killed, as had John *Tibbesone* and his wife at Burton Coggles; half a mark had been extorted from John *Gibbesone* in the neighbourhood of Boston; John *Ingesone* inhabited Grimsby; at Boston again, William *Pellesone* acted as the executor of John *Pellesone*; William *Gunnesone* of Spalding had been falsely imprisoned by the sheriff; William *le Greyuesone* of Bucknall suffered battery; a theft had been perpetrated by William *Benetson* of Linwood near Market Rasen; and Walter *Denesone* of Kirby Laythorpe was accused of homicide.[93]

Before the royal inquest, patronyms and metronyms with *-son* had already insinuated into the county. For example, in 1336, William *Handessone* was involved in a dispute over probate of a will.[94] A year later, Alice *Sessun* acted as executrix of the will of her late husband, Henry *Sessun*.[95] Within the same jurisdiction, Juliana *filia Walteri Edeson'* of Saltfleetby was presented for fornication in 1339.[96]

In Leicestershire, which constitutes an important transitional area, twelve taxpayers in 1327 were identified by vernacular names with -*son*. By 1381, in Gartree Hundred alone, eighty-seven out of 123 patronyms and metronyms were rendered in the vernacular and only a small proportion in the Latin register (*filius*). Throughout the county, more than 350 taxpayers were associated with surnames with -*son*.[97] The 1340s can, however, be defined as the critical time when vernacular forms replaced the Latin register in the county, based on evidence in the rental of the manors of Leicester Abbey in 1341 and the court rolls of Kibworth Harcourt and Barkby.[98]

One of the complicating issues with the distribution of -*son* bynames in the twelfth and thirteenth centuries is the status of *Leveson*. Occurring frequently as a byname, there is a strong probability that what is at issue here is not a patronym with the suffix -*son*, but an insular Germanic (Old English) personal name, *Levesunu*. For example, a licence to compromise a case of battery in 1202 involved Alan *nepos Louesune* (the nephew of *Levesun*).[99] Moreover, a tenant described simply as *Levesune* appeared in a rental of Waltham Abbey at Wrangle and Leake (both in the Parts of Holland in Lincolnshire) in 1229x1241.[100] In that county too, although a century later, Walter *Levesone* was presented before the ecclesiastical court for relapsing into a relationship with Beatrice.[101] Particularly in Wiltshire, where *Levesune* occurred as a byname in the lay subsidy of 1225, the explanation of an insular personal name might be more convincing.[102] This byname or surname developed a quite widespread distribution during the middle ages, so that John *Levesone* performed the duty of a juror in an inquest for the manor of Hampton Meisy (Gloucestershire) in 1317 and Simon *Levesone* was tenant of half a virgate in Yatesbury (Wiltshire) in *c.* 1300.[103] At Pernstead in Sussex, Alice *Levesone* held a messuage and a virgate.[104] In 1268, Simon *Levesone* acted as a pledge in Bedfordshire.[105] Thirteen years later, the thief, Richard *Levesone*, was submitted to capital punishment at the Derbyshire eyre.[106]

In general, therefore, the continuity of bynames with -*son* remained as a trickle with sporadic distribution through the twelfth and thirteenth centuries. In those counties outside the 'North' where the wider presence of -*son* names eventually appeared in the written records, the incipience of this process did not happen until the 1340s, as in rural Leicestershire.[107] The distribution of -*son* bynames in the lay subsidies (tax lists) of 1327 and 1332 is illustrated in Figure 18. The representation is complicated by the non-availability of lay subsidies for this period for some counties, including counties in the 'North'. In lay subsidies before 1327, patronyms and metronyms are almost exclusively constructed in the Latin register. It is only with the intrusion of Middle English vernacular into the tax lists in the second decade of the fourteenth century that -*son* bynames become visible. Furthermore, the data in the lay subsidies are compromised by the threshold for inclusion and exclusion in the taxation. It is fairly evident that a large transect of the peasant population was omitted. It is, indeed, generally amongst such a social group that -*son* bynames would have been most frequent.

The data are sufficient to reveal, however, that -son bynames, although distributed throughout many southern counties, were becoming concentrated in a 'northern' England which extended approximately down to the level of the Wash. In other words, this form of bynames, although concentrated in the northernmost counties, descended on a graduated manner down into Lincolnshire, Leicestershire, Derbyshire, and Staffordshire in particular. Lincolnshire, especially, exhibited a concentration of -son bynames which had diminished by the Poll Taxes of 1377–81, whereas the concentration in Leicestershire in 1327 was confirmed and intensified by 1377–81. The highest density of distribution occurred in the far North, in Cumberland in 1327. What the data of 1327–32 and 1377–81 illustrate in combination is the predominance of -son bynames in the far North, but with a continuation in a graduated fashion down into the north Midlands. In the Midlands, two onomastic cultures coexisted: -son bynames alongside appositional patronyms and metronyms.

The appearance of -son bynames in the North may now be considered, although the most accessible and complete data related to the lower part of the 'North', in the West Riding of Yorkshire. Returning then to the quotation with which this chapter commenced, the writ of the Earl de Warenne in 1279 exempted John *Hobbesone* from the jurisdiction of the aletasters of the large composite manor of Wakefield. It is quite possible that the Middle English vernacular was deployed in this writ because the writ itself was composed in the French vernacular. In a document in the Latin register, the construction of John as *filius Roberti* or *filius Hobbe* was acceptable. In a French vernacular writ, however, composition as *fitzRobert* might have been inappropriate for a peasant. Such might have been the logic behind the written record. This formation in -son remained unusual in the written records of the manor, most of the records, such as the court rolls, being compiled, as was widespread usual for manorial records, in the Latin register. Elsewhere too, instances of the vernacular -son were incidental, but taxpayers in 1297 in Nafferton, Humbleton and Skipsea were identified as *Madersone*, *Loustepsone* and *Knyhtsone*, and in 1301 as *Allotsone* at Pickhill, *Kyngesone* at Carthorpe, *Fadirsone* at Hemlington and *Honderson* at Newton.[108] In 1309, the death of John *Benneson* of Linton occurred.[109] A smattering of patronyms and metronyms with -son had thus made their appearance by the first decades of the fourteenth century.

Vernacular forms of patronymic and metronymic bynames really intruded into the Latin manorial court rolls of Wakefield during the second decade of the fourteenth century. In 1314, John *Sibson* proffered 6d. for a licence to enlarge his booth in Wakefield market.[110] Two years later, Walter *Preesteson* was amerced 1s. for battery.[111] In the same year, 1316, Alice daughter of Richard *Brounesone* exchanged land in Alverthorpe, one of the hamlets of the manor.[112] Richard himself, described by the byname *Brouneson*, attended the court as defendant in a case of trespass in that year too.[113] The recent formation of this patronym is confirmed by a recourse in 1317 to the earlier court rolls in a dispute about dower after Richard's death. In Alverthorpe, Eve, the widow of Richard *Brouneson*, demanded against Richard *de Collay* dower in two and a half acres. Richard invoked to warranty John Broun son and heir of Richard *Brouneson* to confirm that *de Collay*'s father had purchased the land from Richard *Brouneson*. In the reference to the earlier court rolls, all were described as

Broun, not *Brouneson*.[114] Subsequently, however, the byname *Brouneson* persisted. Alice, also of Alverthorpe and daughter of Richard *Brouneson*, appeared in a case of detinue concerning a cow.[115] In 1317, Alice, daughter of Richard *Brounson*, proceeded as plaintiff against Hugh *Brounson*, in a case emanating from Alverthorpe.[116] Code-switching by the *scriptor* of the rolls is demonstrated in 1333 when Robert *filius Johannis* professed fealty for ten acres of free land which he inherited on the death of his father, John *Hobson*.[117]

Returning to *Sibson*, first occurring, as above, in 1314, Thomas *Sabbesone*, of Soland, acquired seventeen acres of land and meadow with buildings a few years later.[118] In Alverthorpe, Juliana, daughter of the *nativus* John *Sibbeson*, was presented for *leyrwite*, having been deflowered before marriage.[119] Whilst Robert *Sabbesone* made default of suit of court from Sowerby, John *Sibbeson* was accused of battery.[120] In 1316, John *Sibbesone* offered 12s. for a licence to acquire land from the lord's waste in Wakefield.[121] A year later, John *Sibbesone* acted as a pledge in Alverthorpe.[122] In 1324, John *Sibbesone* initiated a recognisance for the recovery of a crop of oats and acted as a pledge again.[123]

These two bynames – *Brouneson* and *Sibbesone* – constituted the earliest patronymic bynames to become established in the manorial court rolls of Wakefield, between 1314 and 1316. By 1317, other *-son* bynames were sporadically appearing in the court rolls: Richard *Milleson* who offered 3s. to take three acres for a term of six years in Alverthorpe; Cecily daughter of Adam *Nabbeson*, plaintiff in detinue in Sowerby; Agnes *Dyeson* amerced 2d. for an offence against the vert; and Thomas *Pellesone*, formerly reeve of Sandall, amerced 3s. for hay lost during his reeveship because of defects in the grange's roof.[124] The transitional stage in this vernacular formation in the written record is well illustrated by *Pellesone*, for in the same year, Thomas *filius Pelle* was found guilty of a false suit against Robert *filius Pelle* of Sandall, whilst that Robert *filius Pelle* contributed the merchet for his daughter.[125]

By 1323–4, *-son* bynames proliferated on the manor of Wakefield: John *Gepsone* (for collecting dry wood); John *Elyotson* (default of suit); John *Hudsone*; Robert *Pelleson* (as above); Henry *Moddeson* (admission to one acre); William son of Simon *Juddeson* (theft of a cow); Idonea *Colleson* (hue without proper cause); Thomas *Pelleson* (escape of an animal); Robert *Pelleson* (trespass); John *Nalleson* (debt); Robert *Gelleson* (admitted to one acre); Robert *Pelleson* (plaintiff in covenant); John *Nalleson* (at law about a cart); John *Alicesone* and Henry *le Smithson* (both default of suit); John *Hobbeson* (nuisance); and the wives of William *Dobbeson* and John *Hudson* (brewing).[126] During the late 1320s, the number of different patronyms and metronyms with *-son* in the court rolls expanded rapidly: *Pelleson*; *Nalleson*; *Sibbeson*; *Dobson*; *Podeson*; *le Taillourson*; *Oteson*; *le Smythson*; *Gibson*; *Alcockson*; *Robinson*; *Willeson*; *Judson*; *Alotson*; *Molleson*; *Watson*; *Cristianson*; *Iveson*; *Geppeson*; *Evoteson*; *Hebbeson*; *Colleson*; *Joseson*; *Coliceson*; *Clareson*; *Tibson*; *Hobsone*; *Brounesone*; *Bennesone*; *Daweson*; *Pierson*; *Swaynson*; *Grayveson*; *Malynson*; *Bateson*; *Thoresone*; *Erkynson*; *Childson*; and *Megotson*.[127]

That at least some of these *-son* bynames remained unstable or were recent in genesis is illustrated by a few entries in the court rolls. For example, when John *le Smythson* acceded to three acres in Sowerby for an entry fine of 1s. in 1324, the previous tenant was recorded as William *le Smyth*.[128] Moreover, the marginal status of some of the bearers of bynames with -son is perhaps illustrated by John *Evotesone* who, although placed in mercy for non-suit, was pardoned a fine because he was *pauper* in 1323.[129]

During the two years between Michaelmas 1338 and the same feast day in 1340, a profusion of patronyms and metronyms appeared in the court rolls of the manor of Wakefield: (in order of their appearance) *Willeson; Alotson; Anotson; Isbelson; Wilcokeson; Nelson; Wydeson; Smythson; Evotson; Bateson; Emson; Wilkeson; Moldeson; Penneson; Gepson; Hankynson; Grayveson; Benson; Gemson; Swaynson; Ibbotson; Odamson; Malson; Hanneson; Meggeson; Filcokeson; Michelson; Iveson; Malynson; Dobbson; Daueson; Nickeson; Sisson; Pierson; Erkynson; Tomson; Milleson; Gelleson; Colynson; Watkynson; Hobson; Robynson; Hancokeson; Eliotson; Dikson; Isoudson; Sarson; Edeson;* and *Elcokeson.*[130] Two important comments can be made about these forms: first, the proliferation; but secondly, and as importantly, the variety and range. The importance of the second point inheres in the unusual nature of the large proportion of the forms. The patronyms and metronyms were not restricted to the most common forms of personal name, but were predominantly constructed on the more unusual forms of personal name.

By the 1340s, consequently, -son bynames had become established in the written manorial records of Wakefield. Comparison can be made here with counties to the south where such formations were only just entering the written record to any extent in the 1340s. By 1348–50, the corpus of -son bynames on the composite manor of Wakefield had not only been sustained, but expanded further: *Genison; Moldson; Nabilson (alias Anabelson); Gibbeson; Dikson; Iveson; Smythson; Clerkson; Gibson; Magotson; Danson; Michaelson; Gepson; Eliotson; Malynson; Hobson; Swaynson; Hughson; Jenkinson; Magson; Bateson; Nikson; Watson; Emson; Hobkynson; Hudson; Nelleson; Alanson; Sisson; Robynson; Adamson; Clareson; Elenson; Ellison; Penson; Colynson; Mariotson; Jordanson; Edeson; Philipson; Mokeson; Wilcokson; Tellson; Brounson; Pelleson; Gillotson; Emson; Walkynson; Judson; Taylourson; Saresson; Silleson; Peresson; Alcokson; Clerkson; Rogerson; Tomasson; Hebson; Nicolson; Evotson; Hanson; Gilleson; Preistson;* and *Amereson.*[131] The extent of this proliferation is reflected in the tenants convicted of offences against the vert in 1349 who included: Roger *Edeson;* Hugh *Philipson;* Robert *Magotson;* the wife of John *Dobson;* John *Watson;* John *Colynson;* John *Hughson;* Adam *Gilleson;* Geoffrey *Moldeson;* Richard *Anabelson;* and Thomas *Iveson.*[132] All these bynames had appeared in the court rolls in the early 1330s, complemented by others: *Kirkeshaghson; Dogeson; Ormesson; Gemmeson; Wymarkson; Loucokson; Gamelson; Aggeson; Evotson;* and *Julianeson.*[133]

From these appearances in the court rolls, some associations may be elicited. The supposition can be made that -son bynames were regularly associated with the peasantry – although, of course, that is inherent in the nature of manorial court rolls. What is evident is the proliferation of such formations of bynames amongst the peasantry. That status is perceived in John *Malynson*, involved in a case of battery, who was described as a *pauper* who baked and whose wife brewed.[134] Defined also as a *pauper*, Adam *Magotson*, amerced 6d., followed the occupations of shoemaker and tanner.[135] Thomas *Gilleson* existed as a wage labourer and was thus involved in two cases concerning agreements for ploughing in 1350.[136]

Although many of these -son bynames had developed into hereditary surnames by *c.*1350, some still exhibited features of transience. A small number appeared fleetingly in the court rolls, perhaps associated with marginal inhabitants who appeared in court infrequently.[137] Instability featured also in double patronyms and metronyms: John *Danson Willeson* admitted to three roods of land in Alverthorpe;[138] John *Daweson Willeson* acquired half an acre in Wakefield;[139] John *Jacson Pelleson* against whom a false suit was initiated in 1350;[140] and Richard *Johnson Betson* accused of offences against the vert in 1350.[141] At the very end of the fourteenth century, John *Hogekynson Gybson* was outlawed consequent on an action of trespass in Aston, Yorkshire.[142] In the early years of the next century, the same proscription was directed against Henry *Jonson Wilson* of Crosby Garnet in Westmorland for a debt owed in York.[143] These double patronyms and metronyms resulted from the instability of these *-son* formations over two or three generations.

Although one explanation for the existence of these double forms was the persistent instability of patronymic and metronymic bynames, more complexity was involved. To an extent, the double formation was necessitated by the concentration of patronyms and metronyms in *-son* towards very common forms conceived on frequent forenames, so that it became imperative to distinguish one Johnson from another. That predicament increased during the later middle ages in northern regions. Double forms of byname were thus not comprehensively constituted by double patronyms or metronyms, but included also 'mixed forms': a patronym or metronym followed by another form of byname.

Similar instability was thus represented in John *Nelleson Catelyn* who surrendered a messuage and three acres in 1332.[144] In Northumberland, at Newham, William *Elyson del Hough* made a grant in the early fifteenth century, his description confirming both the instability of patronymic and metronymic compounded bynames, but equally the persistence of syndetic topographical bynames (*del* Hough).[145] As illustrative, but from the periphery of the north, was recorded the manumission of Thomas *Agasson Underthehull* – a combination of metronym and topographical description – at Bilsthorpe in Nottinghamshire in the late fourteenth century.[146] As significant in this example is the association of this compound of metronym and affixed byname with an unfree tenant.

Anecdotal evidence from other manorial court rolls confirms the chronology of the appearance of these vernacular forms of patronyms and metronyms in the early fourteenth century. In 1325, Thomas *Bateson* was selected to a jury of inquisition for Hatfield Chase, although many of the others were denominated in the Latin register as *filius x.*[147] In 1339, such jurors on the manor included Thomas *Pierson* and William *Alotson*, whilst Thomas *Grayveson* was defendant in a plea of land.[148] Appointed to the same position in Fishlake was William *Nalleson* in 1340.[149] Of the same status were Thomas *Nalsun* and Roger *Greyvesun* at Methley in 1331.[150]

Since there is a substantial break in the court rolls of the manor of Conisborough in the early fourteenth century, understanding of the introduction of Middle English vernacular forms in the court rolls is delayed until 1334. At that point, the wife of John *Nicholson* was presented for selling ale in pots and Thomas *Hudeson* and William *Bateson* were both plaintiffs in cases of trespass.[151] From *c.*1339–40, several tenants assumed *-son* bynames. William *Joseson* (once *Josepson*) was distrained to respond to

Richard *Cody*'s plea of debt; he was subsequently involved in pleas of pledge and as a defendant in a case of debt. Thomas *Iueson*, who took a lease of three roods for three years, did not recur in the rolls. William *Bateson* frequently appeared in court: in cases of debt, battery, and trespass, whilst his wife brewed and was prosecuted for defamation. The more serious charge against her, related to the defamation, imputed her connivance in putting out a contract on another tenant's son, which appears to continue a dispute occasioned when William *Bateson*, her husband, accused William *de Edenestowe* of battery for hitting him on the head with a sword. Occurring less often and in less grave circumstances, John *Mabbeson* was amerced for collecting dry wood, Thomas *Perkynson* for offence against the vert, and John son of John *Hebbeson* in a plea of land.[152]

Although the sources are much less plentiful, something of the pattern can be observed on the manor of Hundsworth in the West Riding. There, in 1329, William *Dicson* held half a bovate *ad voluntatem* (in unfree tenure) in 1329.[153] In more complicated manner, William *Preisteson*, whilst holding jointly with John *Smalchar* a messuage and bovate in free tenure, held a messuage and two bovates *ad volun-tatem*.[154] Amongst the small number of tenants on this manor, nevertheless, only a few were attributed *-son* bynames, such as John *Bateson* in 1337 and Richard *Colynson* in 1349.[155]

In the last case, however, we can discern the formation of the patronymic byname in its transition from Latin periphrase to ME byname. Colyn *alias* Colin appeared sequentially in the court of Hundsworth without any byname.

Colyn [sic] *pro uno equo capto in bladis domini*
[Colin for a horse taken in the lord's grain]

Colin [sic] *quia non est prosecutus uersus Ricardum del Lache*
[Colin because he didn't proceed against Richard *del Lache*]

In the same manner, he was involved without a byname for the escape of four oxen and four pigs and acted as a juror on an inquest, all activities between 1327 and 1348.[156] In 1346, Richard *filius Colyn'* [sic] was presented for failing to repair hedges.[157] In 1349 that Richard was inscribed in the court rolls as Richard *Colynson*, presented for his pigs straying in the lord's grain, his beasts in the lord's wood, and his maid mowing the lord's grass.[158]

Returning to 1320, Roger *Allyson* held a toft and haldole in Monk Friston, further north in Yorkshire.[159] In 1332, Simon le *Greyvesone* and accomplices were acquitted of a charge of murder at Cottingham in the East Riding.[160] Thomas *Wallesone* acquired land in Horton in 1323 and at Bolton in 1329 Richard *le Widusone* was a tenant of a bovate.[161]

Equally sparse are the court rolls for the manor of Allerton Mauleverer, but the extant ones reveal something of the progress of *-son* bynames in written form. During his lifetime, William *Todson*, who died in 1345, had been tenant of a messuage and two bovates, although his widow was admitted to only a toft and one bovate.[162] There too, Adam *Betessone* held in 1338 a cottage, garden and croft, enumerated amongst *les cotiers*, and William *le Widowson*, tenant of merely a toft, also belonged in that category.[163] In 1345, he was similarly enumerated with the same holdings and amongst the cottars.[164] In a rental of *c*.1350, John *Hebson* was listed as tenant of two messuages, five bovates and five acres, but William *le Widowson* merely a toft.[165] What, however, is extremely interesting about the Allerton rentals is their linguistic register and the formation of patronymic and metronymic bynames in general. Two rentals are composed in French, one dated 1338 and the other undated (but presumably of similar date).[166] In both rentals, the patronymic and metronymic bynames of the peasantry are unusually rendered as *le fitz x* and *le fyz x*, whilst Middle English vernacular -*son* is employed only exceptionally, so that William *Toddessone* was singularly composed in 1338, alongside *Isolde que feust la femme Will' Anicessone*.[167] The formation of peasant patronyms and metronyms in French appears extraordinary. In the fourteenth-century rentals for Allerton constructed in Latin, in contrast, peasant patronyms and metronyms were composed in that register, as *filius x*. Indeed, it is interesting that, although three tenants in the 1370s were designated Dobson, Nicholson and Hykson, most patronymic and metronymic bynames were still constructed in their Latin formation.[168] At least in the mind of these *scriptores*, therefore, ambiguity persisted in the written form of these bynames even late into the fourteenth century.

Although in the lay subsidy for the North Riding in 1327 most of the patronymic and metronymic forms were rendered in Latin, some intrusive vernacular forms indicated the tendency for the future. At Aton, Robert *Widson* was assessed at 1s. 3d.; Robert *Gingeson* was encountered amongst the taxpayers at Thirlby; Peter *Smitson* paid 1s. 6d. at Thornton Watlass; Robert *Rybson* 1s. 6d. at Kirkleatham; John *Fayraliceson* 1s. at Alverton; and Robert Allotson and John *Wymarkson* slightly more at Ruswarp.[169]

A similar pattern of development of vernacular forms in -*son* can be detected in Lancashire. Adam *Bymmessone* received the lease of a vaccary in Ortner in Wyresdale in 1323.[170] At the same time, a tenant of a single acre in Skerton was identified simply as *Langebaynessone*, without acknowledging any forename.[171] More substantially, William *Wylkessone* held in 1323 a messuage and seven and a half acres in Hest whilst William *Dameelaynessone* acted as a juror a year earlier for an inquest held at Garston.[172] Also acting as jurors were Richard *Mallesone* for an inquest at Wigan in 1323 and Robert *Matteson* at Billington in 1329.[173] By 1332–3, Robert *Dowson*, William *Alcokesson* and William *Gybbesone* were enumerated as tenants of Warrington and John *Dykessone* a tenant of two acres in Amounderness.[174]

A year later, William *Skotsone* performed service as a juror in an inquest at Hornby.[175] Subsequently, in 1325, Alan *Dandessone* reprised the same role at Wigan, although at the inquest at Lancaster on which he performed the same duty in the same year he was described in the Latin register as Alan *filius Dande*, suggesting a transitional time.[176] Jurors at Lancaster in 1333–6 included John *Anotissone* and Alan *le Maystersone*, whilst Peter *Magoteson* appeared in a similar capacity at an inquest in Kirkby in Kendale in 1344.[177] To complete the pattern of this early development of vernacular forms in -*son*, charters referred to *Allecocson* in 1332 at Garston (and in 1336 in the variant *Alcocsone*), *Atkynsone*, *Hullesone* and *Ellotson* there in 1336, *filius Hullesone* at Speke in 1329, followed there by *le Smythesson* in 1333, *Willessone* and *Alokokkissone* in 1334, *Gillesone* at Woolton in 1329 and *Dobson* and *Hulleson* in 1330,

Dauidsone much earlier at Ditton in 1319, *Huttyngsone* at Clitheroe in 1324, *Ibbesone* at Ightenhill in 1324, *le Harperson* at Penwortham in the same year, *Hoggesone* and *Dandsone* at Derby in 1325, *Hullesone*, *Kendalsone*, and *Swaynesone* in Lonsdale Wapentake in 1325–6, and *Tilleson* in Rochdale in 1324.[178]

By the 1340s, some, but by no means all, of these patronyms were developing into family surnames in Lancashire. In *c*.1340, Thomas son of Robert *Hollissone* and his brother Hugh received land in Oxton which had once been held by Thomas *Hollissone* of Oxton. In 1342, Thomas son of Robert *Hullesson*, of which *Hollissone* was a variant, made a grant of a messuage and bovate in Oxton. Incipient heritability was implicit.[179]

By the 1340s, the extent of the penetration of vernacular forms in *-son* can be quantified. Amongst just over 160 tenants holding burgages or fragments of burgages in Liverpool in 1346 were enumerated Adam *Symmeson*, Richard *Diconson*, Richard *Hogson*, Robert son of *Marrotson*, Adam *Janyson*, Robert *Willesson*, William son of Adam *Hokesson*, Adam son of Alan *Coweson*, William *Dobson*, Adam *Stevinson*, John son of William *Hullesson*, Adam *Williamson*, John son of John *Maretson*, Adam *Richardson*, Margery daughter of Alcok *Janson*, John son of Adam *Mariotson*, John son of Richard *Williamson*, Nicholas *Emmokson*, William *Richardson*, John son of John *Phillipson*, John *Adamson*, Richard *Dobson*, Robert *Emmeson*, William son of Thomas *Dawson*, Henry *Hoisetteson*, Adam *Edithson*, Henry *Patennesson*, Richard *Williamson*, Matilda widow of *Mariotsonne*, John *Gyspinsonne* and William son of William *Mariotson* – almost twenty percent of the burgesses.[180] One feature which can be elicited from this enumeration is that the vernacular form in *-son* was already well established in the borough by 1346. Another important aspect is that these vernacular forms with *-son* were not confined to the countryside but had insinuated or endogenously developed in the borough, in the urban context. Whereas in urban places in other regions vernacular forms in *-son* did not infiltrate until the later middle ages, in southern Lancashire these forms were not an irregular feature of urban personal naming. Moreover, the forms encountered embraced formations from both common forenames and more exotic ones. All these characteristics confirm the normative extent of vernacular forms in *-son* in southern Lancashire.

To reinforce the existence of these forms in both urban and rural southern Lancashire, amongst the forty-seven tenants for life in Saltensmore at this time – the mid 1340s – were registered eleven (almost a quarter) with vernacular forms in *-son*: *Symmeson*; *Williamson* (three); *Hebbeson*; *Dawson*; *Adamson*; *Hudson*; *Mariotson*; *Emmock-son*; and *Richardson*.[181] At Wavertree, standard holdings of half a bovate were attributed to tenants with the surnames *Nickesson*, *Tomsonne*, *Maleinson*, *Williamson* (two), *Sandesson*, and Henry *Wilkenssone Dandesun*, whilst Henry *Robinson* was tenant of a quarter of one, so that forty percent (eight out of twenty) had surnames conforming to this pattern.[182]

In this area of southern Lancashire, the composite lordship of West Derby comprised both borough and rural elements, in which burgage tenements belonged to eight burgesses with *-son* surnames (*Dikson*, *Gillesson*, *Tomson*, *Alexanderson*, *Thommesson*, *Katerinesson*, *Gibbeson*, *Gellesson* and *Elisson*). In the rural component, thirty percent of the tenants holding fragments of bovates (seventy-one in total) disported *-son* surnames, comprising *Dik(k)(es)son* (four), *Gillesson* (four), *Thomson*,

Kittessone, Magesson (three), *Hullesson* (three), *Katesson, Adekinson, Dawson, Dobson* and *Rogerson*.[183]

The pattern in other northern locations is more difficult to reconstruct because of the relative paucity of sources. At Shipley in Northumberland, William *Prestsun* attested a charter in 1302.[184] Tenants enumerated at Fawdon in 1332 included William *Batemanson*.[185] At the same time in Hawksdale on the opposite side of the Pennines, William son of Stephen *Da(n)desone* also held only a tiny amount of land.[186]

Similarly, the deficit of sources for county Durham makes exploration of the appearance of vernacular patronyms and metronyms complicated. It is, however, certainly clear that by the middle of the fourteenth century, such bynames were extensive in the court rolls of the manors of the Bishop. In 1358, John Oteson was admitted to a rood of land in Over Hedworth.[187] In that same year, Thomas Rogerson was ordered to repair his tenement at Fulwell and Roger Thomson acted as a personal pledge.[188] At that time too, John Watson brought a case of detinue against Gilbert Jenkynson at Billingham, whilst at Newton Ketton Nicholas Philipson acted as a pledge.[189] At Ackley during that year Walter Rogerson was admitted to a quarter of a bond tenement and at Burdon Thomas Casson received a messuage and thirty acres.[190] Two years later, Thomas Nanson was directed to maintain his cottage at Middle Merrington.[191] During the 1360s, appearances were manifested in the court rolls by John Simson, acquiring a cottage and twelve acres at Jarrow, Thomas Gibson at East Rainton, Hugh Raynoldson at Southwick, John Wydouson, distinctly unfree (*nativus domini*) at West Rainton, Peter Hudson at Piddington, Thomas Louson at Wearmouth, Adam Diotson responding to a plea of trespass initiated by John Doggeson at Wiveston, Robert Malkynson at Dalton, John Nikson at Hedworth, Hugh Patson at West Merrington, John Euotson admitted to a tenement at Scheles, William Colson at Ackley, Thomas Tudowson who formerly held five acres in Hett in Spen, Thomas Wytouson at Wearmouth and, in 1370, John Edeson for illicitly felling an oak.[192] What is exhibited here is the wide variety of personal names incorporated in vernacular bynames with -*son*, continued in the 1370s: Hewmondson; Nanson; Sisson; Edmundson; Saunderson; Uttingson; as well as formations compounded with occupational nouns or nouns of status: Fermourson; Widouson.[193] Even in the late fourteenth century there was no apparent concentration of vernacular patronyms and metronyms on the most frequent forenames (variants of John, William, Robert), but rather a wide variety of forms.

Of course, as illustrated by the frequency of -*son* bynames in the lay subsidy of 1327, this form of byname already featured strongly in Cumberland by the early fourteenth century. In Michaelmas 1300, wages were delivered to Robert *dictus Maystreson* for work in the maintenance of Carlisle castle.[194]

From this extensive, and perhaps tedious survey, several characteristics of vernacular patronymic and metronymic naming in the North are evident. First, the formations are earlier than further south, evident from the first decade of the fourteenth century – and in sporadic cases even earlier – accumulating in the 1320s and 1330s and widespread by the 1340s. The appearance further south is first really apparent in the 1330s, but more particularly the 1340s. Moreover, the densest concentration in lay subsidies occurred in the Cumberland lay subsidy. A second feature of these earlier formations was that the combination of personal names with -*son* was not confined to the most common forenames. Variety is evident, illustrated above, but also by *Gilleson* and *Ormeson* at Childwall in 1350, *le* (sic) *Madoksone* in Liverpool in 1340, *Annotson* in Lea in 1341, *Paulyneson* at Preston in 1337, *Mirresone* there in 1334, *Amerysone* and Lambardsone in Dutton in 1363, *Hullesone* and *Amreson* at Ribchester in 1338 and 1346, *Mallesone* at Aughton in 1336, and *Haynesone* at Kirkdale in 1342.[195] In fact, formations on the most common forenames were in this context irregular and insignificant. For compounds with the most frequent personal names to have become so extensive by the later middle ages suggests that these earlier formations must have been unstable and disappeared.

In all these earlier formations, the personal name elements in the byname or surname were not yet concentrated.[196] That diversity applied equally to the northern -*son* names throughout the fourteenth century. For example, patronyms with -*son* on the Durham episcopal manors in 1382 were constituted from forty-two different etymons. Whilst John, William, Robert and Thomas and their variants were well represented in the hypocorisms (Jon-, Jak-, Wil-, Dob-, Hob-, Thom-) which provided the first elements in compound -*son* names, other personal names provided a profuse number of other combinations, including Alexander (Sander-), Raynald, Gilbert (Gil-, Gillot-, Gib-), Simon (Sim-), Alan (Aleyn-), Matthew (Mathe-), Nicholas (Nik-), Peter (Pier-, Pere-), Theobald (Tebbe-), Lawrence (Law-, Low-), Ralph (Daw-), and Amerey (Emeri-). Another eleven protothemes were contributed by female personal names, although usually less prolifically (that is, usually represented by a single tenant each). Other combinations resulted from status or occupation: Wedowson; Clerkson; Souterson; Sheperdson; Smithson; and Greveson. An inherent variety thus characterised the formation of northern vernacular patronyms and metronyms into the late fourteenth century. Whilst there was some frequency of compounds on the most popular personal names, there was not the concentration that ensued later.

In contrast, concentration had proceeded to influence the formation of vernacular patronyms and metronyms in the East Riding of Yorkshire by the late fourteenth century. Although the protothemes derived from thirty-two male personal names and fifteen female ones, a limited number of male personal names was deployed much more profusely in the bynames and surnames with -*son*: John, William, Thomas, Robert and Richard with their variants and hypocorisms.[197]

Now the protothemes contained within compounded -*son* bynames and surnames usually – even normatively – consisted of hypocorisms: diminutives or pet-forms of personal names. Whilst the etymon of a hypocorism is sometimes ambivalent, it is possible to detect in some northern -*son* bynames and surnames distinctively northern characteristics.[198] In Lancashire in particular, the two formations Hig(g)son and Hanson betray northernness. In the Poll Tax for Lancashire, Hig(g)son existed at Manchester, Oldham, Lostock, Hindley, Formby (Hygynson), Aintree, Thornton, Samlesbury and Westleigh.[199] In this case, Hick (the hypocorism from Richard) had been voiced to Hig(g). In the same source, Hanson was located at Ashton under Lyne, Spotland, Castleton, Withington, Newton le Willows, Atherton, Great Crosby, Walton le Dale, Livesey, Great Harwood, in Lonsdale Wapentake, and at Atherton. The probability here is that Han- is a pet-form of Henry, as it was on the manor of

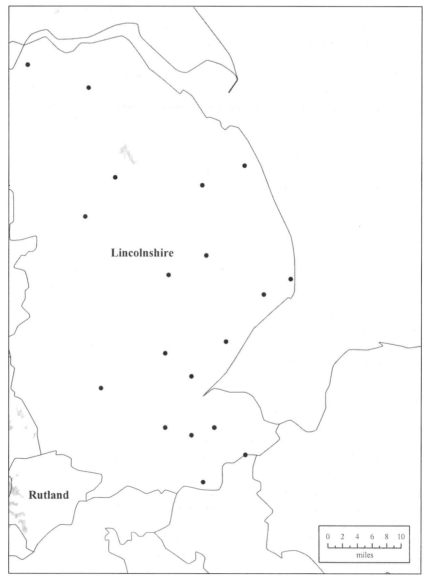

Figure 21 Bynames with -neve: Lincolnshire, 1332

Wakefield.[200] In both cases, the incorporated hypocorisms are characteristically northern, one localised in Lancashire, the other more generally northern.

To a certain extent, patronyms and metronyms belonged to a wider category of Middle English bynames denoting kinship association. Other suffixes indicated relationship to the nuclear family and some even to wider affines (such as *-neve, -stepson* and others). An interesting feature in Lincolnshire is the appendage of the suffix *-neve* to bynames, denoting Middle English 'nephew' (Old English *nefa*). Thus in

1341, John *Douceneue* of Boston complained of extortion.[201] Identification in Yorkshire had occasionally assumed this form, but in Latin construction. In 1218, Utting *nepos Ukeman* was appealed for robbery before the Crown Pleas.[202] Both *Neve* as a byname and *-neve* compound bynames flourished relatively (to other counties) in Lincolnshire in 1332, as illustrated in Figure 21. Most compounds were constructed on personal names, most usually hypocorisms: *Gilneue; Basilneue; Walraneue; Batisneue; Geffreyneue; Robynnef; Beteneue; Elynneue;* and *Edeneue.* Occasionally, the suffix was appended on a byname of status: *Parsonneue* and *Prestneue.*[203] What is significant here is the development of other bynames of kinship relationship with Middle English suffixes outside the six northern counties. Although not as extensive as *-son* bynames in Lincolnshire, *-neve* bynames in that county constituted something of a corpus in the early fourteenth century. Significantly, however, by the late fourteenth century they were much reduced, for in the extant Poll Tax of 1381 were enumerated only Robert Dennysneue at Whaplode and Roger Prestnef at Somercotes.[204]

Another formation involved the affix *-brother*, represented in north Derbyshire, on the periphery of the North, by John Nikbrother, a witness of a charter associated with Eyam in 1372.[205] On the manor of Wakefield, it occurred sporadically, as when Richard *Hannebrothir* was presented for an offence against the vert in 1324.[206] Importantly because of its location in the far North-west, this suffix was attached to a peasant tenant in Hothwait, so that some charters of 1200x1250 constantly referred to land adjacent to the land held by *Gillemichaelbrother* or *Gille Mighelbrother.*[207]

Those forms of byname associated with kinship explored above were not confined to male gender, but importantly female elements were also incorporated in bynames. The compound characteristic is exemplified through Alice *Liteldikdoghter* who surrendered a messuage in Hepworth in Holme in the manor of Wakefield in 1348.[208] On the same manor, illustrative of the marginal nature of some of the female bearers of this form of byname, Alice *Mabdaughter*, a pauper, was presented for brewing.[209] Four other women in 1350 were identified on the manor by the suffix *-doghter*: Agnes *Perkyndoghter* who had been subjected to battery, Alice *Waryndoghter* impleaded for a debt of 16d., and Elizabeth *Pellesondoghter* and Anabel *Jankyndoghter* both for brewing.[210] The earliest occasion of the use of this compound and suffix on the manor of Wakefield belonged to 1326 when Magota *Jeddoxter* of Holne surrendered eight and a half acres of land to establish a remainder in the property.[211] Five years later, Agnes *Dyedoghter* was presented at the assize of ale.[212]

In the West Riding, these suffixes were recorded in an arrangement for the remainder in land to be transferred to Joan *Roberddoghter Wannervill* and Helen *Roberddoghter Wannervill* in Hemsworth in 1361.[213] The persistent flexibility inherent in this form of byname is exhibited in these two females. Similarly, that instability is reflected in the byname of Agnes *Jondoghter* who claimed land in Hatfield Chase in 1348, for the case revealed that her father was John *Thomson.*[214] In fact, in this event is divulged the instability of both patronyms in *-son* and those in *-doghter*.

Bynames of this type continued to exist, although not in any profusion, into the late fourteenth century, for in the Poll Tax for the East Riding, *-doghter* bynames were recorded for singleton female taxpayers at Beverley, Cottingham (two), Bishop Burton, Bentley, Southburn (four females), Eastburn, Tibthorpe (two) and Hutton Cranswick.[215]

This particular associative compound byname had, perhaps, a greater concentration in the most northerly counties. For example, at East Merrington in County Durham in 1365, leyrwyte (the fine for sexual incontinence) was exacted from Diota *Jaksdougter*, reflecting her unfree status.[216] In the following year on another episcopal manor, Wolveston, Agnes *Gibbesdoughter* was presented for brewing.[217] A fine for sexual immorality (leyrwite, as above) was also imposed on Cecily *Dausdoghter* at Coupon in 1371, as also on Agnes *Gillisdoughter* at Wiveston, Agnes *Felicedoughter* and Cecily *Bellesdoughter* both at Harton, all in 1371, suggesting a close association between this form of byname and suffix and unfreedom.[218] Confirmation of the association derives from the leyrwite exacted from Cecily *Wilkinsdoughter* at Newton Beaulieu in 1377.[219] More indeterminate was the status of Agnes *Watsdoughter* who acquired two cottages at Hedworth in 1375.[220] What is visible, however, is the frequent colloquial and written use of *-doughter* identifications in this more northerly area.

More frequent than *-daughter* bynames, *-wif* bynames more usually denoted a widow, although not exclusively. The earliest references in the Wakefield court involved a payment of 3d. by Agnes *Jonkynwif* for brewing in 1324, and resulted also from Amabilia *Hannewyf*'s rescuing seven cows illicitly in 1327, succeeded in the same year by her committing a trespass in Ossett.[221]

Bynames of this formation persisted into the late fourteenth century. In the Poll Tax for the East Riding, *-wif* bynames continued to exist in Beverley, at Cottingham (four female taxpayers), at North Burton, Market Weighton, Wauldby, Kirk Ella, Bishop Burton (two females), North Cave, Newbold, Eastburn, Tibthorpe and Hutton Cranswick.[222] In the middle of the fourteenth century, lands of the bishopric of Durham at Killerby and Wolsingham in County Durham had tenants described as Sybil *Johanswyf* and Alice *Lucydoghter*.[223]

All such formations existed sporadically in southern areas of the country, so that Emma *Custisdouter* contributed 6d. to the lay subsidy at Elton in Huntingdonshire.[224] In the late fourteenth century, the homicide was reported of William the servant of Agnes *Maydoughter*.[225] In 1337, Margery *Woweryswyf* held a messuage and nineteen acres as a *nativa de sanguine* (unfreedom by birth, abject unfreedom) for a rent of 3s. on the manor of Calystock in Cornwall.[226] Contributing tax in Buckinghamshire in 1332, Joan *la Reuewyf* was assessed at 3s. at Bow Brickhill.[227] By 1327, a byname with this suffix had been inherited by William *Kenewyf* at Wetheringsett, assessed at 1s. to the lay subsidy in Suffolk.[228]

Furthermore, this form of suffix appeared quite early in some parts of southern England, if only sporadically. Thus *c*.1206 *Dierewif* was enumerated in Canterbury and in that area too *Relicta Herdewif* – a sort of tautology – owed with others the service of providing one horse for *averhors*.[229] In the same county, at Menstre, *Romescot* was collected from tenants who included *Batewif filia Ade*.[230] It might be speculated that these vernacular forms occasionally intruded into the written record at a time when trilingualism was still a feature.[231]

In Methley in 1364, Adam Prest defended a plea of dower against Alice *Colynwife*, her byname representing the Middle English byname associated with widows.[232] Although not multitudinous, formations with the suffix *-wif(e)* were not unusual in the North, but singularly less frequent outside that region. On the manor of

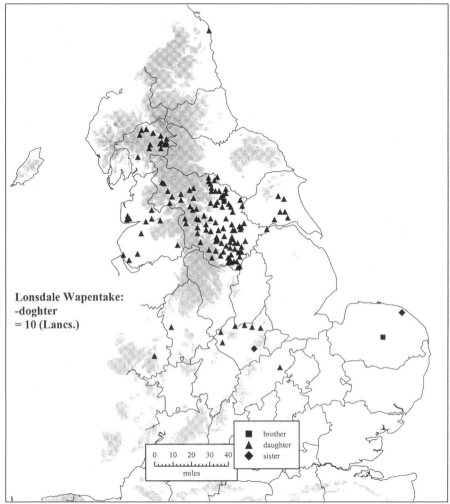

Lonsdale Wapentake:
-doghter
= 10 (Lancs.)

■ brother
▲ daughter
◆ sister

0   10   20   30   40
miles

Figure 22 Bynames with -brother, -sister or -daughter, 1377–81

Wakefield, Juliana *Dikwife* was presented for an offence against the vert, collecting alders and thorns in 1349.[233] In the early fourteenth century, land in Middlewich in Cheshire had been held by Helen *Michelswyfe*.[234]

Whilst the concentration of these Middle English associative bynames remained clearest in the 'North', vernacular kinship bynames occasionally appeared outside the 'North'. The distribution elsewhere is perhaps best realised through the Poll Taxes of 1377–81, represented in Figures 22 and 23. The southernmost extension of these associative kinship bynames is revealed in the extant Poll Taxes in Essex, where Catherine *Presteswyf* inhabited Tolleshunt Knights in 1381.[235] In the case of John Batewyf in Colchester, however, an hereditary surname is encountered.[236] Northwards in Norfolk William *Parsonesbrother* at Mattishall, Cecily *Prestessoster* at

Figure 23 Bynames with -wife, 1377–81

South Repps, and Margaret *Joneswyf* at Bacton reproduced the form as flexible bynames in 1379.[237] Westwards, in central England, the assessment captured Joan *Tymewyf* at Cateby and Agnes *Magotysdowter*, both in Northamptonshire in 1379, as

	-son	Filius	-doghter	Filia	-wif/ -wyf	Relicta/uxor/vidua
N	1850	883	143	345	104	181
Percent	7.6	3.6	0.6	1.4	0.4	0.7

Table 1 Statistics of vernacular suffixes in the 1379 Poll Tax: West Riding of Yorkshire[245]

well as Matilda *Tomyswyfe* in Caldecote in nearby Rutland.[238] More frequent were the occurrences in Leicestershire: Alice *Prestsyster* at Ilston on the Hill; Alice *Beneteswyf* at Hemington; Matilda *Williamesdoughter* at Wymeswold; Alice *Johneswyf* at Thurmaston; Cecily *Thomasdouter* at Hathern; Alice *Hoggedougter* at Grimston; Agnes *Harriwyf* at Saxelby; Agnes *Magotdowter* at Frisby on the Wreake; Agnes *Symmeswyf* at Seagrave; Amice *Jonwif* and Margaret *Robertwif* in Barkby; Joan *Emdoghter* at Gaddesby; Matilda *Rosedoutter* at Bagworth; Joan *Gewyf* at Sutton Cheney; Emma *Parsondoutter* at Congerstone; Joan *Parkyndouter*, spinster, in Thorpe Arnold; Matilda *Dikunwif*, widow, in Saltby; and Emma *Wylkynwyf* in Welby.[239] Particularly concentrated in the northern half of the Leicestershire, the bynames here are also revealed in respect to female status: *-douter* bynames associated with not-married women and *-wif* bynames with widows.[240] Formations with the suffix *-wif* were encountered by the tax collectors in Whaplode (Agnes *Lombyswif*, ambiguously, and Ivetta *Simundwif*) and Somercotes (Helen *Stevewyfe*) in Lincolnshire.[241] In the truncated Poll Tax for Staffordshire, the tax collectors enumerated Alice *Gybonswyf* and Agnes *Mawdoughter* at Gnosall in 1381.[242]

These suffixes of relationship and kinship thus extended throughout wider parts of England, but their particular concentration was in the North. For example, Cecily *Huddesister* held a toft in Bolton in Craven in 1329.[243] Whilst *-brother* and *-sister* bynames of relationship occurred infrequently, but more often in the North, bynames associated with husbands remained particularly rare, but at Holne in Wakefield John *Kithusband* was presented for the assize of bread in 1324.[244]

As can be inferred from Figures 22 and 23, nevertheless, the suffixes indicating a feminine relationship remained inconsiderable in number by comparison with the vernacular suffix *-son*. The inference which might be adduced here is a relative difference in language usage by gender: that women, by and large, continued to be defined in the more prestige form of the Latin register whilst men were accommodated by the lower register of Middle English – or, perhaps, the inverted prestige of using Middle English vernacular.

Table 1 confirms this discrepancy for the taxpayers in the Poll Tax for the West Riding in 1379. In other words, of all the male taxpayers attributed patronyms or metronyms, 68.9 percent received vernacular forms (*-son*) whilst only 31.1 percent were described by Latin forms (*filius x*). By comparison, daughters recognized by patronyms or metronyms were identified in only 25.8 percent of cases in the vernacular (-*doghter*) but 74.2 percent in the Latin register (*filia*). Moreover, only 36.5 percent of widowed taxpayers were recognised by the vernacular -*wif* or -*wyf*, but 63.5 percent by the corresponding Latin formation (*relicta/uxor/vidua*).

The same pattern is reflected in the Poll Tax for Lancashire in which 810 male taxpayers of a total of 5,322 male taxpayers were described with the suffix -*son*, but of the 612 female taxpayers enumerated who had an independent description, only twenty-seven were accorded -*wif/-wyf* epithets and thirty-three -*doghter* descriptions. The two female relationships combined thus accounted for 9.9 percent of independent female taxpayers whereas -*son* descriptions comprised 15 percent of male taxpayers. The distribution is replicated in the surveys of the bishop of Durham's manors in 1382 for here 507 of the 2,938 male tenants had -*son* second names, whilst amongst the 194 female tenants – all therefore inherently independent females – only three were attributed -*doghter* names and five -*wif/-wyf* descriptions. Perhaps coincidentally, all three of the -*doghter* names pertained to females with marginal land: a cottage; a messuage, two acres and one rood; and a cottage and croft. By contrast, twenty-four of these female tenants were described in the Latin register as *uxor* or *relicta* and twelve as *filia*. Accordingly, the higher, more polite register was favoured in describing women.

The extent to which the vernacular forms with -*doghter* and -*wif/-wyf* were concentrated in the North is represented in Figures 22 and 23. Again, the incomplete survival of the Poll Taxes renders the distribution ambivalent, but the concentration is demonstrative, with, interestingly, a clear presence of vernacular forms in the transitional area in Leicestershire.

Now the expanse of these Middle English formations for other relationships than -*son* clearly evokes a non-Scandinavian effect and tends to reinforce the concept of Middle English language use as a vital influence in the formation of -*son* bynames and surnames, if only by allusion to a wider category of naming. Nevertheless, it is impossible to be dogmatic about the chronological appearance of -*son* names in relationship to other suffixes of relationship. It might be argued that vernacular -*son* names appeared first, through a combination of Scandinavian and Middle English language usage, and that -*wif/-wyf*, -*doghter* and other suffixes of relationship developed secondarily in the wake of -*son* formations.

One of the enduring, if marginal, features of patronyms and metronyms with -*son* was their tendency to continue to exhibit instability into the late middle ages, long after other forms of surnames had generally stabilised. Such ambiguity is contained within the Greves descent at Beeley in Derbyshire. In 1324, Giles *de Greves* conveyed to his son, Thomas, a messuage and half a bovate in the field in Beeley called Greves. In 1357, as Thomas *filius Egidii de les Grevez*, Thomas alienated a *placea* of land in the township and in 1359, by the same description, he passed the messuage and land in *les Greves* to his son, John. In 1394, Thomas *filius Egidii del Greves* acquired further lands, but in 1398, a licence was received by Thomas *Gylessone de le Greves* to alienate the messuage and half bovate in le Greves. Over a generation later John Greveys of Beeley conveyed to his brother, William Greveys of Brampton, a tenement with lands which had been held by John's father, Thomas *Gylessone*. It was only after the middle of the fifteenth century that the family surname developed unambiguously as Greves.[246] Such instability in this form of byname is further evidenced by the grant by Richard de Hope son and heir of Robert *Magotessone* de Hope of the reversion of lands in Hope in 1400.[247]

Even in central England, patronyms might continue, in exceptional circumstances, to exhibit some continued instability in the later middle ages long after hereditary surnames had become normative. The manumission of a kinship of *nativi* (unfree tenants) in Anstey in Leicestershire in 1420 illustrates the point.

> *Memorandum quod iij° die mensis Maij anno Regni Regis Henrici quinti post conquestum anglie octauo venerunt ad curiam domini Abbatis Willelmus Edson de Ansty filius Johannis Sareson nuper de eadem Johannes Wylson senior filius predicti Willelmi Edson Thomas Wilson filius predicti Willelmi Robertus Wilson filius eiusdem Willelmi Johannes Wilson filius Willelmi Ricardus Wilson filius eiusdem Willelmi et Willelmus Wilson filius predicti Willelmi Edson de Ansty qui attachiati fuerunt per corpora sua causa natiuitatis Et postea in curia omnes predicti scilicet Willelmus Edson &c per Ricardum Rotheley Abbatem cum Assensu tocius conuentus manumissi in libertatem pro qua uero manumissione fecerunt finem cum dicto Abbate et conuentu pro .C. marcis.*[248]

[Memorandum that on the 3rd day of May in the 8th year of the reign of king Henry V came into the lord abbot's [Leicester Abbey] court William Edson of Anstey son of John Sareson late of the same, John Wilson the elder son of the aforesaid William Edson, Thomas Wilson son of the aforesaid William, Robert Wilson son of the same William, John Wilson son of William, Richard Wilson son of the same William and William Wilson son of the aforesaid William Edson of Anstey, who were summoned by their bodies by reason of their neifty. And afterwards in the court all the aforesaid that is William Edson etc were by Abbot Richard Rotheley with the assent of the convent manumitted into freedom for which manumission they made a fine with the said abbot and convent for 100 marks.

Although complicated by the unfree status of the kinship, the event reflects the occasional fluidity of patronyms even in the early fifteenth century in the central part of England.

Nevertheless, such instances were isolated and unusual in this region. What distinguished the North, particularly the furthermost north, was the extent of that persistent instability of patronyms and metronyms, manifest not only in the change of patronymic or metronymic byname by generation, but also in double bynames.

Surnames in [County] Durham are certainly confusing. The least reliable appear to have been those ending in -son. Names such as Robinson, Saunderson, and Jackson appear regularly in the court rolls but in the early part of our period [the late fourteenth century] they are not used as inherited surnames and simply tell us the names of a man's father (or, sometimes, mother). Thus John the son of William Emmotson is referred to as John Wilkinson in 1407. By the early fifteenth century, however, names of this sort are starting to be hereditary.[249]

Confirmation of the complexity and fluidity of patronyms and metronyms derives from the compound double bynames attributed to some individuals. Although some of these double surnames comprised only one patronym or metronym combined with another form of byname (for example, an occupational byname), double patronyms and metronyms remained more frequent and illustrate the instability of patronymic and metronymic surnames which attempted to reflect descent over two generations. That complication was exhibited on the manor of Wakefield: John *Dauson Willeson* admitted to three roods of land in Alverthorpe;[250] John *Daweson Willeson* who acquired half an acre in Wakefield;[251] John *Jacson Pelleson* against whom a false suit was initiated in 1350;[252] and Richard *Johnson Betson* accused of offences against the vert in 1350.[253] John *Hogekynson Gybson* was outlawed for a trespass at Aston in the West Riding at the end of the fourteenth century.[254] At Crosby Garrett in Westmorland, Henry *Jonson Wilson* was arraigned on an action of debt brought by a citizen and merchant of York in 1417.[255] At Preston in Lancashire an appeal was initiated in 1372 for the murder of William *Roberesson Dawesson*.[256] Eleven of the contributors to the Poll Tax in the East Riding responded to these double patronyms, such as Richard *Jonson Nicolson* at Cottingham. The continuing instability associated with vernacular patronyms amongst some kinship groups in the North thus extended into the late fourteenth century, and occasionally slightly later.

Amongst the profusion of patronyms and metronyms in northern reaches, some had a distinctive northern concentration, particularly Pattison and Atcheson, and their particularity was established in the early-modern north. At Whitburn, Pattison was established in the third decade of the seventeenth century when a child of John and Isabel was baptized, followed by more of their children in 1638–51.[257] James Pattison appeared in the registers in 1659–61.[258] Pattisons continued to inhabit the parish into the middle of the eighteenth century.[259]

Finally, the question must be briefly re-addressed why patronymic and metronymic bynames and surnames became so distinctive of the North. It has been demonstrated that the formation in *-son* was not exclusive to the North, but existed at varying levels, usually not terribly significant, in other regions of England. It is in the North, however, that the major concentration occurred which distinguished the North (and its penumbra) from southern regions. Two influences have been advanced to explain this onomastic phenomenon: the more extensive deployment of Middle English combined with the later flexibility in and of bynames and surnames in the North; and, on the other hand, a persistent Scandinavian influence. Hitherto, these two influences have been proposed by some as antithetical. In particular, the influence of Middle English has been propounded to the exclusion of any Scandinavian context. It would seem, nevertheless, that the two concepts should no longer be regarded as independent and exclusive, but as complementary.

In particular, the continuity of the *-son* element in the twelfth century was quite often extended through compounding *-son* with a Scandinavian name form. Reaney – the proponent of an exclusive Middle English explanation – himself cited *Grimmesone* and *Fornessune* in twelfth-century Yorkshire.[260] In Norfolk in 1138x1147 occurred a reference to Aluric *Carlessone*'s land, unlikely to refer to a pre-Conquest tenant.[261] Pertinently in this present context, Arne *Grimsune* attested a charter to Whitby Abbey, possibly in the early twelfth century.[262] Dugdale mentioned benefactions to St Mary's Abbey, York, by Ulf *Fornesson* and Uchtred *Ulfson*, combinations of insular names, including some Scandinavian elements.[263] More complex is Giselbriht *Scottissune* who attested in the insular component of the witness list a charter of the bishop of Durham to his chamberlain William in which the bishop granted to him in marriage Emma daughter of Unspac with the lands which Unspac had held for the service of half a knight – a charter which has been assigned to 1133x1138.[264] Now *Scottissune* betrays an insular etymology, although not Scandinavian. A similar implication can be elicited from the reference to land held by Peter the priest son of *Brunsune* in 1149x1156, where Brun is an insular element, although *Brunsune*, like *Levesune*, might already have developed into an insular personal name form.[265]

What an exploration of vernacular forms of patronyms and metronyms with *-son* reveals is an expansive north, extending down into the north Midlands. Bynames and surnames with the suffix *-son* were characteristic of this wide northern zone. These names flourished in a particular, northern vernacular environment, probably infused with Scandinavian influence in the *-son* formation. Nevertheless, *-son* naming belonged to a wider process of naming by relationship, although the other suffixes of relationship did not achieve the same frequency as *-son* names. *-Son* names became particularly dominant amongst these names of relationship. A possible reason for failure of development of the other suffixes of relationship was a difference of register in address by gender. The prevalence of *-son* bynames and surnames thus allows a general overview of the geographical scope of a northern zone, as it graduated south into the north Midlands. Within that wider northern zone and within the core of the far North, however, existed singular, localised naming processes and patterns, which betray that the North, although coherent over a wide space and zone, remained also a mosaic of smaller localities and 'sub-regions'.

Notes

1   Bodl. MS Yorkshire Ch. 313
2   C. Clark, *Words, Names and History. Selected Papers* ed. P. Jackson (Cambridge, 1995), p. 370 (original statement by Clark in 1980).
3   P. H. Reaney, *The Origins of English Surnames* (repr. London, 1987), pp. 86–90; R. A. McKinley, *A History of British Surnames* (London, 1990), pp. 110–17; McKinley, *The Surnames of Sussex* (English Surnames Series V, Oxford, 1988), pp. 332–4; C. D. Rogers, *The Surname Detective. Investigating Surname Distribution in England 1086–Present Day* (Manchester, 1995), pp. 221–3; the most recent evaluation of the influences is D. Postles, 'Defining the "North": some linguistic evidence', *Northern History* 38 (2001), pp. 28–46, from which some of the material here is derived.
4   For a detailed consideration of the respective arguments of Reaney, McKinley, and Sørensen about the influence of Middle English language use or Scandinavian honorific influence, Postles, 'Defining the "North"'.
5   H. S. A. Fox, 'The people of the Wolds in English settlement history' in M. Aston, D. Austin & C. Dyer, eds, *The Rural Settlements of Medieval England* (Oxford, 1989), pp. 77–101, for vulnerable locations; for the general demographic conditions, R. M. Smith, 'Human resources' in G. Astill & A. Grant, eds, *The Countryside of Medieval England* (Oxford, 1988).
6   The data are derived from Fenwick, *Poll Taxes* 1.
7   'East Riding Poll Tax'.
8   See below, pp. 40–4.
9   West Riding Poll Tax, 5, pp. 1–51, 241–66, 417–32; 6, pp. 1–44, 129–71, 287–342; 7, pp. 6–31, 145–86.
10   *Bishop Hatfield's Survey.*
11   W. Boyd, 'The Poll Tax of 1379–81 for the hundreds of Offlow and Cuttlestone', *Collections*

for a History of Staffordshire, William Salt Archaeological Society 17 (1896), pp. 155–205. Here and below, some of my figures were collected before the second volume of Fenwick was published.

12　E. Powell, *The Rising in East Anglia in 1381 with an Appendix containing the Suffolk Poll Tax Lists for that Year* (1896), Appendix I, pp. 67–119.

13　T.N.A. (P.R.O.) E179/ 165/1

14　*Cumberland;* T.N.A. (P.R.O.) E179/135/14–16.

15　For an example, the homicide of John *Maggesone* at Loddon in 1343: *Chancery Miscellanea* V (List and Index Society 29, 1970), p. 195. For Suffolk, the outlawry of Richard *Maggesone* of Winfarthing on an action of account 1309x1329: *Chancery Miscellanea* VI (List and Index Society 81, 1972), p. 245.

16　That issue is discussed more substantially in Postles, 'Defining the "North"', pp. 32–7.

17　G. Tengvik, *Old English Bynames* (Nomina Germanica IV, Uppsala, 1938), pp. 147–8.

18　P. H. Reaney, *The Origins of English Surnames* (London, 1967), p. 87.

19　C. T. Clay, ed., *Early Yorkshire Charters* V (YASRS Extra Series 2, 1936), p. 91 (no. 41).

20　J. C. Atkinson, ed., *Cartularium Abbathiae de Whiteby* (Surtees Society lxix, 1879), pp. 35–7 (xxix–xxx).

21　W. Urry, *Canterbury under the Angevin Kings* (London, 1967), p. 247.

22　Urry, *Canterbury under the Angevin Kings,* p. 396 (xiv).

23　For the general context for these conclusions, Postles, 'Defining the "North"'.

24　*Cat. Ancient Deeds* I, p. 496 (C1109).

25　Bodl. MS Norfolk Roll 8.

26　A.H. Denney, ed., *The Sibton Abbey Estates: Select Documents, 1325–1509* (Suffolk Record Society 2, 1960), p. 70.

27　*Cat. Ancient Deeds* I , p. 152 (A1351).

28　*Chancery Miscellanea* VI (List & Index Society 81, 1972), p. 71 (74/5/139).

29　R. McKinley, *The Surnames of Oxfordshire* (English Surnames Series 3, London, 1977), p. 232; the problem here, however, is that the byname might derive from a nickname, as also *Resson* in 1266 cited by McKinley.

30　*Chancery Miscellanea* V (List and Index Society 49, 1970), p. 263.

31　D. W. Sutherland, ed., *The Eyre of Northamptonshire 3–4 Edward III A. D. 1329–30* 1 (Selden Society 97, 1983), pp. 204–5, 219.

32　Sutherland, *Eyre of Northamptonshire,* 1, p. 168.

33　This context is summarized in Postles, 'Defining the "North"'.

34　*Chancery Miscellanea* III (List & Index Society 26, 1967), p. 176.

35　L. R. Poos & L. Bonfield, eds, *Select Cases in Manorial Courts 1250–1550. Property and Family Law* (Selden Society 114, 1998), p. 49.

36　*Cat. Ancient Deeds* I, p. 331 (B1216), 2 (London, 1894), p. 434 (B3731).

37　For his activities there, *Cat. Ancient Deeds* I, pp. 391 (C53), 414 (C293), 442 (C574), 498 (C1121), 518 (C1314).

38　Poos & Bonfield, *Select Cases in Manorial Courts,* p. 62.

39　Poos & Bonfield, *Select Cases in Manorial Courts,* p. 122.

40　E. G. Kimball, ed., *A Cambridgeshire Gaol Delivery Roll* (Cambridge Antiquarian Society Record Series 4, 1978), pp. 38 (7), 54 (330), 65 (52).

41　*Cat. Ancient Deeds* I, p. 350 (B1417), 2, p. 355 (B2986).

42　Poos & Bonfield, *Select Cases in Manorial Courts,* p. 15.

43　W. Palmer, *Cambridge Borough Documents* volume 1 (Cambridge, 1931), pp. 97–131.

44　J. J. Muskett & C. H. Evelyn, *Lay Subsidy for the Year 1327* (Cambridge, n.d.), pp. 3, 7, 8, 18, 22, 23, 44, 50, 58, 60, 64, 69, 70, 73, 86.

45 *Cat. Ancient Deeds* I, p. 230 (B145).

46 R. B. Pugh, ed., *Wiltshire Gaol Delivery and Trailbaston Trials 1275–1306* (Wiltshire Record Society 33, 1978 for 1977), p. 111 (no. 635).

47 Pugh, *Wiltshire Gaol Delivery*, p. 75 (no. 278).

48 Pugh, *Wiltshire Gaol Delivery*, p. 107 (no. 563).

49 M. Clough, ed., *Fitzalan Surveys* (Sussex Record Society lxvii, 1969), p. 15.

50 *Hertfordshire*, pp. 20, 22, 67–8, 95–6, 101, 113, 120.

51 *Gloucestershire*, pp. 27, 32, 45, 59, 63, 77, 86, 97, 105, 107, 111, 112; *Worcestershire* (1327), pp. 15, 19, 20, 24, 27, 36, 47, 64, 66, 67, 69, 70.

52 E. A. Fry, ed., *Abstracts of Inquisitions Post Mortem for Gloucestershire Part V* (British Record Society Index Library 40, 1910), pp. 259, 269, 313, 321, 360.

53 Fry, *Abstracts of Inquisitions* V, pp. 274, 278.

54 L. Boatwright, ed., *Inquests and Indictments from Late Fourteenth Century Buckinghamshire* (Buckinghamshire Record Society 29, 1994), pp. 4, 14, 15, 16, 31, 34, 35, 39, 53, 61, 63, 64, 74, 77, 78, 82.

55 Boatwright, *Inquests and Indictments*, pp. 34, 43. Additionally, John Rosesone acted as a pledge: p. 35.

56 *Buckinghamshire Inquests and Indictments*.

57 R. F. Hunnisett, ed., *Bedfordshire Coroners' Rolls* (Bedfordshire Historical Record Society xli, 1961), p. 40 (90).

58 Hunnisett, *Bedfordshire Coroners' Rolls*, p. 54 (120).

59 Hunnisett, *Bedfordshire Coroners' Rolls*, p. 116 (no. 281).

60 M. K. Dale, ed., *Court Roll of Chalgrave Manor 1278–1313* (Bedfordshire Historical Record Society 28, 1950), pp. 46, 51.

61 E. G. Kimball, ed., *Sessions of the Peace for Bedfordshire 1355–1359, 1363–1364* (Bedfordshire Historical Record Society 48, 1969), p. 41.

62 Kimball, *Sessions of the Peace for Bedfordshire*, p. 48 (45).

63 Kimball, *Sessions of the Peace for Bedfordshire*, pp. 78 (125), 83 (138).

64 Kimball, *Sessions of the Peace for Bedfordshire*, pp. 86 (145), 95 (171).

65 Kimball, *Sessions of the Peace for Bedfordshire* p. 86 (155).

66 *Chancery Miscellanea* III *Bundles 33–57* (List & Index Society 26, 1967), pp. 122, 126, 204, 207 and 216.

67 University of Nottingham Department of Manuscripts Clifton Deeds 62 and 501.

68 T.N.A. (P.R.O.) E179/159/5 mm. 7, 9, 12.

69 R. Stewart-Brown, ed., *Calendar of the County Court, City Court and Eyre Rolls of Chester, 1259–1297* (Chetham Society 84, 1925), pp. 72, 75.

70 J. Varley, ed., *A Middlewich Chartulary* I (Chetham Society 105, 1941), p. 197.

71 Varley, *Middlewich Chartulary* I, p. 133.

72 Varley, *Middlewich Chartulary* I, p. 70.

73 Varley, *Middlewich Chartulary* I, p. 79, II, p. 301.

74 Varley, *Middlewich Chartulary* I, p. 132.

75 G. Wrottesley, 'Extracts from the Plea Rolls A. D. 1294 to A. D. 1307', *Collections for a History of Staffordshire* William Salt Archaeological Society 1 (1886), p. 157.

76 I. H. Jeayes, 'Calendar of the charters … Marquis of Anglesey …' *Collections for a History of Staffordshire* (1937), p. 112 (387).

77 G. P. Mander, 'Calendar of early charters at the Wodehouse Wombourne' *Collections for a History of Staffordshire* (1928), pp. 26–30 (32–3, 35, 38–9).

78 Mander, 'Calendar of early charters…', p. 37 (62).

79 G. Wrottesley, 'Extracts from the Coram Rege rolls and pleas of the Crown, Staffordshire, of

the reign of Edward II, A. D. 1307 to A. D. 1327', *Collections for a History of Staffordshire* William Salt Archaeological Society 10 (1889), pp. 6, 10, 11, 15, 41, 46.

80 D. G. Stuart, 'A rental of the borough of Burton, 1319', *Collections for a History of Staffordshire* William Salt Archaeological Society 4th series 16 (1994), pp. 39–40, 45, 46, 48.

81 G. Wrottesley, 'Extracts from the plea rolls A.D. 1294 to A.D. 1307', *Collections for a History of Staffordshire* William Salt Archaeological Society vii (1886), p. 132.

82 J. Wedgwood, 'The inquest on the Staffordshire estates of the Audleys' *Collections for a History of Staffordshire* William Salt Archaeological Society n.s. xi (1908), pp. 248–51, 255, 257.

83 C. J. Holdsworth, ed., *Rufford Charters* 1 (Thoroton Society Record Series 29, 1973), p. 70 (no. 129).

84 Occasional references can be found for the south of the county: for example, Alan Jonesson, a grantor of land in Repton in 1361: I. H. Jeayes, ed., *Descriptive Catalogue of Derbyshire Charters in Public and Private Libraries and Muniment Rooms* (London, 1906), p. 249 (1976).

85 Jeayes, *Derbyshire Charters*, p. 88 (694).

86 Jeayes, *Derbyshire Charters*, pp. 91 (725), 95–6 (766, 777), 97 (782).

87 Jeayes, *Derbyshire Charters*, p. 80 (616).

88 Jeayes, *Derbyshire Charters*, pp. 176–7 (1434–5).

89 Jeayes, *Derbyshire Charters*, p. 196 (1581).

90 Jeayes, *Derbyshire Charters*, p. 207 (1667).

91 Jeayes, *Derbyshire Charters*, p. 316 (2507).

92 B. McLane, ed., *The 1341 Royal Inquest in Lincolnshire* (Lincoln Record Society 78, 1988).

93 McLane, *The 1341 Royal Inquest*, pp. 11, 23, 33, 93, 98, 124, 129, 130 (nos 45, 105, 367, 934, 986, 1154, 1195, 1211).

94 L. R. Poos, ed., *Lower Ecclesiastical Jurisdiction in Late-medieval England. The Courts of the Dean and Chapter of Lincoln, 1336–1349, and the Deanery of Wisbech, 1458–1484* (British Academy Records of Social and Economic History n.s. 32, 2001), p. 9.

95 Poos, *Lower Ecclesiastical Jurisdiction*, p. 45.

96 Poos, *Lower Ecclesiastical Jurisdiction*, p. 82.

97 Fenwick, *Poll Taxes* 1, pp. 516–637.

98 The chronology is substantiated in D. Postles, 'At Sørenson's request: the formation and development of patronyms and metronyms in late medieval Leicestershire and Rutland', *Nomina* 17 (1994), pp. 55–70

99 D. M. Stenton, ed., *The Earliest Lincolnshire Assize Rolls A. D. 1202–1209* (Lincoln Record Society 22, 1926), p. 94.

100 R. Ransford, ed., *The Early Charters of Waltham Abbey 1062–1230* (Woodbridge, 1989), p. 374 (no. 550).

101 Poos, *Lower Ecclesiastical Jurisdiction*, p. 9.

102 F. A. Cazel and A. Cazel, *Rolls of the Fifteenth and Ninth of the Reign of Henry III of Cambridgeshire, Lincolnshire and Wiltshire and the Rolls of the Fortieth of the Seventeenth Year of the Reign of Henry III for Kent* (Pipe Roll Society n.s. 45, 1983 for 1976–7), pp. 50, 69.

103 E. A. Fry, ed., *Abstracts of Wiltshire Inquisitions Post Mortem* (British Record Society Index Library 37, 1908), p. 279; Fry, ed., *Abstracts of Inquisitions Post Mortem for Gloucestershire* V, p. 165.

104 Clough, *Fitzalan Surveys*, p. 15.

105 Hunnisett, *Bedfordshire Coroners' Rolls*, p. 9 (25).

106 A. M. Hopkinson, ed., *The Rolls of the 1281 Derbyshire Eyre* (Derbyshire Record Society 27, 2000), p. 134 (523).

107 Postles, 'At Sørensen's request', pp. 61–5.

108 *Yorkshire 1297*, pp. 124, 129, 134; *Yorkshire 1301*, pp. 2, 35 and 59.

109 *Chancery Miscellanea* VIII (List and Index Society 105, 1972), p. 143.
110 *Wakefield Court Rolls* III, p. 58.
111 *Wakefield Court Rolls* III, p. 103.
112 *Wakefield Court Rolls* III, p. 128.
113 *Wakefield Court Rolls* III, p. 156.
114 *Wakefield Court Rolls* IV, pp. 33, 40.
115 *Wakefield Court Rolls* IV, p. 55.
116 *Wakefield Court Rolls* IV, p. 204.
117 *Wakefield Court Rolls 1331–1333*, p. 166.
118 *Wakefield Court Rolls* IV, p. 30.
119 *Wakefield Court Rolls* IV, p. 53. For leyrwite, see now, J. M. Bennett, 'Writing fornication: medieval leyrwite and its historians', *Transactions of the Royal Historical Society* 6th ser. 13 (2003), pp. 131–62.
120 *Wakefield Court Rolls* IV, pp. 79, 96.
121 *Wakefield Court Rolls* IV, p. 114.
122 *Wakefield Court Rolls* IV, p. 202.
123 *Wakefield Court Rolls 1322–1331*, pp. 33–4.
124 *Wakefield Court Rolls* IV, pp. 168, 177, 198, 201.
125 *Wakefield Court Rolls* IV, p. 201.
126 *Wakefield Court Rolls 1322–1331*, pp. 3, 5, 6, 10, 12, 23, 28, 30, 33, 36, 40, 41.
127 *Wakefield Court Rolls*, V, pp. 42, 44, 47, 50, 52–9, 62–3, 66–70, 75, 82, 85, 87, 89, 95–6, 100, 103, 108, 112, 120, 122, 128, 130–1, 136, 152, 167, 169, 183, 187, 192.
128 *Wakefield Court Rolls*, V, p. 53.
129 *Wakefield Court Rolls* V, p. 2.
130 *Wakefield Court Rolls 1338–1340*, pp. 4, 9, 12, 15, 17, 18, 19, 23, 24, 30, 42, 52, 57, 58, 61, 65, 69, 72, 77, 85, 88, 93, 98, 104, 110, 117, 118, 121, 137, 146, 193, 200; page numbers relate to first occurrences only.
131 *Wakefield Court Rolls 1348–1350*, pp. 4, 21–6, 28–9, 31–2, 34, 36–7, 40–2, 45, 48–50, 52–4, 57–60, 62–3, 65–6, 72–3, 75, 86, 96, 99, 103, 110, 113, 118, 121, 124, 128, 130–3, 136, 138–40, 145, 149–50, 156, 161–2, 172, 192–4, 201–2, 204, 207–9, 213–16, 220, 225, 229, 235, 238, 245, 247, 250, 260.
132 *Wakefield Court Rolls 1348–1350*, p. 86.
133 *Wakefield Court Rolls 1331–1333*, pp. 6, 7–8, 10, 17, 20, 24, 27, 46–8, 58, 62, 65–7, 70, 72, 79, 97, 114–15, 120, 129, 130, 132, 134–6, 151, 161, 166, 170, 172, 181, 183, 190, 199, 201–3, 206–7, 218–19, 221, 224.
134 *Wakefield Court Rolls 1348–1350*, p. 34.
135 *Wakefield Court Rolls 1348–1350*, p. 34.
136 *Wakefield Court Rolls 1348–1350*, p. 238.
137 L. R. Poos, Z. Razi, & R. M. Smith, 'The population history of medieval English villages: a debate on the use of manor court records' in Razi & Smith, eds, *Medieval Society and the Manor Court* (Oxford, 1996), pp. 298–368.
138 *Wakefield Court Rolls 1348–1350*, p. 95.
139 *Wakefield Court Rolls 1348–1350*, p. 122.
140 *Wakefield Court Rolls 1348–1350*, p. 235.
141 *Wakefield Court Rolls 1348–1350*, p. 251.
142 *Chancery Miscellanea* VIII (List and Index Society 105, 1972), p. 95.
143 *Chancery Miscellanea* VIII, p. 105.
144 *Wakefield Court Rolls 1331–1333*, p. 129.
145 *Cat. Ancient Deeds* II, p. 330 (B2729) (11 Henry IV).

146 *Cat. Ancient Deeds* III, p. 88 (A4625) (1370).
147 Poos & Bonfield, *Select Cases in Manorial Courts*, p. 12.
148 Poos & Bonfield, *Select Cases in Manorial Courts*, p. 135.
149 Poos & Bonfield, *Select Cases in Manorial Courts*, p. 21.
150 Poos & Bonfield, *Select Cases in Manorial Courts*, p. 131.
151 Doncaster Archives Office DD/Yar/C/1/14.
152 Doncaster Archives Office DD/Yar/C/1/15. For *Bateson*'s wife: *Venit inquisitio ad inquirendum si Idonea que fuit uxor Willelmi Bateson diffamauit Willelmum de Edenestan vocando illum falsum et latronem et imponendo ei quod ipse conduxit Thomam de Eland ad occidendum filium suum* ... For the context, P. R. Schofield, 'Peasants and the manor court: gossip and litigation in a Suffolk village at the close of the thirteenth century', *Past & Present* 159 (1998), pp. 3–42.
153 Nottinghamshire Archives Office DDSR 1/2/1.
154 Nottinghamshire Archives Office DDSR 1/2/1.
155 Nottinghamshire Archives Office DDSR 1/6/5,7: the manorial court rolls are, however, sporadic.
156 Nottinghamshire Archives Office DDSR 1/6/5, 7.
157 Nottinghamshire Archives Office DDSR 1/6/6b.
158 Nottinghamshire Archives DDSR 1/6/7: *De Ricardo Colynson pro porcis suis sepe captis in bladis domini* ... *pro ancilla sua que messuit* [sic] *herbam domini.*
159 T. A. M. Bishop, 'Extent of Monk Friston 1320' in *Miscellanea IV* (YASRS 94, 1937), p. 68.
160 *Chancery Miscellanea* VIII, p. 114.
161 *Pudsay Deeds*, pp. 201 (172), 205 (182).
162 York Minster Archives 1.5/37A, 1.5/38.
163 York Minster Archives 1.5/35, 37A.
164 York Minster Archvies 1.5/38.
165 York Minster Archives 1.5/40: the date is suggested by the hand and the numerous cancellations and interlineations of changes of tenants.
166 York Minster Archives 1.5/37A, 1.5/35.
167 York Minster Archives 1.5/37A: Isolda also exceptionally held a messuage and six bovates.
168 York Minster Archives 1.5/39.
169 Colonel Parker, 'Lay subsidy rolls 1 Edward III N. R. and City of York' in *Miscellanea II* (YASRS lxxiv, 1929), pp. 110, 121, 126, 148, 152 and 156.
170 W. Farrer, ed., *Lancashire Inquests, Extents and Feudal Aids* part II (LCRS liv, 1907), p. 127.
171 Farrer, *Lancashire Inquests* part II, p. 129. He was probably the son of Robert *Langebayn*, a tenant there, and his succinct description might reflect his marginal status: p. 174.
172 Farrer, *Lancashire Inquests* part II, pp. 132, 141.
173 Farrer, *Lancashire Inquests* part II, pp. 156, 231. *Mallesone* also occurred in 1328 at Garston: *Norris Deeds*, p. 60 (269).
174 Farrer, *Lancashire Inquests* part II, pp. 240, 241.
175 Farrer, *Lancashire Inquests* part III (LCRS lxx, 1915), p.5.
176 Farrer, *Lancashire Inquests* part III, pp. 15, 23.
177 Farrer, *Lancashire Inquests* part III, pp. 31, 39, 45, 59.
178 *Norris Deeds*, pp. 3–5 (12, 16, 19), 79 (396), 91 (482–3), 148 (817), 149–50 (825, 830), 176 (972); *Lancashire Court Rolls*, pp. 34, 47, 61, 105–6, 113, 133, 136, 138, 141, 147.
179 E. Barker, ed., *Talbot Deeds 1200–1682* (LCRS ciii, 1948), pp. 23–4 (43, 47).
180 Farrer, *Lancashire Inquests* part III, p. 69.
181 Farrer, *Lancashire Inquests* part III, pp. 75–6.
182 Farrer, *Lancashire Inquests* part III, pp. 77–8.
183 Farrer, *Lancashire Inquests* part III, pp. 82 ff.

184 J. Walton, 'The Greenwell Deeds', *Archaeologia Aeliana* 4th series 111 (1927) (extra volume), p. 47 (no. 98).

185 Walton, 'The Greenwell Deeds', p. 69 (no. 149).

186 R. L. Storey, ed., *The Register of John Kirkby, Bishop of Carlisle, 1332–1352, and the Register of John Ross, Bishop of Carlisle, 1325–1332* volume II (Canterbury and York Society lxxxi, 1995), pp. 6, 12.

187 *Halmota Prioratus Dunelmensis*, p. 20.

188 *Halmota Prioratus Dunelmensis*, p. 21.

189 *Halmota Prioratus Dunelmensis*, p. 22.

190 *Halmota Prioratus Dunelmensis*, pp. 22–3.

191 *Halmota Prioratus Dunelmensis*, p. 26.

192 *Halmota Prioratus Dunelmensis*, pp. 26–7, 33, 37–8, 48, 71, 74, 78, 87–8, 90, 98–9.

193 *Halmota Prioratus Dunelmensis*, pp. 102–3, 109, 112, 123, 129, 143, 145, 147, 149, 151.

194 W. N. Thompson, ed., *The Register of John de Halton Bishop of Carlisle* (2 volumes, Canterbury & York Society xii–xiii, 1913), p. 181.

195 *Norris Deeds*, pp. 166, 198; *Hoghton Deeds*, pp. 38, 53, 88, 105, 155, 212, 231.

196 The range of personal names in earlier patronyms and metronyms with -*son* in Leicestershire and Rutland is described in Postles, 'At Sørenson's request' , where unusual personal names formed the first element (prototheme).

197 The descriptive statistics are as follows: for male personal names, N=32, mean=6.5, trimmed mean=5.61, standard deviation=7.02, median=3.5, first quartile=1, third quartile=10.5, minimum=1, maximum=29; for female personal names, N=15, mean=1.6, trimmed mean=1.385, sd=1.056, median=1, Q1=1, Q3=2, min=1, max=5. The numbers relate to the frequency of use of personal names in compounds with -*son*.

198 For the problems of identifying the etymon of some hypocorisms, P. McClure, 'The interpretation of hypocoristic forms of Middle English baptismal names', *Nomina*, 21 (1998), pp. 101–31.

199 Fenwick, *Poll Taxes* 1.

200 Fenwick, *Poll Taxes* 1; for *Han-* on the manor of Wakefield, below pp. 80–1.

201 McLane, *1341 Royal Inquest*, p. 78 (no. 796).

202 D. M. Stenton, ed., *Rolls of the Justices in Eyre … Yorkshire in 3 Henry III (1218–19)* (Selden Society 56, 1937), p. 278 (no. 747).

203 T.N.A. (P.R.O.) E179/135/14, mm. 2, 4, 9, 11, 12, 14, 16, 19; E179/135/15, m. 8; E179/135/16, mm. 8, 11, 17, 20, 21, 24, 26, 27, 35, 36, 37, 48, 50, 55.

204 Fenwick, *Poll Taxes*, II, pp. 13, 55.

205 Jeayes, *Derbyshire Charters*, p. 150 (1224).

206 *Wakefield Court Rolls* V, p. 59.

207 *St Bees*, pp. 181–2, 184 (145–7, 184).

208 *Wakefield Court Rolls 1348–1350*, p. 26.

209 *Wakefield Court Rolls 1348–1350*, p. 115.

210 *Wakefield Court Rolls 1348–1350*, pp. 177, 229..

211 *Wakefield Court Rolls 1331–1333*, p. 95.

212 *Wakefield Court Rolls 1331–1333*, p. 185.

213 University of Nottingham Department of Manuscripts Galway MS 9229.

214 Poos & Bonfield, *Select Cases in Manorial Courts*, p. 137.

215 Fenwick, *Poll Taxes*, pp. 327, 330, 340, 346–50: thus almost replicating the pattern of -*wif* bynames as below.

216 *Halmota Prioratus Dunelmensis*, p. 42.

217 *Halmota Prioratus Dunelmensis*, p. 53.

218 *Halmota Prioratus Dunelmensis*, pp. 105, 108. It may be, of course, a tendentious problem of the source that single females were usually only drawn into court by the payment of leyrwite and so the association between unfreedom and -*doghter* bynames might be an illusion of the source.

219 *Halmota Prioratus Dunelmensis*, p. 140.

220 *Halmota Prioratus Dunelmensis*, p. 131.

221 *Wakefield Court Rolls 1331–1333*, pp. 41, 115, 118, 125, 131.

222 Fenwick, *Poll Taxes*, pp. 326, 330–2, 338–40, 342, 346, 348–50.

223 *Bishop Hatfield's Survey*, pp. 22, 65.

224 *Huntingdonshire*, p. 187.

225 *Chancery Miscellanea Part VI* (List & Index Society, 1972), p. 39 (73/4/167).

226 P. L. Hull, ed., *The Caption of Seisin of the Duchy of Cornwall (1337)* (Devon and Cornwall Record Society new series 17, 1971), p. 104.

227 *Buckinghamshire*, p. 83.

228 *Suffolk*, p. 38.

229 W. Urry, *Canterbury under the Angevin Kings* (London, 1967), p. 350; *Black Book of St Augustine*, part 1, p. 49.

230 *Black Book of St Augustine*, part 1, p. 31.

231 C. Clark, 'People and languages in post-Conquest Canterbury' in Clark, *Words, Names and History. Selected Writings of Cecily Clark* ed. P. Jackson (Cambridge, 1995), pp. 179–206.

232 Poos & Bonfield, *Select Cases in Manorial Courts*, p. 104.

233 *Wakefield Court Rolls 1348–1350*, p. 99.

234 J. Varley, ed., *A Middlewich Chartulary* I (Chetham Society 105, 1941), I, p. 133 (46d.) (1315x1326).

235 Fenwick, *Poll Taxes*, I, p. 246.

236 Fenwick, *Poll Taxes*, I, p. 194.

237 Fenwick, *Poll Taxes*, II, pp. 121, 126, 161.

238 Fenwick, *Poll Taxes*, II, 231, 246, 372.

239 Fenwick, *Poll Taxes*, I, pp. 524, 537–8, 544–5, 551–4, 557, 562–3, 575, 582, 601, 603.

240 The association of -*wif* with widowhood is occasionally explicit: Matilda *Dikunwif vidua* at Saltby and Emma *Wilkynwyf vidua* at Welby in Leicestershire are examples: Fenwick, *Poll Taxes* 1, p. 603.

241 Fenwick, *Poll Taxes*, II, pp. 11–12, 55.

242 Fenwick, *Poll Taxes*, II, p. 485.

243 *Pudsay Deeds*, p. 205 (182).

244 *Wakefield Court Rolls*, V, p. 40.

245 Percentages are the total number of taxpayers with an independent byname or surname (N= 24,469). Chi-square analysis (on the raw numbers) produces a value of 324.034 with two degrees of freedom, significant at the 0.001 level (the critical value at this level of significance is 13.82).

246 Jeayes, *Derbyshire Charters*, pp. 34–5 (251–60).

247 Jeayes, *Derbyshire Charters*, p. 177 (1438).

248 Bodl. MS Laud Misc 625 fo. 14r.

249 T. Lomas, 'V South-east Durham: late fourteenth and fifteenth centuries' in P. D. A. Harvey, ed., *The Peasant Land Market in Medieval England* (Oxford, 1984), p. 291.

250 *Wakefield Court Rolls 1348–1350*, p. 95.

251 *Wakefield Court Rolls 1348–1350*, p. 122.

252 *Wakefield Court Rolls 1348–1350*, p. 235.

253 *Wakefield Court Rolls 1348–1350*, p. 251.

254 *Chancery Miscellanea* VIII, p. 95.

255 *Chancery Miscellanea* VIII, p. 105.

256 *Chancery Miscellanea* IV (List & Index Society 38, 1968), bundle 65/file4/96 (46 Edward III).

257 H. M. Wood, *The Registers of Whitburn* (Durham and Northumberland P. R. Soc. x, 1904), pp. 8–10, 13.

258 *Registers of Whitburn*, pp. 17–19.

259 *Registers of Whitburn*, pp. 33, 40 for example. The observation is based on a perusal of a multitude of printed parish registers published by the various northern Parish Register Societies.

260 Reaney, *Origins*, p. 87. For Forni, G. Fellows-Jensen, *Scandinavian Personal Names in Lincolnshire and Yorkshire* (Copenhagen, 1968), p. 84, and J. Insley, *Scandinavian Personal Names in Norfolk. A Survey Based on Medieval Records and Place-Names* (Uppsala, 1994), pp. 124–5; for Grimr, Fellows-Jensen, *SPNLY*, pp. 105–7 and Insley, *SPNN*, pp. 144–7.

261 C. T. Clay, ed., *Early Yorkshire Charters* V (YASRS Extra Series 2, 1936), p. 91 (no. 41). For Karli in Norfolk, Insley, *SPNN*, pp. 250–1.

262 J. C. Atkinson, ed., *Cartularium Abbathiae de Whiteby* (Surtees Society lxix, 1879), pp. 35–7 (xxix–xxx). For Grimr, see n. 260; for Arne as a hypocorism of a Scandinavian compound name Arn-, Fellows-Jensen, *SPNLY*, pp. 11–12.

263 W. Dugdale, *Monasticon Anglicanum* III, p. 550.

264 M. G. Snape, ed., *English Episcopal Acta Durham* (Oxford, 2002), pp. 156–7 (32b).

265 C. Harper-Bill, ed., *English Episcopal Acta. 6, Norwich, 1070–1214* (Oxford, 1990), p. 91 (110). For earlier instances of *Brun sune*, see D. C. Douglas, ed., *Feudal Documents from the Abbey of Bury St Edmunds* (British Academy Records of the Social and Economic History of England and Wales viii, 1932), pp. 33, 37. The continuation of *-sune* bynames in the survey of the abbey's estates might be important, if, as suggested by Cecily Clark, the date of the survey is revised from 1065x1098 to early in the twelfth century, 'Alfordruncen, Benebrec, Cattenese: some early twelfth-century Suffolk bynames' in D. Hooke and D. Postles, eds, *Names, Time and Place. Essays in Memory of Richard McKinley* (Oxford, 2003).

3

AN EXPANSIVE 'NORTH':
FURTHER CHARACTERISTICS

Although a principal denomination of a North inheres in the concentration and gradation of vernacular forms of patronymic and metronymic bynames and surnames, other features further defined a wider northern onomastic expanse. Whilst some of these characteristics are phonemic – consisting of sounds as transmitted through their written expression (graphemes) – amongst the most interesting are lexical items – items of vocabulary. The distribution of terms for the occupational byname or surname for a fuller has been principally deployed to explain these regional variations: tucker in the south and west; fuller in the east; and walker in the North. It is necessary to recognise, of course, intermediate regions where these terms coincide, so that Walker occurs in the West Midlands. Whilst dialect boundaries are permeable, exploration of some of these features assists in delineating a broad northern onomastic extent.

-man

The addition of the suffix -man to bynames and surnames has a polyvocality or plurality of meanings. One of the significances distinctive, it is believed, of the north is its employment to indicate a servant. When, in particular, combined with a personal name, it has been assumed that the composite byname or surnames indicate that the bearer was a servant – in the wider sense of a waged worker – of the bearer of the personal name. That explanation cannot be exclusively applied to this form of compound byname or surname, but its appearance in the north can be diagnostic of that area. To a certain extent this significance applies too to compound forms with the suffix -knave – and, indeed, occasionally, in unstable bynames, the suffixes were evidently interchangeable.

The associative relationship behind the suffix -man in the North is reflected clearly in an entry in the manorial court roll for the bishop of Durham's manor of Ferry in 1368, in which William *Trollopman* was presented for stabbing William *filius Hugonis* with a knife

Unde Rogerus Trollop respondebit quia habet salarium in manu sua

for Trollop appeared as the employer of *Trollopman*.[1] Although in this particular instance the suffix -man was combined with the surname of the employer to indicate status as a servant, the principle of byname formation was the same as combining forename and -*man*. In Newcastle between 1292 and 1297, land in the *vicus peregrinorum* was conveyed to Robert *Lemmanman*, but that land was later described as the land of Robert *serviens Lemmani de Pampeden*.[2] Here is the direct correlation between a -*man* byname and servanthood.

The process can be illustrated from a particular byname on the manor of Wakefield associated with an important tenant. In 1307, William *Margeriknaue* was pardoned for non-suit in a case of debt because he was the lord's bailiff.[3] In that same year, Adam Gerbode admitted that he owed William *Margeriknaue* half a stone of wool as he had acted as pledge for Henry *le Nunne*.[4] Also in that year, the attorney for an essoin was described as William *serviens Margerie*.[5] Doubtless, the identity was the same, *Margeriknaue* comprising simply a vernacular rendering of *serviens Margerie*. In the following year, William *Margeryman* acted twice again as an attorney for an essoin and William *Margeryknaue* appeared twice as an attorney in the court. Now also in 1308, a pledge at Hiperum, a constituent of the manor, was identified as William *serviens Margerie*, whilst in that same session William *Margeriman* performed as a personal pledge for several other tenants.[6] Described as the servant of Margery, William acceded to one and a half acres of bordland in 1315.[7] The conclusions issuing from these descriptions are that William was or had been a servant of Margery, that he was described in both Latin register and ME vernacular, that the suffixes -*knave* and -*man* imported the same meaning and were interchangeable, and that both suffixes in this specific context reflected servanthood when combined with a personal name.[8] The position of William might be illuminated by the essoin made by Hugh *le Nodder*, attorney of the Lady Margaret de Neyvile, through William *Marjoriman*, with the imputation that not only *Nodder* but also *Marjoriman* was employed by Dame Margaret.[9]

The same etymology might therefore be presumed to obtain in the cases in the Wakefield courts which involved the wife of Henry *Brianman*, presented for brewing in 1349, and at Stanley John *Watknaue* who had acted as a juror.[10] In 1338, Henry had received a pledge in a plea of debt; in the same year he was fined for stray pigs; in 1339 he was fined for brewing.[11] One of the earliest incidences of this form of compound on the manor occurred in 1324, when it was presented that John *Robinman* had been subjected to battery in Holne.[12] This sort of infrequency of mention in the rolls combined with the activities in which he (and his wife) was engaged, suggests the status of a servant.

In 1350, Thomas son of Thomas *Annotknaue* offered a heriot of 3s. for a messuage and sixteen acres of land on the death of his father in April 1350.[13] His father, Thomas *Annotknave* had, with five others, taken the lease of the mills of Holnfirth for an annual rent of £8 in October 1339. That investment might suggest that, although he had been of the status of a servant and although he retained the byname indicative of such, he had graduated to a different life-course stage.[14] One interpretation here might be that Thomas the elder had succeeded after his period of servanthood, but the byname persisted.

That -*knave* and -*man* might have been synonymous is further reflected in the amercement of the wife of Adam *Dobbknave* in 1314 for infraction of the vert and

Hugh *Hervyknave* who defended a case of debt in the manorial court of Wakefield in 1338. In pursuance of the case through 1339, the court rolls then repeatedly identified him as Hugh *Herviman*.[15] This instability of the form is also indicated by Robert *Dyconknave Iveson* who was identified by this periphrasal form of naming in 1339 when he was subjected to battery.[16]

About a decade before the battery of *Robinman*, outlawry was enacted against a migrant from Barnby, Lincolnshire, in the Hustings Court of London: John *Willemesman*.[17] The taxation of 1327 in the North Riding extended to taxpayers named Robert *Andreuman* at Ferlington and Adam *Rogerman* in Norton Conyers.[18] In such a context, the assumption might be made that Robert *Daweknaue*, presented at Thornhill in the West Riding in 1347 had a similar occupational status and etymology for his byname.[19] That implication is certainly corroborated by this appearance being his only suit to the court, suggesting a marginal status. Amongst the smaller tenants at Warrington in Lancashire was enumerated Thomas *Dykknaue* in 1332.[20]

Further north, in Northumberland, the occurrence of this compound formation can be substantiated and its intent supported. In 1342, Henry *dictus Kellawman* son and heir of Robert *de Birdon* granted to William *de Kellawe* junior the attornment of his men in East Birden.[21] In this particular case are combined the instability of bynames and the assumption of a byname suggesting a relationship between lord and man. Another local Northumbrian charter was attested by William *Peresman* de Setone.[22] Similar examples can be elicited for the north-west. In a rental of Unthank in 1328x1332, William *Dauiman* held merely half an acre, consistent with an occupation as a contract labourer. In Newcastle in 1302–3, a *placea* was leased to Robert *Tunnokysman* alias (in 1318) *Tunnokman*.[23]

Conventionally, therefore, these formations existed in County Durham, epitomized by William Thomlynsman, ordered to repair his cottage on the episcopal manor of Wolveston in 1366.[24] His tenure of a mere cottage is perhaps indicative of his status as an employee. Equally interesting in this far northern county is the deployment of the suffix -*mayden* to refer to employed status of females, such as Emma *Androws-mayden* on the episcopal manor of Willington in 1370.[25] Accordingly, Alice *Anesley-mayden* incurred the fine called leyrwite for sexual incontinence outside marriage at Pittington in 1370, implying the combination of servanthood, age at servanthood, unfreedom and singleton status.[26] Those characteristics were reinforced when Matilda *Malkynsmayden* was also placed in mercy for leyrwite at Newton Beaulieu, another episcopal manor in the county, in 1377.[27]

In Ormskirk in Lancashire in 1366, one of the subscribers in the township of Scarisbrick was Richard Thomasmon.[28] This form of byname existed just to the south in the northern periphery in Staffordshire. In one particular instance, the relationship of servanthood is implicit: in the first decade of the fourteenth century, John *Dod* and Richard *Jonesmandod* appeared with others accused of cutting down trees at Pentrich. At Podemore, Thomas *Rogersman* was accused of homicide and about the same time, 1318, Henry *Janekynesmon* fled from a similar accusation.[29] In 1332, Richard *Stevenesman* was assessed at 1s. at Wollaston.[30]

Excluding those illustrative examples, the spatial distribution of these compounds of a personal name and -*man* can now be assessed. In Figure 24 is depicted the location of these compounds as the bynames of taxpayers in the lay subsidies of the late thirteenth and early fourteenth centuries. Advisable, however, is some circumspection, since this taxation was not comprehensive but excluded a large proportion of inhabitants below a taxable threshold. Now, if these compound bynames do represent servanthood or a similar status, then the likelihood is that the extent of these bynames will be concealed by the lay subsidies since these bynames would accordingly have pertained more firmly (although not exclusively) to the less affluent.

In Figure 24, although the number of these bynames is not prolific, they are ostensibly more frequent in the far north, in Cumberland and the North Riding. Their composition is fairly restricted: *Thomasman*; *Randman*; *Walterotman*; *Goceman*; *Wakeman*; *Hoggeman*; *Martinman*; *Robertman* (two); *Henriman*; *Alanman*; *Richardman*; *Maryman/Mariman* (three); *Dauyman*; *Rogerman* (two); *Geffeman*; *Hoggeman* (two); *Roulandman*; *Elyotman*; *Dodeman/Dodemon* (two); *Maggeman*; *Sunneman*; and *Nicolasmon*.[31]

The comparative distribution of compounds of -*man* indicating servant in 1377–81 is illustrated in Figure 25. For purposes of comparison, however, it should be remembered that the capture of the taxation of 1377–81 was more comprehensive than those of 1296–1332. Necessary, however, is a separation of different compounds with -*man*. Ambiguity inheres in some. For example, *Blithman* at Whickham might constitute the servant of an inhabitant with the byname/surname *Blith* or merely consist of a nickname byname/surname.[32] In contrast, *Walkeman* at Greasborough contains some ambiguity, as it might denote an alternative occupational term for *Walker*.[33] Topographical bynames/surnames with -*man* appended expand the ambivalences. Those are the sort of generic problems surrounding the interpretation of the suffix -*man* in the late fourteenth century.[34] Furthermore, where a personal name is attached to the suffix, it might comprise either a byname/surname or a forename.[35] Any consideration of this compounding thus elicits questions.

To some extent, surer ground can be attained by excluding obviously ambiguous elements. Assumptions can be made that in the West Riding Poll Tax of 1379 *Watkynman* at Bolton on Dearne, *Rogerman* at Pontefract, *Perysman* there, *Dobman* at South Kirkby, *Daukeman* at Ousefleet, and *Robertman* at South Elmsall, as examples, might have derived from forenames, even if there is a possibility that the prototheme might have constituted a byname or surname.[36]

We should not assume that compound forms combining a personal name and the suffix -*man* did not exist elsewhere. It is quite evident that they did. The difference is the greater familiarity of this form of compound name in the North. In the Worcestershire lay subsidy of 1280, for example, are encountered the taxpayers John *le Warineknaue*, William *Edemon*, Adam *Watemon*, Richard *Godetknaue*, John *Hykemon*, and, with the feminine genitival -*s*, Juliana *Hykemonnes*.[37] In Gloucestershire in 1327, Thomas *Maryman* was taxed in Gloucester and in the contemporary lay subsidy for Shropshire, Roger *Mabbemon* contributed 1s. 4d. at Marton.[38] *Mariman* occurred as a byname in Derby in 1327.[39] Amongst the jurors for the deanery court held at Skillington, Lincolnshire, in 1338, was Adam *Martynman*.[40] Another *Mariman* was assessed at Chesterton in Warwickshire, but equally interesting in that county's taxation was the appearance of William and Geoffrey *Malleknaue*, included at Long

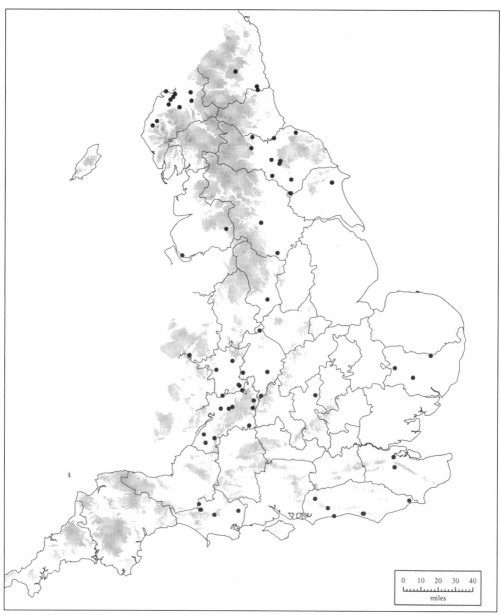

*Figure 24 Compound bynames with -*man*, late thirteenth and early fourteenth century*

Itchington, and a *Saunderknaue* at Tanworth.[41] The byname *Hickeman* or *Hikeman* or
Hykeman represented taxpayers in Fairford, Little Rissington, Frampton, Shurdington
and Hawkesbury, whilst *Janeman* contributed at Broadwell in Gloucestershire.[42] In
Bedfordshire in 1355, Alan *Jonysman* and others broke into a close and committed
battery.[43] There too, John *Hicheman* and Thomas *Hicheman* acted as pledges for a

vagrant, although the following entry in the sessions revealed that they too existed as itinerants, wandering about and armed, the four vagrants anomalously thus pledging for each other.[44] *Hykemon* and its variants was replicated in Warwickshire amongst taxpayers at Lapworth, Great Compton, Polesworth and Billesley.[45] In the manorial and franchisal court of Middleton in Warwickshire in the 1280s, Geoffrey *Jonesmon* was involved in litigation.[46]

For a more comprehensive geographical coverage – but again with the caveat about exclusiveness – resort must again be made to the lay subsidies for other counties, which are included in Figure 24. The geographical extent is revealed, but in many areas of the south there is nevertheless a light density, the exception being the west Midlands (Worcestershire and Gloucestershire).[47]

These compound bynames of servanthood were predominantly attached to males and only occasionally was the equivalent suffix applied to a female. In 1328, Agnes *Hawemayden* was involved in a case of battery in Stanley, a constituent of the manor of Wakefield.[48]

Nevertheless, other compound descriptions obtained in southern areas, amongst which was frequently occasioned a combination of the servant's forename and surname with a periphrase containing the master's forename and *-servant*. For example, the outlawry was exacted of John Romseye 'that was Richardesservant Esket' on an action under the Statute of Labourers initiated by Richard Esket at the very end of the fourteenth century.[49] Under the same statute, John Adam prosecuted John atte Sele 'that was Johanservaunt Adam'.[50] Both actions pertained to the hiring of servants in Bedfordshire. In adjacent Buckinghamshire about the same time, outlawry was imposed on John *Dryvere Robertesservant Power* for poaching.[51] In Wiltshire, in the middle of the fifteenth century, report was made of the abduction of Alice 'that was Thomasservant Semeleye' at Kingston Deverell.[52] In Sussex, the murder of John Wilton at Chichester was attributed to William *Warde alias Stut alias Jonesservant Wilton*, presumably homicide of a master by his servant.[53] In Norfolk in the early fifteenth century, Thomas Codling 'that was Roberdesservant' was outlawed for absconding from the service of Robert Mauteby of Sparham.[54] In the south-west, Richard 'that was Adamesservant Hopper' was outlawed for killing a dog in the late fifteenth century.[55]

Occasionally that sort of formula intruded into more northerly areas, as in the publication of the homicide of Richard *Norman Johannesservant* of Hutton at Hackthorn in Lincolnshire in the late fourteenth century.[56] Across the Trent was reported the homicide of John de Billesby 'that was Willameservant' of Retford in the 1360s.[57] Simply to illustrate the differences of regional formations, in the south-west of England a prominent feature of bynaming consisted of a compound of the the prefix *Dame-* with a female personal name, presumably indicating a servant of a woman. For example, Richard *Damedith* acted as a juror on an inquisition about the manor of Begworth in 1343.[58] In the south-west of Oxfordshire, in Kencot in 1279–80, Robert *Damabeli*, an unfree tenant, held a messuage and a virgate.[59]

What can be concluded about a northern onomastic zone from the evidence of this use of the compound *-man*? Evidently there was no clear dialect boundary for its use for denoting servanthood: the compound was deployed more widely than just northern areas. Nevertheless, it featured more regularly in northern areas and its

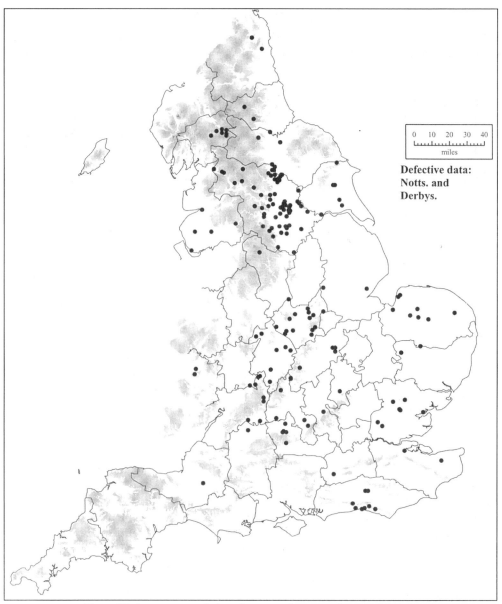

Figure 25 Surnames consisting of a personal name and -man, *1377–81*

formation outside northern areas tended to be unusual. Moreover, outside northern areas, other compound formations competed with -*man*. In fine, we might conclude that the intensive and customary use of -*man* in bynames as a suffix to a personal name denoting servanthood was more characteristic onomastically of an extensive northern zone which extended down into the north Midlands.

Thecker / thacker: dialect lexis

When Thomas Thakker was presented for trespass at Surfleet in south Lincolnshire in the middle of the fifteenth century his surname was redolent of north Lincolnshire.[60] *Thakker* had demonstrably existed as the northern variant of *Thatcher* and had infiltrated into the southern part of the county. At a much earlier time – in 1342 – the death of Roger *le Theker*, who fell on a knife at Belby in Yorkshire, illustrates that this surname had a more general association with the 'North' as an onomastic zone.[61]

The extent to which that obtained can be illustrated for the manor of Wakefield. In 1314, William *le Theker* was presented at the manor court of Wakefield for collecting dry wood and for rescuing beats.[62] In 1315, he was presented again, by the byname *le Theker*, for his persistence in taking dry wood.[63] Whether from the same kinship or another, the daughter of William *Thecker* appeared before the court in 1331 for exactly the same offence.[64] At the same time, the servant (*ancilla*) of Gilbert *Thecker* was also prosecuted for breaking fences.[65] In 1340 Agnes *Thekar* was amerced 2d. for an offence against the vert.[66]

This occupational difference extended into adjacent counties, so that Roger *le Thecker* was assessed for the lay subsidy in the south of Nottinghamshire at Stoke Bardolph.[67] The easterly extension of the byname is represented by Christine *Theker* embroiled in an office cause involving fornication in the deanery court of Lincoln in 1338.[68]

Like other lexicographical items as bynames, *Thakker* extended outside the North into north midland counties, but more in an easterly direction than a westerly one. A contrast might thus be made with *Walker*, for *Walker* extended outside the North mainly in a westerly direction, whereas *Thakker* proceeded mainly in an easterly extension. Thus when charters about land at Womborne (Staffs.) were attested in 1308 and 1320, the witnesses included William *le Thacchere*.[69]

To illustrate the pattern during the fourteenth century, Figures 26 and 27 delineate the incidences of Thacker and Thatcher and their variants in the lay subsidies of the early fourteenth century and in the last quarter. The phonemic divergence was not the sole differentiating characteristic, however, for it is possible that whilst many thatchers in the south employed reed or straw, thackers in the north roofed with stone. For example, on Wakefield manor in 1340 Thomas *filius Juliane* was accused of purloining stone called *Thakston*.[70] In like manner, Henry Stonthacker inhabited Chesterfield in Derbyshire some time before 1363.[71]

Nevertheless, the difference of materials accounted less for the alternative name forms than the impact of dialect – in other words, the materials used were incidental to the regional diversity. Essentially, the difference subsisted in different voicing in OE and Scandinavian forms. Whereas Scandinavian forms sustained the velar pronunciation (*k*), OE tended to the palatal consonant (*ch*).[72] That difference in voicing is commonly associated with other lexical items, most notably *kirk* (northern) and *church* (southern). A more general appreciation of the effect in northern zones is discussed below.

Figure 26 Thakker *and* Thatcher, *late thirteenth and early fourteenth centuries*

Walker: dialect lexis

The general association of the occupational byname and surname Walker with an expansive northern onomastic zone is illustrated by the homicide of William *le Walker* at Hornsea in Yorkshire in 1316.[73] In the 1327 lay subsidy for the North Riding, *Walkers* were itemized at Thirsk, Skuttershelf, Spaunton and at two of the three Appletons.[74] That this occupational byname also extended out into adjacent areas, particularly in a south-westerly direction, is illustrated by a grant by Nicholas *le Walkere* at Longdon in Staffordshire in the late thirteenth century.[75] The distribution of this byname in the lay subsidies before 1332 is represented in Figure 28 and in 1377–81 in Figure 29.

Lister: dialect lexis

As with many other lexical elements, the byname *Lister* was characteristic of the North, but not distinctive of northern-ness in the sense that it extended outside any defined area of the north into other regions. Although, therefore, dialect lexis within the north, it was not confined there. The overall distribution in the late thirteenth and early fourteenth century is illustrated in Figure 30, where it is revealed, for example, that *Lister* extended as far south as Huntingdonshire and Suffolk.[76] Figure 31 reveals the distribution in 1377–81.

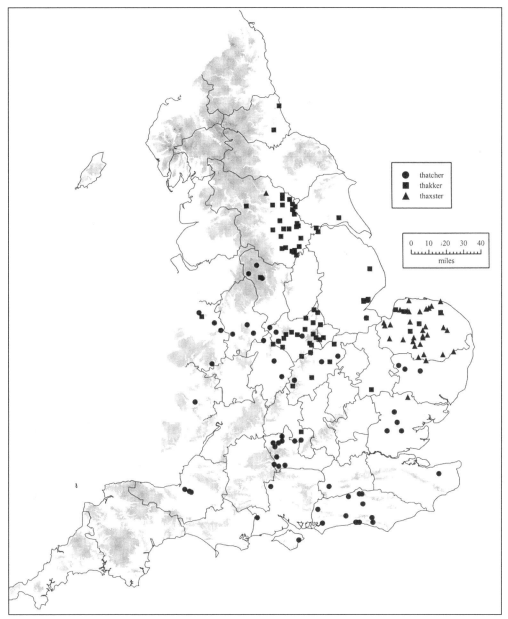

Figure 27 Thakker and Thatcher, 1377–81

Greave/reeve: dialect phoneme

In 1333, Simon *le Greyesone* was acquitted of a murder committed at Cottingham in the East Riding of Yorkshire.[77] Confirmation of the association between forms of greave and the more northerly areas of England is represented by the tenants of land

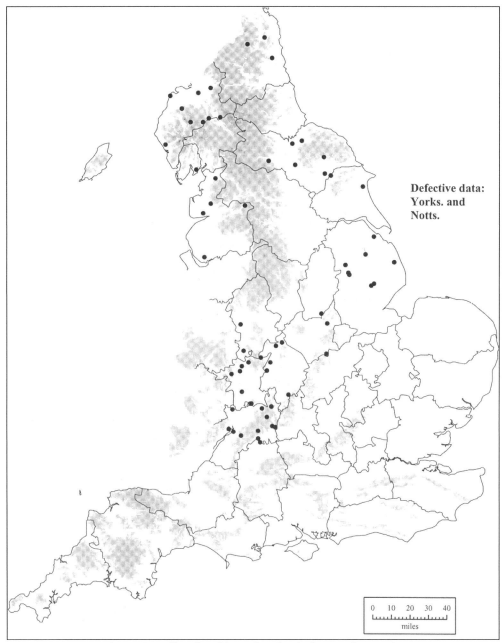

Figure 28 Walker, *late thirteenth and early fourteenth centuries*

at Chester-le-Street in county Durham in the middle of the fourteenth century: John and William *Greveson*.[78] As complicated as they can be, Greave and its variants support a broad definition of a northern onomastic zone. Outside that area, the

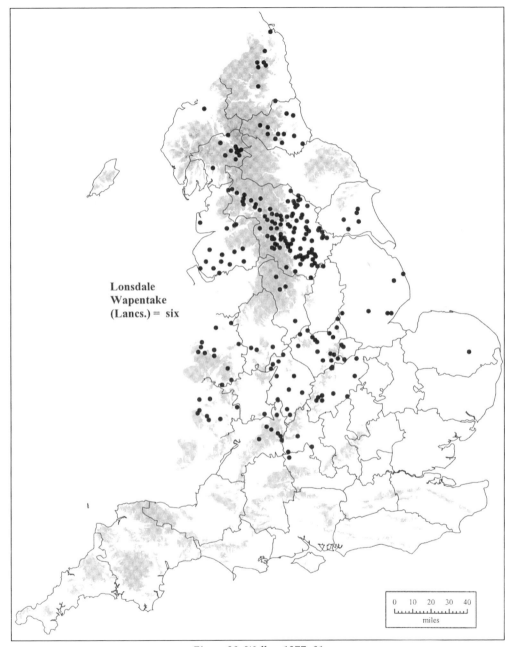

**Lonsdale
Wapentake
(Lancs.) = six**

Figure 29 Walker, 1377–81

manorial office (Latin *prepositus*) was more usually represented in ME by *Reeve*. The difficulty occurs with variants of *Greave* such as *Greue* or *Graue*, since either might conceivably derive from topographical bynames (minim corruption in [*ate*] *Grene*

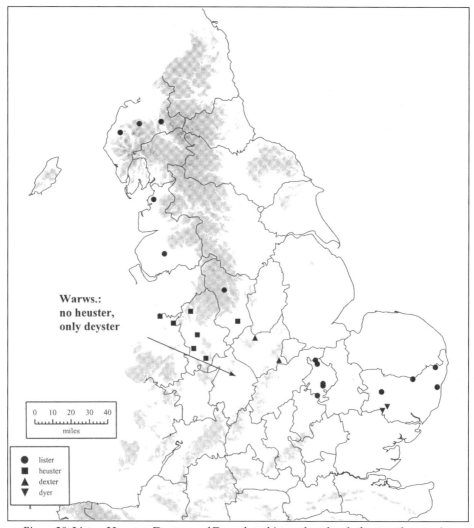

Figure 30 Lister, Heuster, Dexter, *and* Dyer, *late thirteenth and early fourteenth centuries*

Warws.:
no heuster,
only deyster

0 10 20 30 40
miles

● lister
■ heuster
▲ dexter
▼ dyer

and vowel substitution in [*ate*] *Groue*). Through the substitution of *u* for *v*, *Greue* becomes indistinct from *Grene*, although this form of the office was more usually rendered as *Greyue*, so that the -*y*- might be diagnostic. Considered with care, however, *Greave* can be employed to comment on the broad north-south difference. Of course, when topographical bynames retained their syndetic form (with the preposition *atte*) the problem does not obtain.

The south-easterly extension of -*grave* is confirmed in Lincolnshire by repetitive compounds with -*grave* as the second element: *Woodgrayue* (three taxpayers) at Fiskerton in 1332; *Lathegrayue* at Riby; *Woodgrayue* at Lindwood; *Fengrayue* at Wilsby; *Ploghgrayue* at Scrivelsby, Wigtoft and Swineshead; and *Wodgrayue* at Londonthorpe.[79]

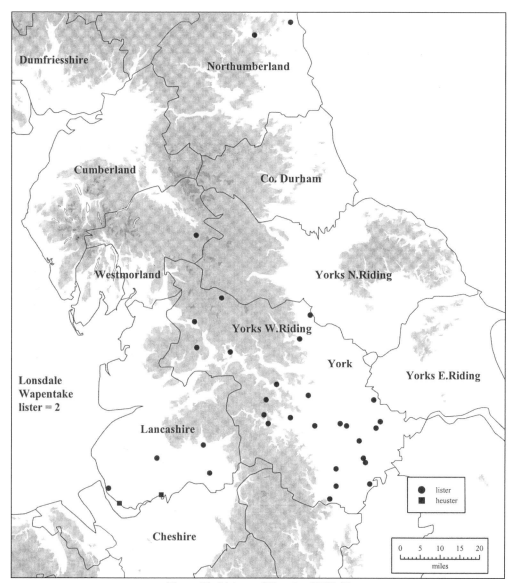

Figure 31 Lister and Heuster, 1377–81

Accordingly, at least as far as her lineage was concerned, Emma daughter of Gilbert *Greyve* of Snartford committed adultery in 1337.[80] Accused of fornication, Joan *Greyve* was arraigned before the same ecclesiastical court as Emma in 1339.[81]

Greave thus furnished a consistent marker for northern-ness, but, like some other lexis, it extended outside the north to define a wider onomastic area. Although not exclusive to the north, it still represented a northern-ness. As Figure 32 illustrates, its extension out from the north was in a south-easterly direction only. In Suffolk,

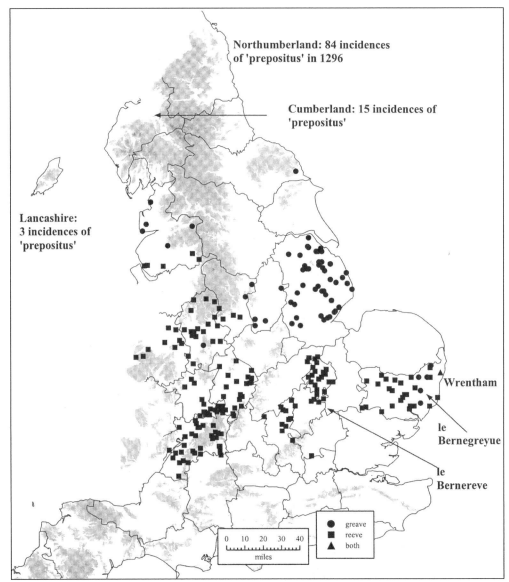

Northumberland: 84 incidences of 'prepositus' in 1296

Cumberland: 15 incidences of 'prepositus'

Lancashire: 3 incidences of 'prepositus'

Wrentham

le Bernegreyue

le Bernereve

	greave
	reeve
	both

0 10 20 30 40
miles

Figure 32 Grave *and* Reeve, *late thirteenth and early fourteenth centuries*

several instances of *Greyve* occurred amongst taxpayers in 1327, but *Reve* predominated.[82] At Wrentham, both forms coincided.[83] The distribution in 1377–81 is depicted in Figure 33.

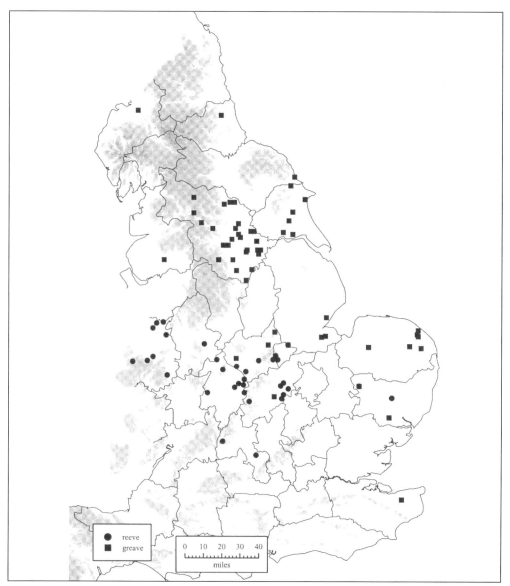

Figure 33 Grave and Reeve, 1377–81

k/c substitution (velar and palatal plosives)

The consonantal substitution of *k* for *c* in northern zones is a familiar phenomenon of late Middle English. From some particular evidence it is apparent that this alteration was not simply a graphemic change but a phonemic one too, affecting the voicing of some bynames and surnames. Indeed, in some other bynames, *k* was inserted in the north in bynames in which the consonantal *c* was later to disappear.

In particular, the final grapheme in insular Old English personal names differed between northern regions and the southern areas of England. Whereas the final consonant in the north was represented as a grapheme – if not voiced as -*rik*, in more southerly areas it was composed as -*rich*. For example, at Alconbury in Hunts., OE Leofric was represented as *Leuerich*.[84] Once again, the transitional area transected the north Midlands. Illustrative of the southern composition was the compilation of bynames from these West Germanic personal names in Gloucestershire: *Godrich, Thedrich, Aylrich, Alfrich, Edrich, Loverich, Wolfrich* and *Serich*.[85] So also in Worcestershire, bynames from these personal names were constituted with final -*rich*.[86] In Shropshire, the same construction was applied: *Eylrych, Edrych, Wolfrych, Oughtrych,* and *Thedrych*.[87] In contemporary Warwickshire too, the grapheme indicated the same voicing: *Goddrich; Aylrych; Alrich; Baldrich; Serich;* and *Edrych*.[88]

Another implication, however, was the introduction of either *k* or *c* to affect the northern pronunciation of some lexis. One example in particular is the occupational byname *Slater*, which was inscribed as *Sklater* or *Sclater*. The northernmost representation is reflected in Thomas and John *Sklater*, both contributors to the Poll Tax in Carlisle in 1377.[89]

The survival of forms with the substituted -*k*- can be illustrated by the later consistency of the surname Skaithlock, originally *Scathelok*. In 1566, William Skaithlocke entered into matrimony at St Nicholas in Durham.[90] There too conjugal contracts were made by Robert Skaithlocke in 1595, but followed by John Scaithlocke in 1602 and John Scathlocke in 1628.[91]

Qu/W

In 1407, a grant was made in Billsborough in Lancashire by John Quyteschonk. A century later, in 1516–18, land in Padiham in that county was the subject of interaction within the Quittaker kinship, involving Joan Quittaker daughter of Laurence Quitakar versus Miles Quittaker and Henry Quittaker, and including, as a witness, Robert Qwittaker.[92] In the parish registers of Prescot (Lancs.) early entries related that Humphrey Qwytefelde son of Henry Qwytfelde of Qwyston was baptized in 1541, Edmund Qwytehedde married in that year, and Margaret Qwytfeld in 1549.[93] The voicing of *W* and *Wh* by *Q*, it has been maintained, was a distinctively northern phoneme, although it occasionally occurred elsewhere.[94]

Despite its attribution to the north, this particular voicing featured not infrequently in Norfolk. In Taverham, for example, John *Qwytfot* effected a release and made a grant of turbary and heath in Felthorpe in the 1330s.[95] As John *Whitfot*, he was the recipient of a messuage and land in the latter vill.[96] The voiced alternative recurred at Felthorpe in the 1360s in the persons of Margaret, daughter and heir of John Qwhytfot.[97] As far south as Southover in Sussex, Robert *Peperquit* attested a thirteenth-century charter.[98]

Nevertheless, the voicing was also characteristic of more northerly areas, including north-west Midlands Middle English, for Hugh *le Quelp* attested a charter relating to Fadile in Cheshire in 1271.[99] Illustrative of this phonemic difference was Evota

Quelspinner of East Merrington in Durham in 1365.[100] In the same locality, at Newton Ketton, Margaret Qwyte was accused of breaking the lord's enclosure.[101] The graphemic representation insinuated into official royal records, thus listing Alice *la quite* amongst the tenants in an inquisition into the manor of Warrington in 1332.[102]

In south-west Yorkshire too, the grapheme was introduced into the written manorial records: illicitly felling wood at Hiperum attracted a fine of 6d. for Adam *le Quelwrigh* on the manor of Wakefield.[103] For contempt of court, John *del Quithill* was amerced 6d. in Stanley in 1313.[104] The redaction of the Poll Tax returns in the late fourteenth century do not preclude the sound substitution. At Lathom and Great Crosby and in Lonsdale Wapentake in Lancashire, those assessed included taxpayers with the surnames *le Quite*, *Quytman* and *le Qwyte*.[105]

In the same manner, the substitution of the phoneme was prevalent in Lancashire, although *w*- forms coincided with *q*-. Whilst Thomas Quyteside was mentioned in association with Lea in 1419, therefore, Richard *Whithevid* was inscribed in a document relating to Colne in 1324.[106] The initial *w(h)*- was used as consistently in Lancashire documents as the alternative, but the written form does not necessarily or comprehensively enlighten us about the language of the speech community. Nevertheless, formations with initial *q*- were a characteristic of Lancashire dialect: Qwelpe and Qwytynggam at Hale in 1447–8 and 1460, Qwytfeld at Woolton in 1492, *le Quyte* in the same place in 1348 succeeded by *de* Quitthefeld in 1372, Qwytfeld in 1385 and 1389 but Whytfeld in 1410 (one form of which, *de Quitfeld*, had occurred earlier there in 1333), *le Quite/Quyt* in Woolton in 1345 and 1348 (but *le Whyte* there in *c*.1320–1340), *de Qwalley* in association with Eccleshill in *c*.1280, and *Qwytesyde* in Liverpool in 1300.[107] In 1332 Alice *la Quite* belonged to the tenantry of Warrington.[108]

It is in particular in the chamberlains' accounts for Newcastle-upon-Tyne from 1508 to 1511, however, that this language use is especially distinctive of a speech community. Amongst the litany of words with initial *qw*, none was as repetitive as the surname of Gilbert Qwhytt, to whom the chamberlains made unremitting payments throughout these years for his service.[109] Additionally, Roland Qwhitt was remunerated for acting as an attorney for the borough in 1510.[110]

The substitution endured into the late sixteenth century at Farnham (Lancashire), where the registers between 1584 and the end of the century referred, *inter alia*, to *Maudilla uxor Qualteri Knasbrough*, *Qualterus Readshaw*, *Qualterus Simpson*, *Alicia uxor Qualteri Dixson*, *Maria filia Qualtheri Knarsbrough*, *Qualterus filius Qualteri Dixson* and *Qualtherus Thorpp*.[111] In the registers of Padiham (Lancashire) at the end of the sixteenth and beginning of the seventeenth century, this substitution occurred in the inscription of the surname Quipp. Most of the baptisms were registered as Quipp, but the burials as Whipp (although not conclusively so), but some serendipitous entries reveal the connection: the burials of Robert Quipp alias Whipp in 1599 and the wife of William Quipp alias Whipp in 1607.[112] These Lancashire examples may be supplemented by David Qwhitfeld, juror in the view of frankpledge for Liverpool in 1551.[113]

Whilst patronyms and metronyms with their vernacular suffix *-son* provided one broad delineating criterion for a northern onomastic zone, other name elements confirmed the definition of a broad northern expanse. In the case of those patronyms and metronyms, the onomastic element extended into the penumbra of the north, dissecting the northern half of the Midlands. That same southerly gradation applied with the other elements, but some of those elements continued to the south-west and others to the south-east rather than expanding southwards in both directions. Those elements, however, complement the patronyms and metronyms in elucidating characteristics which, while formative in northern speech communities, affected the periphery of the north too.

Notes

1   *Halmota Prioratus Dunelmensis*, p. 73. For an analogous situation, see the enumeration of tenants at Liverpool including both John *Fox* and John *Fox Knaue* (sic): W. Farrer, ed., *Lancashire Inquests, Extents and Feudal Aids* Part III (LCRS lxx, 1915), p. 69.

2   A. M. Oliver, ed., *Early Deeds relating to Newcastle upon Tyne* (Surtees Society cxxxvii, 1924), pp. 143–5 (242–3, 246).

3   *Wakefield Court Rolls* I, p. 96 (Alverthorpe); by that byname he appeared as a pledge in 1307: *Wakefield Court Rolls* I, pp. 94, 97.

4   *Wakefield Court Rolls* I, p. 96.

5   *Wakefield Court Rolls* I, p. 106.

6   *Wakefield Court Rolls* I, pp. 166, 169, 174, 178, 179, 180.

7   *Wakefield Court Rolls* III, p. 90.

8   Other references include: William *Margeriknaue* plaintiff in debt in 1307; William *Margeriman* attorney for an essoin in 1309; the same as a pledge in 1309; the same as a pledge for prosecution in 1309; William *Marjoriman* as pledge and bailiff in 1315; *Wakefield Court Rolls* I, pp. 84, 212, 217, 225; *Wakefield Court Rolls* III, pp. 68–9; William *Marjoriman* attorney 1315; the same a pledge in two cases of debt in 1315; a bailiff in 1315; William *Marjoriman* one of the under-bailiffs; William *Marjoriman* admitted detinue of rye; the same a pledge in 1316: *Wakefield Court Rolls* IV, pp. 1, 24, 58, 99, 138–9, 141; he probably died between 1317 and 1323: *Wakefield Court Rolls* V, pp. 23–8.

9   *Wakefield Court Rolls* IV, p. 35.

10   *Wakefield Court Rolls 1348–1350*, pp. 55, 71, 114. In 1331, however, there was the presentment of the daughter of John *Wacknaue*: *Wakefield Court Rolls 1331–1333*, p. 17: we thus have the possibility of either servant of Watte (Walter) or servant of Wack (Walkelin). In 1332, John *Watteknaue* collected dry wood in Stanley: *Wakefield Court Rolls 1331–1333*, p. 62.

11   *Wakefield Court Rolls 1338–1340*, pp. 9, 12, 67, 118, 200.

12   *Wakefield Court Rolls* V, p. 40.

13   *Wakefield Court Rolls 1348–1350*, p. 239.

14   *Wakefield Court Rolls 1338–1340* , p. 123.

15   *Wakefield Court Rolls 1338–1340*, pp. 24, 28 (-knave), 50, 55, 60, 73, 80, 83, 88, 94, 100, 153 (-man).

16   *Wakefield Court Rolls 1338–1340*, p. 124; *Wakefield Court Rolls* III, p. 63.

17   *Chancery Miscellanea* V (List & Index Society 29, 1970), p. 147.

18   Colonel Parker, 'Lay subsidy rolls 1 Edward III N. R. & City of York' in *Miscellanea II* (YASRS lxxiv, 1929), pp. 142, 152.

19   Nottinghamshire Archives Office DDSR 1/6/6a. So also *Aleynknaue* at Ashbourne contained the same imputation: I. H. Jeayes, *Descriptive Catalogue of Derbyshire Charters* (London, 1906), p. 108 (882).

20   W. Farrer, ed., *Lancashire Inquests, Extents and Feudal Aids* Part II (LCRS liv, 1907), p. 240.

21   J. Walton, ed., 'The Greenwell deeds', *Archaeologia Aeliana* 4th series 111 (1927) extra volume, p. 80 (168).

22   Walton, 'Greenwell deeds', p. 42 (87).

23   Oliver, *Early Deeds … Newcastle upon Tyne*, pp. 17 (12), 181 (353–4)

24   *Halmota Prioratus Dunelmensis*, p. 58.

25   *Halmota Prioratus Dunelmensis*, p. 98.

26   *Halmota Prioratus Dunelmensis*, p. 101.

27   *Halmota Prioratus Dunelmensis*, p. 140.

28   *Miscellanies Volume 2* (LCRS 31, 1896), p. 112.

29   G. Wrottesley, ed., 'Extracts from the Coram Rege Rolls and Pleas of the Crown, Staffordshire, of the reign of Edward II, A.D. 1307 to A.D. 1327', *Collections for a History of Staffordshire William Salt Archaeological Society* x, 1889, pp. 6, 29, 43.

30   'Staffordshire 1332', p. 123.

31   *Yorkshire 1301*, pp. 9, 17, 27, 37, 83–4, 85, 120; *Cumberland*, pp. 16, 19, 20, 21, 25, 27, 28, 31, 52, 54, 69; *Northumberland*, pp. 19, 43, 56; *Yorkshire 1297*, pp. 70, 108, 143. *Bateman* has been omitted because of its ambiguity.

32   *Bishop Hatfield's Survey*, p. 97.

33   'West Riding Poll Tax', 5, p. 244.

34   G. Fransson, *Middle English Surnames of Occupation, 1100–1350* (Lund Studies in English 3, 1935), discusses the intentions of the *-man* suffix.

35   That combination might account for Gaytknaue, Styrtanaue, Smytheknaue and other names in 1379: 'West Riding Poll Tax', 5, pp. 13, 33; 7, pp. 152–3, 155, 160, 166, 171.

36   'West Riding Poll Tax', 6, pp. 7, 10, 21.

37   'Worcs. (1280)', pp. 8, 67, 70, 80, 89.

38   *Gloucestershire*, p. 27; 'Shropshire', 8, p. 45.

39   'Derbyshire', p. 81. *Ingemay* in Scarcliffe at that time is probably another example of this form of byname.

40   L. R. Poos, ed., *Lower Ecclesiastical Jurisdiction in Late-medieval England. The Courts of the Dean and Chapter of Lincoln, 1336–1349, and the Deanery of Wisbech, 1458–1484* (British Academy Records of Social and Economic History new series 32, 2001), p. 52.

41   *Warwickshire*, pp. 1, 22, 33–4.

42   *Gloucestershire*, pp. 49, 57, 59, 68, 84, 94, 113. Perhaps *Wakemon* is ambiguous, but the possibility exists that it was produced from *Wa(c)ke-* as a hypocorism of Walkelin.

43   E. G. Kimball, ed., *Sessions of the Peace for Bedfordshire 1355–1359, 1363–1364* (Bedford Historical Record Society 48, 1969), p. 46 (39).

44   Kimball, *Sessions of the Peace for Bedfordshire*, p. 65 (88–89).

45   *Warwickshire*, pp. 11, 16, 58, 77.

46   University of Nottingham Department of Manuscripts MiM 131/1: *Galfridus Jonesmon optulit se uersus Radulphum Mersiche*. He also brewed: MiM 131/2. Otherwise, he rarely appeared in the record of the court.

47   'Kent', pp. 9, 12, 24, 48; 'Derbyshire', p. 12; *Gloucestershire*, pp. 6, 7, 12, 14, 16,17, 24, 26, 30, 111; *Suffolk*, pp. 8, 13, 16, 18; *Warwickshire*, pp. 24, 36; 'Worcs. (1280)', pp. 24, 28, 36, 72, 80; *Buckinghamshire*, p. 16; 'Shropshire 1327', pp. 16, 25; *Sussex 1327*, pp. 6, 19, 31, 49, 51; *Dorset 1332*, pp. 8, 12, 16, 24. *Jakeman* has been omitted as ambiguous.

48   *Wakefield Court Rolls* V, p. 136.

49   *Chancery Miscellanea* III (List and Index Society 26, 1967), p. 125.

50   *Chancery Misc.* III, p. 153.

51   *Chancery Misc.* III, p. 185.

52   *Chancery Miscellanea* VII (List and Index Society 88, 1973).

53   *Chancery Misc.* VII, p. 81.

54   *Chancery Misc.* V, p. 218.

55   *Chancery Miscellanea* VI (List and Index Society 81, 1972), p. 151.

56   *Chancery Misc.* V, p. 38.

57   *Chancery Misc.* VI, p. 39.

58   E. Fry, ed., *Abstracts of Inquisitions post Mortem for Gloucestershire* Part V (British Record Society Index Library 40, 1940), p. 294.

59   E. Stone, ed., *The Oxfordshire Hundred Rolls of 1279* (Oxfordshire Record Society 46, 1968), p. 56.

60   *Chancery Misc.* V, p. 64.

61   *Chancery Miscellanea* VIII (List and Index Society 105, 1972), p. 142.

62   *Wakefield Court Rolls* III, p. 55.

63   *Wakefield Court Rolls* III, p. 84.

64   *Wakefield Court Rolls 1331–1333*, p. 17.

65   *Wakefield Court Rolls 1331–1333*, p. 17. For this form also, Parker, 'Lay subsidy rolls 1 Edward III N. R. & City of York' , p. 158: Alan *le Theker* assessed at 1s. at Spaunton in the North Riding.

66   *Wakefield Court Rolls 1338–1340*, p. 197; see also the instances of *Theker* at pp. 20, 53, 76, 78 and 229.

67   P.R.O. E179/159/5, m. 8.

68   Poos, *Lower Ecclesiastical Jurisdiction in Late-medieval England*, p. 65.

69   G. P. Mander, 'Calendar of early charters &c at the Wodehouse Wombourne' *Collections for a History of Staffordshire* William Salt Archaeological Society (1928), pp. 22, 31 (24, 41–2). An early instance of *thecchere* in the south-east is Wibert *thecchere* in Canterbury in 1175x 1177: W. Urry, *Canterbury under the Angevin Kings* (London, 1967), p. 423 (xlvii).

70   *Wakefield Court Rolls 1338–1340*, p. 201.

71   Jeayes, *Derbyshire Charters*, p. 94 (748).

72   One of the clearest and most succinct explanations is G. Hughes, *A History of English Words* (Oxford, 2000), p. 99.

73   *Chancery Misc.* VIII, p. 152.

74   Parker, 'Lay subsidy rolls 1 Edward III N. R. & City of York', pp. 122, 150, 157, 158.

75   I. H. Jeayes, 'Calendar of the Marquess of Anglesey's ... charters ...' *Collections for a History of Staffordshire* William Salt Archaeological Society (1939), p. 108 (1723).

76   *Huntingdonshire*, pp. 150, 179, 217, 229, 254; *Suffolk*, pp. 47, 60, 81, 215; for *Dyer* in Suffolk, *Suffolk*, pp. 139, 145.

77   *Chancery Misc.* VIII, p. 114.

78   *Bishop Hatfield's Survey*, p. 79.

79   T.N.A. (P.R.O.) E179/135/14, mm. 4, 6; E179/135/15, m. 17; E179/135/16, mm. 10, 16, 20, 34, 35.

80   Poos, *Lower Ecclesiastical Jurisdiction*, p. 5.

81   Poos, *Lower Ecclesiastical Jurisdiction*, p. 86.

82   *Suffolk*, pp. 51, 64, 69, 77, 87, 116

83   *Suffolk*, p. 69.

84   *Huntingdonshire*, p. 220.

85   *Gloucestershire*, pp. 37, 42, 43, 50, 55, 57, 61, 72, 76, 78, 80, 82–4, 88, 92, 96–7, 99, 101, 104, 111, 116.

86   'Worcs. (1327)', pp. 12, 20, 33, 37, 43, 55, 59 (*Hutrich*), 59, 70, 71, 73.

87   'Shropshire', 4, pp. 290–2, 305, 325, 333; 10, p. 139.

88   *Warwickshire*, pp. 23, 40, 47, 55, 63, 68.

89   Fenwick, *Poll Taxes* I, pp. 92–3.
90   H. M. Wood, *The Registers of St Nicholas'* [Durham] (Durham and Northumberland P. R. Soc. xxxii, 1918), p. 4.
91   Wood, *Registers of St Nicholas'*, pp. 12, 14, 23.
92   J. Parker, ed., *Lancashire Deeds* volume 1 *Shuttleworth Deeds* part 1 (Chetham Society n.s. 91, 1934), pp. 114, 117 (C15, C18).
93   J. Perkins, *The Register of the Parish of Prescot* (Lancs. P. R. Soc. 137, 1995), pp. 2, 152, 153.
94   S. Carlsson, *Studies on Middle English Local Bynames in East Anglia* (Lund, 1989), p. 161. For one interesting formation, Parker, 'Lay subsidy rolls 1 Edward III N. R. & City of York', p. 114: *Qillelmus Atebogh* (Pickering, 1327).
95   *Cat. Ancient Deeds* I, pp. 117 (A2755), 131 (A2886), 149 (A3049).
96   *Cat. Ancient Deeds* I, p. 127 (A2850).
97   *Cat. Ancient Deeds* I, pp. 127–8 (A2847, 2863).
98   *Cat. Ancient Deeds* III, p. 34 (A4136). See now, D. Crystal, *The Stories of English* (London, 2004), pp. 141–2 for Norfolk.
99   *Cat. Ancient Deeds* I, p. 424 (B3624).
100   *Halmota Prioratus Dunelmensis*, p. 42.
101   *Halmota Prioratus Dunelmensis*, p. 54 (1366).
102   W. Farrer, ed., *Lancashire Inquests, Extents and Feudal Aids* Part II (LCRS liv, 1907), p. 240.
103   *Wakefield Court Rolls* I, p. 181.
104   *Wakefield Court Rolls* III, p. 2.
105   Fenwick, *Poll Taxes* I, pp. 451, 471, 478.
106   *Hoghton Deeds*, p. 42; *Lancashire Court Rolls*, p. 2.
107   *Norris Deeds*, pp. 112–13, 126, 128, 132, 144–6, 150, 155–6, 158, 160, 168, 177, 195.
108   Farrer, *Lancashire Inquests* Part II, p. 240.
109   C. M. Fraser, *The Accounts of the Chamberlains of Newcastle upon Tyne 1508–11* (Society of Antiquaries of Newcastle upon Tyne, Record Series 3, 1987), pp. 5, 6, 10, 11, 13, 26, 28, 58, 59, 61, 67, 73, 75, 81, 84, 89, 90, 91, 93, 95, 101, 105, 107, 111, 115, 116, 117, 118, 134.
110   Fraser, *Accounts of the Chamberlains*, p. 135.
111   F. Collins, ed., *The Register of Farnham* (London, 1905), pp. 67–9; further examples are at pp. 73–5.
112   J. A. Laycock, ed., *The Registers of the Parish Church of Padiham* (Lancs. P. R. Soc. 16, 1903), pp. 70, 75.
113   J. A. Twemlow, *Liverpool Town Books: Proceedings of Assemblies, Common Councils, Portmoot Courts, etc., 1550–1862. Vol.1, 1550–1571* (London, 1921), p. 32.

4
THE NORTH AS A MOSAIC

Whilst at one level a minimum of cultural coherence was expressed through patronyms and metronyms with the suffix -son and through some other name elements – all of which extended outside the North, but were northern characteristics – at another level, the North exhibited less cultural homology. The North, of course, consisted of multiple smaller topographical, social and cultural *loca*, a patterned mosaic of distinctive speech communities. Whilst the overlying criteria of -son and other common elements obtained here, diversity and variety were also exhibited through different name formations and items.

Lexis 1: topographical -by names

Demarcated by the distribution of this form of byname, north Lincolnshire and the East Riding of Yorkshire, spilling into the North Riding, constituted a dialect area which formed one of the smaller units in the mosaic of the north. This form of byname was exclusive to this small area in the North and was also differentiated from bynames outside the North which purported the same sense.

The byname was composed of a point of the compass with reference to the location of habitation within the village (the -by element).[1] Typically, therefore this form of byname appears as *Northiby*, *Southiby*, *Eastiby* or *Ousterby*, and *Westiby*: living north, south, east or west of the village. This formation might have encapsulated the more convoluted Latin phrase such as: *de uno tofto cum crofto que iacent in exteriori extremitate eiusdem ville versus merediem ex occidentali parte vie*.[2] The distribution of this form of byname is illustrated in Figure 34.[3] The concentration is evident.[4]

The description of one of the bearers of this form of byname can be expressed in detail. Between 1234 and 1251, Peter *Westiby* attested a multitude of charters which proffered benefactions to Guisborough Priory, seventy-one of which related to lands in Guisborough, thirty-two to benefactions to the almoner and the fabric, thirteen to lands in Lowcross, fourteen to lands in Barnoldby, twenty-one to lands in Ormesby, and a few others to Normanby, Cotum and Glasedale.[5] Peter was thus certainly a freeman and his status is confirmed by his other activities, amongst which he made a benefaction of eight acres to the Priory, described as Peter *Westiby* of Guisborough.[6] As one of the Priory's free tenants, he quitclaimed rights to the house.[7] His byname

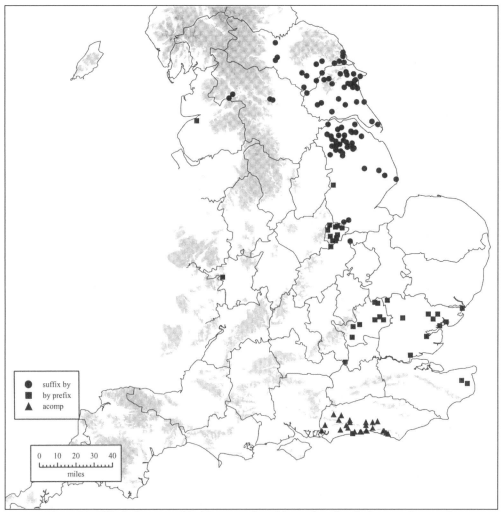

Figure 34 Elliptical topographical bynames, late thirteenth and early fourteenth centuries

was probably already inherited, for he can be identified almost certainly with the
Peter *filius Nicholai Westiby* who transferred two selions to the Priory for the fabric
fund.[8] It is consequently possible that he was the Peter *filius Nicholai* who witnessed
other charters in favour of the Priory.[9] Assiduously, he acquired land in Barnoldby to
convey to the house.[10]

The status of bearers of this form of byname extended, however, across the range
of the peasantry. Two widows, also in Guisborough, Christine de *Westiby* and Emma
de *Westiby*, made benefactions to the Priory.[11] Both widows were of free status. In
contrast, bond tenants received this form of byname in Riccall near Selby where
Agnes *Westiby* held a bovate and Alan *Westiby* four bovates.[12] At Grindale, Thomas
Switheby (south), a tenant of two bovates, and Walter *Donyby* (down), another tenant

Date	N	Mean	Trimmed mean	Standard deviation	Median	Min.	Max.	First quartile	Third quartile
1297	37	22.5	21.5	10.11	18	12	54	14	28.75
1301	23	32.5	29.5	24.72	26.75	5.5	124.5	17	37.75

Notes: numbers (except the standard deviation) are d. to the nearest farthing.

Table 2 Economic status of taxpayers with topographical -by names, 1297 and 1301

(one and a half bovates), both belonged in the unfree category.[13] There too, reference was made to the sons of Nicholas *Doniby* and Thomas *de Westiby*.[14] William *Westiby*, who was a tenant of two bovates in Bugthorpe, also pertained to the unfree tenantry.[15] At Driffeld, the status – free or unfree – of Thomas *Westiby*, a tenant of a toft and two bovates, was also probably unfree.[16] In similar vein, the *nativi* at Sewerby included Geoffrey *Suthibi*.[17] In complete contrast, Walter *Uppiby* (up) held four bovates freely in Burythorpe from which knight service was owed.[18] Whilst knight service at this time did not reflect military status, it is clear that Walter was both free and of fairly substantial economic position.

Also of free status were the various kinships in North Cave with this form of byname. Moreover, their prosopography reveals more about the etymology of this form of byname. Polyfocal settlement at North Cave produced the minor places of North Cliffe and South Cliffe. In the thirteenth and early fourteenth centuries, charters associated with North Cliffe were attested by Robert *Westyby*, Henry *Westibi*, and Roger *Westibi*, who were probably related since in 1330 Robert *Westiby de Northcliff* conveyed to his daughter Constance a toft and croft in North Cliffe which he had inherited from his brother, Henry. Similarly, charters for South Cliffe were witnessed by Roger and William *Suthyby* about the same time.[19]

Despite this kinship clustering at North Cave, the byname seems elsewhere to have been dispersed, with only single representatives in vills, such as Robert *Suthiby* who held land in North Dalton, or William *Westiby*, a tenant in Raventhorpe.[20]

The economic status of taxpayers with this form of byname is illustrated in Table 2.

Those taxpayers with this form of byname who were captured by the lay subsidies thus contributed at varying levels. This formation was not reserved to any socio-economic or socio-legal group; status did not inform the form of byname. The principal characteristic of this form of byname was its geographical concentration in the thirteenth and fourteenth centuries either side of the Humber's mouth.

Extending northwards from the estuary, this form of byname intruded into the southern and eastern area of the North Riding. In the 1327 tax assessment for that Riding, taxpayers were captured who bore a syndetic version: *de Northby* at Osbaldwick and Burneston (two in each vill); *de Westby* at Hutton Buscel; *de Ousteby* at Snainton and Brandsby; and *de Estbi* at Ness.[21]

In that administrative area, almost the most northerly extension for this form of byname was the honor and forest of Pickering. Here, for example, John *Westby* acted as a pledge for an offender against the law of the chase, but was he the John *de*

Westiby also accused of an offence against the venison?[22] Non-attendance at the forest court incurred a fine for Roger *de Ousteby*.[23] Robert and John *de Westby* were accused of the same dereliction.[24] Tenants of the honor in 1322 included Roger *Oustiby*.[25]

The existence of the byname in Lincolnshire is represented in Figure 34 from the lay subsidy of 1332.[26] More graphically is it revealed in Thomas *de Northiby* of Kirton in Lindsey from whom twelve stones of wool were extracted before 1341.[27] Less contentiously, land in Saxby was alienated by William *Southiby* in the second decade of the fourteenth century and John *Suthyby* made a grant of land at Claxby by Normanby in the late thirteenth century, both places located in Lincolnshire.[28]

Despite the relative proliferation of this form of byname through this region before 1350, it had declined in incidence by the late fourteenth century, it appears. In the Poll Taxes of 1377–81, this formation cannot be discovered in either the West Riding or Lincolnshire.[29] In the Poll Tax for the East Riding, the form persisted at Beverley (one taxpayer), Weighton (one), Bishop Burton (five), North Cave (one), Newbold (one). Eastburn (three), Holme on the Wolds (two) and South Dalton (one). Its concentration had intensified, therefore, circumscribed in the East Riding and to the north of the Humber.[30]

To the corpus of this form of byname previously noticed can be added two further formations: Uppiby (up in the town – at Frothingham, Wold Newton, Theakston, Old Malton and Seamer) and Dunyby (down in the town).[31] The compound form thus comprised not only cardinal points of the compass affixed to *-by*, but also vaguer directional elements (up- and down-). The composition thus combined in its Middle English form a Scandinavian deuterotheme (*by*) with Old English prototheme.[32]

What might be considered now are alternative forms of the intent of this byname, not only in the North, but in other areas of Scandinavian influence, and also in areas without a Scandinavian legacy. An alternative formation is clearly visible in Essex, for example. In 1327, taxpayers at West Mersea in that county were designated *Bysouthen* (two), *Bynorthen*, and *Byweston*. That construction was the normative form in Essex, so that encountered also are *Bynorthen* at Dovercourt, *Bysouthen* at Colchester, Brightlingsea, Great Tey, Birch, and Great Dunmow, *Bywesten* at Mundon, and *Oppetoune alias Uppetoune* at Elsenham and Bromfield (two).[33] Two differences occurred here: the formation consisted of a prototheme *by-*, followed by a deuterotheme which consisted of the cardinal point of the compass with the suffix *-en*; and in the construction of *Oppetoune*, the deuterotheme was the Old English *-tun* rather than Scandinavian *-by*. The first construction extended into Hertfordshire, for taxpayers there in 1307 were identified as *Bysouthen* at Standon, Reed, Rebourn (three), and Abbots Langley (as well as *Bysouth* at Therfield [two] and Sacombe) and as *Bynorthen* at Much Hadham and Wheathampstead.[34] This form of byname existed earlier in the county, for Ailward *filius Ricardi Bywesten* found pledges at Barnet in the middle of the thirteenth century that he would remain on the lord's land.[35] In the thirteenth century also Henry *BiWeston* inhabited Elmdon.[36] This form of byname – obviously associated with rural polyfocal settlement – actually migrated into Colchester in the early fourteenth century, where Thomas *Bysouthen* (later *Besouth*) frequently appeared in the portmoot rolls after 1312.[37]

The same formation obtained in Rutland, illustrated by Henry *BiWestoun*, William

ByWestoun and Robert *filius Radulphi ByWestoun*, taxpayers in Morcott in 1296.[38] *ByWestoun* recurred in 1296 at Glaston and Kilpisham, whilst *Byestoun* was attributed to taxpayers then at Stretton, Greetham, Martinsthorpe, Normanton, Glaston, Langham, Pickworth, North Luffenham, and Teigh. *Bynortheton* was evidenced at Caldecote in the same manner and date. At Kilpisham, a more elaborate form existed which reveals the syntactical content of these names: *Byestecross* and *Bywestekirke*. In the Oakham Survey of 1305, William *Byeston* was enumerated at Langham. The formation was probably normative in Northamptonshire as well as Rutland, for Henry *filius Nicholai Byestoun* was accused of the homicide of Geoffrey *filius Gilberti Byestoun* in that county in 1329–30.[39] By the late fourteenth century, the incidence had declined in Rutland, for in the Poll Tax of 1377 the name of only John Byweston at Morcott conforms to this formation.[40] Nor was the formation any more prolific in late-fourteenth century Northamptonshire, although contributors to the Poll Tax of 1379 included William BynotheTheToune at Stanwick and Henry Beyeston at Finedon.[41] The elliptical *by-* as a prefix thus tended to disappear in the later middle ages in this central eastern area of England.

In the very south of the country in Sussex, Adam *Bynortheton* held a virgate in Ferring, but his byname was extremely unusual in the county.[42] In the same vill, enumerated amongst the villeins, Juliana *de Southeton* also held a virgate, whilst at Bishopstone, Robert *de Westetoun* held merely a croft. [43] Nevertheless, such formations remained exiguous in most of Sussex where a different compound existed in the thirteenth and fourteenth centuries, the prefix *by-* replaced by *a-*.[44] Accordingly, at Amberley, two unfree tenants – John *a Northetoune* and Walter *Amiddetoune* – both held virgates.[45] At Denton, Nicholas *a Westeton* was an unfree tenant of two virgates and Robert *Anoppeton* a juror in the manorial court.[46] The topographical formation *a-* with a compass point and *-to(u)n* was concentrated in coastal and west Sussex, as illustrated on Figure 34, comprising *A Westeton*, *A Northeton*, *A Middeton*, *A Sutheton*, *Anestetoun*, but occasionally the alternative formation with the preposition *de* (for example, *de Estetoune*).[47] The elliptical *by-* prefix was sporadically employed in compound topographical bynames, but in slightly different formations: *Byestebrok*, *Byestewater*, *Biestestrete* and *Bysouthebrok*.[48]

On the manors of the Archbishop of Canterbury in Sussex, the same formation applied to a number of tenants. At Slindon, Martin *Anouentun* held half a hide, Alan *an Ouentun* the same quantity, Ralph *an Ounetun* and John *an Nouentun* each a full virgate, whilst at Terring, full virgates were held by Adam *a Northenton* and Alice *de Suthetone* and two virgates by Adam *at Estetone*.[49] At West Angemeryng before 1315 appeared William *a Istetone*.[50]

What is interesting is the survival of the formation, mostly in asyndetic form, in late-fourteenth-century Sussex. In its syndetic aspect, the formation was represented by Roger Awesteton in Sompting in 1379. More profuse was the asyndetic construction, with John Esteton in Beeding, William and Nigel Northeton in Edburton, Robert Westeton in Kingston by Sea, Walter Northeton at Southwick, William Northeton at Steyning, William Westeton at Halnaker, Thomas Southeton at West Harting, Adam, John and Thomas Northetoune at Saddlescombe, John Northeton at Patcham and William Northetone at Pottingdean.[51]

In Worcestershire, the formation was ostensibly different: no suffix was included in the compound to represent the element of the vill or township. The elliptical *by-* was employed as a prefix, but only in association with the compass point. Thus, in 1221, Henry *Bisuthe*, who had killed Arnold *Busudhe*, was outlawed, his status reflected in his lack of chattels for valuation.[52] In Gloucestershire, although the evidence is slender, Simon *Suthinton* contributed to the lay subsidy in 1327 at Wickwar.[53]

Returning to the northern zone, an interesting contrast can be detected in the manor of Wakefield in the designation of locations in polyfocal settlement. The process of formation of topographical bynames in polyfocal settlements is illustrated by Thomas *del Northend* who was amerced 2d. for collecting dry wood, but was also selected for a jury in 1307.[54] Two years later, the formation was reiterated in a similar offence by Henry *del Northend*.[55] As interestingly for the relationship between bynames and village topography, in that year too Richard *del Nethertoun* was amerced in Holne for escapes of beasts.[56]

Where polyfocal settlement induced bynames of habitation reflecting a location by compass point in relation to the vill, different formations obtained in different areas of England. In 'Humberside' the resulting compound consisted of the point of the compass with the suffix *-er* compounded with the noun *-by*, betraying a Scandinavian influence. Within the North that formation was distinctive and marked out the south of the East Riding as a particular unit within the mosaic of the 'North'. In the thirteenth and early fourteenth centuries, the compound topographical form extended down into north Lincolnshire, so that some units within the mosaic of the 'North' actually spilled out of the 'North' as we conceive it.

Lexis 2: *Fox* and *Tod(d)(e)*

In the middle of the fourteenth century, land at Escomb and Blackwell, manors of the bishop of Durham, had been in the hands of tenants named William and Robert *Tod*.[57] Another unit within the mosaic of the 'North' was defined by the varying lexis for fox – *Fox* or *Tod* and variants. Figure 35 illustrates the division of the 'North' into two areas divided across from coast to coast roughly along the line of the River Ribble.[58] Above that line, *Tod* was prevalent, but below the line, in southern Lancashire and the West and East Ridings of Yorkshire, *Fox* predominated. *Fox* constituted, moreover, the normal lexis of bynames in the rest of the country. Whilst the deployment of *Todd* differentiated this area in the far North from the remainder of England, it equally defined a small *espace vécu* within the North.[59] Perhaps the wider difference is best illustrated by John *Voxhunte clericus* assessed to the Poll Tax in Canterbury in 1381 by comparison with Thomas *Todhunter* who contributed 11s. 10d. to the lay subsidy at Threlkeld in Cumberland in 1332.[60]

The North Riding in particular constituted a significant zone where *Tod* and *Fox* intermixed. In the 1327 lay subsidy, almost equal numbers of taxpayers were named *Tod* and *Fox*, the former exceeding the latter by five to four, all assessed within the range of 6d. to about 1s. 6d.[61] Presentments for offences in the forest of Pickering

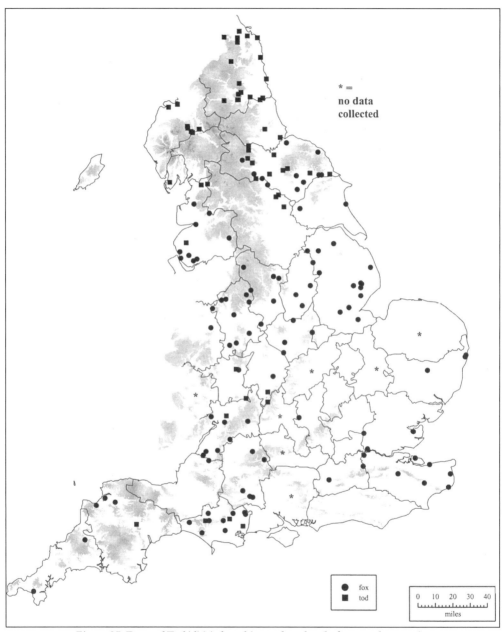

Figure 35 Fox *and* Tod(d)(e), *late thirteenth and early fourteenth centuries*

confirm how this area featured as an imprecise boundary zone. In the early fourteenth century, William *Todd* held part of a messuage in Pickering.[62] Perhaps the same tenant, described as William son of Robert *Todde*, was accused of an offence against the venison in 1322.[63] In 1332, Richard *Todde* was assessed to the lay subsidy in this

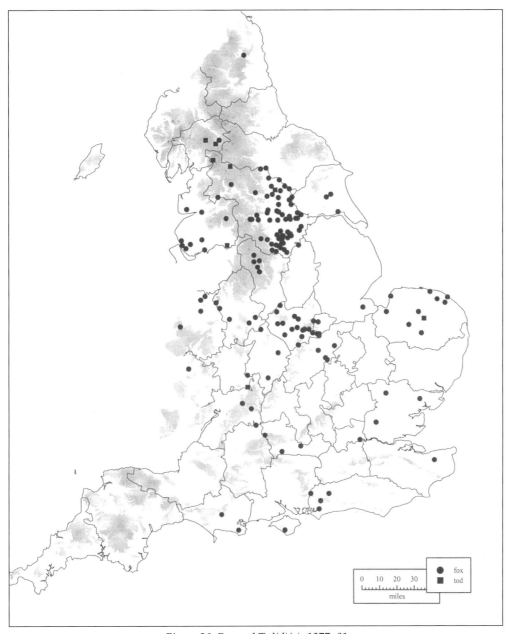

Figure 36 Fox and Tod(d)(e), 1377–81

vicinity.[64] About that time, John *Todd* acted as a pledge for an offender against the law of the chase.[65] In comparison, about the same time, John *Foxsone* was pardoned his offence because he was estimated to be *pauper*, but he died during the process.[66] Subsequently, several other *Fox* tenants were presented for poaching: John *Fox*; Jordan

Fox; Henry *Fox*; William *Fox*; Simon *Fox*; Peter *Fox*; and Robert *Fox*: all contemporaneously.[67]

The distinction can be illustrated by compound *-fox* bynames in the West Midlands and other locations, for example. In Warwickshire, Reginald *Wytfox* was killed in 1221, whilst John *Colfox* ('black fox') of Bordesley committed homicide and was received into the household of Philip *Urlesheued*.[68] At the same time, John *Colfox* was outlawed in Worcestershire for hamsoken and wounding.[69] *Colfox* recurred in the person of a taxpayer at Little Drayton in Shropshire in 1327, whilst another contributor in 1332 in Wiltshire was identified by the byname *Vayrfox* ('fair fox').[70] Just below the 'northern zone', Hulle *Colfox* appeared in the courts of Chester in the 1260s.[71]

Tod, nevertheless, occasionally appeared outside the North, but its occurrence in those other places might be explained by a different etymology. One possibility is revealed by the byname *le Todder* at Ford in Sussex in 1327.[72] More probably, however, Tod outside the North derived from OE *tāde* (toad). Such an explanation might account for Tod in Gloucestershire, for although it occurred there in the thirteenth and fourteenth centuries, *Fox/Vox* featured in Hanham Abbots, Tetbury, Stowell, Horfield, Brookthorpe, Stoke Gifford, Longhope and Old Sodbury in 1327.[73] Again, *Tod* existed at two places in Warwickshire in 1332, although *Fox* was predominant, so that another derivation for *Tod* might be expected.[74]

An apparently early occurrence of *Tod* – Everard *Tod* – appeared in a rental of Canterbury in 1163x1167, but it too might be explained as deriving from *tāde*.[75] The nearby and contemporary existence of John *Toddi* – or *Totty* – Edward *Totty*, Bartholomew *Totty* and William *Totty* also suggests an alternative etymology.[76]

In assessing the extent to which Fox intruded into the 'North', the homicide by Roger *Fox* at Bold in Lancashire in the last decade of the thirteenth century is indicative, for that county consisted predominantly of Fox bynames except for the extreme northern edge.[77] *Fox* thus predominated in most of Lancashire, as with William *Fox* in Rochdale in 1323, another William *Fox* and a Robert *Fox* in Penwortham in that year, another Robert *Fox* in Waddington in 1324, William and John *Fox* in Liverpool in 1313–31, William *Fox* in Derby in 1323, and another William *Fox* in Amunderness in 1325, complemented by Emma *del Foxholes* in Rochdale in 1325.[78] Accordingly, several of the tenants of Liverpool in 1346 displayed this byname: Alexander, John, William, and Nicholas *Fox*, as well as John *Fox Knaue*.[79]

Similarly in the northern area of Yorkshire, Thomas *Fox* of Middleton quitclaimed a selion to Warter Priory.[80] In Hundsworth in the West Riding, Adam *Fox* pastured his pigs in the lord's wood in 1345.[81] In the first decade of the thirteenth century, Thomas *Fox* attested charters relating to Pontefract in the same sort of area.[82]

The dominance of *Tod* in a 'far' North is exhibited in the hall moot rolls of the bishop of Durham. Since Durham, as a Palatinate, remained exempt from the lay subsidies, the hall moot information has a double significance. A toft in Billingham in County Durham, on an episcopal manor, was formerly held by Gilbert *filius Johannis Tod* as recorded in the court roll in 1296.[83] In 1347, Robert *Todd* was enumerated as one of the coalminers in Ferry in County Durham.[84] In that same vill, Robert *Todd* surrendered a bond tenement in 1366.[85] The same Robert sought authorisation for agreement to compromise a personal action in Ferry in 1369.[86] The difference was defined further at Cumdivock and Linstock in Cumberland in a rental of 1328x1332; in the former place, William son of Henry *Tod* held a small amount of land and in the latter vill, Hugh *Tod* held a messuage and three roods.[87] In the middle of the fourteenth century, John *Todd* – along with Adam *Sturdysone* – stood as a manucaptor in Carlisle.[88]

At Ouseburn, appurtenant to Allerton Maulever in the northern part of the North Riding, the prevalence of *Tod* was also exhibited. William *Todde* senior had died by the mid 1330s, as his widow, Alice, prosecuted a case of debt in the manorial court.[89] She acted as the executor of William's will, attempting to recover 1s. 3d. owed for three bushels of rye which Robert had purchased from her late husband. About a year and a half later, William's son, William *Todde* junior, acknowledged that he had withdrawn suit to the lord's mill and was amerced 3d.[90] By 1338, this younger William had become identified as William *Toddessone*, holding a messuage and two bovates in the rental of that year – illustrating also the transition to patronymic forms of byname (at least in the written record, but in this particular case also in common usage).[91] This William *Todson* was apparently dead by 1345, since his widow was recorded as holding a messuage and one bovate.[92] Illustrated here is the differentiation of Yorkshire between a predominant part where *Fox* was normative and a small extreme north-western area of the county where *Tod* was encountered.

That *Tod* was also customary in Northumberland is divulged by Crown Pleas in the county in the late thirteenth century. About 1279, Agnes *Tod* was suspected of homicide, whilst in an unrelated incident, Stephen *Todde* was murdered on Heaton moor.[93] In the same year, Peter *Tod* of Berill fell from his horse and drowned in the River Tyne, but in a more heinous event Adam *Tod* was killed by two other men.[94]

By the late fourteenth century, however, the porous boundary between areas of predominance of Fox and Tod had become less distinct. Contributors to a subscription in Ormskirk in 1366 included not only Matilda Fox, a byname anticipated here, but also the widow of John Todd, and Alan Todd.[95]

Nevertheless, the concentration of Tod continued to be located in the far North, illustrated by the frequency of the name's appearance in the Quarter Sessions rolls of county Durham. In 1472, Adamer Tode, of Darlington, husbandman, became embroiled in an altercation in Aycliffe.[96] In the following year, James and William Tod were accused of keeping greyhounds contrary to their status, and in the same year Thomas Tod, of Langley, attended the sessions.[97] In 1556 Edward Todd of Frosterley, yeoman, appeared at sessions, whilst in the following year the close of John Todd junior at Burtree ford was at issue.[98] The status of yeoman was attributed to John Todd, of North Auckland, in the roll of 1556.[99] When the extant rolls recommence in 1596 after a long hiatus, a case of assault involved Thomas Todd, of Chopwell.[100] From East Boldon, John Todd was to attend court about a case of assault in 1600.[101] The same offence was the concern when John Todd, of Escomb, was required to come into court in 1602.[102] At the same sessions, Richard Tode, yeoman, was presented for conducting the trade of butcher at Gateside without having served an apprenticeship.[103] Amongst the multitude of cases of assault, that crime was perpetrated against Thomas Todd at Whickham in 1606.[104] In 1623, one of the ewes of John Todd, of East Boldon, was

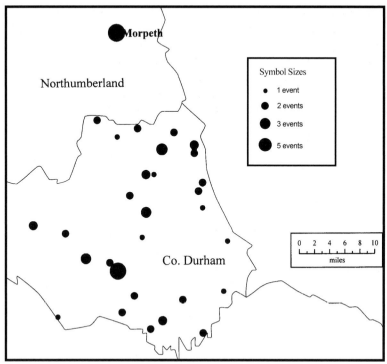

Figure 37 Todd in County Durham, 1641–2

purloined, whilst in the following year it was reported that the status of yeoman also pertained to Geoffrey Todd, of Denton.[105]

During this time, Robert Todd was appointed one of the special bailiffs of the bishop of Durham in Darlington.[106] Before then, the marriage of Richard Todde had been recorded in 1540 at St Nicholas, Durham, the registers there referring further to Thomas Todd in 1615 and William Tood in 1617.[107] In comparison, Nicholas Foxe had intruded into Durham, his marriage registered at St Nicholas in 1544.[108] One of the jurors in 1596 was William Todd, of Herrington, gent., and he was succeeded in that role by Thomas Todd, of Redworth, juror in 1617 and by John Todd in 1624.[109] Corbridge too had its own Todd kinship in the seventeenth century.[110]

By the second decade of the seventeenth century, recusants were being consistently presented at the Durham county quarter sessions. Amongst the presentments in 1615–16 for non-attendance at church were enumerated Dorothy Todd, wife of Nicholas Todd, of Shadforth, yeoman, Margaret Todd, of Hawthorn, Anthony Todd, of Great Unsworth, yeoman, and another Margaret, wife of Lancelot Todd, of Stillington, yeoman.[111]

A fuller conspectus of the distribution of Todd in County Durham can be achieved through the Protestation Oath of 1641, which involved all males aged eighteen and over. Todds were enumerated in thirty-two places in Durham as well as in the two locations in Northumberland which were returned, Morpeth and Berwick (Figure

37). Whilst the density of Todds was usually low – one to three adult males in each location – some higher concentrations existed: four in Monkwearmouth; five in each of Escombe, Auckland and Lumley; seven in Washington; and twelve in Morpeth.[112] By comparison, only two Foxes had insinuated themselves into this part of the North: one each at Wolsingham and Gateshead.[113]

On the opposite side of the Pennines, Margaret and Nicholas Tod/Tood were baptised in Croston parish church in 1539 and 1546 respectively.[114] In Morland both Alexander Todd and Thomas Todd had issue sons baptised as Thomas in 1539.[115] One of the Thomas Todds was buried there in 1547, as was Nell Todd in 1567.[116] East of the Pennines, but further south, William Todd and Agnes Tode were registered as buried in Farnham in 1576–77.[117]

('Anomalous') Heuster

Intruding into southern Lancashire, the occupational byname *le heuster* (*le hewster*) also represented the extension of North-west and West Midlands dialect into the northern zone, marking off a southerly dialect difference. So Henry le Hewster occurred in association with Garston in 1357, where it recurred in 1384.[118]

Vowel substitution: *a/o*

What created a general division within the northern zone was the employment of different vowel sounds. The extension of the deployment of *o* from North-West Midlands and West Midlands dialect into Lancashire up to the Ribble formed a western region which contrasted with north and east of the Ribble. Now, of course, the distinction cannot always be accurately discerned, especially when relying on printed texts, but also when scrutinising manuscripts in cursive hands. Nevertheless, the cumulative evidence supports the regional difference.

The distinctiveness is manifest in particular bynames in Lancashire south of the Ribble. For example, in 1341 one of the jurors at Prestcote was Robert *del Bonk*.[119] Consequently, allusions were made to John *dil Bonke* in Rochdale in 1323, Agnes *dil Windibonk* there a year later, Richard *de Wyndibonck* at Penwortham in 1324, William *de Bonk* at Waddington in that year, Adam *dil Bonk* in Speke in 1327 and 1341–3 but earlier in 1317 Richard *del Bonke*, Richard *del Bonke* at Garston in 1342, Stephen *dil Bonk* in Hale in 1350 and 1369 preceded there by Richard *del Bonke* in c.1290, and Robert *del Bonk* in Salford Wapentake in 1324.[120] Enumerated amongst the free tenants of Hale in 1323 were John *del Bonk* who held a messuage and eight and a half acres, Robert *del Bonk*, holding a messuage and seven acres, and Richard *del Bonk*, tenant of a messuage and twelve acres.[121]

More demonstrative is the difference in Figure 38 in which the distribution of *del bonk* and *del bank* in the early fourteenth century is plotted. The division between North-west Midlands *o* and the *a* of Cumberland is quite apparent. Less clear, however, is the demarcation at the Ribble, but that results from the relative paucity

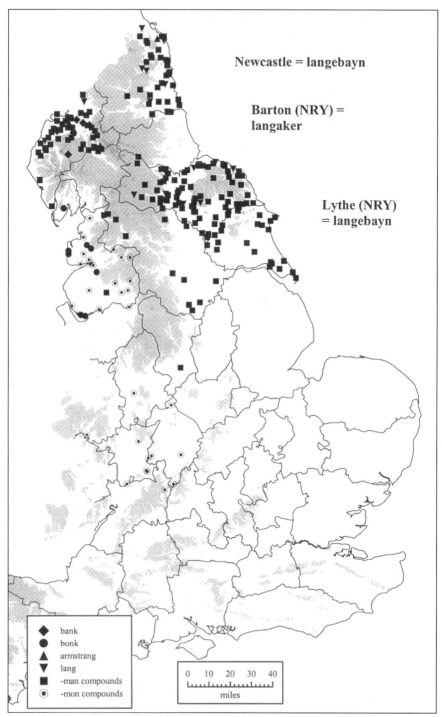

Newcastle = langebayn

Barton (NRY) = langaker

Lythe (NRY) = langebayn

◆	bank
●	bonk
▲	armstrang
▼	lang
■	-man compounds
◉	-mon compounds

0 10 20 30 40
miles

Figure 38 Vowel substitution a/o, late thirteenth and early fourteenth centuries

of the data. Whilst *del bank* appeared at Stainton, Wetheral, Threlkeld, Raughton, Carlatton and Waverton in Cumberland, in contrast taxpayers were simultaneously described as *del bonk* in Whittle, Speke, Hale, Bispham, Ulverston, Garstang, Claughton, Ribby and Layton in Lancashire.[122]

Another form of the distinction was the representation of *-man* in bynames, although transcription of this phoneme is particularly fraught. In the extent of Liverpool in 1346 are encountered Thomas *Hardmon*, Edward *Chapmon*, and Eustace *Chapmon*.[123] *Chapmon* recurred in William at Preston in 1335 and 1361, John at Inskip in 1356, Edward in 1325 at Liverpool where Richard *le Chapmon* also resided simultaneously and Adam in Amunderness in 1324.[124] At that last place resided in 1324 Henry *le Chapmon* and William *le Chapmon* each of whom held half a burgage tenement.[125]

Other forms of *-mon* compounds conformed to the regional variation. At Lea resided William *le Herdemon* in 1323, at Preston in 1368 Adam Hirdemonsone (but once in 1371 as Hirdmanson on the cusp of the dialect transition), Henry *Laghmon* at Walton le Dale in 1318, Adam *Dodemon* in Rochdale in 1324, Robert, Gilbert and John *le Mon* at Ightenhill in 1323–4, Adam *Laghmon* in Bowland in 1324, John *Fremon* in Up Holland in 1326, William *Godmon* and Roger *le Stedmon* in Lonsdale Wapentake in 1325, Richard and John Godemonson in Garston in 1357–1384 and 1406 respectively, John *Nicolasmon* there *c*.1300, Thomas *le Herdemon* at Liverpool in 1330, Henry *Laghmon* at Clitheroe in 1324, William *le Uncouthmon* in Amunderness in 1325, Roger *le Stedemon* and Robert *Coltemonson* in Lonsdale Wapentake in 1325, William *Fairmon* in the same wapentake in 1325–6, Richard *le Uckermon* in Penwortham in 1323, and William *Largemon* in Salford Wapentake in 1326.[126] Singleton was the habitation in 1323 of William *le Herdemon* and Alan *le Herdemon*, both of whom held a house.[127] Nine years later, the tenants of Warrington included Richard *Herdmon* and in the following year Adam *Morleghmon* was recorded as holding thirty acres in Amounderness.[128] In addition, the customary form in Lancashire featured in the byname of Henry *Whitshonk* at Penwortham in 1323 and Robert *del Sonde* in Lonsdale Wapentake in 1325.[129]

Now with reference to *-mon*, its extension from West and North-west Midlands dialect into Cheshire and southern Lancashire can be easily demonstrated (subject to reliance on the editorial accuracy of printed transcriptions). Throughout the lay subsidy for Derbyshire in 1327, for example, the *-mon* formation proliferated: at Ash, Ible, Repton, Drakelowe, Spondon, Mackworth, Eckington, and Alfreton. By contrast, *-man* appearered only at Derby, Chellaston and Mackworth.[130]

In contrast, north of the Ribble and on the eastern side of the Pennines, the voicing of the vowel was *a*, illustrated by Eva *del Stanes*, a cottager at Allerton in the North Riding in 1345.[131] A few years later, Isolda *del Stanes* was presented there for not furnishing ale for the lord.[132] At Holne in the manor of Wakefield, Henry son of John *del Standbank* surrendered four and a half acres of land in 1323.[133]

The substitution of medial *a* for *o* was included also in some nickname bynames east of the Pennines. In the North Riding, tax was contributed at Pickering by John *Lange* in 1327.[134] Another *Lang*, John at Patrick Brompton, delivered 1s. for the same tax and at Ormsby 2s. was collected from Walter *Lang*.[135]

By the late fourteenth century, however, some considerable levelling had apparently taken place in the sense that through much of Lancashire in the Poll Taxes voicing as *a* was more dominant that *o*.[136] Voicing as *o* seemingly persisted only sporadically. The direction of influence of the revised voicing cannot be determined from the available evidence, but it is likely the retention of voicing of *o* persisted longer in the south of the county under the more direct influence of North-west West Midlands dialect. Where voicing as *o* continued, it did so predominantly in the form of the suffix -*mon*, but also *Bonk*. Thus -*mon* compounds were preserved at Walton le Dale, Cuerdale, Samlesbury, Livesey, Blackburn, Thornley, in places in Lonsdale Wapentake for which there is a composite return, Bickerstaffe, Rixton, Hindley, Liverpool, Scarisbrick, Bury, Hundersfield, Castleton, Pilkington, Chorlton, Prestwich, Glazebrook, Haydock, Lathom, Great Sankey, Kirkby, and Bootle, with an emphasis on the south of the county.[137] Similarly, but less extensively, *dil/del Bonk* (or a compound) was maintained at Great Harwood, Whalley, Atherton, Turton, Bedford, Astley and Hale.[138]

In parts of Derbyshire the shift of the voicing of the vowel had also happened by the late fourteenth century. Amongst the Poll Tax contributors in Derby the surnames of eight had apparently the suffix voiced as -*man*, but only seven as -*mon*.[139] Similarly through the High Peak, -*man* superseded -*mon* by this time, with the contrast between twenty-five surnames with -*man* and seventeen with -*mon*, but the last are concentrated in a few parishes, most particularly Ashford.[140]

Apparently, therefore, throughout the North-west Midlands, the voicing as -*mon* was being displaced by East Midlands -*man*, as East Midlands dialect gradually extended an influence as a standard form of Middle English. Nevertheless, the implementation of -*a*- for -*o*- persisted in the north-east, repetitively in the chamberlains accounts for Newcastle-upon-Tyne, in which, for example, disbursements were made to William Snawball for lading twenty-six loads of lime in 1510.[141]

Pinder (Pynder) and *Punder*

Quite surprisingly one of the phonemic items demarcating two different sub-regions of the North was the variation in development of reflex -*y*-. Especially was this relevant on the eastern side of the Pennines, dividing a northerly sub-region of *Punder* from a Yorkshire region of *Pynder/Pinder*. The ubiquity of Pinder in the West Riding is pervasively illustrated by the Poll Tax of 1379. Here Pynder or Pinder were recorded at Adwick le Street, Wales, Wadworth, Fishlake, Pollington (two), Norton, Reedness (two), Ousefleet, Fockerby (two), Greasborough (two), Stubbs Walden, Little Smeaton, Snaith, Peerston, Scosthorp, Skipton, Halton, Ingleton, Upper Poppleton, Wighill, Oxton, Copmanthorpe, Pontefract, Skellow, Nether Poppleton, Edlington (two), Ravenfield, Barnsley (two), Monk Fryston (two), Selby, Criggleston, Thornhill, Mirfield (three), Hipperholme, Rigton, Wike (three), Leeds, Sicklinghall, Little Ribstan (two), Nun Monkton (two), Ripley, Marton, Stockfield, and Aismunderby (two).[142] Substantiation of the form in the West Riding can be found in the Wakefield court rolls, in which, for example, Geppe *le Pynder* of Stanley was prosecuted for trespass in 1298.[143] A quarter of a century later, Robert *Johanstepson le Pynder* was amerced for non-suit.[144] From this

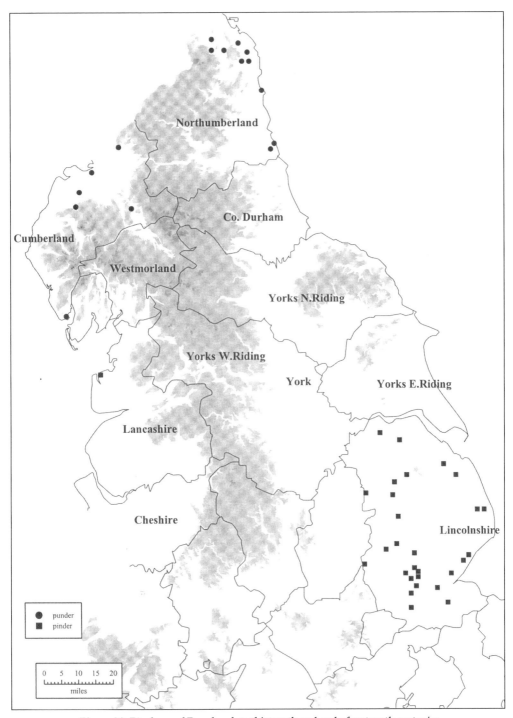

Figure 39 Pinder *and* Punder, *late thirteenth and early fourteenth centuries*

tedious listing of places, the widespread distribution of this occupational byname or surname will be evident, correlative with the importance of the manorial and village office in a pastoral economy where the control of livestock was essential. What is equally significant, nevertheless, was the comprehensiveness of the form *Pinder* or *Pynder*.

Now, those same conditions of pastoral economy and livestock husbandry obtaining further north, the occupational byname and surname featured widespreadly there too. The difference, however, was contained in the Middle English transition of Old English reflex -*y*- to -*u*-, so that in this more northerly area *Punder* assumed dominance. Examining, for example, Bishop Hatfield's survey of the Durham episcopal estate just two years after the 1379 Poll Tax, tenants designated *Pundere* were listed at Cockerton, Chester le Street, Ryton, Whickham (four), North Auckland (three), Bedlington, Wearmouth, and Cornforth.[145] Its existence can be extended back to the *Ponder* who, as an unfree tenant at Aycliffe, was elected reeve in 1364 and the *Punder* at Wolviston arraigned in the manorial court in 1357.[146]

On the eastern side of the Pennines, therefore, two dialect areas were demarcated by the sounding of OE reflex -*y*- in the ME occupational byname and surname *Pinder/ Pynder* and *Punder*. Surprisingly, the byname or surname does not feature strongly contemporaneously in any form west of the Pennines. Although Eve *Punder* contributed to the Poll Tax for Ravenstonedale in Westmorland in 1379, there is no other substantive evidence.[147] Amongst the contributors to the Poll Tax in Lancashire were enumerated a le *Pynder* at Cronton, another at Ribby, one at Hardhorn, a le *Pynner* at Great Harwood, and a *Pynder* amongst the undifferentiated Lonsdale Wapentake. If reliance can be placed on this small corpus, it can be suggested that the northern counties were divided into an upper area characterised by *Punder* and a lower region where *Pynder/Pinder* extended upwards from the north Midlands. Were this the case, then *Punder* represents a far northern dialect phoneme (Figure 39).[148]

Notes

1   K. Cameron, 'Bynames of location in Lincolnshire subsidy rolls', *Nottingham Medieval Studies* 32 (1988), pp. 156–64.

2   Bodl. Fairfax MS 7, fo. xvi verso (cartulary of Kirkham Priory).

3   The dispersed references in southern Lincolnshire derive from BL Add MS 40,008, fos 290r and 291r (Liolf *de Suthiby*, a tenant at Scottlethorpe, and Guy *de Suthiby*, a tenant of meadow in Edenham).

4   The references are collected from: BL Add MS 40,008 (cartulary of Bridlington Priory) (e.g. fo. 22v Gilbert *Oustyby*, a tenant of a toft at Hilderthorpe, and fo. 195r Henry *Northyby* at Cowton); P.R.O. E179/135/14–16 (Lincolnshire lay subsidy, 1332); W. Brown, C. T. Clay, M. J. Hebditch and M. J. Stanley, eds, *Yorkshire Deeds* (10 volumes, YASRS 39, 50, 63, 65, 69, 76, 83, 102, 111 and 120, 1909–55), 3, pp. 69 (no. 203), 84 (no. 262); 4, p. 134 (nos 453–6); 6, p. 127 (no. 419); 7, pp. 84–93 (nos 240–69); M. T. Martin, ed., *The Percy Cartulary* (Surtees Society 117, 1921), pp. 156–7 (ccclxxxii–ccclxxxv) and 178 (dxxxviii); *Yorkshire 1301*, pp. 3, 47, 52, 57–8, 61–2, 70, 72, 74, 79, 112–14; *Yorkshire 1297*, pp. 23, 120–2, 125–6, 130, 132–3, 135, 137, 139–42, 147, 149 and 153–4; Manchester, John Rylands University Library, Phillipps Charter

258 (Thomas *Sutinby* in Laytham); T. A. M. Bishop, 'Extents of the prebends of York (c.1295)', *Miscellanea IV* (YASRS 94, 1937), pp. 3, 5, 6, 11, 27, 28; *Pudsay Deeds*, pp. 105, 128, 212–34.

5   W. Brown, ed., *Cartularium Prioratus de Gyseburne* (2 volumes, Surtees Society, 86, 89, 1889–92), 1, pp. 24–85, 145–61, 172–90, 198–215, 238–62; 2, 5, 117, 197; three charters which involved Peter were dated Purification 1235, Easter 1251, and 1251: 1, pp. 143–4, 147 (nos ccxli, ccxliii, cclv).

6   Brown, *Cartularium Prioratus de Gyseburne*, 1, pp. 1, 56 (no. cxxvii).

7   Brown, *Cartularium Prioratus de Gyseburne*, 1, pp. 56–7, 74 (nos cxxix, cxxx, clxxx).

8   Brown, *Cartularium Prioratus de Gyseburne*, 1, p. 157 (no. ccxciii).

9   Brown, *Cartularium Prioratus de Gyseburne*, 1, pp. 160, 176, 178.

10   Brown, *Cartularium Prioratus de Gyseburne*, 1, pp. 203, 209 (nos ccccxvii, ccccxxx–ccccxxxii).

11   Brown, *Cartularium Prioratus de Gyseburne*, 1, p. 57 (nos cxxxi–cxxxii).

12   Bishop, 'Extents of the prebends of York', p. 3.

13   Bishop, 'Extents of the prebends of York', p. 5.

14   Bishop, 'Extents of the prebends of York', p. 6.

15   Bishop, 'Extents of the prebends of York', p. 11.

16   Bishop, 'Extents of the prebends of York', p. 27.

17   Clay, *Yorkshire Deeds*, 6, p. 127 (no. 419).

18   R. H. Skaife, ed., *The Survey of the County of Yorkshire taken by John de Kirkby, Commonly called Kirkby's Inquest* (Surtees Society 49, 1867), p. 270.

19   Clay, *Yorkshire Deeds* 6, pp. 84–93 (nos 240–69); the later of the charters are dated 1313–33.

20   Bodl. Fairfax MS 9, fos 92r, 98r–v.

21   Colonel Parker, 'Lay subsidy rolls 1 Edward III N. R. & City of York' in *Miscellanea II* (YASRS lxxiv, 1929), pp. 108, 112, 113, 115, 141, and 156.

22   R. B. Turton, ed, *The Honor and Forest of Pickering* (North Riding Record Society n.s. II and IV, 1895 and 1897), I, p. 147; II, p. 57.

23   Turton, *Honor and Forest of Pickering*, II, pp. 25, 32, 35.

24   Turton, *Honor and Forest of Pickering*, II, p. 26.

25   Turton, *Honor and Forest of Pickering*, II, p. 204.

26   T.N.A. (P.R.O.) E179/135/14–16.

27   B. McLane, ed., *The 1341 Royal Inquest in Lincolnshire* (Lincoln Record Society 78, 1988), p. 74 (no. 755).

28   *Cat. Ancient Deeds* II, pp. 379 (B3211), 551 (C2738).

29   Fenwick, *Poll Taxes* II, pp. 1–60; 'West Riding Poll Tax.'

30   'East Riding Poll Tax'. Its survival is also represented in the early fifteenth century by Margaret widow of Thomas Northiby *de Gymlyn*: Bodl. MS Yorkshire Ch 339.

31   Clay, *Yorkshire Deeds* 7, p. 87 (no. 250) for *Dunyby* in North Cave.

32   D. N. Parsons, 'How long did the Scandinavian language survive in England? Again' in J. Graham-Campbell, R. Hall, J. Jesch and D. N. Parsons, eds, *Vikings and the Danelaw. Select Papers from the Proceedings of the Thirteenth Viking Congress, Nottingham and York, 21–30 August 1997* (Oxford, 2001), pp. 299–312, esp. 305–6.

33   *Essex.*

34   *Hertfordshire*, pp. 26, 42, 45, 46, 66, 79, 117, 142, 143, 146.

35   A. E. Levett, *Studies in Manorial History* ed. H. M. Cam, M. Coate & L. S. Sutherland (repr. London, 1963), p. 323.

36   *Cat. Ancient Deeds* II, p. 59 (A497).

37   I. H. Jeayes, ed., *Court Rolls of the Borough of Colchester* volume 1 *(1310–1352)* (Colchester, 1921), pp. 74, 91 (for example).

38 The whole of this paragraph is based on D. Postles, *The Surnames of Leicestershire and Rutland* (English Surnames Series 7, Oxford, 1998), pp. 38–9.

39 D. Sutherland, ed., *The Eyre of Northamptonshire 3–4 Edward III A.D. 1329–1330* (2 volumes, Selden Society 97–8, 1983), 1, pp. 207–8.

40 Fenwick, *The Poll Taxes*, II, p. 371, but note also William Byestcrosse at Clipsham (p. 363).

41 Fenwick, *The Poll Taxes*, II, pp. 240, 251 (but BynotheToune is not unambiguous, possibly denoting beneath the vill).

42 W. D. Peckham, ed., *Thirteen Custumals of the Sussex Manors of the Bishop of Chichester* ... (Sussex Record Society 31, 1925), p. 75. The Thomas Byeston, vicar of Edmonton in Surrey in the late fourteenth century, may have been a clerical migrant: *Cat. Ancient Deeds* I, p. 437 (B3758).

43 Peckham, *Thirteen Custumals*, pp. 73, 92.

44 M. T. Lofvenberg, *Studies on Middle English Local Surnames* (Lund Studies in English xi, 1942), enumerated only a small number of these bynames in Sussex in 1296, restricted to those few with the fuller preposition such as *atte sutheton* and *atte notheton*: pp. 139, 207.

45 Peckham, *Thirteen Custumals*, p. 57.

46 Peckham, *Thirteen Custumals*, pp. 101–2.

47 *Sussex 1327*, pp. 110–15, 117–18, 122, 127, 134, 137–8, 140, 144, 146, 147–8, 162, 164–5, 167–70, 172, 174–80, 185, 190, 192, 193, 195, 200, 203, 212.

48 *Sussex 1327*, pp. 113, 127, 146, 148, 180, 195, but see also 140 (*a Suthewatere*).

49 B. C. Redwood and A. E. Wilson, eds, *Custumals of the Archbishop's Manors in Sussex* (Sussex Record Society lvii, 1958), pp. 1–3, 23. See also M. Clough, ed., *Fitzalan Surveys* (Sussex Record Society lxvii, 1969), p. 7 (*Anoueton*). In these cases, one must assume that the *u* represents *v* indicates a fricative f.

50 *Cat. Ancient Deeds* I, p. 232 (B166).

51 Fenwick, *Poll Taxes*, II, pp. 584–7, 590, 597, 599, 615, 621, 623.

52 D. M. Stenton, ed., *Rolls of the Justices in Eyre: Being the Rolls of Pleas and Assizes for Gloucestershire, Warwickshire and Staffordshire 1221 and 1222* (Selden Society 59, 1940), p. 597 (no. 1232).

53 *Gloucestershire*, p. 112.

54 *Wakefield Court Rolls* I, pp. 85, 88. He was presented in 1314 as Thomas *del Northend* for further offences against the vert and for escaped animals: *Wakefield Court Rolls* III, p. 61.

55 *Wakefield Court Rolls* I, p. 209 (1309).

56 *Wakefield Court Rolls* I, p. 215 (1309).

57 *Bishop Hatfield's Survey*, pp. 13, 45.

58 For the 'North', *Cumberland*, pp. 5, 8, 16, 23, 26; 'Lancashire', pp. 97, 100; *Northumberland*, pp. 2, 9, 16–18, 20, 31, 33, 39, 41, 48, 59, 97, 109, 120, 123–4, 132, 134, 174; *Yorkshire 1301*, pp. 2, 8, 11, 23, 58, 64, 83–4, 95, 113; *Lancashire Inquisitions*, p. 204 (for *Tod* and variants); 'Lancashire', pp. 2–3, 6, 17, 19, 79; *Yorkshire 1301*, pp. 33, 49, 54, 57, 61, 78, 92; 106, *Yorkshire 1297*, pp. 16, 128; *Lancashire Court Rolls*, pp. 16, 40, 43, 69–70, 122, 143, 195–7 (*Fox*). For all other counties, only lay subsidies have been examined: T.N.A. (P.R.O.) E179/159/5, mm. 1, 7, 8 (Notts.); E179/135/14–16 (Lincs.); *Devon*, pp. 20, 23, 75, 99, 119; *Wiltshire*, pp. 1–2, 49, 63, 82, 84, 91; *Essex*, pp. 11, 34, 92, 102; *Huntingdonshire* (nil); *Buckinghamshire*, p. 11; *Surrey*, pp. 2, 57; 'Worcs. (1280)', p. 21; 'Kent', pp. 85, 88, 94, 99, 117; 139, 157, 165; 'Staffordshire 1332', pp. 197, 201, 206, 217–19, 222, 227, 230, 252; 'Derbyshire', pp. 49, 56, 68, 91, 95; *Gloucestershire*, pp. 48, 53, 66, 73, 81, 83, 90, 101, 107, 112; *Warwickshire*, pp. 17, 19, 39; 'Worcs. (1280)', pp. 67–8; *Suffolk*, pp. 36, 69, 93; 'Shropshire', pp. 135, 198; *Sussex*, p. 137; *Dorset 1332*, pp. 9–10, 14–15, 22, 31, 42, 50, 75–7, 81, 92, 105; 'Leicestershire' [Claybrooke, Thurlaston, Cold Overton, Wymeswold]; T.N.A. (P.R.O.) E179/165/1 (no data). For Cornwall, however,

the caption of seisin of 1337 has been used: P. Hull, *The Caption of Seisin of the Duchy of Cornwall (1337)* (Devon and Cornwall Record Society 17, 1971), pp. 17, 52.

59   For the term *espace vécu*, P. Claval, *An Introduction to Regional Geography* (Oxford, 1998), esp. pp. 45–6.

60   Fenwick, *Poll Taxes*, I, p. 428; *Cumberland*, p. 4.

61   Parker, 'Lay subsidy rolls 1 Edward III N. R. & City of York', pp. 111, 113, 123, 127, 135, 139, 155, 156.

62   R. B. Turton, ed., *The Honor and Forest of Pickering* (North Riding Record Society new series II and IV, 1895 and 1897), I, p. 34.

63   Turton, *Honor and Forest of Pickering*, I, p. 95.

64   Turton, *Honor and Forest of Pickering*, II, p. 153.

65   Turton, *Honor and Forest of Pickering*, II, p. 39.

66   Turton, *Honor and Forest of Pickering*, II, p. 26.

67   Turton, *Honor and Forest of Pickering*, II, pp. 61, 64, 65.

68   Stenton, *Rolls of the Justices in Eyre … Warwickshire 1221*, pp. 337 (no. 740), 377 (no. 864), 379 (no. 870).

69   D. M. Stenton, ed., *Rolls of the Justices in Eyre: Being the Rolls of Pleas and Assizes for Lincolnshire 1218–9 and Worcestershire 1221* (Selden Society 53, 1934), p. 546 (no. 1104).

70   *Wiltshire*, p. 24; 'Shropshire', pp. 1, 136.

71   R. Stewart-Brown, ed., *Calendar of the County Court, City Court and Eyre Rolls of Chester 1259–97* (Chetham Society new series 84, 1925), p. 11 (no. 76).

72   *Sussex*, p. 137.

73   *Gloucestershire*, pp. 67 (Childwicksham), 83 (Wotton St Mary). Compare *Fox/Vox* at pp. 48, 53, 73, 81, 90, 100, 107, 112.

74   *Warwickshire*, pp. 17, 19.

75   W. Urry, *Canterbury under the Angevin Kings* (London, 1967), p. 228.

76   *Black Book of St Augustine*, part 1, pp. 18–19, 22–3, 41.

77   P.R.O. Chancery Miscellanea 65/4/92.

78   *Lancashire Court Rolls*, pp. 16, 40, 43, 69, 122, 143, 148; *Norris Deeds*, pp. 195–7; Farrer, *Lancashire Inquests and Feudal Aids* Part II, p. 90; Part III (LCRS lxx, 1915), p. 1.

79   Farrer, *Lancashire Inquests, Extents and Feudal Aids* Part III, p. 69.

80   Bodl. Fairfax MS 9, fo. 63r.

81   Nottinghamshire Archives Office DDSR 1/6/6b.

82   R. Holmes, ed., *The Chartulary of St John of Pontefract* (2 volumes, YASRS 25, 30, 1899–1902), I, p. 195 (nos cl–cli).

83   *Halmota Prioratus Dunelmensis*, p. 8.

84   *Halmota Prioratus Dunelmensis*, p. 19.

85   *Halmota Prioratus Dunelmensis*, p. 55.

86   *Halmota Prioratus Dunelmensis*, p. 78.

87   R. L. Storey, ed., *The Register of John Kirkby Bishop of Carlisle 1332–1352 and the Register of John Ross Bishop of Carlisle 1325–1332* (Canterbury & York Society 81, 1995), pp. 2, 14, 19.

88   *Cat. Ancient Deeds* II, p. 518 (C2425).

89   York Minster Archives 1.5/1: *Alicia que fuit uxor Willelmi Todde de parua Useburn' querens in placito debiti optulit se versus Robertum le Webster.*

90   York Minster Archives 1.5/1: *Willelmus Todde Junior calumpniat de secta molendini subtracta venit et cognouit hic.*

91   York Minster Archives 1.5/37A (dorse).

92   York Minster Archives 1.5/38.

93 W. Page, ed., *Three Early Assize Rolls for the County of Northumberland Saec. XIII* (Surtees Society 88, 1891), pp. 312, 315.
94 Page, *Three Early Assize Rolls … Northumberland*, 342, 347; see also Nicholas *Tod de Liom* in the same year: 350.
95 *Miscellanies Volume 2* (LCRS 31, 1896), pp. 110, 116.
96 C. M. Fraser, ed., *Durham Quarter Sessions Rolls 1471–1625* (Surtees Society cxcix, 1991), p. 51.
97 Fraser, *Durham Quarter Sessions*, pp. 57, 61.
98 Fraser, *Durham Quarter Sessions*, pp. 89, 94.
99 Fraser, *Durham Quarter Sessions*, p. 86.
100 Fraser, *Durham Quarter Sessions*, p. 101.
101 Fraser, *Durham Quarter Sessions*, p. 122.
102 Fraser, *Durham Quarter Sessions*, p. 132.
103 Fraser, *Durham Quarter Sessions*, p. 132.
104 Fraser, *Durham Quarter Sessions*, p. 151.
105 Fraser, *Durham Court Rolls*, pp. 314, 328.
106 Fraser, *Durham Quarter Sessions*, p. 226 (1612).
107 H. M. Wood, ed., *The Registers of St Nicholas's Church in the City of Durham* I (Durham and Northumberland P. R. Soc. 32, 1918), pp. 1, 19.
108 Wood, *Registers of St Nicholas's*, p. 2.
109 Fraser, *Durham Quarter Sessions*, pp. 98, 271, 321.
110 H. M. Wood, *The Registers of Corbridge* (Durham & Northumberland P. R. Soc. xxiv, 1911), pp. 6–8.
111 Fraser, *Durham Quarter Sessions*, pp. 248, 266–7.
112 H. M. Wood, ed., *Durham Protestations or the Returns made to the House of Commons in 1641–2 for the Maintenance of the Protestant Religion for the County Palatine of Durham* (Surtees Society 135, 1922), passim and pp. 9–10, 32–3, 46–7, 64–7, and 192–4.
113 Wood, *Durham Protestations*, pp. 22, 108.
114 H. Fishwick, ed., *The Registers of the Parish Church of Croston* (Lancs. P. R. Soc. 6, 1900), pp. 161, 169.
115 J. Anderson, *The Registers of Morland* I (Cumberland and Westmorland P. R. Soc., 1957), p. 2.
116 Anderson, *Registers of Morland* I, pp. 188, 197.
117 F. Collins, *The Register of Farnham* (London, 1905), p. 66.
118 *Norris Deeds*, pp. 81, 84.
119 Farrer, *Lancashire Inquests, Extents and Feudal Aids* Part III, p. 52.
120 *Lancashire Court Rolls*, pp. 17, 22, 41, 71, 153; *Norris Deeds*, pp. 6, 7, 25, 31, 80, 96, 101, 109,
121 Farrer, *Lancashire Inquests, Extents and Feudal Aids* Part II, p. 94.
122 'Lancashire', pp. 4, 8, 22, 25, 29, 69; *Cumberland*, pp. 8, 27, 52, 54, 59, 60, 68, 93.
123 Farrer, *Lancashire Inquests, Extents and Feudal Aids* Part III, p. 69.
124 *Hoghton Deeds*, pp. 53, 56, 230; *Lancashire Court Rolls*, pp. 86, 88, 118.
125 Farrer, *Lancashire Inquests, Extents and Feudal Aids* Part II, p. 107.
126 *Hoghton Deeds*, pp. 36, 56–7, 173; *Lancashire Court Rolls*, pp. 20, 31, 34, 41, 55, 68, 73, 110, 113, 122, 134, 139, 164; *Norris Deeds*, pp. 66, 81, 89, 197.
127 Farrer, *Lancashire Inquests, Extents and Feudal Aids* Part III, p. 115.
128 Farrer, *Lancashire Inquests, Extents and Feudal Aids* Part II, pp. 240–1.
129 *Lancashire Court Rolls*, pp. 40, 134–5.
130 'Derbyshire', p. 81 (Derby)
131 York Minster Archives 1.5/38.
132 York Minster Archives 1.5/9: *Presentatum est per balliuum quod Isolda del Stanes non facit*

seruicium suum domino de eo quod non dat domino ceruisiam sicut deberet et sicut alii tenentes domini solebant dare.

133 *Wakefield Court Rolls* V, p. 2.

134 Parker, 'Lay subsidy rolls 1 Edward III N. R. & City of York', p. 114.

135 Parker, 'Lay subsidy rolls 1 Edward III N. R. & City of York', pp. 128, 147.

136 This statement relies on the difficulty of distinguishing the graphemes of the vowels in the Poll Tax: Fenwick, *Poll Taxes* I, pp. 442–78.

137 Fenwick, *Poll Taxes* I, pp. 444–78.

138 Fenwick, *Poll Taxes* I, pp. 447, 448, 458, 467, 472, 476; mention should also be made of del Lone at Worsley and Litherland: pp. 468, 478.

139 Fenwick, *Poll Taxes* I, pp. 97–100. Here also the transcription of *a/o* is difficult.

140 Fenwick, *Poll Taxes* I, pp. 100–113, esp. 110 (Ashford).

141 C. M. Fraser, *The Accounts of the Chamberlains of Newcastle upon Tyne 1508–11* (Society of Antiquaries of Newcastle upon Tyne, Record Series 3, 1987), p. 175.

142 'West Riding Poll Tax'.

143 *Wakefield Court Rolls* I, pp. 47–8.

144 *Wakefield Court Rolls* V, p. 2.

145 *Bishop Hatfield's Survey*, pp. 15, 35, 36, 40, 81, 91, 94, 95, 97, 126, 134.

146 *Halmota Prioratus Dunelmensis*, pp. 19, 36.

147 Fenwick, *The Poll Taxes* II, p. 703.

148 Fenwick, *The Poll Taxes* I, pp. 442, 443, 447, 451, 475.

5
PERSONAL NAMES IN THE NORTH

During the twelfth century a general transformation in English naming processes and patterns occurred.[1] It has also been suggested that this transformation was more precocious for the *nomen* of males, whereas female names tended towards a higher corpus of traditional names, since either female names remained a repository of traditional culture or female role models were persistently of insular origin.[2] Amongst males, insular personal names (mainly, but not exclusively Old English and Anglo-Scandinavian items) were rapidly supplanted by newly introduced forms of personal name, mainly, but again not exclusively, Continental-Germanic and Christian names. More women, however, continued to be given insular personal names, because first the new aristocracy was predominantly male, so that intermarriage with indigenous females was inevitable (but was equally an important strategy for legitimation of the acquisition of estates by 'conquest') and thus female exemplars for naming bore traditional names. Secondly, as a result, women remained the repository of a traditional culture.

This transformation should be problematized, nevertheless, for it was complex. One of the potential complexities is regional variation and, not least, how regional differences should be interpreted. It seems clear that insular names persisted in some regions, such as some parts of the West Midlands, longer than elsewhere, even amongst the naming of males.[3] It is, however, the North, however defined, which might present the greatest ambiguity. It might be helpful to present an analysis of the evidence of personal naming in the North up to *c*.1250 and then to consider the possible interpretations of that evidence.

In the late eleventh century, some localized parts of the North were an intense confusion of naming etymologies, a co-mingling of Norman, Breton, Godoillic, Scottish, Old English and Anglo-Scandinavian name forms – thus betraying persistent insular as well as exogamous influences from a variety of directions.[4] Such a confusion of naming and thus cultural processes has been identified in the North in the late eleventh century in the upper levels of free society. It will be suggested here that the persistence of the insular tradition in naming extended longer, well into the late twelfth century, and that it endured at lower social levels.

The importance of insular actors at some levels of society has also been more recently established.[5] For example, the English provided the substantial number of the Domesday jurors. Moreover, reliance on English officials was significant into the

1130s.[6] As an example of this feature might be cited the attestations to an *actum* of Geoffrey, bishop of Durham, transferring to his cathedral monks half a carucate of land in 1133x1141, in which about a quarter of the witnesses were described in insular terms: Dolphin *filius Uhtredi*; Maldred *filius Dolfini*; Burnulf *filius Arkilli*; and Gamel *filius Aelferi*.[7] It has also long been recognized that there was a stronger survival of insular families in the regions where resistance to new overlordship was most intense, including, and perhaps especially, the North.[8] An example of the continuation of insular male role models in the North is the descent of the family of Gospatrick, succeeded by Uchtred (*de Alverstain*), then Thorphin (*de Alverstain*), the *nomen* in the family becoming 'new' only with the accession of Alan *filius Torphini* in the late twelfth century, and then assuming a Breton *nomen*.[9]

The importance of less significant insular families into the middle of the twelfth century was also important in the North. For example, when Robert *de Sarz* endowed Fountains Abbey in 1135x1153, the attestations involved *inter alia* Audkill *prepositus*, Gamel *filius Suani*, Stainulf *clericus*, Acc *filius Thor'*, Rainkill *filius Stainbern'*, Ketel *filius Siwardi*, Ulf *de Serleshau*, Orm *filius Heremeri* and Uchtred *filius Wallef'*.[10] Indeed, insular families were themselves benefactors of this great Cistercian house: Wallef *filius Archilli*, a free tenant (*homo*) of the archbishop of York, granted land by 1139–40, his overlord's charter of confirmation attested by Wallief (Waltheof) *de Stotleia* and Hulchill (Ulfkill) *prepositus*.[11] The significant amount of half a carucate had been received by the abbey from Ulf *filius Roschilli* and some time in the late twelfth century Dolfin *de Clotherun*, son of Godwin *de Cluderun* an earlier benefactor of Fountains, provided more land for the abbey.[12] Fountains had furthermore acquired lands from Torfin *filius Gospatric'* and Godwin *de Cludum*.[13]

Amongst the lower peasantry, reference was made in 1175x1195 to two assarts which had been held by Orm *Anglicus*, associating insular personal name with ethnicity.[14] To illustrate the variety of social level of insular names in the far North, charters relating to the barony of Dilston in Northumberland were attested by important free tenants in 1154x1160, by Walef (Waltheof) *filius Alden'*, by Ultred *filius Bertrami* (an interesting hybrid source of naming) and Cospatrick *Hamel*.[15]

This continuing importance of insular free families in Yorkshire into the middle of the twelfth century receives confirmation from the honour of Mowbray. When, in 1147x1155, Alice *de Gant*, female member of the baronial family, transferred a wood to Fountains, her charter was witnessed *inter alia*, by Wlric, Leuric (Leofric), and Siward.[16] Her augmentation of this endowment with land near Redley, 1144x1156, included in its attestation clause Uctred *filius Wallef'*, Ketel *filius Siwardi*, Gamel *de Stodley*, Uctred *homo Nod'* and Aldelin *filius Uctredi de Stodley*.[17]

On the same honour, Roger de Mowbray confirmed to Huctred (hypercorrect Uchtred) *filius Gamelli* all Uchtred's assarts in Brimham (Yorkshire) in 1147x1157.[18] The record of a settlement in the court of Roger de Mowbray in 1154x1157 had amongst its attestors Ketel *prepositus de Masham*, but also manifested hybridity of naming amongst the other witnesses: Richard *de Malesart'* and his brother Huctr' (Uchtred), Jernagen *de Tanef'* and his brother Dolf' (Dolfin).[19] When the archbishop of York issued a confirmation to Fountains for its acquisition of the vill of Herleshow, his *actum* was attested by Uctred *filius* Wallef' and Swein *de Torentona*, although some transitional impetus was also demonstrated in the other witnesses, Richard *filius Autchil'*, Richard *filius Archilli*, and Bernard *filius Gamelli*.[20] Some twenty years later, an agreement between Fountains and Roger de Mowbray was attested by Mr Swain and Uchtred *forestarius*.[21] Subsequent to that accord, Nigel de Mowbray, perhaps in 1175x1176, made a confirmation to Fountains, witnessed *inter alia* by Gamel *de Dunesfort*, Thorphin *filius Roberti filii Copsi* (another interesting hybrid succession of names), and Osbert *de Scipwic*.[22] As late as *c*.1181 Fountains benefited from a gift of Bramley from Swain *de Tornetun*, Swain having purchased it from Roger.[23]

Past the middle of the twelfth century, the insular free tenantry of Yorkshire maintained a valuable role. In the honour of Mowbray they attested the charters of their baronial tenant-in-chief, including his benefactions to the principal religious houses. Some of these free tenants, moreover, were themselves benefactors of Fountains. Others were confirmed in their lands or received new lands from the tenant-in-chief of the barony. What is ostensible is that there was no compulsion on or attraction for these free tenants in changing their name forms to newly-introduced items. It is equally clear that these free peasants were at least the second (and perhaps later) generation since the introduction of the new name forms.

We can, indeed, observe how insular personal names continued to be transmitted through several generations of an insular family in Yorkshire without any inducement to change to a new style of personal name. At Ilton (Yorkshire) also within the honour of Mowbray, the tenant in 1066 was Archil; in 1086, the holder of the two carucates was Gospatric, from whom they descended to Dolfin, who had issue three sons, Torfin, Swein and Uchtred, these last three tenants of Ilton and Hebden from Roger de Mowbray some time after 1138 into the middle or late twelfth century. It was only with the next generation – the third since 1066 – that Uchtred's son was accorded a new name form, the Christian (saint's) name, Simon.[24] Now, although that transformation of name form was introduced in the mid to late twelfth century, nevertheless three generations had elapsed since the tenant of 1066. Since much significance has been placed on the flexibility of personal names – hypothetically mutable with every generation – this persistence over several generations reflects a reluctance immediately to discard a tradition of insular naming.[25] Moreover, it does not appear that the free peasantry was disadvantaged in any way by this retention of insular name forms, for these tenants continued to be confirmed in their lands or receive additions. It might therefore be speculated that the Mowbray family acceded to or expected its northern tenants to be distinguished by insular name forms.

The composition of the names of the lower peasantry, as far as we can ascertain, also continued to include a corpus of insular personal elements. Of course, the principal problem is access to the names of the lower peasantry, for manorial records survive poorly for many northern areas and when they do survive, exist from only a later time. Access to the names of the lower peasantry thus depends on contingent references in charters, such as this one to Warter Priory.

Totam mansuram matris mee et suam mansuram que fuit Segge et duas alias mansuras cum ipsis hominibus Henrico scilicet et bondo fabro cum filiis suis Edricum [sic] album [sic] et Humfridum [sic] papilun et yuonem [sic] filium Ailwy.[26]

[The whole messuage of my mother and her house which was Segge's and two other houses with those men, that is, Henry and Bond *faber* with their sons, Edric *albus* and Humphrey *papilun* and Ivo son of Ailwy].

Here incidental access is allowed to some of the lower peasantry in Yorkshire, referring back to insular personal names of Segge, Bond, Edric and Ailwy. Another charter to Warter Priory divulged that Ailwin had held two bovates and related back to Reginald son of Bonde.

Quas Ailwin [sic] aliquando tenuit et messuagium meum cum crofto et pomerio adiacente [sic] inter petrum clericum et Reginaldum filium Bonde.[27]

[(two bovates) which Ailwin once held and my messuage with croft and orchard lying between Peter *clericus* and Reginald son of Bonde]

By the time for which manorial records are extant, the major transformation of personal naming – that is, of the *nomen* – had already elapsed. Consequently, the evidence for the time of the transition is sporadic, dispersed and incomplete, allowing only an impression rather than a complete and comprehensive account of personal naming in the north.

When Roger de Mowbray ordered some of his tenants to make direct payments to the canons of Hirst in 1148x 1166, his charter enumerated *inter alia* Ketel, Lefwin and his co-tenant Wlmar, Gamel *filius Normani*, Elwin *de Humelt'*, Ernui *filius Spratlini*, Lefwin *Baseus*, Eilward, Wlmar *Rudda*, Berewald and Swein.[28] In notifying his tenants of Acaster (Yorkshire) of his gift to Selby Abbey in 1143x1153, Roger gave direction to Leising and Chetell.[29] Tenants of six bovates which Roger gave to Selby in 1160x1184 were called Agamund and Elfriad or Elfuat, whilst half the tenants listed at (North) Cave in 1170x1184 comprised Gamel (half a carucate), Gamel *prepositus* (two bovates), and Thoche (i.e. Toki) *filius Lete* (two bovates).[30] At South Cave at the same time, three of seven tenants of Roger were named Lewin, Godwin and Seward.[31] Even more of his tenants at Grewelthorpe (Yorkshire) disported insular names, each holding one or two bovates: Swein *Neubonde*; Gamel *de Birnebem*; Hulf (hypercorrect Ulf or Wlf) *filius Dune*; Gamel *Eltebroder*; Thorbrant *filius Accheman'*; and Thorbrant *filius Orm'*.[32] Swein *filius Dune* was the tenant in Thirsk attorned to St Leonard's, York, by Roger in 1160x1182.[33]

Durham

For the Durham episcopal estates in the twelfth century, we are fortunate to have a manorial survey, Boldon Boke of 1183.[34] Unlike contemporary surveys from southern estates, however, it largely omits the names of tenants, but with exceptions. A proportion of tenants is named, but in itself that inconsistency raises questions about the status of these named tenants. By and large, it might be assumed that these tenants are more significant, but it is not exclusively so, for some cottagers were attributed names. Despite this inconsistency, it is possible to present the evidence of insular names in tabulated form.

The size of many of the tenements of these tenants with insular personal names

Manor	Names	Tenure	Other description
Bedick	Ulkill	sixth of a knight's fee	
Clevedon	Ketel	2 bovates	riding service
Clevedon	Osbert *filius Leising'*	80 acres	
Burdon	Elfer *de Birdena*	2 bovates	riding service
Houghton	Leveric *prepositus*	2 bovates	
Sutton	Saddoc	1 bovate	
N. Shirburn	Ulkill	2 bovates	riding service
Shireburn	Arkill	2 bovates	previous tenant
Shireburn	Watling and his wife Sama	4 bovates	
Middleham	Arkil	4 bovates	
Stockton	Elwin	toft	*cotmannus*
Stockton	Godwin	toft	*cotmannus*
Stockton	Suan *faber*	toft	
Preston	Orm *filius Toki*	½ carucate	
Quesshow	Toki	2 bovates	
Quesshow	Orm	2 bovates	brother of Toki
Midridge	Ulkill	1 bovate	*cotmannus* [sic]
Midridge	Anketill	2 bovates	
Thickley	Ail'	?	*cotmannus*
Escombe	Ulf *Raning*	6 acres	former tenant
West Auckland	Aldred	1 bovate	
West Auckland	Uchtred *forestarius*	1 bovate	
West Auckland	Godmund	1 bovate	
West Auckland	Edwin	toft	
West Auckland	Elstan *drengus*	4 bovates	dreng
Stanhope	Bernulf *de Pec*	60 acres	
Stanhope	Gamel *filius Godrici*	60 acres	
Stanhope	Thore	60 acres	
Stanhope	Ethelred	15 acres	
Stanhope	Osbert	15 acres	
Stanhope	Aldred *faber*	12 acres	
Stanhope	Arkill *Hubaldus*	9 acres	
Stanhope	Collan	6 acres	

Table 3 Insular personal names in Boldon Boke 1183 (continued on the next page)

Stanhope	Meldred *faber*	toft and croft	
Stanhope	Ilving	4 acres	
Stanhope	Meldred	toft	
Langchester	Liulf	60 acres	
Langchester	Ulkill	20 acres	
Langchester	Meldred	20 acres	
Langchester	Orm	8½ acres	
Crawcrock	Meldred *filius Dolfini*	land	previous tenant
Westlikburna	Turkill		owed rent of hens
Westlikburna	Eadwin		owed rent of hens
Westlikburna	Patrick		owed rent of hens
Norham	Suartbrand	1 carucate	
Norham	Elfald *Langstirap*	½ carucate	

Table 3 Insular personal names in Boldon Boke 1183 (continued)

suggests that they were substantial tenants and some were of free status. Moreover, some tenants bearing Continental-Germanic (CG) personal names represented a transitional generation, such as William *filius Uttingi* who held half a carucate at Preston, William *filius Ormi* with a carucate in Carlton, Walter *filius Sigge*[35] with two bovates at Great Halghton, Richard *filius Ulkilli* with half a carucate at Norham, and Robert *filius Gospatricii* and Arnald *filius Uctredi* who owed rents of hens at Netherton. Furthermore, the bishop had leased Little Slickburn to a group of peasant *firmarii* including Edmund *filius Edmundi*, John *filius Patricii*, Laurence *filius Edmundi*, and Thomas *filius Edmundi*, reflecting (in the first) the persistence of insular names or (in the case of the other three) a recent change.

Northumberland

Material for Northern naming during the twelfth century occurs in unsystematic sources in the sense that it survives less in manorial surveys than documents which necessarily provide only an impression of naming: charters; miracle narratives; and the pleas recorded in 'criminal' jurisdiction in royal courts. The earliest, but perhaps most eclectic of these sources, are the miracle narratives surrounding Godric of Finchale. Of 237 narratives, however, only 133 stated the names of the pilgrims to the numinous place. Moreover, 153 of the supplicants were female. The narratives extend through the middle of the twelfth century, perhaps to c.1175.[36] By and large the supplicants were of lower status, although the overall complexion was mixed. From the narratives, some fifty-five different female names emerge, of which the most frequent were the ambiguous *Adeliz* (Alice, seven occurrences), followed by the new Matilda (six), *Eda* (five) and Agnes (four). Amongst the non-insular names were also Mabilia (twice), and, once each, Wimarc, Avelina, Hawise, Emelina, Beatrice, Mabilia, Emelotha, Emma, Cecily, Isabel, Johette, and Margaret. Whilst such a purposive sample might be considered unrepresentative, it did comprehend a considerable element of new forms of female name. Nevertheless, the insular forms also remained extensive, if none was as frequent as Alice, Matilda, Eda or Agnes. Sierith (thrice) exhibited some popularity, reflected in its later persistence, alongside Heccoc and Siwine (both also three), followed by, twice each, Sungiva, Tunnoc, and Eluuina. Some names perceived to be frequent, were reflected only once each, such as Goda, Brictiva and Edith. Overall, the corpus of female names continued to include a high proportion of insular forms, but was obviously already in transition.

Amongst male pilgrims to the holy *locus*, Continental-Germanic names had already established a more considerable presence: Hugh, Robert and William three incidences each, Gilbert, Elias, Henry, and Richard two each, with single appearances of Ralph, Baldwin, Gervase, and Roger. Christian names were represented by two Johns, Breton by a single Alan, and Crusading by Jordan (if such be its etymology). It is, nevertheless, important to provide a further context for these names, for the two Gilberts were of higher status, *dispensator* and *clericus*; although one of the Hughs was a shepherd, another was a *minister*, and the third the *homo* of Fulk Painel. Of the three Williams, one was a monk of Durham and another a priest. One of the Henrys was a *clericus*, as was Gervase, whilst Alan was of knightly status, a lord. Jordan was son of Elias *Escollande*, a benefactor of Finchale Priory, and equally both Richards were of wealthy status (a *primogenitus* of a *dives* and the other *dominium possidens*). In fact, the preponderance of newer forms of names is comprehended by higher status.

In contrast, Alsi was a reeve, but we have little evidence of the status of the other bearers of insular names, except for Waltheof who was of seignorial status, lord of a vill. Those names comprised Crin, Wilgrun, Edric, Acke, Edulf, Godric, Elsi, Gamel, Iggi, and Uchtred, all once each. Moreover, some belonged to youths, reflecting the persistence of the names: Edulf, for example, was a *juvenis*. Acke was the son of Pace and Gamel the offspring of Carl. One of the Henrys was son of Uchtred, as was one of the Roberts, and one of the Johns a son of Sigar, reflecting recent generational change.

In the case of Æthelwold, he too was a reeve, administering a local property for the bishop of Durham. Accused of malversation, he elected the bilateral ordeal, trial by battle. However, his fear increasing as the day of battle approached, he supplicated before Godric. These events passed some time before 1162.[37]

On balance then, male insular *nomina* continued to be as prominent at the lower social levels as female, it seems, although the sizes of the two samples are disparate. It is possible to examine some of these individuals in a little more detail, particularly the women. In some cases, it is certainly true that males with new forms of name had taken in marriage females with insular names; thus Walter *minister episcopi* was the husband of one of the Sieriths, whose daughter was named Aviza, as William de Waltham had married Eccoc, their offspring being William.[38] Another Sierith, a *matrona*, was the wife of the reapreeve, Elias, a Sungiva wife of Norman, Emma wife of Leofric, but equally Edoc was married to Seman *faber*, Avelina to Richard, Agnes to Gospatrick, but with the status of a lady, and Margaret was the daughter of the lord Waltheof. One Eda was the daughter of a Durham man, an Alice was a *puella*, an

Eleuuiua a servant (*ancilla*), and Emelotha a young girl (*puellela* or *juvencula*), Aldusa poor, Eda a young woman (*femina*) aged 23, Tunnoc the daughter of Ferthan, Agnes a young girl (*puella*), Alice another *puella*, and Bothilda also poor. Ekke of Hardwick was of similar lowly status, for she had only two lambs. No discernible pattern seems to emerge from this prosopography.

On the other hand, the persistence of insular names amongst males was itself propagated by the saint's cult itself. As a result of her child's swollen body, Emelotha *de Wideslade* conveyed the boy to Finchale, and in gratitude for his recovery renamed her child Ralph *Godric*.[39]

Additional context can be introduced for Northumberland, in particular for the urban environment of Newcastle upon Tyne. There, urban inhabitants with insular personal names continued to act significantly in the borough in the middle of the twelfth century. On the foundation of the hospital of St Mary in *c*.1150, the charter was attested by *inter alia* Ailred *de Ponte*, Uchtred, Bernulf *prepositus*, Thorald, Turolf, Gamel *longus* and Elred *clericus*. All these witnesses must have belonged to at least the second generation after 1066.[40] In 1163x1180, the hospital acquired land held by Edwin *tinctor* in Westgate from Hugh *de Elentina* and his wife, Alice *de Greinevill'*, whose charter was attested by *inter alia* Edric *Palmer*, Patrick *de Calvirdoun*, Edulf *Dun* and Ailred *capellanus*.[41] Another Edric, *de la barre*, attested a charter recording a grant in Pilgrim Street in 1180x1185.[42] Another charter of *c*.1200 was witnessed by Elgi *de Goseforde*.[43]

Yorkshire

By the early thirteenth century, Yorkshire was characterised in part by the persistence – at whatever level – of a corpus of distinctive insular personal names.[44] Before the royal courts, the free tenants Landric, Dolfin and Eluric were convicted of disseisin of common of pasture in Tanfield and Landric son of Oswald of disseisin in Doncaster.[45] In the fragmentary Crown Pleas of 1208, Swein *Belle* appeared as a pledge, Haldan *filius Willelmi* (an interesting recursion to an insular name form), appealed as an accessory and Gamel *de Winkesleye* as a pledge.[46] In the previous year, Quenilda *de Carleton'* had been vouched to warranty by her husband, Waldulf.[47] Such names recur amongst those involved in the Crown Pleas held at York in 1218–19, whether as plaintiffs, those appealed, or convicted felons. In the majority of cases, it is likely that those involved are from lower social groups. Thus, when Utting *de Folifant* was found guilty of killing Elias *de Lidel'*, his chattels were appraised at only 17d.[48] Many of the males involved in these pleas still held insular names, whilst other pleas reveal a recent generational change in naming in patronymic descriptions.

When Orm and William, men of the abbot of Beauchief, were murdered, Uchtred *de Brincliffe* found the perpetrators. When Walter son of Gamel *de Farnl'* was found drowned, it was his father, Gamel, who discovered the body, illustrating the recent transition from insular OE and Anglo-Scandinavian personal names.[49]

Transition is reflected in many other pleas, as when William *filius Saxi* was appealed for murder or when Bernard *filius Bernolfi* appealed Robert *filius Ukeman'*

Arkell *de Breddal'*	found murdered
Auty *plumbarius* (of Leeds)	found murdered
Auty *le paumer*	appealed as accessory to murder
Gamel *Gosenoll*	accessory to battery/robbery
Gamel *filius Gamelli*	held a messuage and had been pilgrim to Jerusalem
Gamel *garcio*	
Gamel (a certain Gamel)	found dead
Leolf	accessory to robbery
Leofric	fell from his cart and died
Ketel *de Saghe*	convicted murderer
Orm *de Grinlinton'*	accessory to murder
Swan *de Criggleston'*	
Swan *de Bretton'*	appealed for murder but acquitted
Swan *de Stodfeld*	accessory to battery
Swan *de Hesinton'*	fell from his horse and died
Swan *de Chinkel'*	appealed for murder
Swan *de Wadinton'*	accessory to murder
Uchtred *de Bramle*	found murdered
Ukeman	found murdered
Utting *de Folifant*	convicted of murder
Utting *nepos* of Ukeman	appealed for robbery
Utting *scutehod*	outlawed for robbery
Utting *filius Leuer'*	fell from his cart and died
Utting *de Ilketon*	was appealed for rape

Table 4 Insular personal names in Yorkshire Crown Pleas 1218–19

and his nephew, Utting, for robbery. The two sons of Ulf, Walter and Adam, were outlaws for the same offence of theft. Thomas *filius Eylsi* was a pledge. Agnes daughter of Uchtred *de Nid* was an appellor for rape and Hugh son of Aylsi *de Drictlington'* was another appellor. Walter *filius Derman'* brought an appeal for battery, and Emma *filia Edric'* even more seriously for homicide. The two sons of Heremer, Thomas and Gilbert, were appealed. The pledges found in another case were Robert *filius Dolfin'* and Peter *filius Auty*, but Geoffrey *filius Grimkell'* was attached.

Walter *filius Toly*	pledge
Thomas *filius Siwardi*	appealed for rape
William *filius Edrici*	appealed for battery
Alan *filius Uctred'*	fell from cart and died
Adam *filius Waldef'*	appealed for theft
Nicholas *filius Bernolfi*	plea of waste
Anketin *filius Wulmer'*	his body found dead
William *filius Dolfini de Spanton'*	appellor for the murder of his son
Hugh *filius Ukeman'*	outlawed for murder
Thomas *filius Akkeman'*	outlawed for battery
Thomas *filius Elsi le poter*	outlawed for murder
Thomas *filius Eylsi*	his body found dead
Galiena daughter of Kenwald' *de Wusseburc'*	appellor for rape
Robert *filius Gemelli de Wusseburc'*	appealed for rape
Henry *filius Ormi*	appealed for murder
William *filius Edwardi de Claverle*	his body found dead
Robert *filius Arkelli*	ditto
Richard *filius Dolfini*	ditto
Alan and Thomas *filii Alsy*	
Richard *filius Dolfini de Elmesh'*	
Robert *filius Ulfi*	
John *filius Swani de Upton*	
Ralph *filius Ormi*	
Herbert *filius Herewardi de Sutton'*	
Geoffrey *filius Herewardi de Barnebi*	appellor
Simon *filius Aki de Hetele*	appellor for robbery
Stephen *filius Gospatricii de Preston'*	outlawed for murder

Table 5 Patronyms with insular personal names in the Yorkshire Crown Pleas

Of higher position were Peter the son of Wulmar who held nine acres in Greasborough and Henry the son of Eylsy who held twenty-two acres in Wombwell. In litigation about four bovates in Melmerby, six daughters, Golle, Maud, Emma, Beatrice, Isolda, and Agnes, were the offspring of Ulf *de Westone*. Adam *filius Waldef'* was encountered again as the defendant in a plea of dower relating to two bovates in Carlton Husthwaite.[50]

These names appeared in the earlier 'civil' pleas and assizes for the county, fragments of which have been published. So in 1204 Gernegan *de Tanfeld* impleaded Landric, Dolfin, Elvric and William *filius Patricii* along with others concerning common of pasture in Tanfield.[51] Haldan *filius Willelmi* (an interesting reversion to an insular name form) was appealed as an accessory and Gamel *de Winkesleye* acted as a pledge, in 1208.[52]

The recent transition is reflected in some of the assizes of *mort d'ancestor* which depended on establishing the previous tenant who died seised of the land: Uchtred *pater Arnaldi* in half a carucate in Follifoot in 1204; Horm *pater Ricardi de Torp* in seven acres; Ketel *pater Willelmi de Doctton'* in two bovates in Grafton in 1204; all these cases represent insular personal names held at the end of the twelfth century by free tenants of considerable land.[53] In a plea of *novel disseisin* between two more free tenants in 1205, the litigants were Geoffrey *filius Lefwini* and Roger *filius Lefwini*.[54] Robert *filius Uctred'*, moreover, introduced a plea about a substantial amount of land, six bovates in Langton, in 1204.[55] These assizes confirm that insular personal names continued amongst the substantial free tenantry, were not marked out as deficient in social honour, and were not confined to the unfree tenantry or the lowest social groups.

The corpus of the names is expanded, however, by the Crown Pleas, for David *filius Siward'* was appealed of a breach of the peace in 1208.[56] Alan *filius Dering'* killed Benedict the clerk and he was probably of low status, for he held no chattels.[57] Two unfortunate incidents involved the accidental deaths of William *filius Harding'* in the R. Wiske and William *filius Forn'* who fell from his horse, both in 1208.[58]

The proliferation of such names in the Crown Pleas suggests a strong survival of male insular personal names into the late twelfth, if not the early thirteenth century. Consequently, Richard *de Claiton*'s sons, Alan and Walth [eof], were provided with names from both cultural traditions, perhaps at the very end of the twelfth century, for on the death of Waltheof, Alan brought an appeal, before the war, but he was found to be under age.[59] Such names were becoming encapsulated in bynames, as when Roger *Tosty* of Marton appealed Robert *Tosty* of battery.[60] In that same year, Robert *filius Copsi* was appealed for wounding, his accessory, allegedly, Hugh *filius Copsi*.[61]

The evidence provided by cartularies is likely to be different and perhaps even more eclectic. Charters legally involved only free tenants and, when the charters represented mainly benefactions to religious houses, the donors were potentially of a stratum which had some disposable land. Secondly, in the case of attestations the inclusion of males with insular personal names was even more contingent. It is probable that bearers of insular personal names belonged to a stratum less likely to be vouched to witness charters so that attestation clauses with insular personal names probably only indicate a submerged population. What charters do reveal is the persistence of insular personal names amongst the free and also amongst the significant free tenants. Thus Henry *de Willardby*, whilst giving to Bridlington Priory half a carucate, also confirmed the previous benefaction by Adelard, his father, of the advowson of Willardby and half a carucate. Charters of Henry's succcessors divulge that he had three children, Adelard, his son and heir, Henry, and Agnes.[62] Thus the OE personal name Adelard had continued in a knightly family and was further extended by the naming of a son for his grandfather, whilst the second son assumed the father's name. In another gift by Adelard *de Willard'* to Bridlington, the land provided abutted on the toft of Alemann *faber* and mention was made of the croft of Adelard *Cuuing*.[63] In the early thirteenth century, Beatrice *de Killom* married first John *de Brigham*, but second Edulf *de Killum*.[64] Beatrice held at least two bovates and a toft. In Burton Fleming, Eilward *filius Edwaldi* received three bovates and two tofts from Theobald *de Wikham*, part of a knight's fee.[65] These tenants with insular personal names thus belonged to the upper stratum of the peasantry holding considerable amounts of land.

Warter Priory acquired two bovates from Adam *Murdac*, which two bovates Ailwin used to hold (*Quas Ailwinus aliquando tenuit*) and, in the same benefaction, a messuage was described as lying between that of Peter *clericus* and Reginald *filius Bonde*.[66] Warter also received a toft and furlong in Seaton from Gilbert *filius Edrici de Seton'* as well as an exchange of lands with German *de Hay*, lord of Acton.[67] Drax Priory received a bovate and toft from Colswann *de Happlesthorp'*.[68] Such transactions suggest that insular personal names were not undignified nor confined to the unfree peasantry and that they were persistently used amongst males into the early thirteenth century.

For Yorkshire, it is not possible to quantify the persistence of insular personal names, but there is sufficient evidence to affirm that these names continued to the end of the twelfth century at all levels of peasant society, including amongst substantial free tenants. The material suggests that they persisted at a fairly high numerical level. Since substantial free tenants constantly bore these forms of name, it seems unlikely that in the North any social dishonour was attached to the names before the early thirteenth century. Importantly, the names were retained by males as well as females, with no apparent distinction by gender.

Donors to St Bees and Furness

Other expositions of the general transformation of naming practices in England in the twelfth century have suggested the importance of downwards cultural conflation, predicated on cultural imitation of superiors. Below it will be maintained that such conflation was by no means the only influence on cultural situations, but here it will be demonstrated that at a middling level of society insular personal names persisted into the late twelfth century. Whilst Stenton, Williams and Lewis have demonstrated respectively the revival of the fortunes of English families in the early twelfth century or the significance of a level of an English administrative cadre in the realm generally, through to the 1130s, in the North insular personal names continued in use at the

Actor	Date	Action	Beneficiary	page	no
Uccheman *de Chertmel*	1170x1180	witness	Furness	303	15
William *filius Uchtredi*	1170x1180	ditto	ditto	ditto	15
Uchtred *filius Gamelli*	1170x1180	ditto	ditto	ditto	15
Hutred *de Austwic*	*c.*1177, 1177x1193	ditto	ditto	301, 304	12, 16
Waltheof	12th cent.	ditto	St Bees	28, 30, 32, 34–6, 39	1–3, 5–7, 9–10
Ketel	ditto	ditto	ditto	ditto	ditto
Siward *presbiter*	ditto	ditto	ditto	ditto	ditto
Chetell	ditto	ditto	ditto	ditto	ditto
Gospatrick *filius Ormi*	1145x1179	donor	St Bees	60, 62	32–3
Elwin *de Egremundia*	1185x1201	witness	ditto	65,67	35–6
Thomas *filius Gospatricii*	1185x1201	ditto	ditto	ditto	ditto
Alan *filius Gospatricii*	1185x1201	ditto	ditto	ditto	ditto
Adam *filius Gospatricii*	1185x1201	ditto	ditto	ditto	ditto
Gamel *prepositus*	1158x1160	ditto	ditto	84	53
Orm *de Yreby*	1185x1201	ditto	ditto	92	61
Waltheof	*c.*1185	ditto	ditto	113	84

Table 6 Insular personal names in charters to some religious houses (continued on the next page)

Orm *filius Rogeri*	late 12th cent.	ditto	ditto	113	85
Waltheof *de Dena*	*c.*1185	ditto	ditto	117	88
Waltheof *filius Thome clerici de Dene*	1178x1184	ditto	ditto	137	100

Table 6 Insular personal names in charters to some religious houses (continued)

same level into the late twelfth century. Donors and witnesses to charters to religious houses in the North included numerous who still bore insular personal names, represented, for example, in charters to St Bees and Furness Abbey in the further North. As one instance, in 1165x1177, Waltheof *filius Edmundi* made a benefaction to Furness of Newby, his charter witnessed *inter alia* by Elias *filius Gamelli*, Thomas *filius Swani*, Uchtred *de Austwyk*, Ulf *filius Ormi* and Dolfin brother of that Ulf.[69] Some degree of status is represented by Torfin who made a benefaction to Easby Abbey before the honorial baronage of the court of the honour of Richmond in 1162x1194.[70] In *c.*1200, the benefaction of Robert *de Stalmine* and his son, Peter, to Furness Abbey, of a carucate in Stalmine was attested as the first five witnesses by Osbern *filius Ethmundi*, Ralph *filius Bernulfi*, Hucc *prepositus*, Robert *filius Hucce*, and Ulv (Ulf) *filius Uvieti*.[71] In this case, an important transaction, transferring a considerable amount of land for this time, was witnessed by a group of freemen who either had insular personal names or whose immediate predecessors had borne insular personal names, so that persons with insular personal names retained some status locally and there had been no complete transformation from insular to newer forms of personal name by the turn of the century.

Moreover, the importance of these lay freemen inheres also in their attestation of charters of knightly families such as the de Boivilla and Morevilla families, or in the case of Waltheof, Ketel, Siward *presbiter* and Chetell, a charter of William Meschin. Gospatrick *filius Ormi* conferred the vill of Salter on St Bees, in 1145x1179, reflecting his substance. Not only did insular personal names persist amongst the English families of middling status, however, for elements within the secular clergy continued to bear insular personal names in the late twelfth century: Gospatrick *sacerdos de Keltona* (1145x1179); Dolfin *presbiter de Camertona* (1145x1179); Gospatrick *clericus de Derann'* (1158x1160); Waltheof *persona de Briggaham* and Waltheof *decanus* (both 1178x1184), as examples.[72]

In some of the instances of Latin patronymic forms of naming, whilst the father's name was Continental-Germanic or Christian, the son's renewed an insular personal name. Even in the early thirteenth century, insular personal names were socially entirely acceptable, represented, for example, in Gospatrick *filius Willelmi de Fel* who made a benefaction of a toft in Lancaster to Cockersand in 1200x1240, or Grimbald son of Herbert *de Ellale* who provided a rent of 100s. to the same religious house in 1209x1235.[73] Indeed, Grimbald, the son of Herbert, had issue Walter whose son was another Grimbald (1240x 1268).[74] Similarly, some families felt no social or cultural impetus to discontinue insular personal names, for Grimbald *de Soureby* confirmed to the same religious house the land which had been donated by his father, Grimbald, the status of the younger Grimbald reflected in his further benefaction of a bovate with his body for burial.[75] In the north-west, the transition from insular personal names to C-G and Christian names appears to be firmly located in the late twelfth century rather than earlier, according to the evidence in the charters to Cockersand. Illustrative of this process is Bernard *filius Akke* who made several benefactions in nine separate charters to Cockersand between 1205 and 1230, comprising 15a. 3r. and unspecified land, so that his father was living in the late twelfth century.[76] Similarly, between 1190 and 1230, Waltheof *de Pulton* conveyed to this religious house by five separate charters twelve acres, six selions, a messuage and toft.[77] These benefactions were confirmed by Waltheof's son, William, in 1220x1268.[78] The manner in which freemen with insular personal names were still predominant into the early thirteenth century is reflected in a memorandum in the house's cartulary, describing the provenance of lands in a gift by a certain Ralph (*fl.* 1236x1246), for his immediate predecessors in the lands had been attributed insular personal names:

> *Habemus etiam cartam Suani filii Michaelis factam dicto Radulpho de ista terra et cartam Suani filii Roberti de Hoton factam Suano filio Michaelis de ista terra.*[79]

> [We have indeed a charter of Suan son of Michael made to the said Ralph about this land and a charter of Suan son of Robert *de Hoton* made to Suan son of Michael about this land.]

In this area, therefore, there was no cultural stigma against insular personal names in the early thirteenth century, exemplified by Gospatrick *filius Roberti filii Sigge* who had issue four sons, Robert (named for his grandfather), Gospatrick (named for his father), Hugh and Ranulph.[80]

The cartulary thus reflects the continuation of some of these names amongst the free tenantry of the region and that persistence is evident at lower social levels, for example in the cursory rentals of the house in 1251, where the tenants enumerated included Uchtred *Kempedale*, Grimme *Stanistrete*, Grimbald *de Barton*, another Uchtred, Uchtred *de Warton*, Brun *de Mora*, Uchtred *de Loxum*, Brun *de Bonka*, Grimbald *de Forton*, Uchtred *de Hildreston*, Waltheof *filius Rogeri*, Swain *de Katon*, Grimbald *de Elhale*, and Orm *filius Astini* as well as those reflecting a recent transition

Uchtred *filius Haldani*	tenant of at least half an acre	1205x1225	III, ii, 931 (2)
Swein	held land in Warton	1212x1246	I, i, 192
Hardwin	tenant (*homo*) of Thomas in Melling	1190x1212	II, ii, p. 536
Orm *Dragun*	used to hold a toft in Ainsdale	1190x1213	II, ii, p. 573

Table 7 Insular personal names in the Cockersand cartulary (continued on the next two pages)

Swein *filius Osberti de Frekelton'*	gave an acre in Freckleton	1200x1212	I, i, p. 199
Swein	tenant (*homo*) of Matilda (attorned)	1217x1221	I, i, p. 232
Elsi	tenant of a croft	Before 1212	I, i, p. 192
Flint	Ditto	Ditto	Ditto
Grimbald *de Elhalle*	attested charters re-land in Forton	1200x1240	II, i, pp. 351, 358
Uchtred *de Kempedale*	gave one and a half acres in Hutton	1220x1250	II, i, pp. 422–3
Uchtred *de Derbychyre*	held land in Hutton	1268x1279	II, i, p. 447
Alan *Hardingsun*	tenant of land	1210x1226	III, ii, 398–9 (63)
Robert *filius Gilmichael de Lathebot'*	donor (6 separate charters)	1194x1219	III, ii, 940–4 (1–7)
Waltheof *filius Alfredi*	tenant of land	1194x1219	ibid.
Gospatrick	tenant of land	1194x1219	ibid.
Waltheof *albus*	tenant of an assart	1194x1219	ibid.
Benedict *filius Waldevi filii Anketini de Bland*	donor	1235x1268	III, ii, 961 (11)
German *de Bland*	donor	1200x1250	III, ii, 962 (12)
Orm *filius Thor'*	(i) tenant of 7.5 acres (ii) donor	1200x1250 1184x1190	III, ii, 962–3 (12–13), 997 (1), 1010–1011 (1)
Orm *filius Ade de Kellet*	donor	1222x1229	III, ii, 984–5 (9)
Uchtred *filius Osolfi*	donor	1184x1190	III, ii, 1001–2 (2–3)
Gospatrick *filius Gilmichael' de Burton*	quitclaim	1200x1220	III, ii, 1008 (5)
Gospatrick *filius Roberti filii Sigge*	donor	1190x1210	III, ii, 1017 (2)
Uchtred *de Kempedale*	donor	1220x1250	II, i, 422 (18)
Gamel *filius Sesar' de Thorp'*, Gamel *de Torp'*	donor, attested for Bretherton	1184x1212	II, i , 471, 478–9 (11–13)

Gamel *forestarius*	attested for Cuerden	1199x1220	II, i, p. 492
Edric *de Sivirdeleie*	gave land	1199x1220	II, ii, p. 627
Orm *de Haidoc*	gave land in Ince	1190x1199	II, ii, p. 673
Gospatric *de Chorlton*	gave half his demesne in Chorlton, held land there in thanage	1200x1223	II, ii, p. 707
Dolfin *de Urwilham*	gave land in Irlam	1184x1190	II, ii, p. 719
Waltheof *de Quitinton' filius Hutredi*	gave land in Withington	1184x1210	II, ii, p. 730
Siward *de Longetre*	donor	1190x1219	II, i, 513 (3)
Gospatrick *filius Warini de Kiuerdale*	donor	1190x1220	II, i, 518 (1)
William *filius Hutredi filii Suani*	donor	1242x1268	I, ii, (Chetham Society, n.s. 39, 1898), 190 (1)
Suan *filius Osberti de Frekelton'*	donor	1200x1212	I, ii, 199 (5); his son was Richard: *ibid.*, 199 (6)
Orm *filius Rogeri*	donor	early 13th cent.	I, ii, 214
Grimbald *filius Willelmi de Slen'*	donor	1230x1268	I, ii, 260 (13)
Jordan *filius Torphini de Gairstang*	donor	1246	I, ii, 276 (6); Torphin had held 1 bovate and 6 acres from the rectory of Garstang.
Siward *filius Uccke*	donor	1185x11901	I, ii, 114 (1); his son was Richard, who *fl.* 1205x1233: *ibid.*, 116.

Table 7 Insular personal names in the Cockersand cartulary (continued)

in the early thirteenth century, such as Dikre *filius Alwardi*, Dothe *filius Uchtredi*, John *filius Ulfi*, Dobbe *filius Dolphini*, William *filius Uchtredi* and William *filius Thorphini*.[81]

The persistence of insular personal names is perhaps exemplified by the charter of Edgar in favour of his sister Juliana who married Ranulph *de Merlay*, the two siblings being children of earl Gospatrick. Edgar's charter was attested by Ostred *presbiter*, Grimbald *de Merlay*, William *filius Elef'*, Sewert *filius Liolf'*, Liolf *filius Liolf'*, Cospatric *filius Leuenoc'* and Cospatric *de Horsley*. The witness list represents a different and vital insular culture at the time of the event, *c*.1167.[82]

'Hybrid' personal naming

In the area around Canterbury in the late twelfth century, a certain Edwin named his sons Leffelm and Godfrey, so conferring on one a new continental-Germanic personal name, but to the other a traditional insular personal name.[83] Edwin did not abandon the cultural tradition of his own name, but he did tentatively adopt the new name forms introduced into England after the Conquest. In short, he adopted a 'hybrid' solution to the naming of his sons. In investigating the symbolism and meaning of his action – assumed by others, but often invisible to us – we need to consider all the instances where this 'compromise' occurred. This attitude to naming has, however, particular resonances in the 'north'.

We can consider a particular example of this compromise in naming in northern England. In 1154x1174, Toc son of Toc conveyed land in Durham to the nuns of Newcastle.[84] He was conjoined in this benefaction by his brother, Alan. Here then a father disporting an insular Scandinavian personal name (Tokí) retained this name for one of his sons, but attributed to his brother a Breton personal name. Confronting the dilemma at an early time, 1135x1139, two siblings had been named Wallief *de Stotleia* and his brother, Richard, a measured response to adapting to a new situation.[85]

Exemplifying this approach too, Dolfin accorded to one of his sons an insular personal name, Meldred, on another a PCeltic form, Patrick, and on another son a continental-Germanic item, Robert. Meldred attested three *acta* of bishop Hugh of Durham, Robert one and Patrick another, in 1154x1174.[86] Now, the status of Meldred was reflected in Hugh's confirmation to him sometime after 1163 of the vills of Winston, Winlaton, Sunderland Bridge and Newsham, combined with a portion of the forest for an annual rent of £20 and services in exchange for a quitclaim of his right in other lands. Meldred was deceased by 1179 and had succumbed to a new form of name for his son, Robert.[87] Apparently, therefore, the kinship had some local importance, perhaps as local officialdom, but Dolfin resisted the temptation to convert completely to new name forms and ensured the persistence of insular naming. The influences involved here are complicated: patrilinear naming converging with attachment to an insular personal name. Nevertheless, many kinship groups must have been confronted with exactly this dilemma.

In that area too, in 1200x1212, Swein *filius Osberti de Frekelton'* alienated an acre between the land which Swein *de Frekelton'* and his brother, Roger, had given to

Cockersand Abbey.[88] When Dolfin *de Urwilham* gave land in Irlam to Cockersand in 1184x1190, his charter divulged that his brother's name was Simon.[89]

If we move to southern Lancashire, there are encountered charters relating to the kinship of Hugh *de Whiteword* which allow a reconstruction of his nuclear family. He had three sons, to two of whom were consigned new name forms, one continental-Germanic (Hugh), a patrilinear approach to naming of one son, and one Christian, Michael. To the third, however, Hugh allocated the insular Scandinavian personal name, Swain. Swain received half a bovate in Tong from Hugh *quasi heredi meo* (to him as if my heir), so he was probably the younger son and Hugh, named in patrilinear manner, the eldest. Married with Agnes, Swain had issue Richard.[90] Attestations of a charter relating to Barton in 1200x1206 reveal that Grimbald had issue Herbert, Grimbald and Richard. Here again patrilinear naming and the repetition of an insular form are compounded, but the reassertion of the insular form in hybrid naming was reiterated in the same vill.[91]

In early-thirteenth-century Yorkshire, Richard *de Claiton'* had issue two sons, one named Alan who, although under age, attempted to bring an appeal for the death of his brother, Waltheof. Although Richard, with a continental-Germanic name form, had allocated a Breton name to one of his sons, on the other, presumably the eldest who had been killed before 1215, he imposed an insular name, presumably without any dishonour or disparagement.[92] When, it was reported, Geoffrey *Norman* of Skelton drowned after tumbling from a boat, his body was located by his brother, Gamel, and at the same time, Thurstan *filius Jacobi* was imprisoned for murder.[93]

Now this last patronym alerts us to the reversion of some fathers with new forms of name to insular name-forms. Sometime before 1268 Orm *filius Rogeri* alienated land in Ashton (Lancashire).[94] In Cuerdale in Lancashire in 1190x1220, Gospatrick *filius Warini de Kiuerdale* conveyed land to Cockersand Abbey.[95] Continuing in the same vein, Cockersand Abbey also received from Grimbald *filius Willelmi de Slen* in 1230x1268 all his land in Claughton.[96] In the middle of the thirteenth century, the justices in eyre in Northumberland heard the appeal of Waldef *filius Alani*; to them was reported that Utting *filius Ade* had stabbed William; and they were also informed about the misdeed involving Siward *filius Jacobi*.[97] It is therefore not surprising that the Crown Pleas of Yorkshire in the early thirteenth century furnish further examples: the Haldane son of William accused of battery; the Gikel son of Warin appealed for rape; and the Gamel son of Richard arraigned for battery.[98]

The revival of insular personal names within kinship groups was occasionally even more complex. At Framlington in Northumberland, Meldred Pigaz was the son of John Pigace, the father thus resurrecting a very particular insular personal name for his son. Nevertheless, John designated his other son Richard.[99]

Amongst these revivals of insular name forms, the bearers were not consistently insignificant, but pertained to the substantial free peasantry. Making a benefaction of a bovate in Thornton to Fountains Abbey, Thorald *de Thornetun'* requested burial in the abbey. In another charter, he was described as Thorald *filius Ricardi* and as tenant of two bovates with a toft and croft in Thornton. This status therefore firmly located him in the upper echelon of the free peasantry of Yorkshire.[100] Ostensibly in these cases no social or cultural dishonour seems to have been experienced by reverting to insular name forms; these forms had become an integral part of the conventional corpus of names in the northern zone.

Interpretation

From this evidence, it is apparent that there was no cultural homology in the North for much of the twelfth century, but that different cultural traditions of naming coexisted and persisted for some generations into the late twelfth century and with residual levels amongst the peasantry into the early thirteenth. Considering the spatial aspects, one possible explanation might be centre (core)-periphery differences, with naming processes changing more rapidly in the core areas, but exhibiting residual traces in the peripheral areas. Such an interpretation is problematic, however, because of the relationship between core and periphery and defining each in relation to the other. Viewed from inside, the north of England might have retained a greater affinity with southern Scotland for much of the twelfth century. Peripheral areas might also be considered to be creative because of their liminality rather than culturally residual.[101]

Since naming processes and patterns continued to represent cultural heteroglossia over several generations and perhaps a century after the Conquest, cultural theories which are constituted around an homologous culture seem inappropriate, thus excluding, for example, Geertzian interpretive anthropology, which depends on 'thick description' from single cultural variables, such as names, to elicit the total nature of a culture. Although Geertz, in one statement, requires only a minimum of cultural coherence, yet it is apparent that his interpretation does predicate an homologous culture. That extensive degree of cultural coherence manifestly did not exist in the twelfth-century North. Rather than 'thick description', a more appropriate conceptualisation might be William Sewell's 'thin coherence', which allows beneath a 'dominant' discourse of culture, cultural variants which might be residual, oppositional or resistant, allowing space for those cultural undercurrents perceived by cultural materialists.[102] Nevertheless, the question remains as to the precise nature of these cultural expressions: residual, oppositional or resistant? Attractive as is the temptation to regard them simply as residual, perhaps some case might be advanced for their oppositional or resistant nature to a dominant discourse of culture, that of the new overlords. It is, of course, possible that recursive repetition of names (in the manner of Bourdieu's *habitus* or Giddens's structuration) might have sustained cultures that were entirely residual, but the process of naming is in itself an act of considerable agency. It is inherently intentional and is an expression of wider allegiances and associations, if not identities. On the other hand, the strategies available to the Northern peasantry for resistance were limited and circumscribed; indeed, it is probable, as de Certeau maintained, that such social groups do not have access to strategies, only tactics, and so naming is a tactic of resistance, the only form of cultural dissonance available to the Northern peasantry.[103] In that perception, agreement is possible with Aceto that 'more important is the fact that this community reveals a naming system that has been developed, used and maintained to signify minority ethnic and linguistic identities ... a specific cultural group is likely to display ethnic or alternative names that contrast either etymologically or phonologically with those drawn from the ambient language of power.'[104] In other words, naming allowed access to a counter-hegemonic praxis, action through language,

Name	Northumberland	Durham	Yorkshire
Acke, Aki[105]	●		●
Adelard[106]			●
Ailward		●	
Ailwin			●
Akkeman[107]			●
Aldred		●	
Arketill[108]		●	
Arkill[109]	●	●	●
Auty[110] [Outy]		●	●
Bernolf, Bernulf[111]		●	●
Bond[112]			●
Brigtmer	●		
Copsi			●
Colswann[113]			●
Crin[114]	●		
Cuthbert	●		
Dering			●
Derman[115]			●
Dolfin[116]	●	●	●
E[a]dwin[117]		●	
Edmund[118]		●	
Edric	●		●
Edulf[119]	●		●
Edwald			●

Table 8 The corpora of insular personal names in three Northern counties in the twelfth century (continued over the next three pages)

Edward	•		•
Elfer		•	
Elfald		•	
Elgi[120]		•	
E[y]lsi/Aylsi	•		•
Elstan	•	•	
Elvric			•
Elwin		•	•
Ethelred		•	
Figge[121]		•	
Forn[122]			•
Gamel[123]	•	•	•
Godmund[124]		•	
Godric[125]	•	•	•
German			•
Gikel			•
Godwin[126]		•	
Gospatrick	•	•	•
Grimkell[127]			•
Grund			•
Harold			•
Haldan[128]			•
Harding[129]			•
Hauell			•
Heremer[130]			•
Hereward[131]			•
Iggi	•		
Ilif [Ylif]	•		
Ilving		•	

Kenwald			•
Ketel[132]		•	•
Landric			•
Lefsy			•
Lefwin[133]			•
Leising		•	
Leofric		•	•
Leolf[134]			•
Meldred	•	•	
[H]Orm[135]		•	•
Osbern		•	
Oswald[136]			•
Osward[137]			•
Pace	•		
Patrick	•	•	•
Ravenkill			•
Saddoc		•	
Saxi[138]			•
Saxelini			•
Seman[139]	•		
Sigar[140]	•		
Siward	•	•	•
Snebern			•
Snell[141]			•
Suartbrond[142]		•	
Swa[i]n[143]	•	•	•
Thore		•	
Thorald	•		•
Thurstan			•

Toki[144] [Tocc]	●	●	
Toly[145]			●
Torolf			●
Tosti			●
Turkill[146]		●	
Uchtred[147]	●	●	●
Ukeman [Uccaman]			●
Ulf[148]		●	●
Ulkill[149]		●	●
Unspak			●
Utting	●	●	●
Waltheof	●		●
Watling		●	
Westmund			●
Wigan			●
Wlfric			●
Wulmer			●

Table 8 The corpora of insular personal names in three Northern counties in the twelfth century

that extended for longer and more widely in the far north, so that even in the early thirteenth century peasants with insular name forms visibly populated this environment. Since these insular name forms persisted so late (by comparison with southern areas of the country), a few, like Uchtred, continued in the vocabulary of personal naming through the middle ages. Whilst initially expressions of a counter-hegemonic culture, no doubt they were later merely assimilated as non-signifiers into a neutral lexis and corpus of names.

Patterns of insular naming in the twelfth century

Whilst Table 8 exhibits the corpus of insular personal names which persisted in the north, it does not fully reflect the distribution of particular insular names. Although many of these personal names existed throughout the north – especially the profuse Uchtred and Waltheof – a few remained more localized. Particular to this category were Gospatrick and Gilmichael and, to a lesser degree, Grimbald. In general, insular

Germanic and insular Scandinavian personal names extended throughout the far north, whereas insular Celtic forms were spatially more focused.

Gilmichael remained mainly confined to the far north-west of England. In 1190x1212, Roger *filius Gilemichel'* had held a bovate in Carlton in Amounderness.[150] In Medlar, nearby, Gilmicael had held a bovate some time before 1220x1268.[151] In Amounderness too Robert *filius Gilmichael'* alienated a bovate in Prees in 1190x1212.[152] The persistence of Gospatric in the far north-west is represented by Gospatric *de Chorlton*, a minor lord, who held in thanage in Chorlton and alienated land from his demesne called Bexwic to Cockersand Abbey in 1200x 1223.[153]

Whilst there were localized distinctions in some of the names, the overall characteristic of the North consisted in a wider variety of insular name forms which persisted into the late twelfth century and also a distinctive corpus of names in general by comparison with southern areas. Partly, the corpus was expanded by insular Scandinavian personal names, but even the composition of insular OE names differed from the south. Additionally, names of other etymology were invasive in the far north and north-west.

Concentrating on insular Old English (OE) personal names, in Newcastle, Elstan *filius Edrici* attested local charters in 1220x1230.[154] Utting extended throughout Yorkshire, represented in the criminals before the Yorkshire Crown Pleas in 1218–19, Utting *de Folifant* and Utting *nepos Ukeman'*, as related above.[155] Uckman too recurred in Yorkshire and other northern parts, Ukmann *sutor* holding a small amount of land alongside Gamel *Neubond*, Gamel *filius Pycot'*, and Godric *Ruskel* in Spofforth, whilst in Eastanby Thomas *filius Uccaman'* acquired eight acres of land.[156] In Catton in Yorkshire the tenantry included Robert *filius Uckemani* and Avice *filia Uckeman'*.[157] Almost as extensive as Uchtred (see below) was Waltheof in its variants and elisions. How that personal name developed into a byname is illustrated by Adam *filius Waldef'* who made an appeal about theft and was himself appealed for theft as Adam *Walthef*.[158] Although not as frequent, Dolfin was established as a distinctly northern insular personal name, illustrated by the Dolfin (without byname) who held a toft in Buckden in Yorkshire.[159]

Amongst Scandinavian forms of personal name, Grimbald had a particular resonance in the north. Gamel was profuse in Yorkshire, but extended outside into other parts of the north and indeed into other regions of the Danelaw. Its prolific extent in Yorkshire can be illustrated by Gamel *filius Golle* and Gamel *venator*, both tenants simultaneously in Catton.[160] Charters relating to land in Catton at the same time – the end of the twelfth century – were attested also by Swain *de Tornet'* and Gikel *de Baldethi*, the former expansively distributed, the latter less so but distinctive.[161] The persistence of these insular Scandinavian forenames into the late twelfth and thirteenth centuries was associated in great part with the survival of a free peasantry in these areas, not least in Yorkshire. Thus Gamel *filius Ulfcel'* alienated land in Yeland and Swain *faber de Grethland'* acquired land in Lindley for 28s.[162] That independent free peasantry perpetuated insular Scandinavian personal names throughout northern areas.

One particularly northern insular personal name, although not profuse in its distribution, was Maldred or Meldred.[163] One of its most noticeable bearers was the Maldred or Meldred *filius Dolfini* (deceased before 1179) who attested *acta* of Hugh, bishop of Durham, in 1154x 1166, confirming the association of insular personal names, local free tenants, and lower officialdom.[164] In the late twelfth and early thirteenth century, Meldred (without a byname) held land in Gateshead.[165] Also in Northumberland, at Framlington, Meldred *Pigaz* of that vill, confirmed a benefaction of land to Brinkburn Priory.[166] Further south, at Broughton in the West Riding, Meldred *de Broctona* held two bovates and assorted small amounts of land.[167]

It was especially in Cumberland that the constant heteroglossia of names continued to be remarkable. Here diverse cultural traditions intersected and were represented in names. Simply in charters in favour of Lanercost Abbey in the late twelfth and early thirteenth centuries, mention was made of Uchtred *filius Leuenod'*, Haldan *de Wydene*, Uchtred *filius Ricardi*, Duncan *de Lasceles*, Brice *de Thirlewall'*, Thomas *filius Sunolf'*, Thomas *filius Gospatricii*, Deremann, Bueth *Barn*, Robert *filius Bueth'*, Leissing, Gamel *de Walton'*, Uchtred *filius Boeth'*, Gillecrist *filius Ricardi Brun*, Elstan *molendinarius*, Hegret, Uchtred *de Tueregles*, Thomas *filius Drake* (i.e. *Draconis*), William *filius Hudardi* and Gille *Bueth*.[168] In this cultural heteroglossia, insular Germanic personal names (for example, Uchtred, Deremann) intermingled with Scottish influences (for example, Bueth, Duncan), insular Scandinavian (for example, Haldan) and newly-introduced continental forms of both unusual and common incidence.

As a contested space in the Solway basin, subjected to a diversity of influences over its transformations and political dominations, it is not surprising that Cumberland remained an area of onomastic heteroglossia.[169] Undoubtedly too the extension of the lordship of the Gospatric-Waltheof connection into the twelfth century assisted in the persistence of insular name forms, which would explain the context, for example, of the charter about Bridekirk of Waltheof *filius Gospatricii comitis* attested by Swain *presbiter*, the brothers Liof and Uchtred who were sons of Uchtred, Waltheof *filius Buet'*, Uchtred *filius Gamel'* and Ulf *filius Gamal'*, followed by that of Alan *filius Waldevi filii Cospatricii Comitis* witnessed by, amongst the lay attestors, Uchtred *filius Uchtredi*, William *filius Waldevi*, Egelward and Orm, sons of Dolfin, Chetel *filius Ulfchil'* and Chetel *filius Roberti*.[170] Scottish influence is equally evident in the notification by the archbishop of York of the consecration of the bishop of St Andrews before July 1127 which, whilst attested by Waltheof *de Croiland*, was also attested *de Scotia* by Aimar *miles*, Alden *filius Alwald'*, Ulchil *filius Merevin'*, Ulchil *filius Meldred'* and Gillecolm *Nogedac*.[171]

One important influence in that persistence of both diversity and traditional forms might have emanated from the names of the clergy. Whilst it has been suggested that women acted as bearers of traditional culture, a similar role might have been performed by the clergy until the late twelfth century.[172] The status of the secular clergy and the significance of parochial organization were in transition in the twelfth century.[173] It is probably of consequence that Ailwin *presbiter* attested an *actum* of Thomas, archbishop of York, in 1112x1114, although almost fifty years had elapsed since the Conquest.[174] Certainly, it is possible to accumulate numerous examples of the secular clergy with insular name forms in the twelfth century, although the material is merely impressionistic: Gamel *presbiter* (1167x1202 and 1200x1221);[175] Dolfin *presbyter* (1154x 1158);[176] Patrick *presbiter* (1163x1174);[177] Haldan *diaconus* (1154x1195);[178] Thorald *presbiter*;[179] Swain *capellanus* (c.1188);[180] Swain *presbiter*; [181]

Æthelwald *clericus* son of Erlaf *sacerdos*, and Acca *presbiter*.[182] When Pontefract Priory benefited from the munificence of Swein *filius Ailrich'*, a prominent insular-named donor of the advowson of Silkstone, six bovates of land, the chapel of Cawthorne, another two bovates, and two-thirds of his demesne tithes, the notification of his generosity by the archbishop of York was attested by Edwin *presbiter et persona de Derefeld'* and Ulf *presbiter et persona de Adewic'* as well as the insular-named Dolfin *de Wolvlay* and Saxi *de Horbiri*.[183]

Formation of bynames from insular personal names

By the late thirteenth and early fourteenth centuries, bynames from insular personal names contributed marginally to the corpus of bynames from personal names. In the Cumberland lay subsidy of 1332, just over 130 taxpayers were identified by bynames derived from personal names, twenty-nine (twenty-two percent) of which consisted unambiguously of insular etymons. Merely forty-two bynames emanated from personal names amongst Lancashire taxpayers in 1332; amongst these contributors, nine (twenty-one percent) belonged to an insular category – but we must beware the stochastic variation inherent in such small numbers. Earlier, in the Northumberland taxation of 1296–7, out of 162 taxpayers with bynames from personal names, forty-nine (thirty percent) consisted of insular forms. For Yorkshire, two taxation lists are available in print: 1297 and 1301 which slightly overlap in geographical coverage but also extend over different parts of the county. In that of 1297, 278 of the assessed were identified by bynames from personal names, eighty (twenty-nine percent) of whom had an insular etymon. Similarly in the taxation list of 1301, 114 (twenty-seven percent) out of 418 taxpayers with bynames from personal names had an insular origin. Demonstrated by these figures is the substantial proportion of bynames from personal names which consisted of an insular item, between twenty and thirty percent.

Using the tax lists is not unproblematic, however, for inclusion in the lists was decided by personal wealth surplus to subsistence above a determinate level. In fine, the lists comprehended, on average, about 40 percent of male tenants and, in part of Yorkshire, for example, probably an even lower proportion. Now, it is quite possible that bynames derived from insular personal names extended further amongst the poorest, although it has been concluded above that some of the substantial free tenants of the twelfth century disported insular *nomina*. Consequently the tax lists may be an under-enumeration of bynames derived from insular personal names.

Dominant in the rank order of these bynames from insular personal names were *Bond(e)* (twenty-eight taxpayers) and *Swein* (fifteen) (usually a variant like *Swan*). Neither is uncomplicated, since both could possibly have evolved from another etymology: *bond* an unfree tenant and *swein* from servant or 'man of'. Nevertheless, at this conjuncture, in the late thirteenth and early fourteenth century, the alternative etymology would have been represented in the syndetic form: *le bond* and *le swan*.[184] It therefore seems fairly conclusive that both developed from insular personal names. Successively in rank order, the corpus then comprised: *Colstan* and *Harding* (ten);

Derling and *Gamel* (nine); *Leofric* (in its variant *Laverok, Leveroke* and *Leverock*) and *Derman* (seven); *Thorald* and *Osbern* (six); *Wlf/Ulfe, Dolfin, Waltheof* (in its variants *Waldef, Waltef, Waltheu, Waldive* and *Waldeve*), and *Utting* (five). The remainder recurred between one and four times, producing a very wide range of bynames: *Lewyn; Brandolf; Grimbald; Slabrand; Thorbrand; Haldan; Gilibrond; Unwin; Ketil; Elwald; Grim; Ayrike; Brand; Colbayn; Toly; Thurkill; Aylmer; Dunkan; Bruning; Tock; Dunning; Gykel; Alsy; Torkard; Swartbrand; Fegge; Kemball; Forn(e); Thorgot; Hereward; Osmund; Aky; Hughtred; Ailward; Harold; Skeggolf; Arkel; Goderick; Leolf; Godwin; Patrick; Tosty; Orm; Wygot; Torfyn; Hamund; Sigrym; Unwin;* and *Cudbert.* Thus more than sixty different insular personal names were converted into bynames, an extremely wide corpus. Amongst the items differentiating the northern zone from southern areas was the relatively inconspicuous level of the insular Old English personal names *Goderick* (*Godric*) and *Godwin*, which revealed a stronger presence in other areas as personal names in eleventh- and twelfth-century England.[185] Distinctive of the norther zone was the transformation of a significant number of Scandinavian personal names into bynames, more particularly *Bond* in Yorkshire but also the general level of conversion, and specific insular Germanic (OE) personal names such as *Leofric, Waltheof, Dolfin,* and *Utting*.

Persistence of bynames from insular personal names

The survival of these bynames from insular personal names into the late fourteenth century can be more accurately measured through two particular sources: the Poll Taxes of 1377–81 which were much more inclusive and comprehensive than the lay subsidies of the early fourteenth century; and the manorial surveys of the episcopal estates of Bishop Hatfield of Durham, which compensate for the exemption of the Palatine from the Poll Taxes. Addressing Durham first, forty-six of about 200 tenants with bynames from personal names were identified by insular etymons. Nonetheless, the repetition of tenants according to the different status of land which they held, confuses the enumeration. The twenty-three percent level represented here is thus an impressionistic proportion.

Such complications do not compound analysis of the Poll Taxes, levied on a per capita basis. On the other hand, these assessments are geographically defective in their survival. What has to be contended, however, is the propensity for bynames from personal names to evolve during the fourteenth century into patronymic and metronymic forms, so that the corpus of bynames from personal names in some areas is particularly narrow by the last quarter of the century. To illustrate that outcome, in Carlisle, the only location for which the taxes are extant in Cumberland, fewer than ten taxpayers disported bynames incorporating personal names by comparison with a much higher proportion of those with patronymic or metronymic forms of byname. It is therefore of little consequence, because of the slender size of the population with bynames from personal names, that *Haldene* and *Ketill* contributed to the corpus.

A particular name: Uchtred

In a case of debt in 1320, Ughtred *de Gevelston* impleaded the rector of Clifton (Cumberland).[186] Almost forty years later, Ughtred Penneson was killed at Bradford (West Riding of Yorkshire).[187] Not only was Uchtred a frequent forename throughout the 'North' in the twelfth century, it persisted into the late middle ages with some consistency. Whilst it does not represent the fortunes of insular naming in general, this personal name indicates that in the particular insular and vernacular environment of northern regions, it was possible for an insular personal name to become a conventional item in the corpus of personal naming.

Of course, Uchtred was not exclusive to the 'North', but continued to exist elsewhere, but more sporadically. Huchtred held land in Senle (Herts.), where also significantly Hereward *Cobbe* also held eight acres.[188] In Essex, a plea before the royal justices was invoked by Uchtred *filius Rogeri* against Isabel *filia Uctred'*, with the surrogate Adam *filius Uctred'*.[189] Here indeed, it appears that an insular name had been conferred on a son by a father with a continental form of name, the implications of which are discussed above. The heirs of Huctred *de Merisco* held three and a half acres of land in Ores in Kent in the twelfth century.[190] Uchtred *de Stok'* attested a charter in the West Midlands in the early thirteenth century.[191]

In the late twelfth century in particular this *nomen* appeared in diverse areas. In 1170x1182, on the Worcester episcopal estates, one Hutred held an assart at Wick, another held a virgate in Kempsey jointly with Alured *palmere*, another, Huctred *de Bromhale* was a tenant in Kempsey, an Utred without a byname held a virgate in Fladbury, and another Utred the same amount of land in Crawcumbe.[192]

Diametrically to the east, a Huctred attested a charter relating to East Bergholt (Suffolk) before September 1188.[193] Possibly in the 1120s, Uhtred *diaconus* had performed the same role for a benefaction to Eye Priory.[194] In the same area Huctred *de Mora* was a tenant whilst Hutred *cementarius* attested another charter. The former was probably identifiable as the Uchtred *de Morua*, a villain tenant at Stoke in 1136x1150s.[195]

This insular personal name thus sporadically developed into a byname in other locations, so that William *Outred* granted land in Wycombe in Buckinghamshire in the 1330s.[196] More particularly, *Outred* became established as a concentration – a small clustering – in the Parts of Holland and Kesteven in south Lincolnshire. In those Parts in 1332, *Outred* was represented by John and William *Outered* at Quadring (assessed at 1s. and 1s. 9d.), Robert *Outred* at Gosberton (6s. 8³/₄d.), Guy *Outred* at Pinchbeck (11s.), Roger and Simon *Houtred* at Moulton (2s. 6d., 8³/₄d.), William *Houtared* at Sutton (4s. 3¹/₄d.), and Andrew and John *Outred* at East Deeping (1s. 6d., 2s. 4d.).[197]

What was characteristic about *Uchtred* in the North, however, was its continuity in use and its relatively more frequent occurrence. Its earlier proliferation amongst insular personal names can be assessed impressionistically. When Alice *de Gant* made a benefaction to Fountains Abbey in 1144x1156, comprising land near Redley, her charter was witnessed by Uchtred *filius Wallef'*, Uchtred *homo Noel'*, and Aldelin *filius Uctredi de Stodlay*. It is in fact apposite to point out that this charter which was also attested by Ketel *filius Siwardi* and Gamel *de Stodlay* represents the continued association of Alice, of a baronial family, with an insular environment, reflected also in the attestation of another of her endowments to Fountains of a wood at Littley also in Yorkshire, to which the names of Wlric, Leuric, and Siward were subscribed as witnesses.[198] In 1147x1157, Uchtred *filius Gamelli* was confirmed in all his assarts in Brimham in Yorkshire by Roger de Mowbray.[199] This Uchtred attested *acta* of the archbishop of York of 1151x1153 confirming benefactions to Nun Monkton Priory.[200] Rather surprisingly, another charter relating to York was witnessed by Uchtred *Malaherba*, a rather bizarre combination of insular forename and Anglo-Norman *cognomen*.[201] This Uchtred had held land in York *c*.1160–82.[202]

In the second decade of the thirteenth century, Agnes daughter of Uchtred *de Nid* brought an appeal for rape.[203] Reported to the same justices in 1218–19 was the casualty which befell Adam *filius Uctred'* who fell mortally from his cart.[204] Then too Uchtred *de Brincliffe* discovered the bodies of the homonymous brothers William and William slain by Orm and William, servants of the abbot of Beauchief.[205] Another appeal was brought by Sybil against Adam for the murder of her husband, Uchtred *de Bramle* before the same justices.[206]

Also in the early thirteenth century, two bovates of land in the East Riding had been held by Uchtred and his nephew Geoffrey.[207] Even at the end of the thirteenth century in northern Yorkshire, the insular personal name continued to be favoured. Henry son of Uchtred held a toft and croft in Heslington and an Uchtred (without a byname) a toft and bovate in Driffield.[208]

The status of some of the free peasants named Uchtred can be detected in a charter of Uchtred *filius Dolfini*. Since his charter relating to Burnaby was attested by Thomas *filius Swani*, William *filius Ketelli de Munteon'* and Richard *filius Siwardi*, and Uchtred's own son and heir, conjoined in the grant, was named Herbert, a transition was occurring. Nevertheless, Uchtred retained some status as a free peasant, for in his quitclaim to Fountains he negotiated spiritual benefits for himself and Herbert:

> *Et nos in uita nostra erimus participes fraternitatis et communis beneficii ecclesie de font' et post decessum nostrum monachi persoluent plenarium seruicium pro nobis sicut fieri solet pro monacho uel conuerso domus de font'*[209]

Indicative of the position of another Uchtred, Uchtred *filius Ramkilli*, was his benefaction to Fountains Abbey of twelve acres in one grant and additions in other charters in Heaton.[210]

Pontefract Priory's charters also provided a stage for peasants with this insular personal name, as when Uchtred *de Walleya* attested one of the priory's charters relating to Marsden in 1216.[211] Other instruments for Midgley were witnessed in the late twelfth century by Uchtred *de Birkewait* and Uchtred *de Mirefeld*.[212] Associated with Scarborough were the instruments attested by Uchtred *de Wiverdethorph*.[213]

Moving into the county and bishopric of Durham, bishop Hugh in 1154x1195 confirmed to Uchtred son of Uchtred *de Wdeshende* land in Little Lumley given to Uchtred by Uchtred *de Lumleya*.[214] In 1190x1195, Hugh transferred to Simon *hostiarius* all the land in Heighington which Uchtred *filius Ormi* had once held; since the consideration was forty marks, the land must have comprised a substantial amount.[215]

The influence of kinship on perpetuating this particular insular personal name might be detected in Hugh's (1154x1195) confirmation of land in Lumley to Uchtred son of Uchtred *de Wdeshende*, the land having been received by Uchtred from another Uchtred, Uchtred *de Lumleya* and his brother, Osbert.[216]

Further north, in Northumberland, Uchtred *de Eslinton'* acted several times as a witness in charters in favour of Brinkburn Priory relating to lands in Over Felton, Bockenfield, Eshott, and Little Framlington in 1244–1263.[217] In that county in 1279–80, Uchtred *filius Hugonis* fell from his horse and drowned and the house of Uchtred *de Vall'* was burgled.[218] The persistence of this name into the late thirteenth century in Northumberland suggests its acceptance into the conventional corpus of personal names. Indeed, that surmise seems to be confirmed by the relationship between one Uchtred and his father Hugh. Moreover, the persistence of these insular names into the late thirteenth century in Northumberland is represented also by Waldef (Waltheof) *filius Dolfini* who was accused before the same justices of killing his wife, Agnes, in the fields of West Swinburn.[219]

The forename was represented too in the urban north, in Newcastle. Here, in the early thirteenth century the wardens of the Tyne bridge conveyed land to Uchtred *pontenarius* – for maintenance of the bridge, a position of some importance, for allusion was also made to him as Uchtred *Brige Wrigte* in 1250x1259.[220] In the middle of that century, 1240x1251, Brightmer son of Uchtred *Nedelmoder* sold land in the borough to Walter *Peper*. Here we encounter not only the persistence of Uchtred as a forename, but the continuity of an insular tradition of naming in both Uchtred and Brightmer.[221] Land in nearby Gateshead was acquired *c*.1260 by Uchtred *Suiller*.[222]

In the middle of the thirteenth century, Uchtred son of Robert *de Buetteby* was captured as a cattle rustler, attempting to sell two oxen and a cow at Corbridge market.[223] The acceptance of the insular personal name is confirmed by its attribution to the son of a father with a Continental-Germanic name, Robert. The same justices in eyre in the county heard that Uchtred *faber* of Buckland had been mortally injured by a stray arrow, that Uchtred Burnel had discovered the body of Mariota, of the death of Uchtred *carpentarius* and of Uchtred *le brasur*'s case of burglary.[224]

Any assessment of the extent of the survival of the forename depends on the recitation of such illustrative evidence. It was reported to the royal justices in Yorkshire that Herbert *filius Uctred'* in 1208 found a corpse which had drowned.[225] In 1216, Uchtred *de Walleya* attested a charter concerning Marsden in the West Riding.[226] In the late twelfth century, another Uchtred in Yorkshire had named his son Elias, a free tenant of a messuage and fourteen acres in Bolton, but the charter was witnessed by Uchtred lord of Paththorn.[227] For land in Over Felton in Northumberland a charter of 1263 was attested by Uchtred *de Eslinton'*, who had also witnessed charters concerning land at Bockenfield, Eshott and Little Framlington in 1245.[228] Belonging to the same peasant status was Uchtred *Long*, tenant of two bovates in Kirkleatham in Yorkshire.[229]

Across the Pennines, the insular forename extended through the border area. When Adam *de Tindale* made a benefaction to Lanercost Priory in 1164x1168 his written instrument was attested by Uchtred *filius Leuenod'* and Uchtred *filius Ricardi*.[230] As late as 1270x1289, Uchtred *de Tueregles* witnessed a charter relating to land in Dumfries.[231]

Thus persisting equally in the far north-west, Uchtred was manifest in transactions in land in the late twelfth and early thirteenth centuries in Amounderness. In Eccleston, in 1242x1268, a perch of land was renounced by William *filius Hutredi filii Suani*.[232] Before then, in 1200x1230, Robert *filius Hutredi* made a benefaction of four acres in Cottam and some time before 1268 Adam *filius Hutredi* furnished all his land in Halton to Cockersand Abbey.[233] One of the tenants (*homines*) of Matilda in Whittingham was Richard *filius Hutredi* who was attorned to the abbey in 1217x 1221.[234] The abbey also acquired one and a half acres from Uchtred *de Kempedale* in Hutton in 1220x 1250.[235] In the same vill Ughtred *de Derbyshyre* – and so seemingly not originally of this region – held land in 1268x1279.[236] At nearby Cuerden, Uchtred *Balle* was a tenant in 1212x1250.[237] Another Uchtred had been a tenant in Wrightington some time before 1259x1268, where also Waltheof had held a house.[238] Together with Ramkell and Tokke (Toki), Uchtred was a tenant in Ainsdale, each holding a toft before 1190x1213.[239] There too, about the same time, Uchtred *filius Suani* – if not the same Uchtred as above – held a headland.[240] Another benefactor of Cockersand Abbey, in 1184x1210, Waltheof *de Quitinton'*, indeed domiciled in Whithington, was the son of another Uchtred.[241] In the south of the county, Uchtred *clericus filius Gospatrik' de Samlesbury* held land in Whalley confirmed to him by Roger de Lacy, constable of Chester.[242] Another *clericus*, Uchtred *clericus de Whalleye* attested a charter relating to Spotland.[243]

Nor is it surprising that the name was revived within a peasant kinship which had adopted newer names, as represented by Uchtred *filius Andree* who, conjoined with his wife, sold two and a half acres of land in Pontefract to the priory there.[244] Furthermore, the personal name was not confined to the peasantry, for in the region of Bolton in North Yorkshire in the late twelfth century, to Uchtred *de Paththorn* pertained the lordship of Pathorn (*dominus de Paththorn*).[245] It was also established as a byname in the context of a lower status, in, for example, the form of the Roger *Uchtred* who along with Roger *Haldan* attested a charter in favour of Pontefract Priory relating to land in Scarborough.[246]

It is not anomalous, consequently, that Ughtred developed into a surname in the later middle ages, but interesting that it was associated with a gentle family. In the late fourteenth century, Sir Thomas Ughtred, knight, acquired Lepington manor.[247] The Ughtred family had connections with this place in the late thirteenth century for Robert *Uhttred*, knight, had attested a charter relating to this Yorkshire village in the first decade of the fourteenth century.[248] Sir Robert *Ughtred*, knight, made transactions in land in Foston in 1293–4.[249] Incidentally, how paradigmatic some of these names became of Northern society is perhaps reflected in the Benedictine monk, Uchtred of Bolton, a monk of Durham Cathedral Priory who studied at Oxford in the 1360s.[250]

Finally, in addition to its relatively more frequent occurrence in the North, what is also distinctive of the northern persistence of this byname, derived from the phonemic representation of the *nomen*, is the voicing of the fricative phonemes in the North. Whereas in Worcestershire, in south Lincolnshire and in other areas in the Midlands the *c* or *g* was omitted – thus *Utred* or *Outred*, or hypercorrectly *Hutred* or *Houtred* – in the North the phoneme was included and sounded – *Ughtred, Uctred*. The bynames and surnames resulting in the different regions thus diverged.

Hypocorisms in written materials

In 1307, at Holne on the manor of Wakefield, *Litel Dobbe* of Carlecotes was presented for the escape of eight beasts. Such informality of naming – reflecting colloquial usage – was generally deployed sporadically throughout the Latin register in the Wakefield rolls.[251] From time to time, however, the clerks employed colloquial forms of identification more profusely in these court rolls. Indeed, what the written materials from the North demonstrate overall is a greater propensity for the colloquial form of naming to infiltrate into the written record. Hypocorisms in particular are not uncommonly encountered in these written sources in the North, whereas in other regions their intrusion into the written record remained extraordinary. Whilst written records in the North were composed in the same Latin register as in the south, an environment in which Middle English had a greater impact on the recording of names – as in the bynames indicating relationship or those derived from occupation – allowed also the penetration of colloquial forms of naming more liberally into the written record.

Three further characteristics of this phenomenon in the North can be perceived. First, the hypocorisms appeared in the written record from an early time, and secondly, they pervaded a variety of forms of document – charters, court proceedings, tax lists *et al*. Exemplary is Watte *Withtolf'* who acted as an attorney for an essoin in the pleas before the King in Yorkshire in 1201.[252] Northern hypocorisms thus infiltrated into the formal record even of the *curia Regis*.[253] In like manner, still at this early time, other Yorkshire pet-forms entered into the formal record of the pleas of the Crown: in 1218–19 Dobbe *Winter* was outlawed for homicide; Custe *filia Willelmi* issued an appeal for rape; Masse *faber* was appealed for battery and robbery; another Dobbe discovered the drowned body of his brother in the river Derwent; Gotte *le Taillour* was slain by William; Dobbe *de Deneby* appealed Dande *Colly* for breach of the peace; and Dike *Dale* was suspected of robbery.[254] In the same record of the proceedings of this high-level court, the vill of Adwick gave testimony that a certain Dawe was responsible for a homicide.[255] Their persistent use in the speech community resulted in their infiltration into royal financial records, in which references were recorded to Hiche *filius Simonis* and Hande *de Thirlewelle* in 1218–19, Wilkin *Rous* in 1220–1, and Gemme *frater* Gilberti, Hulle *frater Willelmi* and Hudde *del Crag* in the 1250s.[256]

It is possible to attribute the intrusion of the pet-forms to the less formal character of court records, but more likely to have exerted the principal influence was the colloquial environment in which the local speech community referred to people habitually by informal names which through the sheer force of these speech acts entered into the written record. The third characteristic is that, although the high proportion of female diminutive forms has been remarked upon in northern lists (including taxation records), male hypocorisms were deployed as frequently in other records.

Descriptions in charters (and their copies in cartularies) also made references by hypocorism, although more often when referring to tenants rather than grantors or beneficiaries, one example being Dikke *filius Magge* in a charter replicated in the

Whalley Coucher.[257] In the same cartulary, charters recited that Orm *de Faleng'* had five sons, one of whom, Robert, was alluded to by that polite register, but also by the hypocorism Dobbe.[258] In a charter relating to the area around Middlewich in Cheshire, reference was made to Dawe *de Wetenhale* in 1260x 1277.[259]

More expansively, the rental of 1251 of Cockersand Priory contains numerous hypocorisms in what would, at least further south, have been a record of some formality, so that the profusion of hypocorisms perhaps suggests, as with the Wakefield court rolls below, less reluctance to use hypocorisms in written records in the North. Amongst the male tenants of Cockersand in 1251 thus occurred eleven Dobbes, two each of Hudde/Houde and Hulle, three of Dik(k)e/Dikre, and single incidences of Goppe, Alecok, Beke, Bimme, Kitte, Doge, Gille, Willekin, Lawe and Gibbe.[260]

Superficially, such an area of investigation may seem trifling, but its importance has been intimated by both Cecily Clark and Peter McClure, not precisely in a medieval context, but in a wider perspective.[261] Perhaps a consideration of the medieval evidence can be deemed worthwhile, not least for its significance for northern culture. It is, of course, our misfortune that the usage of such designations is largely confined to the speech community and that medieval records, whatever their provenance, are still, to some extent, formal and thus predominantly exclude these more colloquial forms – but not exclusively, it must be added.[262] Whether court rolls or taxation lists, the records are formal to the extent that their writers employed the highest register of language, Latin, and the *nomen* is almost universally inscribed in its Latin form.

In fact, of course, it is quite apparent that hypocorisms were widely used in Middle English personal naming, from the evidence of bynames and surnames derived from personal names and in patronymic forms, which almost exclusively incorporate as an element a hypocorism, and from the evidence of literary texts.

And þat a wiste by Wille to Watekyn he tolde hit
And al þat he wiste by Watte tolde hit Wille aftur[263]
Further on, Langland described alliteratively:

Dawe þe dikere, with a dosoyne harlotes...
Hicke þe hackenayman hit his hod aftur
And bade Bitte þe bochere ben on his syde...
Robin þe ropere aryse they bisouhte[264]

Consequently, the formal Latin, even at its lowest level, largely conceals the hypocorisms of the speech community – or apparently so.[265] In an entirely male context (admissions to the freedom of the borough of Leicester), the local clerks, although employing Latin (but also some French in a lower register), did employ some hypocorisms. In 1196, in the first extant roll, the admissions or pledges included Wilke *Waterman*, Wilke *Smalbon*, *Colinus de foleuille* (thus a Latinization of the French hypocorism Colin), in 1198 Wilke *Ouernon*, Hiche *de Sadint'*, Viel *filius Ailvin* [sic] *de derbi* (Viel being a hypocorism of Vitalis), in 1208 Wilke *Ston*, in 1210 Wilke *filius Rogeri clerici*, and in 1219 Coste *Sanne*.[266] Although exceptional in their incidence in the rolls, these hypocorisms reflect more accurately the naming of people within the speech community. Occasionally, the formal register of the rolls adopted Latinized forms of hypocorisms, so that on Merton College's manor of Kibworth Harcourt in the late thirteenth century, the peasant Robert Sibile the younger was constantly identified in the court rolls as *Paruus Robertus*.[267]

Inadvertent introductions of hypocorisms might intrude into quite formal records. For example, the survey of the estate of the Bishop of Ely compiled in 1222 is engrossed into a volume and written in a very well-formed charter hand. The formal Latin text renders the *nomina* in extended Latin form. When, however, a marginal memorandum was added in an early-fourteenth-century hand, it reverted to an informality not exhibited in the original engrossment: *De Hicche uenatore .xv.s.* The formal *Ricardus* of the original text is counterpoised against the transgressive hypocorism of the addition.[268]

Outside the North, pet-forms of names occasionally insinuated into royal documents with local origins. Thus a villein tenant enumerated at Tidenham in Gloucestershire in 1306, at the lower end of the size of holdings, was recorded in an inquisition *post mortem* as Tibbe *de Fraxino* in 1306.[269] At Alberbury in Shropshire, a taxpayer assessed at 1s. 1d. was identified simply as Judde without any byname.[270] Hypocorisms were inserted into written records in other areas of England, but unusually.

As remarked above, even the formal records of the dispensation of royal justice might not always be completely immune from intrusions of the naming processes of the speech community. In 1212, Wille *Brun*, accused of homicide, purged himself by trial by water and abjured the realm.[271] In the same formal record of the proceedings of the royal justices, Hobbe *Kittere* was also outlawed for murder in 1221 in Worcestershire and Hobbe *Golightly* hung in the same year in adjacent Warwickshire because he was a recognized thief.[272]

Consequently, these forms intruded into the records of royal inquisitions in Lancashire in the early fourteenth century.[273] So Joppe *de Aula* was tenant of a plot of land in Chipping in 1310 and Hull son of Robert was described as holding a messuage, quarter of a burgage and some selions of land in West Derby in 1323.[274] There too in 1323, Dauwe *faber* was attributed one and a half acres of land.[275] Also in West Derby, Gille son of Hugh, Dicon, and Hulle son of John were recorded as holding small amounts of land in 1323.[276] Another Dicon, son of Fille, was a tenant of a messuage and substantial land in Crosby in 1323, and there too in the same year Hogge son of Bymme held similar land.[277] At Everton at the same time, Dike *faber* also held that same amount of land.[278] A messuage and smaller amount of land was held in Skerton then by Lambe son of Bunte, whilst Dande *de Couhop* developed a cattle herd in Blackburnshire.[279]

Whilst pet-forms were thus not absent entirely from written records outside the North, what is distinctive of the northern onomastic zone is their profusion in written records. Some indication of their liberal usage in written records is contained in the rolls of the city and county courts of Chester in 1259–60. Pledges were extended in 1259–60 by Hulle *de Alperam*, Dawe *prepositus*, Silke *de Weston*, Hiche *Fleg'*, Honde *serviens*, Adekin son of Honde, Hobbe *Poket* and Hobbekin *de Bagal'*.[280] Contemporaneously in that forum, Hulle son of Geoffrey was accused of the theft of oxen

Hypocorism	Byname	Date	Litigation	Page[291]	Comment
Hanne	*de Wlvedale*	1274	leased mill	3	
	de Goukethorp	1275	took land	30	
	de Nortwode	1277	pledge, timber	161, 165	
	de Bothemley	1277	battery	165	
	prepositus	1277,1285	pledge	165, 199	
	Packe	1277	false measure	179	
	garcio	1284		183	
	Sossan	1284	pledge	184	
	de Hyperun	1286	pledge	213	
	de Holgate	1296	trespass	245	
	le Pinder	1297	pledge	281	Henry *le Pinder* 1297 in battery, p. 282
	Bassard	1297	theft of sheep	287	
	molendinarius	1297	transferred land	290	
Hannecok	*(le) Nonne*	1285–6, 1297	pledge, transferred land, brushwood	203, 223, 225, 266, 292	Henry *le Nonne*: leased land, transferred land, juror, 1286, 1297; pp. 204, 216, 225, 279-80
	ultra rivulum	1286	plaintiff	211	
	le Harpor	1286	defendant	211	Henry *le Harpor* in the same case: pp. 212, 214
	Coltenote	1297	*licencia concordandi*	297	

Table 9 Hanne in medieval Wakefield

and Judde *Chubbe* of theft and murder.[281] Two other defendants for lesser offences were Hulle *Colfox* and Honde *SeliSaule*.[282] In a case of battery, Brun *de Bikerton'* impleaded Philkin *de Bikerton'* and his brother, Hobekin, all denoted by their hypocorisms.[283] Accusations of thefts and robberies were levelled against Wilkin *de Horton*, Geffe son of Robert, and Wilkin *le Best*.[284] Although the former Wilkin and also Geffe were described as 'under age', none of the other felons identified above were other than mature adults, so hypocorisms were not merely attached to the young. Indeed, Honde *de Aldeton* was described as bailiff.[285] Another Honde – Honde *le yetter* – was involved in a dispute about free common in a mine.[286] Amongst those accused of illicitly raising a hedge was enumerated Dik son of Emma *de Honeford*, whilst also in 1260 Wilkin son of Edda appeared as a defendant and another Wilkin – Wilkin *Witinhod* – was remanded in custody.[287] When Hulle *Pitte* died from falling from a tree, his body was discovered by Adekin *Redbird*.[288] Two other dead bodies were happened upon by Hanne *Bakestre*.[289] The body of a *garcifer* named Wilkin involved suspicion of murder, but Hulle *de Newhall* died accidentally on his way to Wich.[290] The *scriptor* of the court rolls in 1259–60 thus recognized the short forms of the forenames of numerous – but not all – litigants and pledges, his inscription reflecting colloquial speech.

The most frequent occurrence of hypocorisms occurred in the court rolls of the manor of Wakefield in the late thirteenth century. Depending on the clerk who wrote the rolls, there is a proliferation of these colloquial forms. Distinctive amongst the repeated hypocorisms are Hanne and Han(ne)cok, reflecting colloquial forms of Henry, as indicated in the tabulation above.

Other frequent male hypocorisms in the Wakefield court rolls in the last quarter of the thirteenth century included: Nelle; Alcok; Hycke; Geppe; Luvecok; Gelle; Hudde; and Bate; whilst there was occasional usage of Heyne, Hulle, Hebbe, Huchun, Wilkoc, Jacke, Hudde, Hobbe, Watte, Nik, Wylle and Dande.[292] In the court rolls of a few months in 1286 alone, for example, are encountered Geppe *del Dene*, Gelle *Pymerige*, Gelle *Cussyng*, Hyk *serviens*, Gelle *Alcok*, Hancok *Nonne*, Locok *de Heppewrth*, Heyne *Forestarius*, Alcok *del Clyf*, and Hanne *de Holgate*.[293] In later rolls, there was a reversion to the more formal recording of forenames in their full Latin equivalents, but occasionally relapses reintroduced hypocorisms. Thus in 1339, Nabbe *Hare* offended against the vert in Hipperholme and Nabbe *Ploghman* raised the hue and in 1340 in Stanley the consummately named Dik *Riccard* – suspiciously suggesting a nickname – was presented for not making suit of court.[294]

The Wakefield court rolls of the late thirteenth century thus reveal that hypocoristic forms of address were rife amongst the peasantry, such that some of the clerks of the rolls felt compelled frequently to record those forms rather than the more formal *nomen*. What remains unclear is whether these more colloquial forms were employed through all social groups or were confined to the peasantry. Is it possible that the peasantry, by some inverse form of cultural independence, marked themselves off by this continuous use of hypocorisms and that these colloquial forms of address were distinctive of an independent peasant cultural tradition which was not emulative?[295]

Here, however, gender is reasserted, for, in some records at least, there seems to be less reluctance to attribute hypocorisms to females than to men, although it must be stated that the proportion of females assigned such hypocorisms is still small and the Wakefield court rolls and the Cockersand rental illustrate that male hypocorisms were not totally excluded from written records, at least in the North. If, for example, we take the Poll Tax of 1379 for the West Riding of Yorkshire, very few men indeed are identified by a hypocorism, but hypocorisms are not unusual amongst females. Magota is by far the most common, but not isolated.[296] Taking, for example, the borough of Pontefract, there were twelve Magotas, two Sibotas, four Emmotas, a Flissota, two Ibotas, two Cissotas, a Diota and an Elisota; and thus the Poll Tax enumerated there Emmota *Seruiens*, Magota *Seruiens*, Cissota *Tresch*, Cissota *Seymster* and Diota *de Bongate*. Most of these women were not, however, singletons, but married.[297] In general, the corpus of these female hypocorisms in the West Riding Poll Tax seems to include Cissota, Diota, Elisota, Elota, Emmota, Evota, Flissota, Gillota, Ibota, Isota, Magota, Mariota, Phillipota, Senota, Sibota, and Tillota.

The nomen in the North

From this accumulative, but admittedly impressionistic, evidence, it is apparent that the North remained marked off by distinctive categories of *nomen*. Not only was it characterized by particular forms of insular personal name, but also by a longer persistence of those *nomina*. Consequently, some – paradigmatically Uchtred – became absorbed into the continuous process of naming and bynaming. Whilst the level of survival was not absolutely high, it certainly exceeded continuity in southerly regions. Whilst hypocorisms were presumably employed throughout the country, what differentiates the North is their penetration into semi-formal written records, those documents composed in dog-Latin. Both phenomena seem associated with a special vernacular environment in the northern zone.

Notes

1   C. Clark, 'Women's names in post-Conquest England: observations and speculations', *Speculum* 53 (1978), pp. 223–51 repr. in C. Clark, *Words, Names and History. Collected Papers* ed. P. Jackson (Cambridge, 1995), pp. 117–43; M. T. Clanchy, *England and its Rulers 1066–1272. Foreign Lordship and National Identity* (London, 1983), p. 57.
2   Clark, 'Women's names'.
3   D. Postles, 'Cultures of peasant naming in twelfth-century England', *Medieval Prosopography* 18 (1997), pp. 25–54.
4   J. Insley, 'Some aspects of regional variation in early Middle English nomenclature', *Leeds Studies in English. Studies in Honour of Kenneth Cameron* n.s. 18 (1987), pp. 183–99.
5   C. P. Lewis, 'The Domesday jurors', *Haskins Society Journal* 5 (1993), pp. 17–44.
6   A. Williams, *The English and the Norman Conquest* (Woodbridge, 1995), pp. 71–125.
7   H. S. Offler, ed., *Durham Episcopal Charters* (Surtees Society clxxix, 1968), p. 122.
8   F. M. Stenton, 'English families and the Norman Conquest' repr. in his *Preparatory to Anglo-Saxon England* ed. D. M. Stenton (Oxford, 1970); Williams, *English and the Norman Conques*, pp. 96–7.

9   J. C. Atkinson, ed., *Cartularium Abbathiae de Whiteby* volume 1 (Surtees Society lxix, 1879), pp. 35–7 (nos xxix–xxx), Alan's benefaction being *c*.1174. Gospatrick had a Welsh etymology.
10   Farrer, *Early Yorkshire Charters*, I, p. 65 (64).
11   Farrer, *Early Yorkshire Charters*, I, p. 62 (63).
12   Farrer, *Early Yorkshire Charters*, I, pp. 75, 83 (74, 83).
13   J. Burton, *English Episcopal Acta V York 1070–1154* (Oxford, 1988), pp. 87–8 (114).
14   Farrer, *Early Yorkshire Charters*, I, p. 59 (57).
15   Farrer, *Early Yorkshire Charters*, I, pp. 33–4 (37).
16   D. E. Greenway, *Charters of the Honour of Mowbray, 1107–1191* (British Academy Records of Social and Economic History n.s. 1, 1972), p. 75 (101).
17   Greenway, *Mowbray Charters*, pp. 78–9 (106).
18   Greenway, *Mowbray Charters*, p. 252 (396).
19   Greenway, *Mowbray Charters*, p. 81 (109); below for a brief consideration of 'hybridity' in naming.
20   Burton, *EEA V York*, p. 86 (113).
21   Greenway, *Mowbray Charters*, p. 85 (112).
22   Greenway, *Mowbray Charters*, p. 93 (123).
23   Greenway, *Mowbray Charters*, p. 102 (133).
24   Greenway, *Mowbray Charters*, pp. 250–2 (392–5).
25   R. Bartlett, *The Making of Europe. Conquest, Colonization and Cultural Change, 950–1350* (Harmondsworth, 1994), pp. 271–80, for this mutability and contemporary transformations of personal naming.
26   Bodl. MS Fairfax 9, fo. 7v. (*Donatio Willelmi filii Astini de cultura sua de Trehauleghe cum aliis tenementis*).
27   Bodl. MS Fairfax 9, fo. 9v. (*Donatio Ade Murdac de .ij. bouatis terre*).
28   Greenway, *Mowbray Charters*, pp. 154–5 (219).
29   Greenway, *Mowbray Charters*, p. 172 (254).
30   Greenway, *Mowbray Charters*, pp. 173–4 (259) (i.e. two of five tenants), 230 (343).
31   Greenway, *Mowbray Charters*, p. 231 (360).
32   Greenway, *Mowbray Charters*, pp. 233–5 (364–5).
33   Greenway, *Mowbray Charters*, pp. 201–2 (308–9).
34   W. Greenwell, ed., *Boldon Buke. A Survey of the Possessions of the See of Durham made by Order of Bishop Hugh Pudsey in the Year M.C.LXXXIII* (Surtees Society, 25, 1852).
35   Greenwell, *Boldon Buke*, p. 19: but one wonders whether this represents confusion of long *s* and *f*, so that the patronym is derived from Figgi.
36   Reginald of Durham *Libellus de Vita et Miraculis S. Godrici, Heremitae de Finchale* ed. J. Stevenson (Surtees Society 20, 1847), p. 463 (ccx) is dated 1175.
37   R. C. Van Caenigem, ed., *English Lawsuits from William I to Richard I* (2 volumes, Selden Society 106–7, 1990–1), II, p. 364 (no. 403).
38   *Libellus de Vita et Miraculis S. Godrici*, pp. 422–3 (clii, cliv).
39   *Libellus de Vita et Miraculis S. Godrici*, pp. 434–5 (clxxvii).
40   A. M. Oliver, ed., *Early Deeds relating to Newcastle upon Tyne* (Surtees Society cxxxvii, 1924), p. 9 (1).
41   Oliver, *Early Deeds ... Newcastle upon Tyne*, p. 36 (45).
42   Oliver, *Early Deeds ... Newcastle upon Tyne*, p. 44 (58).
43   Oliver, *Early Deeds ... Newcastle upon Tyne*, p. 68 (95).
44   G. W. S. Barrow, 'Northern English society in the twelfth and thirteenth centuries', *Northern History* 4 (1969), pp. 1–28.

45 C. T. Clay, ed., *Three Yorkshire Assize Rolls for the Reigns of King John and King Henry III* (YASRS xliv, 1911 for 1910), p. 1.

46 D. M. Stenton, *Pleas Before the King or his Justices, 1198–1212* IV (Selden Society 84, 1967), pp. 95, 103 (3411, 3448).

47 Stenton, *Pleas before the King or his Justices* III (Selden Society 83, 1967), p. 5 (2523).

48 D. M. Stenton, ed., *Rolls of the Justices in Eyre being the Rolls of the Pleas and Assizes for Yorkshire in 3 Henry III (1218–19)* (Selden Society 56, 1937), p. 272.

49 Stenton, *Rolls of the Justices in Eyre for Yorkshire 1218–19*, p. 242 (649).

50 Stenton, *Rolls of the Justices in Eyre for Yorkshire 1218–19*, pp. 26–7 (57), 29 (60), 35–6 (80) and 70–1 (172).

51 Stenton, *Pleas before the King or his Justices* III, p. 125 (no. 895).

52 Stenton, *Pleas before the King or his Justices* IV, p. 103 (no. 3448).

53 Stenton, *Pleas before the King or his Justices* III, pp. 141–2 (nos 936–7).

54 Stenton, *Pleas before the King or his Justices* III, p. 140 (no. 934).

55 Stenton, *Pleas before the King or his Justices* III, p. 156.

56 Stenton, *Pleas before the King or his Justices* IV, p. 101 (no. 3439).

57 Stenton, *Pleas before the King or his Justices* IV, p. 101 (no. 3440).

58 Stenton, *Pleas before the King or his Justices* IV, pp. 108 and 111 (nos 3465 and 3481).

59 Stenton, *Rolls of the Justices in Eyre for Yorkshire 1218–19*, p. 214 (no. 536).

60 Stenton, *Rolls of the Justices in Eyre for Yorkshire 1218–19*, p. 382 (no. 1062).

61 Stenton, *Pleas before the King or his Justices* IV, pp. 113 and 117 (nos 3488 and 3505).

62 BL Add. MS 40,008, fos 76r–83r.

63 BL Add. MS 40,008, fo. 88r.

64 BL Add. MS 40,008, fos. 141r–142r.

65 BL Add. MS 40,008, fo. 43r. (*propter homagium suum et seruicium … unde quinque Carucate terre faciunt feudum unius militis*).

66 Bodl. Fairfax MS 9, fo. 9v.

67 Bodl. Fairfax MS 9, fos 44r–45r.

68 Bodl. Top Yorks. MS c 72, fos 70v–71r.

69 J. Brownbill, ed., *The Coucher Book of Furness Abbey*, II, ii (Chetham Society 2nd ser. 76), p. 296 (5).

70 C. T. Clay, ed., *Early Yorkshire Charters* 5 (Yorkshire Archaeological Society Extra Series 11, 1936), p. 59 (149): *coram baronibus in placitis Richem' recitari feci*.

71 Brownbill, *Furness*, II, i (Chetham Society n.s. 74, 1915), p. 232 (1).

72 J. Wilson, ed., *The Register of the Priory of St Bees* (Surtees Society, 126, 1915), pp. 62 (32), 84 (52), 137 (100–1).

73 W. Farrer, *The Cartulary of Cockersand Abbey...*, III, i (Chetham Society 56, 1905), pp. 770–1 (10) and 823 (5).

74 Farrer, *Cockersand*, III, i, pp. 779 (22) and 783 (28).

75 Farrer, *Cockersand*, III, i, pp. 771–5.

76 Farrer, *Cockersand*, III, ii (Chetham Society n.s. 57, 1905), pp. 931–7 (2–10).

77 Farrer, *Cockersand*, II, i (Chetham Society, n.s. 40, 1898), pp. 453–7 (8–13).

78 Farrer, *Cockersand*, II, i, p. 457 (13); it's not clear how these events relate to *Cockersand*, I, i, p. 190: Waltheof *de Pulton'* quitclaiming half a bovate in 1240x1268.

79 Farrer, *Cockersand*, II, i, p. 421 (15).

80 Farrer, *Cockersand*, III, ii, p. 1017 (2).

81 Farrer, *Cockersand*, III, iii, pp. 1219–29.

82 J. T. Fowler, ed. *Chartularium Abbathie de Novo Monasterio* (Surtees Society lxvi, 1878), pp. 268–9.

83   G. J. Turner & H. E. Salter, eds, *The Register of St. Augustine's Abbey, Canterbury, Commonly Called the Black Book* (2 volumes, British Academy Records of Social and Economic History 2–3, 1915, 1924), part 1, p. 23.

84   M. G. Snape, ed., *English Episcopal Acta* 24 *Durham 1153–1195* (Oxford, 2002), p. 90 (104).

85   J. Burton, *EEA* V*York*, pp. 40–1 (44).

86   Snape, *EEA* 24 *Durham*, pp. 12, 23, 29, 68, 84 (13, 33, 75, 97).

87   Snape, *EEA* 24 *Durham*, p. 84 (97).

88   Farrer, *Cockersand*, I, i, p. 199.

89   Farrer, *Cockersand*, II, ii, p. 719.

90   W. A. Hulton, *The Coucher Book or Chartulary of Whalley Abbey* (4 volumes, Chetham Society 10–11, 16, 20, 1847–9), III, pp. 653, 656–7, 662, 664, 686 (19, 22–3, 28, 31, 57).

91   See above, pp. 68.

92   Stenton, *Rolls of the Justices in Eyre for Yorkshire 1218–19*, p. 214 (536).

93   Stenton, *Rolls of the Justices in Eyre for Yorkshire 1218–19*, p. 328 (901).

94   Farrer, *Cockersand*, I, i, p. 214.

95   Farrer, *Cockersand*, I, ii, p. 518.

96   Farrer, *Cockersand*, I, i, p. 260.

97   W. Page, ed., *Three Early Assize Rolls for the County of Northumberland, Saec. XIII* (Surtees Society 88, 1891), pp. 104, 113, 115.

98   Clay, *Three Yorkshire AssizeRolls*, pp. 32, 36, 38.

99   W. Page, ed., *The Chartulary of Brinkburn Priory* (Surtees Society xc, 1892), pp. 72–5 (lxxx–lxxxi, lxxxiii).

100 Bodl. MS Rawl 449, fo. 139r: *una cum corpore meo ibidem sepeliendo*.

101 These issues which are much exercising geographers are succinctly explained now by R. A. Dodgshon, *Society in Time and Space. A Geographical Perspective on Change* (Cambridge, 1998), esp. pp. 1–20.

102 William H. Sewell, 'The concept(s) of culture' in V. E. Bonnell & L. Hunt, eds, *Beyond the Cultural Turn* (Berkeley and Los Angeles, 1999), pp. 35–61.

103 M. de Certeau, *The Practice of Everyday Life* (Berkeley and Los Angeles, 1984); for a slightly more action-centred resistance, James C. Scott, *Domination and the Arts of Resistance. Hidden Transcripts* (New Haven, 1990); Scott, *Weapons of the Weak. Everyday Forms of Peasant Resistance* (New Haven, 1985).

104 M. Aceto, 'Ethnic personal names and multiple identities in Anglophone Caribbean speech communities', *Language in Society* 31 (2002), p. 603.

105 J. Insley, *Scandinavian Personal Names in Norfolk. A Survey based on Medieval Records and Place-Names* (Acta Academiae Regiae Gustavi Adolphi lxii, Uppsala, 1994), pp. 2–8; G. Fellows-Jensen, *Scandinavian Personal Names in Lincolnshire and Yorkshire* (Navnestudier 7, Copenhagen, 1968), pp. 3–5.

106 O. von Feilitzen, *The Pre-Conquest Personal Names of Domesday Book* (Nomina Germanica 3, Uppsala, 1937), p. 184; T. Forssner, *Continental-Germanic Personal Names in England in Old and Middle English Times* (Uppsala, 1916), p. 8: possibly C-G.

107 Insley, *SPNN*, p. 8; Fellows-Jensen, *SPNLY*, pp. 5–6.

108 Insley, *SPNN*, pp. 19–23; Fellows-Jensen, *SPNLY*, pp. 14–16.

109 Insley, *SPNN*, pp. 22–3 for this contracted form of Ar(n) ketil and the difference of syncopated and unsyncopated forms.

110 Insley, *SPNN*, pp. 86–8; Fellows-Jensen, *SPNLY*, p. 44.

111 Feilitzen, *PCPNDB*, p. 200: possibly either OE or Anglo-Scand.

112 Insley, *SPNN*, pp. 98–107; Fellows-Jensen, *SPNLY*, p. 60. Bóndi as a personal name is not frequent in Yorkshire.

113 Insley, *SPNN*, p. 279; Fellows-Jensen, *SPNLY*, pp. 179–80.
114 Feilitzen, *PCPNDB*, p. 219: O Ir etymology.
115 Feilitzen, *PCPNDB*, p. 233: OE etymology.
116 Feilitzen, *PCPNDB*, pp. 225–6: Anglo-Scand. etymology.
117 Feilitzen, *PCPNDB*, p. 233: OE etymology.
118 Feilitzen, *PCPNDB*, p. 233: OE.
119 Feilitzen, *PCPNDB*, p. 242: OE Ealdwulf.
120 Prior's Kitchen, Durham, 1 Finc 1 (1197x1217): Elgi held 2 bovates.
121 Presumably from Anglo-Scand *Feggi*: Insley, *SPNN*, p. 121; Fellows-Jensen, *SPNLY*, p. 81.
122 Insley, *SPNN*, pp. 124–5; Fellows-Jensen, *SPNLY*, p. 85. Apparently frequent in Yorks.
123 Insley, *SPNN*, pp. 129–31; Fellows-Jensen, *SPNLY*, pp. 89–95. Frequent in Yorks. and Lincs.; less so in Norfolk.
124 Insley, *SPNN*, pp. 154–6, where Anglo-Scand and OE etymons are considered.
125 Feilitzen, *PCPNDB*, pp. 266–9: OE.
126 Feilitzen, *PCPNDB*, pp. 269–73.
127 Insley, *SPNN*, pp. 142–3; Fellows-Jensen, *SPNLY*, pp. 107–8: more frequent in the northern Danelaw than East Anglia.
128 Insley, *SPNN*, pp. 186–92; Fellows-Jensen, *SPNLY*, pp. 126–8. Widespread in England.
129 Feilitzen, *PCPNDB*, pp. 287–8: OE.
130 Feilitzen, *PCPNDB*, p. 290.
131 Feilitzen, *PCPNDB*, p. 290.
132 Insley, *SPNN*, pp. 256–63; Fellows-Jensen, *SPNLY*, pp. 166–70. Frequent throughout England.
133 Feilitzen, *PCPNDB*, p. 317: OE.
134 Insley, *SPNN*, pp. 289–90; Fellows-Jensen, *SPNLY*, pp. 188–9.
135 Insley, *SPNN*, pp. 314–15; Fellows-Jensen, *SPNLY*, pp. 204–6. More frequent in northern England.
136 Feilitzen, *PCPNDB*, p. 340: OE.
137 Feilitzen, *PCPNDB*, pp. 340–1.
138 Insley, *SPNN*, pp. 323–4; Fellows-Jensen, *SPNLY*, pp. 227–8; Feilitzen, *PCPNDB*, p. 352.
139 Feilitzen, *PCPNDB*, p. 353: OE.
140 Insley, *SPNN*, pp. 325–6; Fellows-Jensen, *SPNLY*, pp. 230–1.
141 Feilitzen, *PCPNDB*, p. 368, had only Snelling.
142 Insley, *SPNN*, p. 354; Fellows-Jensen, *SPNLY*, pp. 274–5.
143 Insley, *SPNN*, pp. 356–60; Fellows-Jensen, *SPNLY*, pp. 276–82.
144 Insley, *SPNN*, pp. 371–6; Fellows Jensen, *SPNLY*, pp. 287–8.
145 Insley, *SPNN*, pp. 377–9; Fellows-Jensen, *SPNLY*, pp. 289–90.
146 Insley, *SPNN*, pp. 414–19; Fellows-Jensen, *SPNLY*, pp. 309–11.
147 Feilitzen, *PCPNDB*, p. 398: OE.
148 Insley, *SPNN*, pp. 437–9; Fellows-Jensen, *SPNLY*, pp. 321–4.
149 Insley, *SPNN*, pp. 433–7; Fellows-Jensen, *SPNLY*, 325–7. Syncopation of the second element to -*kel/-kil* predominated in the northern Danelaw, whereas the uncontracted form -*ketel* was concentrated in East Anglia.
150 Farrer, *Cockersand*, I, i, p. 141.
151 Farrer, *Cockersand*, I, i, p. 172.
152 Farrer, *Cockersand*, I, i, pp. 200–1.
153 Farrer, *Cockersand*, II, ii, p. 707.
154 Oliver, *Early Deeds … Newcastle upon Tyne*, pp. 117, 119 (183, 190).

155 Stenton, *Rolls of the Justices in Eyre ... Yorkshire in 3 Henry III (1218–19)*, pp. 272, 278 (732, 747).

156 M. T. Martin, *The Percy Chartulary* (Surtees Society 117, 1921), pp. 61 (cxvii), 108 (ccxcvii).

157 Bodl. MS Rawl 449, fos 98r–v.

158 Stenton, *Rolls of the Justices in Eyre ... Yorkshire in 3 Henry III (1218–19)*, p. 365 (1011, 1014).

159 Martin, *Percy Cartulary*, p. 127 (ccclxxxvi). For its occasional occurrence further south, Dolfin had held land in Warwickshire before 1185x1204: *Cat. Ancient Deeds* III, p. 74 (A4507).

160 Bodl.MS Rawl 449, fo. 94r.

161 Bodl. MS Rawl 449, fo. 94r.

162 Bodl. MS Rawl 449, fos 117r, 118r.

163 P. H. Reaney, *A Dictionary of British Surnames* ed. R. M. Wilson (3rd edn, Oxford, 1997), p. 309 (*sv* Mildred, Meldred) explains the etymology of insular OE *Mildðrwð*, the female saint, but its encounter in the north is normally masculine, and his explanation seems therefore not appropriate to the northern context. Maldred was more pertinently indicative of Scottish influence.

164 Snape, *EEA* 24 *Durham*, pp. 12, 23, 29 (13, 33). Williams, *The English and the Norman Conquest*. For this Meldred, see above.

165 Oliver, *Early Deeds ... Newcastle upon Tyne*, p. 113 (175–6).

166 Page, *Brinkburn Chartulary*, pp. 72–4 (lxxx–lxxxi).

167 R. Holmes, ed., *The Chartulary of St John of Pontefract* (2 volumes, YASRS 25, 30, 1899–1902), II, p. 673 (549).

168 J. M. Todd, ed., *The Lanercost Cartulary* (Surtees Society 203, 1997), pp. 62 (10), 76 (24), 78 (25–6), 85 (32), 86 (33), 98 (45), 99 (46), 100–102 (47–50), 109 (57), 129 (81), 136 (90), 151 (110–11), 154 (114), 163 (126), 163 (126), 189 (121), 334 (285), 398–9 (A1), 404–5 (A5).

169 The configurations of *Cumbria* are elucidated by C. Phythian-Adams, *Land of the Cumbrians. A Study in British Provincial Origins A.D. 400–1120* (Aldershot, 1996).

170 W. Brown, ed., *Cartularium Prioratus de Gyseburne, Ebor. Dioeceseos* (2 volumes, Surtees Society 86, 89, 1889–92), 1, pp. 318–19 (mcxl, mcxli).

171 Burton, *EEA* V *York*, p. 53 (63).

172 Clark, 'Women's names'.

173 See, for example, M. Brett, *The English Church under Henry I* (Oxford, 1975), pp. 219–21.

174 Burton, *EEA* V *York*, p. 20 (9).

175 Todd, *Lanercost Cartulary*, pp. 90 (36), 156 (116).

176 Snape, *EEA* 24 *Durham*, p. 25 (27).

177 Snape, *EEA* 24 *Durham*, p. 30 (34).

178 Snape, *EEA* 24 *Durham*, p. 71 (77).

179 Page, *Brinkburn Chartulary*, p. 28 (xxvi).

180 Brown, *Cartularium Prioratus de Gyseburne* 1, p. 218 (dccclxxva).

181 Brown, *Cartularium Prioratus de Gyseburne* 1, p. 318 (mcxl).

182 Brown, *Cartularium Prioratus de Gyseburne* 1, pp. 318–19 (mcxli).

183 Holmes, *Chartulary of St John of Pontefract* II, p. 462 (ccclxxviii).

184 That etymology – from *Le Swan/Swon/Sweyn* (OE) – is, for example, represented in Huntingdonshire and Suffolk: *Huntingdonshire*, pp. 7, 57, 63, 72, 76, 87, 93, 96, 99, 299; *Suffolk*, pp. 13, 14, 48.

185 C. Clark, 'Willelmus rex? Vel alius Willelmus?', *Nomina* 11 (1988 for 1987), pp. 7–33

186 W. N. Thompson, ed., *The Register of John de Halton Bishop of Carlisle* (2 vols, Canterbury & York Society xii–xiii, 1913), I, p. 202.

187 *Chancery Miscellanea* VIII (List & Index Society 105, 1972), p. 117.

188 *Cat. Ancient Deeds* I, p. 123 (A1061).
189 Stenton, *Pleas before the King or his Justices*, IV, p. 39 (2858).
190 Turner & Salter, *Register of St. Augustine's Abbey, Canterbury*, part 1, p. 106.
191 R. R. Darlington, ed., *The Cartulary of Worcester Cathedral Priory: (Register I)* (Pipe Roll Society 38, 1968), p. 72 (127).
192 M. Hollings, ed., *The Red Book of Worcester: Containing Surveys of the Bishop's Manors and Other Records Chiefly of the 12th and 13th Centuries* (Worcester Historical Society, 1934–50), pp. 58, 84, 86, 147, 420.
193 C. Harper-Bill, ed., *Dodnash Priory Charters* (Suffolk Record Society, Suffolk Charters 16, 1998), p. 35 (3).
194 V. Brown, ed., *Eye Priory Cartulary and Charters* (Suffolk Record Society, Suffolk Charters 12, 1992), p. 123 (136).
195 R. Mortimer, ed., *Stoke by Clare Cartulary, BL Cotton Appx. xxi* (4 volumes, Suffolk Record Society, Suffolk Charters 4–6, 1982–4), I, pp. 28, 119, 131 (137, 144).
196 *Cat. Ancient Deeds* I, p. 394 (C90); an action of account was initiated by John Outred of Wycombe (Bucks.) about the same time: *Chancery Miscellanea* III (List & Index Society, 1967), p. 179.
197 T.N.A. (P.R.O.) E179/135/14, mm. 5, 6, 7, 9, 11, 12, 15; E179/135/15, m. 3.
198 Greenway, *Mowbray Charters*, pp. 75 (101) and 78–9 (106).
199 Greenway, *Mowbray Charters*, p. 252 (396).
200 Burton, *EEA Acta* V *York*, pp. 97–8 (125–6).
201 Farrer, *Early Yorkshire Charters*, I, p. 61 (58–9).
202 Farrer, *Early Yorkshire Charters* I, p. 192 (235).
203 Stenton, *Rolls of the Justices in Eyre*, p. 284 (768).
204 Stenton, *Rolls of the Justices in Eyre*, p. 352 (969).
205 Stenton, *Rolls of the Justices in Eyre*, p. 201 (492).
206 Stenton, *Rolls of the Justices in Eyre*, p. 245 (643).
207 BL Add MS 40008, fo. 33r.
208 T. A. M. Bishop, 'Extents of the prebends of York (*c.*1295)' in *Miscellanea* IV (YASRS xciv, 1937), pp. 25, 28.
209 Bodl MS Rawl 449, fos 90r–v. The content of the charter suggests the resolution of some dispute.
210 Bodl. Rawl MS 449, fo. 106v.
211 Holmes, *Chartulary of St. John of Pontefract* II, pp. 364–5 (cclxxxiiid).
212 Holmes, *Chartulary of St. John of Pontefract* II, pp. 426–7 (cccxxiii–iv).
213 Holmes, *Chartulary of St. John of Pontefract* II, pp. 523, 541, 632 (ccccii, 432, 490).
214 Snape, *EEA* 24 *Durham* p. 140 (166).
215 Snape, *EEA* 24 *Durham*, p. 125 (148).
216 Snape, *EEA* 24 *Durham*, p. 140 (166).
217 Page, *Brinkburn Chartulary*, pp. 28, 55, 61, 64 (xxvi, lvi, lxii, lxvi).
218 Page, *Three Early Assize Rolls*, pp. 319, 344.
219 Page, *Three Early Assize Rolls*, p. 344.
220 Oliver, *Early Deeds … Newcastle upon Tyne*, pp. 74 (104), 118 (186).
221 Oliver, *Early Deeds … Newcastle upon Tyne*, p. 98 (146).
222 Oliver, *Early Deeds … Newcastle upon Tyne*, p. 109 (169).
223 Page, *Three Early Assize Rolls*, p. 77.
224 Page, *Three Early Assize Rolls*, pp. 88, 98–9, 104.
225 Stenton, *Pleas before the King or his Justices* IV, p. 96 (3414).
226 Holmes, *Chartulary of St. John of Pontefract* II, p. 365 (cclxxxiii).

227 *Pudsay Deeds*, pp. 87, 89 (2, 4).

228 Page, *Brinkburn Chartulary*, pp. 28, 55, 61, 64 (xxvi, lvi, lxii, lxvi).

229 Brown, *Cartularium Prioratus de Gyseburne* I, p. 109 (dcclxxvi).

230 Todd, *Lanercost Cartulary*, p. 62 (10).

231 Todd, *Lanercost Cartulary*, p. 253.

232 Farrer, *Cockersand*, I, i, p. 190.

233 Farrer, *Cockersand*, I, i, pp. 226, 228.

234 Farrer, *Cockersand*, I, i, p. 232.

235 Farrer, *Cockersand*, II, i, pp. 422–3.

236 Farrer, *Cockersand*, II, i, p. 447.

237 Farrer, *Cockersand*, II, i, p. 490.

238 Farrer, *Cockersand*, II, i, pp. 504–5.

239 Farrer, *Cockersand*, II, ii, pp. 578, 584.

240 Farrer, *Cockersand*, II, ii, p. 573.

241 Farrer, *Cockersand*, II, ii, p. 730.

242 Hulton, *Whalley Coucher Book* I, pp. 286–7; perhaps identical with Uchtred *de Samlesbury* at *Whalley Coucher* III, pp. 835–6 (vi–viii); IV, p. 1071 (iv).

243 Hulton, *Whalley Coucher* III, pp. 745, 747 (xxii, xxiv), 847 (xxii); IV, p. 953 (xvii).

244 Holmes, *Chartulary of St John of Pontefract* II, p. 572 (477).

245 *Pudsay Deeds*, pp. 87, 89 (2, 4).

246 Holmes, *Chartulary of St John of Pontefract* II, p. 665 (543).

247 *Cat. Ancient Deeds* I, pp. 31, 41, 42–3, 49 (A357, 359, 365, 374, 420).

248 *Cat. Ancient Deeds* II, p. 31.

249 Martin, *Percy Cartulary*, p. 130 (cccxcvi).

250 G. L. Ripple, 'Uchtred and the Friars: apostolic poverty and clerical dominion between FitzRalph and Wyclif', *Traditio* xlix (1994), pp. 235–58.

251 *Wakefield Court Rolls* I, p. 113 (1307).

252 Stenton, *Pleas before the King or his Justices* III, p. 51 (512)

253 See also Stenton, *Pleas before the King or his Justices* III, p. 14 (130).

254 Stenton, *Pleas before the King or his Justices* III, pp. 238 (616), 248 (654), 292 (798), 304 (836), 319 (875), 325 (891), 378 (1046).

255 Stenton, *Pleas before the King or his Justices* III, p. 205 (505).

256 W. Farrer, ed., *The Lancashire Pipe Rolls of 31 Henry I, A.D. 1130, and of the Reigns of Henry II, A.D. 1155–1189; Richard I, A.D. 1189–1199; and King John, A.D. 1199–1216* (Liverpool, 1902), pp. 259–60, 285, 291, 296.

257 Hulton, *Whalley Coucher* III, p. 772 (lix).

258 Hulton, *Whalley Coucher* III, p. 770 (lvii).

259 J. Varley, ed., *A Middlewich Chartulary* (2 volumes, Chetham Society 105, 108, 1941–44), II, p. 281 (143h).

260 W. Farrer, ed., *Cockersand* III, iii, pp. 1219–29.

261 Peter McClure, 'Nicknames and petnames: linguistic forms and social contexts' and Clark, 'Nickname creation: some sources of evidence, "naïve" memoires especially,' both in *Nomina* 5 (1981), pp. 63–76 and 83–93.

262 Thus, see Alexander Rumble, 'The status of written sources in English onomastics,' *Nomina* 8 (1984), pp. 41–56, esp. 47.

263 *William Langland Piers Plowman the C-text* ed. Derek Pearsall (Exeter, 1994), p. 112 (Passus VI, ll 70–1).

264 Pearsall, *William Langland Piers Plowman the C-text*, pp. 126–7 (Passus VI, ll. 369–90).

265 It would be foolhardy here to attempt to establish a chronology of the use of hypocorisms

on the lines of Jean Germain, "Les prénoms à Namur (Wallonie) de la fin du xve siècle au xviie siècle" in *Actes du XVIe Congrès International des Sciences Onomastiques 1987* ed. J-C Boulanger (Quebec, 1990), p. 279.

266 M. Bateson, ed., *Records of the Borough of Leicester* volume 1 *1103–1327* (Cambridge and London, 1899), pp. 12–14, 16–17, 20, 22 and 24.

267 Postles, 'Notions of the family, lordship and the evolution of naming processes in medieval England', *Continuity and Change* 10 (1995), p. 187.

268 BL Cotton MS Tib. II, fo. 117 [Somersham].

269 E. A. Fry, ed., *Abstracts of Inquisitions Post Mortem for Gloucestershire* Part V (British Record Society Index Library 40, 1910), p. 67.

270 'Shropshire', 10, p. 128.

271 F. W. Maitland, ed., *Select Pleas of the Crown 1 (A.D. 1200–1225)* (Selden Society 1, 1887), p. 63.

272 Maitland, *Select Pleas 1*, pp. 87, 101.

273 W. Farrer, ed., *Lancashire Inquests, Extents and Feudal Aids* Part II (LCRS liv, 1907).

274 Farrer, *Lancashire Inquests, Extents and Feudal Aids*, pp. 14, 84.

275 Farrer, *Lancashire Inquests, Extents and Feudal Aids*, p. 90.

276 Farrer, *Lancashire Inquests, Extents and Feudal Aids*, p. 91.

277 Farrer, *Lancashire Inquests, Extents and Feudal Aids*, p. 96.

278 Farrer, *Lancashire Inquests, Extents and Feudal Aids*, p. 97.

279 Farrer, *Lancashire Inquests, Extents and Feudal Aids*, pp. 128, 198.

280 R. Stewart-Brown, ed., *Calendar of the County Court, City Court and Eyre Rolls of Chester, 1259–1297* (Chetham Society ns 84, 1925), pp. 4 (11), 5 (19), 9 (63), 15 (106), 19 (127), 23 (157), 25 (177–178).

281 Stewart-Brown, *Calendar of the County Court*, pp. 4, 10 (13, 16, 68).

282 Stewart-Brown, *Calendar of the County Court*, pp. 11, 14 (76, 101).

283 Stewart-Brown, *Calendar of the County Court*, p. 15 (108).

284 Stewart-Brown, *Calendar of the County Court*, pp. 13, 19, 28 (98, 134, 203).

285 Stewart-Brown, *Calendar of the County Court*, p. 19 (130).

286 Stewart-Brown, *Calendar of the County Court*, p. 21 (144).

287 Stewart-Brown, *Calendar of the County Court*, pp. 19, 23, 28 (135, 157, 201).

288 Stewart-Brown, *Calendar of the County Court*, p. 24 (169).

289 Stewart-Brown, *Calendar of the County Court*, p. 24 (173).

290 Stewart-Brown, *Calendar of the County Court*, p. 28 (204, 209).

291 *Wakefield Court Rolls* I.

292 *Wakefield Court Rolls* I, for example: Nelle *le Syur, de Wynter, de Soureby, ad boscum, de Thorneleye* (pp. 2, 12, 21, 162); Alcok *de Dundreland, carpentarius, de Litilwode, de Wlvedale, del Clif* (pp. 6, 13, 17, 33); Hycke *Schym, garcio, serviens* (pp. 8, 204, 262); Geppe *de Wytewrth, de Litelwode, le Sahar, del Dene,* John son of Geoffrey *de Littelwode* who paid an entry fine of 12d. for 2 acres of land from his father Geppe in 1286, thus associating Geppe with Geoffrey, *de Aula, le Folur, le Colier* (pp. 12, 27, 42, 178, 184, 216, 222, 268, 272, 275); Gelle *molendinarius, Pymerige, Cussing, de Stanley, Quintin* (pp. 78, 216–17, 220–2, 228, 274, 290, 294, 299, 301, 303); Gille *Quintin* appeared also as Gilbert *Quintin* when he carried off seven cartloads of wood in 1297 (p. 301), thus associating hypocorism and formal *nomen*. The hypocorism Hebbe is connected to Herbert in the person of Hebbe *de Botterlye* a juror in 1286, but described as Herbert *de Butterlay* when a pledge in the same year: pp. 210–211. In the same manner, Nik *Keneward*, a pledge in 1286, must have been the father of Adam son of Nicholas *Keneward*, involved in an action of trespass in 1296: p. 241.

293 *Wakefield Court Rolls* I, pp. 216–17, 219, 222–3, 225, 230, 233, 245.

294 *Wakefield Court Rolls 1338–1340*, pp. 48, 124, 247.
295 For these questions in the context of 'cultural consumption', J. Storey, *Cultural Consumption and Everyday Life* (London, 1999), esp. pp. 36–60.
296 For this issue now, Peter McClure, 'The interpretation of hypocoristic forms of Middle English baptismal names,' *Nomina* 21 (1998), pp. 101–32, which also considers the syntactical processes in the formation of hypocorisms, but not the social and cultural processes considered by Storey, *Cultural Consumption*.
297 'West Riding Poll Tax'.

6

NORTHERN OCCUPATIONAL BYNAMES?

When Adam *Botchecollok* proffered 18d. in 1315 for licence to receive a curtilage and half an acre of land from Adam *Strekayse* in Holne on the manor of Wakefield, an unusual occupational byname was recorded in the court rolls of the manor.[1] The Middle English compounded occupational byname *Botchecollok* is infrequently attested anywhere but was held by at least two suitors to the court of the composite manor of Wakefield, for Thomas *Bochecollok* was admitted to a lease of a messuage and seven acres of land in Holne in 1332.[2] Significantly, the byname recurred across the Pennines in south Lancashire some time before 1284.[3] Essentially, it must have connoted an occupation similar to that of a tinker and that byname was certainly also employed on the manor – for Gilbert *le Tincker alias Tinckler* was sufficiently irascible to merit two summonses to the court in the previous year (1314), for night-walking and for receiving malefactors in the town at night.[4] On his presentment for night-walking, it was alleged that he was disobedient to the law, but had insufficient chattels to be distrained. In *Tincker*'s case, his impecuniousness was consistent with his trade. That too appears to apply to *Botchecollok*, for the holding that he received was located at the marginal end of landholding on the manor. Adam thus represented the lower echelons of early-fourteenth-century society, where impermanent employment combined with a small amount of land, and the resulting occupational byname was construed in the Middle English vernacular as a compound rarely encountered. How far was this patterning of occupational naming distinctive of a Northern environment – at least at this time? Did marginal landholding and transient occupations lead in northern areas to unusual Middle English compounded occupational bynames?

Associated with this vernacular compound description of occupational bynames might have been the continued association of occupational bynames with the trade practised by their bearers – in other words, occupational bynames in the North retained instability in so far as they continued to be attached into the late fourteenth century to the actual occupation of those whom they identified. How far were these attributes of occupational bynames more persistent in the North than elsewhere, thus betraying a northern distinctiveness?

ME compounded bynames

Producing exceptional occupational bynames from northern documents presents
few difficulties, reflected in *Botchecollok* above. One of the jurors in an inquisition at
Lancaster in 1325 was identified as Simon *le Collokwryht*.[5] A witness to a charter in
Newcastle-upon-Tyne in 1323 was described as John *Shapacape* and he was elsewhere
identified as a burgess in 1332.[6] In fact, these ME compounded occupational bynames
extended back at least into the early thirteenth century in the North, attested in the
outlawry of Simon *le siuewright'* in Yorkshire in 1218–19.[7]

On the manor of Wakefield, in 1331–2, John *Dishbynder* was amerced 3d. for
taking firewood and 10d. for other offences against the vert, and subsequently
surrendered his messuage and ten acres in Sowerby.[8] In 1339 he was amerced 1d. for
trespass in the lord's wood, whilst in 1340 William *Disshebinder* offended against the
vert on the manor by chopping wood.[9] Such creative Middle English occupational
bynames – creative as to the extent of their compounding and formation – existed
more widely on this composite manor of Wakefield. In 1348, John *Stonebrekar*
purchased a licence to quarry for coal in Holne.[10] Amongst the tenants in the 1330s
was enumerated Adam *le bordewright*.[11]

On the same manor in 1338, William *Swinlibbar'* became involved in a plea of pledge
in Sandal and during the following year the court rolls recorded the involvement of
Emma *le* (sic) *Swynlibbar'* in another case of debt, Thomas son of Robert *Swynlibber*
concerned with the same type of transaction, and the admission of Elias son of Robert
Swynlibber to twelve acres and three and a half roods of land in Sandal.[12] Now, it seems
more than likely that the bynames *Swynlibber* and *Grislibber* were synonymous, for in
1338 Thomas son of Robert *Grislibber* attended the court in a case of debt.[13] Not only,
therefore, was there a highly unusual occupational byname, but also, despite the
repetition of one particular form, it exhibited some instability: *Swynlibber* and *Grislibber*,
both purporting the gelding of pigs. To these formations can be added Peter *Geldegras*
[sc. *Geldegris*], a free tenant in Tadcaster in the thirteenth century.[14]

In the late thirteenth century, 1270x1289, in a charter relating to Dumfries,William
Grindegret, burgess, conveyed to his brother John *Grindegret*, houses in that borough.[15]
Amongst the principal burgesses in Newcastle-upon-Tyne in the 1330s and 1340s was
John *Shapacape*, who in 1338 had licence under the Statute of Mortmain to assign 100s.
of land and rent to establish a chantry and from whom wool was purveyed in 1348.[16]

Of course, not all these unusual occupational bynames were confined to the
northern zone, for Middle English exceptional forms occurred throughout the
country: Richard *Bakewastel* of la Hale in Hampshire in 1345; Rose *Grindecobbe* widow
of William *Grindecobbe* of St Albans at the time of the Black Death; and John le
Wymppelwebbe of Long Marston who was deceased by 1324.[17] Inventive Middle
English compounds appeared intermittently in a variety of places. Thaxted (Essex)
in 1393 had its principal cobbler or clouter, Robert *Tounsowter*.[18] Equally, compounded ME occupational bynames pervaded the periphery of the north: William
Waynfulofwoll assessed for taxation of 5s., a considerable amount, at Glossop in
Derbyshire in 1327, undoubtedly metonymic and also a social comment on his
acquisitiveness.[19]

-maker bynames

Another aspect of northern occupational bynames is the earlier adoption of the suffix -*maker* in the vernacular environment. In many other regions, compounds with -*maker* developed only in the later middle ages, but in northern records their adoption is more precocious. On the manor of Wakefield in 1297 Richard *le Potmaker* was accused of housebreaking and theft of money.[20] Before then, the -*maker* compound had been introduced into the composite manor at Rastrick in the person of Adam *le Melemakere* and Robert *le Melemaker*, defendants in a plea of land and for an escape.[21] Apparently Adam *le Melemaker* had recourse to torture in 1286.[22] In 1317, the court rolls of the manor of Wakefield recited the crime of burglary by Robert son of Cecily *Melemaker* of Huddersfield.[23] On the manor of Conisborough near Doncaster, Ralph *le Arkemaker* compromised in a case of debt and he had also performed the office of reeve of Clifton in 1334–5.[24]

Since they were Middle English compounds and later in their formation, these -*maker* bynames were both creative and unusual, designed to indicate either newer trades or to fill interstices in the lexis of occupations. Before the late middle ages, they remained infrequent, and their introduction was not confined to the North: one of the taxpayers at Little Hormead in Hertfordshire in 1307 was designated by the byname *le Chesemaker*.[25] Particularly in the urban occupational context of Norwich, these seemingly novel trades introduced new -*maker* bynames: Hugh *le Gerthmakere* in 1289; John *le Pastemakere* who sold kosher meat in the same year; Robert *le Myteynmaker* then too; and John *le Pantermakere* from Cambridge, not in tithing and so probably a recent migrant, in 1300. Alongside these created -*maker* names occurred other compounded ME occupational bynames in this urban environment, reflecting new trades: William *le Lacebreydere* in 1300; Robert *le Quernhacker* in 1313 and Thomas *le Glaswryth* at the same time.[26]

Not surprisingly, therefore, -*maker* bynames featured as significantly in the North as in any other area, producing unusual and complex formulations. Thus in 1367 Robert *Sausmaker* inhabited Wearmouth.[27] For a rent of 2s. and a boonwork in autumn, Hugh *Panyermaker* received a cottage and garden in Newton in the North Riding in 1357.[28] At the end of the fourteenth century, Thomas *Matrasmaker* of Warter committed a homicide at Middleton on the Wolds.[29]

Another *Matrysmaker*, Peter, inhabited Beverley in 1381, alongside a small concentration comprising John *Pouchemaker*, Thomas *Mustardmaker*, and William *Bruchemaker*, although a few such names occurred in adjacent rural areas, such as *Maysemaker* at Cottingham and *Sylemaker* at South Cave.[30] Similarly, the urban context sustained others with -*maker* compounds in 1379: at Pontefract another *Musterdmaker*, another *Pouchmaker* and a *Cardemaker*, whilst at Rotherham a *Netmaker* and *Arkmaker*; another *Mustardmaker* in Ripon; at Doncaster a *Nettemaker* and *Slaymaker*; and in the smaller urban centre of Tickhill, a *Colermaker*.[31]

Compound names of this ilk (although by no means exclusive to northern areas) were likely to be easily received into the vernacular environment of writing in northern England, particularly in urban contexts where the specialization of trades and occupations advanced during the later middle ages. Their composition suggests that they functioned more as bynames than hereditary surnames even into the late fourteenth century, which complements the persistence of eponymous occupational bynames in northern reaches.

Eponymous occupational bynames

At the tourn court of Wakefield in 1349 two men were presented for following the trade of shoemaker (and, in one case, the allied occupation of tanner), fined respectively 8d. and 6d.: John *sutor* and Michael *sutor*.[32] When confronting the question of the social meaning of occupational bynames, two hypotheses are encountered. Long ago, Tengvik suggested – as no more than a rule of thumb – that occupational bynames were transformed into hereditary surnames around 1350.[33] Not completely at variance, but also not consistent with Tengvik, Goldberg intimated that occupational bynames continued to exhibit sufficient instability in the late fourteenth century – in the Poll Taxes of 1379 and 1381 – for the bynames to be considered as generally eponymous with the trade or craft of their bearers – in other words that occupational bynames had not yet stabilized into hereditary surnames by 1380, and especially not in the North.[34] There is then the proposition that occupational bynames remained unstable and attached to individuals almost to the end of the fourteenth century and that this persistent instability was particularly associated with the North.

For investigating this proposal, reliance must mainly be invested in the Poll Tax returns of 1379 for the West Riding.[35] Assuming some approach to completeness in those returns comprehending persons over the age of fourteen, 7,649 taxpayers were enumerated with occupational bynames or surnames. In less than ten percent of these instances was the actual occupation of the bearer of the occupational bynames denoted: that is, for about 685 taxpayers we have both the occupational bynames and the occupation. Ignoring issues of dual occupations and by-occupations, for 378 of these 685 the occupational byname and the listed occupation were in most cases eponymous and in others synonymous. By eponymous is meant that the occupational description was exactly the same as the occupational byname (e.g. webster and *Webster*) and the import of synonymous is that the occupational description was a cognate of the occupational byname (thus marshall and *Smyth*, for example). When we have both occupational description and occupational byname, therefore, in 55 per cent of cases, there was a concordance between them, but in 45 per cent of cases the occupational description was different from the occupational surname (in this latter case, for example, wright and *Carter*). What these figures from the West Riding Poll Tax impute is a transitional period (deferred into the late fourteenth century) when occupational bynames were in the process of being transformed into occupational surnames – that is, hereditary, family surnames.

What must now be assessed is how far that process was consistent with or differed from, first, other regions of the North, and, second, with other areas outside the North. Unfortunately, the data for other areas are not as plentiful as those from the West Riding. For example, the returns for the East Riding provide only four occupational descriptions and in none of those cases were those descriptions coincident with the occupational byname. More consistency is exhibited in the Lancashire returns, but the correspondence is still marginal. Occupational descriptions were included in those returns for some taxpayers in Lonsdale Wapentake, consistently in Liverpool, and sporadically in Pennington, Knowsley, Rixton, Bickerstaffe, Atherton, Hindley, Parr, Eccleston, Ashton-in-Makerfield, Lowton and Scarisbrick. Amongst all these dispersed occupational descriptions, only some ten correlated with the occupational byname: three websters at Rixton, fleshewer, barker, bower, chaloner and smith in Liverpool, and smith, cooper and tailor in the other places.[36] Additionally, taxpayers in Formby were predominantly described as fisher folk (*piscatores*) although none had a byname derived from that occupation.[37] Partly because of the deficiencies of the 1379 Poll Tax for Westmorland, no correlations occur between occupational byname and description.

We are consequently reliant on the West Riding returns to depict the continuing association between occupational bynames and the occupational status of their bearers in the North. From that evidence, it can be inferred that the final quarter of the fourteenth century marked a transition for occupational bynames in the North, with a transition from bynames attached to individuals to hereditary, family, surnames. Since 55 percent of occupational descriptions accorded with the description of the taxpayer in those instances where it was revealed, the process of transition was in train rather than nearing completion.

If we compare the West Riding information with data from other areas of the country, it becomes clear that that process of change had already largely occurred elsewhere. Whilst in Leicestershire some occupational bynames did correlate with the occupational description where it was divulged, that correspondence was marginal by comparison with the West Riding. In the 1381 Poll Tax for Leicester-shire, merely forty-one occupational bynames were consistent with occupational status, five of which belonged to Melton Mowbray, a small town in the north-east of the county. In Lincolnshire, the existence of eponymous occupational bynames was as sporadic and inconsistent: the defective data for Lindsey reveal only five eponymous occupational bynames (*Miller, Marchall, Couper, Taillor* and *Dyker*); more profuse were those bynames in Kesteven (*Wright; Skynnere; Couper* – two; *Mason* – two; *Plomer; Walker; Fissher; Tyler; Lymbrenner; Cartewright; Chaloner; Fletcher* – two; *Taillour* – five; *Barbour; Cotiller; Sherman* – two; *Goldsmyth; Horner; Litstere;* and *Glover* – comprehending almost thirty taxpayers in the Poll Tax); almost as frequent were they in Holland (*Smyth* – seven; *Wryth* – two; *Tailour* – six; *Couper* – three; *Walker* – two; and *Bladsmyth*).[38]

Certain occupations particularly might have been associated with continuing flexibility of occupational byname, one of which was *molendinarius*. For example, in 1338 Robert *molendinarius* was arraigned in the deanery court of Lincoln at Hainton as the lessee of two mills – one water and one wind – for withholding tithes of the mills.[39] When John *Smyth* surrendered a cottage and twelve acres of land called *le Smythland* in Wistow in 1365, he transferred the tenancy to Richard *Smyth*.[40] As late as the third quarter of the fifteenth century, a fulling mill in Westmorland was occupied by Robert Walker and his co-tenant John *Banys*.[41] Although it is possible that this association occasionally emanated from inheritance of the occupation, the

quantity of correlation between byname and occupation (where indicated) in the
Poll Tax confirms the continued instability of occupational bynames further north.

How, however, we interpret Richard Plumber of Newcastle in 1511 will remain a
conundrum. It is evident from the chamberlains' payments to him for his service
that he was indeed a plumber: supplying lead; making pipework; work on the
conduit; and providing solder.[42] Might we presuppose here that at this late time he
was attributed a byname congruent with his occupation, thus reflecting a continued
instability – at the margins, at least – of northern occupational (and other forms of)
second naming?

-herd names

In 1363, the death was reported in Cumberland of John *Calfhird* whilst ninety years
earlier William *Hogghird* was suspected of burglary in Northumberland.[43] Impressionistic as it occasionally is, although supported by some evidence, northern zones were
characterized by a greater intensity and variety of occupational bynames with the
suffix *-herd*. Essentially, this influence on naming was connected to the importance of
livestock husbandry in the northern region. That effect was transmitted in two ways:
in nickname bynames (as chapter 8); and in occupational bynames.

In terms of the corpus of occupational bynames, the distinctiveness of a northern
area is aggregate – that is, it is the cumulative evidence of bynames from livestock
occupations and their overall impact which marks off a northern zone. Other areas
displayed specialized occupational bynames derived from livestock husbandry, but
not on the aggregate scale of the North in general. In particular, the variety of
occupational bynames associated with bovine husbandry in the northern zone
illustrates the significance of vaccaries and managed bovine husbandry in some
northern areas.

Particularly northern amongst these was *Nethird* (OE *neat*, ox), which also
extended, however, eastwards into the north Midlands.[44] Before the deanery court at
Market Rasen in Lincolnshire, for example, Robert *Nethird* of Wellingham was
presented for fornication with Alice *Diker* in 1340.[45] In the hamlet of Alverthorpe on
the enormous manor of Wakefield Henry *le Nautherde* assumed a lease for twelve
years of one acre for an entry fine of 18d. in 1316.[46] In 1307, Henry *le Bouthirde* [sic]
(probably *le Nouthirde*) was presented for an escaped animal in Wakefield.[47] Two
years later, Henry *le Nautehird* was employing female servants in Wakefield.[48] In
Wakefield too German *le Nauthyrd* was amerced 2d. for an escaped beast, also in
1309.[49] Further north, at Wearmouth, Alice Nouthird assumed the bond tenement
which had been held by her late husband, Alan Nouthird, in 1358.[50]

Although occupational bynames from livestock husbandry were not exclusive to
the north, the greater engagement with livestock in northern zones encouraged a
proliferation of these bynames, so that they constituted a characteristic of northern
areas. Illustrations of this aspect are profuse in the lay subsidy for the North Riding in
1327. At Skelton, Thomas *Lamhird* was assessed for 1s. 6d.[51] Continuing the category
of sheep husbandry, Walter *Wetherhird* contributed just over a shilling at Wickham,

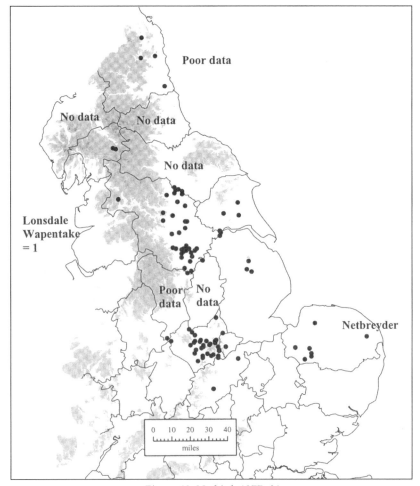

Figure 40 Nethird, 1377–81

whilst Agnes *Wetherhird* made her payment at Helmsley; Juliana *Schephird* at Hovingham; John *Lambhird* at Herlesey; William *le Quyhird* (that is, eweherd) at Souneby; Henry *Lambhird* at Iversley; William *Tophird* (that is, tupherd) at Danby; and John *Lambhird* at Deighton.[52]

Although this variety of bynames from sheep husbandry occasionally developed in other areas where sheep-farming became very specialized, in the north there existed also other locales with *-herd* bynames emanating from wider livestock involvement. In some Cotswold villages in the early fourteenth century, bynames from specialized sheep husbandry evolved. In the 1327 lay subsidy for Gloucestershire, for example, are enumerated taxpayers named *le Wetherherde* at Rodmarton, Gotherington, and Toddington, as well as, from non-sheep husbandry, *le Coltherde* at Tetbury, and *le Gosherde* at Aylburton.[53]

More distinctly northern, however, was the combination with other *-herd* forms,

Occupational byname	Number of occurrences
Shephird	197
Nethird/Nouthird/Nauthird	49
Hird	44
Cowherd	37
Swineherd	28
Hine	28
Oxhird, Oxynhyrd	12
Lambhird	9
Calfhyrd	6
Ewehyrd, Yowhyrd, Euerhyrd	6
Geldhyrd	5
Gaythyrd	3
Wetherhyrd	2
Colthyrd	2
Hoghyrd	1
Tuphyrd	1
Mewhyrd	1
Suehyrd	1
Gaytknave	1
Styrkhyrd	1
Hoghyrd	1

Table 10　Rank order of bynames from livestock occupations in the West Riding in 1379

Occupational byname	Number of occurrences
Shepherd	14
Herdemon	9
Hird	4
Hine	3
Couherd	2
Yuwhird	1
Nawthird	1
Lambhird	1
Del Oxenhouce[69]	1

Table 11　Occupational bynames associated with livestock husbandry in the Lancashire Poll Tax

especially from specialized cattle husbandry. Moreover, because of the importance of livestock in northern areas, townships appointed common herds which increased the corpus of -*herd* forms.[54]

In the North Riding, for example, taxation was extracted in 1327 from John *Stirkhird* at Cropton; Robert *Stirchird* at Kirkbymoorside; Robert *le Couhird* at Crechale; Richard *Oxenhirde* at Burton; Henry *le Couhirde* at Kildale; William *Oxhird* at Grenhow; William *Stirkhird* at Hackness; and John *Stirkhird* at Uggilbardby.[55] The presence of these bynames was, as might be expected, particularly significant within the honor and forest of Pickering in the early fourteenth century. There, presentments were initiated for offences against the vert and venison against: John *le Calvehird* in 1332; Adam son of John *le Nouthird* in 1305; and John *le Stirkhird*.[56] Some acted as pledges for offenders, thus John *Wetherhird*, John *Styrkhyrde*, and Henry *Yowhird*.[57] Others appeared in court because they had assarted or made enclosures: John *Le Wetherhirde*; John *Stirkhirde*; and Henry *Youhirde*.[58] Finally, the names of some were inscribed on the court rolls for non-suit – Richard *le Hoghurde* and Richard *le Cowhurde* – whilst others were taxed in the lay subsidy of 1332 – Simon *Styrkhird* and John *Styrkherd*.[59]

Other, miscellaneous occupational bynames of this category emphasized the influence of livestock husbandry on the formation of bynames in northern areas. At Houghton, Richard *le Hoghird* was assessed for the lay subsidy of 1327.[60] More firmly associated with northern localities was the byname *Stodhird*, represented by Reginald *Stodhird* at Carlton and Richard *Stodehirde* at Scargill in 1327.[61]

Significantly, most of these bynames from livestock husbandry had already been transposed into the vernacular in the 1327 lay subsidy for the North Riding. Few bynames remained in their Latin form. Their conversion into vernacular forms suggests a close familiarity which was conveyed to the *scriptores* of the lay subsidy rolls.

On the manor of Wakefield, numerous -*herd* bynames are encountered in the court rolls in the late thirteenth and early fourteenth centuries. Allusion has been made to Henry *le Nautherde*. In 1286, William *le Geldehyrd* had committed an offence against

Occupational byname	Number of occurrences
Shepherd	20
Cowhird	3
Hird	3
Lambhird	3
Nouthird	2
Studhird	2
Del Cowhous[70]	2
Oxhird	1
Yuwhird	1

Table 12 Occupational bynames associated with livestock husbandry in the Westmorland Poll Tax

the venison in Sowerby.[62] Some years later William *le Horshird* acted as an attorney for an essoin there.[63] About the same time – 1309 – Hugh *Lambehird* attended the court as defendant in a plea of trespass in Horbury.[64] Indicted for, but acquitted of, theft, Thomas *le Geildhirde* appeared at the tourn court of Halifax in 1298.[65] For default of suit to the tourn in 1309, Adam *le Oxhird* was amerced.[66]

Considering the Poll Tax of 1379 for the West Riding of Yorkshire, a rank order of occupational bynames *in the vernacular* can be constructed for that area.

Although the data are impoverished because of the defectiveness of the Poll Tax for Northumberland, the pattern of these bynames there replicated some of the variety of the West Riding: Shephird (seven taxpayers); Nethird (three); Couhird (two); and Oxinhird, Wethirhird and Lamhyrd (all once).[67] In Lancashire, however, the data are much less impressive, so that the principal item of interest is the relative frequency of Herdemon as a generic occupational byname. Additionally, court rolls of some Lancashire manors and charters mentioned John *le Geldehird* in Ightenhill, Simon *le Hyrd* in Bowland, and Roger *le Noutherde* in Skerton, all in 1324.[68]

Further north, in Westmorland, the Poll Tax – defective, however – reveals a pattern similar to Lancashire with the predominance of Shepherd and a less imposing range of other occupational terms related to livestock husbandry.

A similar pattern obtained in the Poll Tax for the East Riding of Yorkshire, where Schephyrd dominated with eighteen taxpayers, followed by two Net(e)hyrds, and a single Swynhird and Lambhyrd.[71] Although county Durham had the status of exemption from the Poll Tax, it is nevertheless possible to reconstruct an impression of this category of occupational byname from Bishop Hatfield's contemporary survey of the episcopal manors. Dominated again by Shephird (twenty-one tenants), the bynames comprehended also Cowhird (three), Stodhird (three), Swynhird (two), Hirde (two), Gaythird (one) and Calvehird (one).

As interesting as their formation, however, is their later transmutation, involving the conversion of final -*d* to -*t* (dental suffix variation) (as well as the loss of the aspirant -*h*- in both and, in Calvert, the substitution of fricative *v*/*f*). Amongst these developments are encountered the surnames Calvert, Stoddart, and, through a different process, Coward. In Calvert and Stoddart there was a mutation of the dental suffix stops. How these forms persisted can be estimated from entries in parish registers. The registers for St Nicholas, Durham, for example, contain entries for Denis Stodderte in 1606 and Christopher Calvert in 1626.[72] Variants of these bynames from livestock husbandry are revealed in the parish registers of Whitburn. In 1629 and 1632 were recorded John Colterd and Barbara Coltard, although John to whom reference was made in 1640–6 was entered as Cowtherd.[73]

Hogherd (and its variants, Hoggherd(e)) became an established surname in Shap in Westmorland in the late sixteenth century. Four children of William Hogherd – commencing with John in 1562 to William in 1568 – were entered in the baptism register, although Jenet died in early childbirth.[74] William died in 1590.[75] Richard Hoggherd, who married Margaret Newton in 1579, had issue William and John in 1580 and Henry in 1589.[76] More informative still are the registers of Askham between 1567 and 1617, for in this registration the surname varied between Hogert, Hoggart, and Hoggard(e). In 1567, Jenet Hogert was registered as baptized, the ceremony performed for Dorothy Hoggart in 1570. Some eight years later, Alice Hoggarde, wife of Hugh, was interred. Perhaps the same Hugh Hoggard married (secondly) Jenet Smyth in 1580, but one of their sons, John, died in childbirth. Hugh Hoggard was buried in the parish in 1596, three years before the interment of Thomas Hoggard. In 1610, baptism was conferred on Richard Hogart son of Richard, and three daughters of Robert, Margaret Hogart, Mary Hogart and Jenet Hogart, were successively initiated by this ceremony into the Anglican church in 1612, 1615 and 1617.[77] Hoggerd or Hoggert persisted in the north-west also at Brough, where the burials were recorded of Margaret Hoggerd in 1572, Thomas Hoggert the following year, and Margaret Hoggert, widow, in 1582.[78]

As extensively distributed was Geldherd in its variant transformations, Geldert kinship groupings existing in Gisburne in Yorkshire in the late sixteenth and early seventeenth centuries. Indeed, they continued in three of the settlements in the parish: Paythorne, Agden and Gisburne itself.[79] Only a few years after the commencement of the extant registers, the baptism was celebrated of Margaret daughter of Richard Geldert in 1564.[80] Subsequent Gelderd christenings featured at regular and compressed intervals in the register between 1564 and 1579.[81] During this period, four Geldert fathers produced progeny: Richard, Henry, William and Thomas. Geldert burials were similarly memorialized in the register during the same time, beginning with Edmund Geldert.[82]

Ripon, although an urban entity, equally hosted -herd formations of surname. Burials were occasioned in 1592 and 1593 respectively of Leo Gelderd and James Calvert. In 1599, new Gelderd progeny was welcomed to the world with Alice and Elizabeth.[83] Rites of passage were celebrated for Gelderds in the rural neighbourhood at Giggleswick-in-Craven, where Peter Gelderd was interred in 1563 and Elizabeth Gelderd married four years afterwards, as did Helen Gelderd in 1574 and Thomas Gelderd in 1588. Another Thomas Gelderd was another spouse whose wedding was celebrated there in 1607.[84]

Across the Pennines, Geldert developed into a focal surname in Aldingham in the late sixteenth century. After the baptisms of Isabel, Agnes and Leonard Geldert in 1571–2, fourteen other children were baptized with this surname up to Agnes Geldert in 1599. Although not the dominant surname in the parish, it was still firmly established amongst the population.[85]

In the vicinity, at Giggleswick-in-Craven, Calverd was inscribed in the registers on the burial of Edward Calverd in 1563.[86] It was there too that Henry Calvert married in 1573, as did Leonard Calverde in 1613.[87] Calverd developed into a local surname at Monk Fryston by the late sixteenth century, where William and Mary Calverd, children of David Calverd, appeared in the parish registers in 1580, postdating the baptism of Margaret Calverd there.[88]

Some particular occupational bynames

Within the corpus of occupational bynames in the northern zone, some should be considered especially northern, although uncompounded terms. Amongst these distinctive lexical items are *Kydder/Kidder* and *Badger*, denoting in particular, itinerant trading activity, differentiated from the profusion of *Chapman* elsewhere. Consequently, in the Poll Tax for the West Riding in 1379, taxpayers identified by the byname or surname *Kydder* existed at Laughton en le Morthen (two), Mexborough, Tickhill, Snaith, Guisborough, Settle, Giggleswick, Adwick le Street, Clapham, Ingleton (two), Acaster Selby, Ecclesfield, Wath on Dearne, Whiston, Hemsworth, Carlton (two), Drax, Brotherton, Leeds, and Nun Monkton, whilst *Baggers/Badgers* inhabited Snaith, Rawcliffe, and Morton.[89]

Occasionally, these bynames can be observed at an earlier time, although infrequently. So it was a rare occasion when Amabel *la Badger* and the wife of Adam *le Badger* paid for brewing in 1315 on the manor of Wakefield.[90] In 1307, furthermore, Henry *le Bagger* had received two and a half acres of land in Holne.[91]

Although therefore a scattering, these occupations would eventually develop into essential and integral aspects of the organisation of the Yorkshire woollen industry. Quite simply, however, the difficulty of extending their existence back into an earlier manifestation is the ambiguity of the Latin occupational term *mercator* which might conceal a range of vernacular options, *chapman*, *kidder*, and *badger* included.[92]

Perhaps the occupational byname and surname *Colier* was not so definitively circumscribed to northern regions, but, although it might have featured in other areas with early (sea) coal mining, its diffusion in the northern zone was distinctive. It also manifested a continuing association with the activity – as an eponymous byname. At the tourn court of Wakefield in 1316, therefore, Ralph *le Colier*, alongside William *Cokewald*, was amerced 1s. for digging for coals on the King's highway to Dewsbury to the aggravation of travellers.[93]

Metonymy

Since language use involves so much metaphor and metonymy, bynaming in particular deployed those characteristics. As has been maintained, metaphor and metonymy provided a conceptual framework for lived experience and language. Metaphor and metonymy thus combined the imaginary or imaginative – the poetic – with the conceptual framework of the ordinary, the quotidian, the way in which *la vie quotidienne* is negotiated. Bynames of nickname derivation, but also monikers imputing occupation, imported heavily metaphor and metonymy, and particularly was that so of the North.[94]

Now in the case of occupational bynames, metonymy was more germane than metaphor: the part signified the whole. Introduced into those metonymic bynames, moreover, was the element of irony, deliberately to shame, humiliate or discipline. Not for the first time, bynames from the composite manor of Wakefield illustrate this exercise of bynames. The byname *Sourmilk* developed into a hereditary byname there. In 1307 Michael *Sourmylk* received two acres of waste land in Sowerby for an entry fine of 1s., but the fortunes of Thomas *Sourmylk* in the same court were less favourable for he was presented for an escape of oxen at Hiperum.[95] Both John and Michael *Sourmilk* were presented in 1314 for escapes of beasts at Sowerby.[96] Receiving four acres of land in Sowerby in 1315 John *Sourmylk* offered an entry fine of 3s.[97] In the same year, Michael *Sourmilkes* of Midgley proferred an entry fine of 10s. to receive three acres of new land from the waste in Sowerby wood, at the same time that Thomas *Sourmylk* was amerced 2d.[98] In the following year, Michael *Sourmylke* redeemed a purpresture which he had made eight years previously by payment of a fine of 2s. 6d.[99] In 1325 Ivo *Sourmilk* was amerced 2d. for an escaped beast, whilst he was selected for an inquest in 1331.[100] In 1348 in Sowerby within the same composite manor, Richard *Sourmilk* was distrained in a plea of debt.[101] About the same time, interestingly, Thomas *Prest* admitted that he unjustly detained 9s. as a pledge for Richard *Sourmilk* for the sale of a cow and mare.[102] In the following year, Anabel *Sourmilk* paid 2d. for licence to brew.[103] Subsequently, Richard *Sourmilk* was recorded as a tenant of villein land in Sowerby in October 1349 and then too he acknowledged a debt of 13s. 4d. (a mark) for the purchase of grain.[104] Within the same manor of Wakefield, it was recorded for the hamlet of Stanley in 1323 that Alice *Sourhale* was indebted in 4s. 8d. by an agreement by which she had consented to withdraw from marriage litigation.[105]

Metonymic stricture characterised a prominent burgess family in Hull, John and Robert *Rotenhering*. In 1293, John held a tenement in the borough, but he had consolidated his urban property further by 1310. By 1320, he had accumulated several burgage properties, which he still held in 1347. Robert's tenure of urban property first became apparent in 1305 and he expanded the amount so that he too was a successful tenant in the rental of 1347.[106]

Metonymy was complicated, however, for some bynames with metonymic content could have been inscribed with meanings of occupational activity or nickname imputations. Of course, the taxonomy of bynames and surnames always presents ambiguities at the margins of classification. Indicted in 1309 for burglary, having purloined a robe and jewelry, Maude *Panyerbagge*'s moniker is redolent of the accoutrement of her criminal activity.[107] Although he occurred but once in the Wakefield court rolls, as a juror in Thornes in 1286, John *Hokebeg'* {i.e. *Hokebeger*} was apparently named after his soliciting activity about Hocktide.[108] Adam Hokbegger, assessed for the Poll Tax in Great Musgrave in Westmorland in 1379 as a married man, confirms this form of byname.[109]

Not all metonymic bynames occasioned social critique, for some – although not too many – had perhaps more positive imputations. A positive interpretation might be attributed to William *Swetemylke*, tenant of a toft at Great Marsden in Lancashire in the 1320s, if it is assumed that he furnished a nutritious foodstuff. On the other hand, the byname might have been derogatory if he was accorded it because he habitually drank milk rather than ale.[110]

In a different code, French, the metonymy associated with the knightly and gentry family *Graindorge* introduces another social level of metonymic occupational bynames, although it is impossible to differentiate occupational and nickname etymology. In 1268, William *Graindorge* attested a charter relating to Midhope in the West Riding.[111]

Similar ambiguity inheres in the byname *Wytlof*, attached to Adam, a juror on the manor of Wakefield in 1298: did it import a superior diet or his superior product?[112]

On the same manor in 1307, Joan *Whytelof* was amerced for the escape of her pigs.[113] That same ambivalence influences any interpretation of the byname of Michael *Thirlebacon*, accused of battery in 1307.[114]

Waste- and *spille-*

Although not necessarily derived from occupational activity, compounded bynames incorporating *waste-* or *spille-* are associated with economic involvement and with social stricture: in both cases the prototheme, whether French (*waste-*) or ME (*spille-*) signified 'to waste'. Again, although not exclusive to the 'North', their directness is consonant with language use in northern regions. For example, the death of Thomas *Spilbrede* was reported in Cumberland in the middle of the fourteenth century.[115] In Skelton in Yorkshire, William *Spillebrede* quitclaimed his right in a toft to Guisborough Priory.[116] At the turn of the fourteenth century, John *Spilbrede* was killed at Ireby in Cumberland.[117] A minor peasant, recorded sporadically in the court rolls, John *Spillewod* inhabited the manor of Wakefield in the early fourteenth century.[118] Default of suit by Roger *Spillewod* was presented to the tourn of the same manor in 1315 and he was involved as plaintiff in a case of trespass in 1316.[119] Within that manor, in the hamlet of Ossett, William *Spilnubir* and William *Spilwode* were amerced for the escape of animals.[120] *Spilwode* was transformed into the code-mixed William *Spilletimbre* when he was significantly fined 3d. for an offence against the vert in Ossett in the following year.[121] In a similar transmutation, Richard *Spiltimbir* surrendered three acres in Sowerby in 1331.[122] There the byname persisted for in May 1349 the wife of Roger *Spilwod* was presented as a common brewer.[123] *Spillewod* existed as an ignoble byname in other woodland areas of the West Riding, refracted through Roger *Spillewod* at Hundsworth who was unsuccessful in his case of detinue in 1326.[124]

Such disciplinary epithets had existed earlier and in the Midlands, for in 1211 one of the burgesses admitted to the freedom of the borough of Leicester – and thus in an urban not a rural context – was designated without deference *Spillecorn*.[125] The unforgiving social critique of that negligence with grain was reiterated in John *Spilhaver*, assessed in the lay subsidy at Guisborough (Yorks. W. R.) at merely 6d., but whose byname indicated a renown for the loss or destruction of oats, a commodity of fundamental importance in parts of the 'North'.[126]

In all these bynames of social critique, the sense of wastage was associated with fundamental and essential commodities. Occasionally, however, the social criticism might have been implicitly directed at ostentation as in the case of Adam *Spilgold* of Holm Cultrum in Cumberland, assessed at 51d. This byname, Spillgyld, recurred in Cumberland in 1354, in the person of Thomas, a legatee under the will of the rector of Melmerby.[127]

Although occasional in their incidence, and even though not confined to the 'North', these ME formations of bynames implying social critique of waste were consistent with language use in the 'North'. Their inherent directness and criticism of waste and loss had a vernacular bluntness.[128]

Spare-

Although compound bynames with the initial verbal form *spar(e)-* might not have pertained uniquely to the northern zone, their recitation there seems much more frequent than in other locations. Again, whilst these verbal compounds were not prolific, they were distinctive. Their bearers seem to have been elusive, suggesting that marginal villagers were assigned these bynames. For default of suit to the lord's mill at Raistrick in 1316, Adam *Sparbottre* was amerced 6d.[129] Enumerated amongst the taxpayers of the North Riding in 1327, at Malton, John *Sparwatere* was assessed at a modest level.[130]

Overview of occupational bynames

Code-switching in occupational bynames was not absent from the North, despite the particular vernacular ME environment which was pervasive there. In 1218–19, for example, the murder was recorded of Walter *le oisillur* (fowler) in Yorkshire.[131] That was not an isolated record of this byname in this code, for a charter relating to a bovate of land in Bonnington in the East Riding recited the service of Robert *le oysillur* and his heirs in the early thirteenth century.[132] What was, nonetheless, significant about northern occupational bynames was their association with a vernacular environment. Their composition in Middle English facilitated compounding which allowed creativity. Compound bynames tended to endure longer than simpler forms and to be associated with the individual. Occupational bynames in northern areas, indeed, remained flexible and unstable longer, in general, than further south. Furthermore, the distinctive rural economy of northern uplands – with an emphasis on livestock husbandry even if within mixed farming – contributed a specialized lexis of *-herd* bynames and surnames which, although some featured elsewhere, made a deeper impression further north.

Notes

1   *Wakefield Court Rolls* III, p. 80. This byname does not appear in either Fransson's or Thuresson's compendia of occupational bynames and surnames.
2   H. Kurath *et al.*, eds, *Middle English Dictionary* vol 1 (A–B) (Ann Arbor, 1952), p. 1001 (*bocchen* – to patch up, mend); vol 2 (C–D), *s.v. collok* (drinking vessel, tankard); *Wakefield Court Rolls 1331–1333*, p. 41. He added another acre and a half in 1326 in Holne but later surrendered two acres and one rood in Thong in Holne: *Wakefield Court Rolls* V, p. 92; *Wakefield Court Rolls 1331–1333*, p. 113.
3   *Norris Deeds*, p. 212 (1220).
4   *Wakefield Court Rolls* III, pp. 52, 66.
5   W. Farrer, ed., *Lancashire Inquests, Extents, and Feudal Aids* Part III (LCRS lxx, 1915), p. 10.
6   A. M. Oliver, *Early Deeds relating to Newcastle upon Tyne* (Surtees Society cxxxvii, 1924), pp. 99, 177, 182 (147, 339, 358).
7   D. M. Stenton, ed., *Rolls of the Justices in Eyre ... Yorkshire in 3 Henry III (1218–19)* (Selden

Society 56, 1937), p. 245 (641). On the tendency to word-formation by compounding in Germanic languages in general, G. Hughes, *A History of English Words* (Oxford, 2000), p. 60.

8 *Wakefield Court Rolls* V, p. 183; *Wakefield Court Rolls 1331–1333*, pp. 67, 129.

9 *Wakefield Court Rolls 1338–1340*, pp. 118, 200.

10 *Wakefield Court Rolls 1348–1350*, p. 26. See G. Fransson, *Middle English Surnames of Occupation, 1100–1350* (Lund, 1935), p. 182 (*stonhewere* in Yorkshire and Lancashire).

11 *Wakefield Court Rolls 1331–33*, p. 193.

12 *Wakefield Court Rolls 1338–1340*, pp. 25, 40, 46, 57.

13 *Wakefield Court Rolls 1338–1340*, p. 31.

14 M. T. Martin, ed., *The Percy Cartulary* (Surtees Society 117, 1921), p. 19 (xxiv).

15 J. M. Todd, ed., *The Lanercost Cartulary* (Surtees Society 203, 1997), p. 253.

16 *Northumberland Charters*, p. 338, n. 5.

17 *Cat. Ancient Deeds* I, pp. 271 (B604, B606), 532 (C1468), II (London, 1894), p. 463.

18 K. C. Newton, *Thaxted in the Fourteenth Century* (Chelmsford, 1960), p. 58.

19 'Derbyshire', p. 59.

20 *Wakefield Court Rolls* I, p. 288.

21 *Wakefield Court Rolls* I, pp. 15, 26.

22 *Wakefield Court Rolls*, I, p. 234. See also p. 171 where he was plaintiff in battery. Incidentally, this chronology would be consistent with the *isolated* reference to Matilda *Bowestrengmakere* who acquired a tenement in Gosford Street in Coventry: *Cat. Ancient Deeds* III, p. 58 (A4356).

23 *Wakefield Court Rolls* IV, p. 181.

24 Doncaster Archives Office DD/Yar/C/1/4.

25 *Hertfordshire*, p. 55.

26 W. Hudson, ed., *Leet Jurisdiction in the City of Norwich during the XIIIth and XIVth Centuries* (Selden Society 5, 1892), pp. 25, 28, 31, 52, 53, 55, 59.

27 *Halmota Prioratus Dunelmensis*, p. 66.

28 York Minster Archives 1.5/10: *Hugo Panyermaker cepit de domino unum cotagium cum Gardino in Neuton' Habendum ad voluntatem domini.*

29 *Chancery Miscellanea* Part VIII (List & Index Society 105, 1974), p. 137.

30 'East Riding Poll Tax', pp. 322, 324–6, 330, 343.

31 'West Riding Poll Tax', 5, pp. 26, 47, 51, 263; 6, pp. 4–5, 44; 7, pp. 12, 22.

32 *Wakefield Court Rolls 1348–1350*, p. 114: *sutor* is the Latin description for a cobbler or clouter.

33 Tengvik, *Middle English Surnames of Occupation.*

34 P. J. P. Goldberg, *Women, Work, and Life Cycle in a Medieval Economy. Women in York and Yorkshire c.1300–1520* (Oxford, 1992), pp. 43–4.

35 Goldberg was more concerned with urban occupational structures.

36 Fenwick, *Poll Taxes* I, pp. 457–60.

37 Fenwick, *Poll Taxes* I, p. 461.

38 Fenwick, *Poll Taxes* II, pp. 4–60.

39 L. R. Poos, ed., *Lower Ecclesiastical Jurisdiction in Late-medieval England. The Courts of the Dean and Chapter of Lincoln, 1336–1349, and the Deanery of Wisbech, 1458–1484* (British Academy Records of Social and Economic History n.s. 32, 2001), p. 61.

40 *Halmota Prioratus Dunelmensis*, p. 38.

41 *Cat. Ancient Deeds* VI, pp. 100–1 (12 Edward IV).

42 C. M. Fraser, ed., *The Accounts of the Chamberlains of Newcastle upon Tyne 1508–11* (Society of Antiquaries of Newcastle upon Tyne, Record Series 3, 1987), pp. 153, 155, 177, 178, 180, 183, 189, 232.

43 T.N.A. (P.R.O.) Chancery Miscellanea Bundle 53, File 1, No. 33; W. Page, ed., *Three Early Assize Rolls for the County of Northumberland Saec XIII* (Surtees Society lxxxviii, 1891), p. 313.

44 B. Thuresson, *Middle English Occupational Terms* (Lund Studies in English xix, 1950), p. 57, suggests *nethirde* in Yorkshire and Lincolnshire and *noutherd* in Cumberland and Yorkshire.

45 Poos, *Lower Ecclesiastical Jurisdiction in Late-medieval England*, p. 111.

46 *Wakefield Court Rolls* III, p. 102.

47 *Wakefield Court Rolls* I, p. 63.

48 *Wakefield Court Rolls* I, p. 194. In 1309, he offended against the vert: p. 204.

49 *Wakefield Court Rolls* I, p. 197.

50 *Halmota Prioratus Dunelmensis*, p. 20.

51 Colonel Parker, 'Lay subsidy rolls 1 Edward III N.R. & City of York' in *Miscellanea II* (YASRS lxxiv, 1929), p. 107.

52 Parker, 'Lay subsidy rolls 1 Edward III N.R. & City of York.', pp. 113, 117, 118, 119, 120, 122, 151, 153.

53 *Gloucestershire*, pp. 53–4, 75, 79, 92.

54 For a later example, the burial of William Kid, the 'common herd' of Long Houghton in 1709: H. M. Wood, *The Registers of Long Houghton* (Durham & Northumberland P. R. Soc. xxxvi, 1926), p. 124.

55 Parker, 'Lay subsidy rolls 1 Edward III N.R. & City of York', pp. 113, 115, 122, 123, 147, 155, 156.

56 R. B. Turton, ed., *The Honor and Forest of Pickering* (North Riding Record Society n.s. II and IV, 1895 and 1897), I, pp. 66, 84–5; II, p. 62.

57 Turton, *Honor and Forest of Pickering*, I, p. 143; II, pp. 29, 54.

58 Turton, *Honor and Forest of Pickering*, I, pp. 160, 165–6, 169; II, p. 54.

59 Turton, *Honor and Forest of Pickering*, II, pp. 25, 153, 154.

60 Parker, 'Lay subsidy rolls 1 Edward III N.R. & City of York', p. 112.

61 Parker, 'Lay subsidy rolls 1 Edward III N.R. & City of York', pp. 124, 132.

62 *Wakefield Court Rolls* III, p. 159.

63 *Wakefield Court Rolls* I, p. 192.

64 *Wakefield Court Rolls* I, p. 205.

65 *Wakefield Court Rolls* I, p. 40.

66 *Wakefield Court Rolls* I, p. 212.

67 Fenwick, *Poll Taxes* II, pp. 266–71; the analysis pertains only to the listings of taxpayers by vill, excluding therefore the list of jurors' names. Amongst the jurors' names, *Calverd* is omitted in the listings as Gunnerton's return is not extant: p. 266. The distribution map for *Nethird* (Figure 40) does include jurors' names.

68 *Lancashire Court Rolls*, pp. 33, 64, 89.

69 Fenwick, *Poll Taxes* I, p. 450: undoubtedly occupational rather than 'topographical'.

70 Fenwick, *Poll Taxes* II, p. 702: presumably occupational rather than topographical.

71 'East Riding Poll Tax', pp. 321, 333–5, 337, 340–4, 346, 349–52.

72 H. M. Wood, ed., *The Registers of St Nicholas' Church* [Durham] (Durham & Northumberland P. R. Soc. xxxii, 1918), pp. 16, 22.

73 H. M. Wood, *The Registers of Whitburn* (Durham & Northumberland P. R. Soc. x, 1904), pp. 6–8, 9–11.

74 M. E. Noble, *The Registers of the Parish of Shap* (Kendal, 1912), pp. 2, 5, 15, 16, 24.

75 Noble, *Registers of the Parish of Shap*, p. 105.

76 Noble, *Registers of the Parish of Shap*, pp. 30, 72, 93.

77 M. E. Noble, *The Registers of the Parish of Askham* (London, 1904), pp. 2, 5, 15, 17, 25, 33, 35, 137, 139, 142, 145.

78 H. Brierley, *The Registers of Brough under Stainmore* I (Cumberland and Westmorland P. R. Soc., 1923), pp. 141, 146.

79   S. Simpson & J. Charlesworth, *The Parish Register of Gisburne* I (Yorks. P. R. Soc. 114, 1943): pp. 236, 239, 240, for example, mention their habitations.

80   Simpson & Charlesworth, *Parish Register of Gisburne*, p. 2.

81   Simpson & Charlesworth, *Parish Register of Gisburne*, pp. 5–9, 11, 12.

82   Simpson & Charlesworth, *Parish Register of Gisburne*, pp. 223–6, 229 (Edmund, John, Henry, John, William, John and Robert – all consistently Geldert).

83   W. J. Kaye, ed., *The Parish Register of Ripon* I (Yorks. P. R. Soc. 80, 1926), pp. 47–8.

84   J. Foster, ed., *The Registers of the Antient Parish of Giggleswick-in-Craven* I (Settle, n.d.), pp. 20, 42, 71, 130; see p. 56 for the burial of Agnes Keldarde there in 1579.

85   H. S. Cowper, ed., *The Registers of Aldingham in Furness* (Lancs. P. R. Soc. 30, 1907), pp. 6, 9, 11, 15, 17–20, 23–4.

86   Foster, *Registers … Giggleswick-in-Craven* I, p. 12.

87   Foster, *Registers … Giggleswick-in-Craven* I, pp. 39, 142.

88   J. D. Hemsworth, ed., *The Registers of Monk Fryston* (London, 1896), pp. 24, 27.

89   'West Riding Poll Tax'.

90   *Wakefield Court Rolls* III, p. 81.

91   *Wakefield Court Rolls* III, p. 102 (1307).

92   *Kyder* spilled out into adjacent Derbyshire where it occurred at Drakelowe in 1327, singularly unusual in its vernacular rendition: 'Derbyshire', p. 50.

93   *Wakefield Court Rolls* III, p. 124.

94   G. Lakoff & M. Johnson, *Metaphors We Live By* (Chicago, 1980, repr. 2003).

95   *Wakefield Court Rolls* I, pp. 85–6 (1307).

96   *Wakefield Court Rolls* III, p. 65.

97   *Wakefield Court Rolls* III, p. 73.

98   *Wakefield Court Rolls* IV, pp. 11, 145.

99   *Wakefield Court Rolls* IV, p. 121.

100 *Wakefield Court Rolls* V, pp. 67, 190.

101 *Wakefield Court Rolls 1348–1350*, p. 21.

102 *Wakefield Court Rolls 1348–1350*, pp. 51–2.

103 *Wakefield Court Rolls 1348–1350*, p. 55.

7

NORTHERN TOPOGRAPHIES

Introduction: issues

In charters relating to vills within the vicinity of Whalley in the fourteenth century, the participants, including witnesses, involved William *del Hakkyng* who attested instruments associated with Eccleshall and Melver in 1342.[1] This William *del Hakkyng* witnessed another charter for Wilpshire about the same time.[2] As prolific in these arrangements was Nicholas *del Slakk*, once described as *clericus*, for he attested charters between *c.*1330 and *c.*1340 which conferred land in Castleton, and he was once conjoined in the witness list with William *del Slakk*.[3] Nicholas *del Slakk* also corroborated charters relating to Whitworth between 1321 and 1336.[4] Yet another attestor of Whitworth charters, but at the turn of the fourteenth century, was Michael *del Schagh*, a tenant there, whose son, John *del Schagh* succeeded him as a tenant in the vill some time before 1321x1324.[5] Another witness to charters relating to land in Castleton at this time was Adam *del Clogh*.[6] Around Whalley, John *del Clogh* performed the same role in the 1330s.[7] These topographical bynames were characteristic of this part of Lancashire.

Considering a single manor in Lancashire, Tottington, in 1323–4, appearances were manifested in the manorial court by peasants designated *dil Stoke, dil Barres, dil (H)ewod, dil Both, dil Birches, dil Dame, dil Rodes, dil Wode, dil Shagh, dil Hogh, dil Grene, dil Lawe, dil Mosse,* and *dil Stones.*[8] Within a single manor, consequently, a very wide variety of topographical features informed peasants' bynames, some of which were distinctive to southern Lancashire.

Topographical bynames were extremely sensitive to region for a number of reasons: variation in regional topographies; dialect lexis for topographical terms; and dialect phonemes.[9] These influences combined to produce a distinctive corpus of topographical bynames and surnames in the North, with sub-regional variation because of intensely localized topographies. Despite usually being consigned to the 'Highland Zone', the North contained wide topographical variation.

One subset can be immediately highlighted because it slightly differentiated parts of eastern Yorkshire from the remainder of the North and was evocative of some topographical bynames elsewhere. One of the taxpayers in the North Riding in 1327 was identified as Thomas *del Loft*.[10] At Coverham, 1s. was levied in 1327 from Alexander *del Howe*, whose topographical byname was replicated in this tax listing in Hugh *del Howe* at East Hauxwell, Robert *del Howe* at Stokesley, and William and Robert *del Houw* at Sourby.[11] This distinctive corpus of topographical bynames is completed by *del Wold*, comprising William *del Wold* at Croft and Robert *del Wold* at Sutton in 1327.[12]

The significance of topographical bynames and surnames thus inheres in the variation of topography eliciting a variety of bynames in different broad regions and even more localization of bynames in sub-regions. One feature of topographical bynames and surnames is consequently difference of lexis – of vocabulary. Other variations obtained too. Throughout much of England, the preposition in syndetic forms of topographical bynames predominantly consisted of Middle English *at(t)(e)*. Whilst in asyndetic formations of surnames the preposition was omitted (producing, for example, Wood rather than Atwood), the prepositional element might in some cases be incorporated in hereditary surnames, such as Atwell. In those areas, the French prepositional prefix *del* or *de la* remained subsidiary. In some parts of the North, however, *del* and *de la* apparently superseded Middle English prepositions in topographical bynames, perhaps truncating the formation of asyndetic forms of surname in the Atwell form. This feature is explored in more detail below.

Perusing the court rolls of the composite manor of Wakefield elicits another subset of topographical bynames, some consistent with those in parts of Lancashire, others more particular to the area of Wakefield. In 1298, Richard and Jordan *del Ker* acted as pledges in Stanley within the manor.[13] In the same year, but at Holne within the manor, Robert son of Matthew *del Scoles* gave 6d. to receive two acres of land in *le Scoles*, for which his pledge was Adam *del Scoles*.[14] Then too, Hanne *del Schawe* was placed in mercy for an escaped beast at Sowerby, whilst Gelle *Quintin* proceeded against Richard *del Ker* in a plea of trespass.[15] Also placed in mercy for an escape, at Hiperum, was John *del Clogh*.[16]

Perhaps more instantly recognisable with northern topography was Michael *del Crag* who held land in Triermain in 1263x1271, in the extreme north-west.[17] In this area of the north-west developed other distinctive topographical bynames, exemplified in Robert *del Gill*, one of the customary tenants (*gresmen*) at Dalston Magna in 1328x1332.[18]

Some of these bynames were incipiently developing into family surnames in the early fourteenth century, including del Hakkyng at Billington near Whalley in Lancashire where William del Hakkyng was succeeded by his son, Bernard del Hakkyng and by John del Hakkyng.[19] This process of stabilization can be observed too in the del Clogh kinship in the same area. Adam del Clogh attested a charter relating to Stanworth in 1335 and another contemporary charter referred to land which was defined as *le Clogh*.[20] Indeed, Adam regularly witnessed charters relating to Stanworth and Billington.[21] More pertinently, in 1316, Robert *Clogh* granted land in Clitheroe to Adam *del Clogh* and in other charters it transpired that Adam's son was John *del Clogh*.[22] During the early fourteenth century, this byname also exhibited some signs of becoming a family name.

Another aspect of these topographical bynames is that they were not confined to the lowest social groups. Assuming that jurors for royal inquisitions belonged to a social stratum above the lowest social degree – i.e. were law-worthy and had some dignity – jurors at Rochdale in 1323 included William *del Slak* and Nicholas *del Slak*, at Preston in 1324 and 1325 Hugh *del Hackyng*, at Lancaster, Mitton and Preston in

1325 and 1329, William *del Hackyng* at Billington in 1329, Hugh *del Flaskes*, and at Preston in 1334 John *del Clogh*.[23] Previously an inquisition had reported in 1310 that Bernard *del Hackyng* held a moiety of a bovate in thegnage tenure in Wilpshire.[24] The frequency of attendance on juries by some of these men with topographical bynames implies some status, at middling social level.[25]

Now with these uncompounded and generic topographical terms, little ambiguity is involved. Nevertheless, one of the principal problems of topographical bynames in particular *pays* with a pattern of dispersed settlement – which existed in profusion in the northern zone – is the status of minor place-names derived from topographical features. Again, the composite manor of Wakefield provides a useful illustration. In 1298 at Sowerby, Alota *del Wytelie* allowed an escape of a beast, whilst Richard *del Sandforth* acted as a pledge then.[26] More pertinently, perhaps, Cecily *de Briggehuses* proffered 6d. to receive for the term of her life a toft in *Brigghuses* which Adam *le Milner*, her late husband, had held. Her pledge, moreover, was Roger *de Breggehuses*.[27] A year later, at Hiperum, Saundre *de Briggehuses* acquired six acres of land from Hanne son of William *de Briggehuses*.[28] Some ten years later, at Rastrick, Henry *del Briggehous* acceded to a bovate of land for a term of twenty years.[29]

A decade earlier – in 1306 – Richard *del Rodeker* was presented for an escaped animal, and an inquisition was convened to determine whether he, as Richard *del Rediker*, had broken the lord's fold in Sowerby in 1307.[30] A year later, Eva *del Wolfker* and Cecily *del Wytestones* were amerced, one for an escape, the other for brewing.[31] In 1316, the jury of inquisition for Sowerby included John *del Asschenhirst*.[32] For escapes in the same hamlet proceedings were instituted against Robert *del Grenehirst* and Richard *del Bredinsikes* about the same time.[33] About that very time, Thomas *del Wolfker* made a payment of 1s. to enlarge his curtilage; William and Adam *del Hyngyndrode* appeared in court; John *del Stonyleghe* was arrested as a common thief; and John *del Noteschaghe* acted as a pledge.[34] In 1317, the plaintiff in a plea of debt, Thomas *del Castelsted*, persuaded William *del Estwode* to be his pledge.[35] Perhaps this feature is characterized best in the transaction between Robert *del Gledholt* and John *del Gledholt* in 1309, Robert acquiring a full bovate from John.[36]

All these topographical terms became consolidated as minor place-names in the large, composite manor of Wakefield. In localities with dispersed settlement, the distinction between bynames derived from topographical features and those with a toponymic origin in minor place-names is confused and complicated. No strict delineation is possible.

The lexical components

Confronting any discussion of the early formation of topographical bynames, particularly in terms of understanding dialect lexis, is the complication of register – since some bynames continued to be recorded in written records in their Latin form. Even when topographical bynames were predominantly rendered in the lower register, Middle English vernacular, the limited frequency of Latin forms confounds interpretation. Occasionally, the conundrum is resolved by two taxpayers in the same township or unit of assessment being recorded in two registers, allowing comparison. Thus at Barniston in 1301, two taxpayers were designated differently *ultra rivulum* and *overthebeck*, which appear as synonyms.[37] In other cases, assumptions can be allowed: a presumption that *ad portam* equates *to atte gate/yate* or *ad ripam* to the repetitive *de la* or *atte bank*.[38]

Despite their relative infrequency and their occasional occurrence in other areas of England, some Scandinavian lexical items, particularly Old Norse (ON), provided the 'north' with a distinctive topographical vocabulary: *bek* (a stream);[39] *kar* (brushwood or wet ground);[40] *lund* (*lundr*) (a small grove or wood);[41] and *scale* (*skalí*) (a temporary hut).[42] Additionally, the lexis was distinguished by other particular items: *bothe* (a vaccary);[43] *boure* (a cottage);[44] and *flash* or *flask* (swampy ground).[45]

The prolific extent of topographical bynames in northern settlements can be

acres 1	fairhalghes 1	lache 3	shore 1
applegarth 3	fairhurst 1	lane (*ad venellam*,	side 3
appleyard 2	fald 3	lone) 6	sike 5
ash 2	fall 4	lanend 1	slack 4
bank (bonk) 35[46]	fanside 2	lathe 7	slene 1
bar 1	fell 5	laund 1	snape 2
barn (berne) 3	fermhed 1	law 8	spen 1
bergh 3	fern 1	lee (legh) 9	spinney (*ad*
berye 2	filde (feld) 5	ley 1	*spinam*) 4
birch (birk) 8	filding 1	lidgate 5	stall 1
Blacklache 1	flaskes 3	lightbirkes 1	ster 1
booth 5	flat 1	longhouse 1	stock 1
botehil 1	ford 7	low 1	stones (stanes) 6
bothel 1	forest 1	lund 3	storches 1
bottom (bothem) 2	fossey 1	lyth 1	street (street,
bow 5	frith 1	mare 2	estrete) 5
bower 3	garth 9	marrais 4	stub 2
boys 1	gate (yate) 28	marre 3	style 2
bracken 1	gate end (gathende)	marsh (*de marisco*)	swin 1
brand 1	1	3	tern 4
bridge (brigg, *ad*	gill 16	marsh (*mersh*) 7	thorn 1
pontem) 27	gillhead 1	meadow 2	thwait 2
bridge end	green (grene, *de*	meer 7	tithes 1
(brighend) 1	*viridi/e*) 49	meles 1	topping 7
bridgehead 1	greendike 1	mill 2	torp 1
brookhouse 1	hale 6	mire 7	town 2
broom 7	hams 1	moor 31	townend 15
burn 6	haweld 1	moorhouse 1	trees 1

Table 13 Lexical elements in topographical bynames: lay subsidies in northern counties, 1296–1332 (continued opposite)

cahowe 1	hay 4	moriley 1	underhou 6
castle 10	head (heued) 5	moss 3	undertree 1
chapel 1	headrow 1	oak (ak, ayk) 2	underwood 5
chemine 1	heath 7	oldfield 1	vale 1
childers 1	hedge (heg(ges)) 2	outgang 1	wald 6
clay 8	held 3	park 3	walhus 1
cliffe 9	henges 1	pele 1	wall (de vallibus) 7
clogh 2[47]	hesk 1	place 2	wathe 1
close 1	heskes 1	poll (pull) 4	well 30
coppedhurst 2	heugh 2	prees 1	west end 2
cot 1	hevening 1	qwoux 1	whomme 1
cote 23	hey 14	rake 1	wich 4
coteslact 1	hill (hull) 76	rawe 1	willows (de
cotgarth 1	hirne 2	ridding 9	salicibus, wylies,
crag 5	hoga 7	ridge (rigg, righ) 2	willews) 5
croft 5	hole 2	roche 1	wind (wend) 2
crogarth 1	hollin 5	rode 2	windmill 1
crokdike 1	holme 7	row 1	wodehouse 2
crokwath 1	holt 3	sale 7	wood (wode, de
crook 3	hope 4	sands 4	silva, de bosco) 29
cross 9	how (hou) 24	scales 3	woodland 1
dale 13	hurst 2	scoles 3	woodside 1
dam 1	kar (ker) 9	see 13	work (wreck) 2
dene 2	keld 3	seller 1	wra (wro) 42
dike 9	kirk 15	seves 1	
doustes 1	kirkeyard 1	shaw (shagh) 7	
edge (egge, eghe) 9	kirkland 1	sheepshiel	
elders 1	kirkstyle 1	(schepscale) 1	
eles 1	knoll 5	sheil (schale,	
estir 1	knot 1	scales) 9	
eves 2	kulnekar 1	ship 1	
ewood (ewode) 4			

Table 13 *Lexical elements in topographical bynames: lay subsidies in northern counties, 1296–1332 (continued)*

illustrated further from their occurrence in the Wakefield court rolls in three years between 1331 and 1333.[48] Excluding complex forms which might denote minor place-names, almost forty generic elements appeared in bynames there.

By the end of the 1330s – in the two years Michaelmas 1338 to the same feast in 1340 – the number of topographical items had proliferated even further, encompassing not only repetition of the forms of 1331–3, but additionally: *bank; boure; brome; clay; court; feld; frith; heth; hirst; holok; holyns; lane; lawe; lunn; park; rokes; scoles; shagh; slak; snape; stones; storthes;* and *ternes.*[49]

Now, omitted from the Wakefield listing of 1331–3 is *del Holyns*, which might have

barre	elme	mere	
birkes	grene	mersh	weld
bothe	haghe	more	well
bothom	hill	mount	wode
boure	hole	okis	wro
brigge	holme	rode	wyke
brok	holne	spen	
clif	ker	stehelle	
dam	klogh	stok	
dene	lone	thwong	
eeves	lidyate	tounend	

Table 14 Topographical elements in bynames on Wakefield manor, 1331–3

had significance within the corpus of topographical bynames in the West Riding, associated with holly as a resource for animal feed.[50] So in 1316 John *del Holyns* was amerced for constructing a bank on Sandall common.[51] Contemporaneously, Margery *del Holyns*, also of Sandall, alienated seven acres of land with buildings in *Holinthorp*.[52]

Since *clogh* featured so extensively in southern Lancashire, it is not surprising that it also extended into north-west Derbyshire, where two taxpayers denominated *del Clogh* were assessed in 1327 at Chapel en le Frith, and also into north Staffordshire where a *del Clough* was taxed at Leek in 1332.[53] A charter referring to land in Offerton in Derbyshire was attested by Thomas and Richard *del* Clogh in 1335.[54] It remained, however, more prevalent in the north-west, particularly in Lancashire, epitomised by John *del Clogh*, juror at Preston in 1334.[55] This topographical byname might have intruded into the south-west of Yorkshire, represented perhaps by John *del Cloych* at Sowerby in 1298.[56] In North Yorkshire, we have to consider the possibility of some variation, as with Richard *del Cloc* in Pickering in 1327.[57]

Language, codes and dialect

The lexical composition of topographical bynames also divulged some dialect features, not least in the byname *del Schel* (Old Norse – ON), as associated with the unfree tenant Henry son of Adam *del Schel* who was manumitted in 1350 in Northumberland.[58] One of the broader characteristics of topographical bynames and surnames is thus how they represented different languages for the lexis of topographical terms consisted of a palimpsest. Whilst the terms were largely constituted by Old English (OE) derivations, some Brythonic topographical terms persisted, and the lexis of OE topography was expanded by Scandinavian items. It is perhaps uniquely in the far northern zone that a palimpsest of this extent existed. Amongst Bryhtonic formations in bynames and surnames featured *tor*, but more particularly *crag*.[59] Complementing the topographical lexis from Scandinavian (especially Norse) origin were the elements *beck, kar/ker, fell, gill, garth, snap(e), storth* and *toft*.[60]

How these Scandinavian terms infiltrated into the lexis of topographical bynames and surnames is again demonstrated by the Wakefield court rolls. In 1315, Richard *del Ker* was accused by the other villeins of living an immoral life amongst them, allowing a harlot, formerly exiled by the steward, to return to cohabit with him; although Richard pretended that she was a child-nurse, he was disbelieved by the inquisition, amerced half a mark, and bound over for good conduct.[61] This topographical byname was widely distributed in northern areas to indicate rough pasture or swampy ground.[62] In isolation, its occurrence in the Wakefield court rolls is unsubstantial, but it pertained to an iterative corpus of Scandinavian topographical lexis in bynames there. In the following year, William *del Snap* (Scandinavian 'pasture') acted as a tourn juror.[63] Previously, in 1308, three pledges for keeping the peace included William *del Storthes* (brushwood).[64]

In their profusion, Scandinavian topographical terms far exceeded the Brythonic forms which survived. Not surprisingly, the Brythonic lexis was largely circumscribed in the western and particularly the north-western corner of the northern counties. In the early fourteenth century, taxpayers in the north-west comprehended *del Crag(g)* at Westby and Claughton in Lancashire and Denton in Cumberland.[65] Thus at Orton in Westmorland, the contributors to the Poll Tax included a taxpayer identified as *del Cragge*.[66] At Skerton (Lancs.) in 1323, Robert *del Krag* held a messuage, fifteen acres and three roods of land.[67]

Prepositions

Initially, it might be considered that the preposition associated with topographical bynames and surnames has but limited significance. One aspect of that import has been suggested above: how some surnames incorporated the syndetic form with *atte*. In the secular term of the formation of surnames, that variation had an impact at the margin. In respect to the demarcation of regional language use in the middle ages, however, prepositions assumed more importance.

In northern areas, the dominant preposition was *del*, *dil* or *de la* by comparison with *atte* in southerly regions. The comparative use of these two prepositions divided a northern onomastic region from a southern one. Figure 41 illustrates how this difference was configured. The preposition *de la* and its elided variants were employed almost exclusively in northern counties. Moreover, in the western side of the north, its deployment extended down to the middle of Staffordshire and Derbyshire: in other words, this preposition continued to be used habitually in the upland areas of the West Midlands.

In the East Midlands, however, a different pattern obtained, for here forms of *de la* did not normatively continue below the Humber, so that *atte* was predominantly used in Lincolnshire, for example, even in Lindsey in the north of the county. Occasional appearances of *de la* in the north of the county intimate that some slight influence penetrated into northern Lincolnshire: so are listed Alice *de la Boure* and Ivette *de la Boure* at Alkborough in 1332.[68] Such occurrences were, however, exceptional. The extent of the difference is exemplified in the lay subsidy for

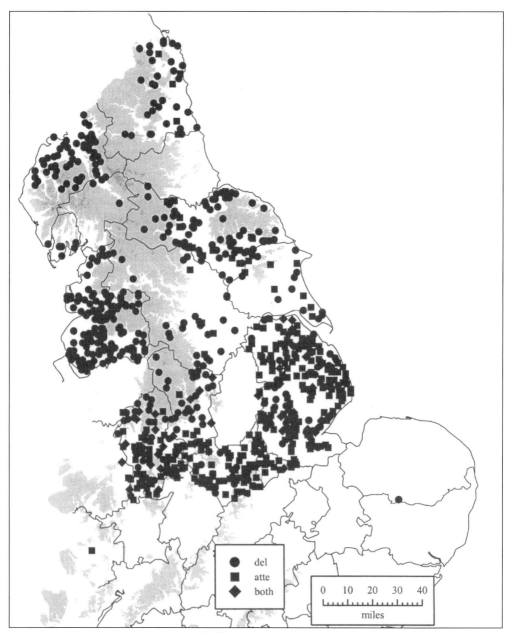

Figure 41 Prepositions in topographical bynames, late thirteenth and early fourteenth centuries

Hertfordshire in 1307 in which merely fifty out of 550 topographical bynames were preceded by the preposition *del* or *de la* by comparison with 500 introduced by *atte*.[69]

Since Figure 41 is predicated on data in the lay subsidies of the late thirteenth and early fourteenth century, it might be objected that what is encountered here is the predilection of particular *scriptores*, especially in Exchequer redactions of the rolls. That assumption, however, seems mistaken. The uniformity across the northern zone and into the north-west of the Midlands by comparison with an equal consistency in the use of *atte* in the north-east Midlands, implies that the tax records duplicated the language of the speech communities. Particular *scriptores* did not disrupt the general language use.

Nor does it seem evident that the preposition was appropriated as a form of self-fashioning. Peasants with topographical bynames regularly appearing in the manorial courts of southern Lancashire comprehensively retained the preposition *dil*. Indeed in these court rolls, topographical bynames never adduced the preposition *atte*, although the principal topographical elements remained common topographical features: (*dil*) *accres*; *asshes*; *barres*; *birches*; *bonk*; *bothe*; *brek*; *brokes*; *clif*; *clough*; *crok*; *dale*; *dame*; *dene*; *doustes*; *egge*; *ferns*; *filde*; *grene*; *hethe*; *hill/hull*; *helme*; *(h)ewod*; *hogh*; *hokes*; *holt*; *holyns*; *how*; *ker*; *lache*; *lawe*; *legh*; *lydyate*; *mos*; *parke*; *pulle*; *rodes*; *rydyng*; *scale*; *scoles*; *shagh*; *shore*; *sikes*; *sonde*; *stede*; *stoke*; *stones*; *ton*; *welle*; *wode*; *wyche*; and *yate*. Apparently, therefore, the employment of *del* or *dil* did not signify an attempt by any social group or individuals exclusively to define their status.

One potential explanation of the difference in the use of prepositions might be a supposition that most topographical bynames and surnames in a northern zone reflected the position that many topographical elements were or were incipiently minor place-names: for example, *del wodhous* might have represented either a topographical feature or what was regarded as a minor place-name.[70] Such a presumption, although explaining some instances, is largely irrelevant, since the preponderance of topographical bynames with the preposition *del* comprised mundane topographical features: *del lathes*; *del bank*; *del wraa*; *del brom*; *del grene*; *del felle*; *del hill* and similar elements.[71]

The practical language use in these bynames can be substantiated from other forms of record which may be assumed to relate to the speech community more closely. In charters and court rolls referring to Lancashire, for example, *del* and *dil* comprise the omnipresent prepositions. Charters relating to Speke in the early fourteenth century thus involved parties and witnesses designated *dil bonk*, *dil doustes*, *dil euese*, *del ferns*, *dil accris*; at Garston *dil ferns*, *del mos*, *dil grene*, *del hull*, *del dale*, *del brokys*, *del grene*, *del ford*, *dil wode*, *del crosse*, *del lake*, *del more*, and *del lunt*.[72] Referring to these topographical features, bynames were persistently and exclusively formed with the preposition *del* or *dil* to the exclusion of *atte*. The frequency of *del* extended also into Cheshire, illustrated by *del Lowe*, *del Schagh*, *del Broc* and *del Holt*, recurrent in charters relating to Middlewich and appurtenant places in the early fourteenth century.[73] Preference for this preposition was thus inherent in a particular late medieval northern language usage within a particular speech community.

The extent of conformity to the norm can be evaluated in more detail. In the Cumberland lay subsidy of 1327, 167 taxpayers were attributed topographical bynames with the preposition *del*. Merely two had such bynames with the preposition *atte*: *attestall* and *attetounhend*.[74] As will be considered further below, *townend* was normatively prefixed by *atte*, even in regions of the dominance of *del*. The corpus of lexical items constituted merely topographical features unlikely to have produced minor place-names: *(del) ayk* (one); *bank* (seven taxpayers); *bek* (three); *bothel* (one); *bow* (four); *brig* (one); *brighend* (hypercorrect, two); *brom* (three); *burn* (one); *cote* (five); *cragg* (one); *croyce* (one); *dale* (one); *fald* (three); *feld* (two); *fell* (five); *fenside* (two); *garth* (four); *gate* (two); *gill* (nine); *grene* (seven); *hames* (one); *heued* (four); *hill* (four); *holme* (five); *how* (eight); *lathes* (five); *law* (one); *leys* (two); *meles* (one); *mir* (one); *more* (three); *mos* (one); *place* (two); *polle* (one); *rakes* (one); *riddyng* (one); *rigg* (two); *sandes* (three); *sc(h)ales* (five); *sik* (one); *stanes* (one); *tern* (four); *toun* (one); *thwayt* (one); *wald* (one); *wood* (five); *wodsid* (one); and *wraa* (eleven). Two emphatic points ensue: the prepositional form was almost exclusively *del*; and the items did not constitute minor place-names, but were genuinely topographical bynames.

Considering the same exercise for Lancashire taxpayers at the same time, 232 were described by topographical bynames with the preposition *del*, by comparison with just two taxpayers attributed such bynames with the preposition *atte* (ambiguously *Astebrok* and *Altencotes*).[75] As in Cumberland, the lexical items are distinctly topographical without any imputation of minor place-names: *(del) accres* (one); *asshes* (two); *bergh* (three); *berne* (three); *birches* (seven); *bonk* (ten); *bothe* (three); *boure* (one); *brigge* (five); *brok(es)* (three); *car/kar* (five); *clif* (three); *clogh* (two); *cote* (one); *crag/krag* (three); *croft* (three); *crok* (two); *crosse* (three); *dale* (one); *dene* (two); *doustes* (one); *egge/eghe* (nine); *eves* (two); *ewode* (four); *fall* (one); *ferns* (one); *filde* (three); *flaskes* (one); *ford* (seven); *frith* (one); *gate/yate* (three); *grene* (seven); *hale* (six); *held* (two); *heth* (four); *hey* (five); *hirne* (one); *holm* (one); *holt* (three); *howe* (two); *hull* (five); *hurst* (one); *kirke* (two); *knoll* (five); *lathes/lache* (four); *law* (one); *legh* (six); *lone* (one); *lund* (one); *mere* (one); *mire* (four); *more* (eight); *mosse* (two); *merssh* (three); *pull* (one); *rodes* (one); *rydyng* (seven); *scales* (three); *scoles* (one); *shagh* (seven); *shore* (one); *sik* (one); *slak* (three); *snape* (two); *spen* (one); *street* (one); *storches* (one); *stubbe* (one); *thorn* (one); *toun* (one); *trees* (one); *walle* (one); *wich* (four); *wode* (eleven); and *wraa/wroo* (three).

In Northumberland, topographical bynames prefixed with *atte* appeared more frequently, accounting for eleven taxpayers (*attedikes* [two], *attemer*, *attemore*, *attetonheud*, *attehill*, *atteredside*; *atteburn*, *attelidegat*, *attegat* and *attestanes*).[76] The preposition *del/dil*, however, comprehended sixty-four taxpayers with topographical bynames in the same list, 1296–7. As consistently as in Cumberland and North-umberland, the items concerned topographical features which would not have constituted minor place-names: *(dil) both* (two); *burn* (four); *clay* (three); *cote* (one); *dal* (one); *dene* (one); *flat* (one); *gren* (six); *hill* (six); *hay* (five); *heugh* (one); *hope* (one); *how* (two); *ley* (two); *low* (five); *mere* (one); *ridding* (one); *sale* (three); *schel* (two); *swin* (one); *side* (one); *vale* (one); *wal* (one); *well* (one); and *wra* (two).

Amongst the taxpayers in the East and North Ridings of Yorkshire in 1301, 136 were identified by topographical bynames with the preposition *del* and thirty-four with the same form prefixed by *atte*.[77] The latter consisted of *(atte) ak* (one), *appelgarth* (one), *beck* (six), *garth* (one), *gate/yate* (four), *hou* (three), *hesk* (one), *kelde* (three), *kirck* (one), *kirkestile* (one), *lych* (one), *mar* (one), *outgang* (one), *sandes* (one), *stiell* (two), and *tounende* (five). Indicating that the elements did not consist of minor place-names, the corpus combined with *del* included: *bank* (nine), *bayle* (one), *berye* (two), *bour* (one), *boys* (one), *bowe* (one), *brend* (one), *brig* (one), *bynkes* (one), *chymine* (one), clay (two), cote (nine), croke (one), dam (one), dale (six), estir (one), ellers (one), flaskes (one), forest (one), gille (four), grene (sixteen), hay (four), hegges (one), heskes (one), hille (twenty), hole (one), holyn (one), hope (one), how (five), kragg (one), lathe (one), laund (one), marrays (two), mare (one), mere (one), more (one), pele (one), sale (one), scoch (one), seves (one), slack (one), ster (one), street (one), twait (one), wald (two), wathe (one), welle

Form[86]	Number
syndetic with *del*	666
syndetic with *de*	345
syndetic with *at(te)*	174
asyndetic	255

Table 15 *Composition of topographical bynames and surnames in the West Riding Poll Tax, 1379*

(three), westende (one), wyndmillen (one), wode (one) and wra (three).

In a previous taxation completed in 1297, largely collected in the West and East Ridings, eighteen topographical bynames with *atte* were exceeded by eighty-seven combined with *del*. The corpus associated with *del* comprised: (*del*) *apelyerd* (one); *bank* (two); *barre* (one); *birke* (one); *bothem* (one); *brom* (one); *brigge* (one); *clay* (two); *clif* (one); *cote* (four); *croft* (one); *dike* (three); *estrete* (one); *fall* (three); *fossey* (one); *gathende* (one); *gill* (one); *grene* (ten); *hale* (one); *heth* (two); *hille/hulle* (nineteen); *hirste* (one); *hole* (one); *holyn* (two); *how* (one); *ker* (four); *lane* (one); *lund* (two); *meer* (one); *mire* (one); *more* (one); *oldfeld* (one); *redwed* (one); *rodes* (one); *sale* (one); *sik* (one); *stan* (one); *stockes* (one); *werk* (one); and *wra* (one). With the exception of *oldfeld*, none of these items was likely to refer to a minor place-name, nor were those topographical bynames preceded by *atte*: (*atte*) *bek* (one); *cotes* (one); *gathende* (one); *hale* (one); *henges* (one); *lane* (one); *lidgate* (four); *mar* (one); *see* (one); *tounhend* (one); and *wend* (one).

Now, considering locally-produced records (the manorial and franchisal courts of Wakefield), about thirty-five topographical bynames featured in the rolls in 1331–3, all but six of which contained the preposition *del*. The exceptions were constituted by *attetounend* (predictably), *atteeves*, *attewell*, *attebarre*, *attestehelle*, and *atteelme*.[78] In two years from late 1338 to late 1340, the manor court rolls contained just over fifty different topographical bynames, only the following of which assumed the preposition *atte*, whilst the remaining fifty were compounded with *del*: *attonende*; *attebarre*; *attekirk*; and *attestighel*.[79]

Principal amongst the *atte* compounds remained *Attebarre*, represented by John *Attebarre* of Alverthorpe. It is possible that the employment of the preposition *atte* was consonant with his status as a *nativus*.[80] In 1314, this John *Attebarre* attended the court of Wakefield for the hamlet of Alverthorpe as a plaintiff in debt and pledge.[81] The possibility is thus encountered that the bynames of the unfree were associated here with *atte* and those of the free with the higher register of *del* – but that is purely speculative, predicated on insufficient evidence.

In East Anglia, for comparison, Carlsson estimated that the preposition *del* predominated before 1275, but that its prominence persisted towards the middle of the fourteenth century only in Suffolk, whereas *del* had by then been replaced by *at(te)* in Norfolk.[82] By contrast, *del* continued to dominate throughout the North.

Now, in the Wakefield manorial court rolls occurred some of those topographical bynames – a small proportion from the total corpus there – which appear to be distinctively 'northern': John *del Slak* involved in a plea of covenant in 1338; Joan *del Clogh* in 1339 and William *del Clogh* in 1314; Robert *del Bank*, plaintiff in trespass and Henry *del Bank* in 1339; and William *del Lawe* amerced 2d. for trespass against the vert in the same year.[83]

Since topographical (and other forms of) bynames retained their syndetic form into the late middle ages, the preposition *del* or *dil* persisted into the Poll Taxes of 1377–81. In Northumberland, for example, taxpayers were assessed whose names were rendered as *del Schele* (in Abshiel and so thus corresponding to the feature), *del Byres*, *del Wode*, *del More* (four), *del Mere*, *del Brig'*, *del Marche*, *del Grene* and *del Grave*.[84] In the 1380s, indeed, Thomas *del Growe* inhabited Hunshelf in the West Riding.[85]

Through into the late fourteenth century, the preposition *del* characterized topographical bynames and surnames in the northern zone. Analysis of the Poll Tax for the West Riding in 1379 allows a very detailed examination of the composition of topographical bynames and surnames.

What is apparent here is the extensive survival not only of syndetic forms, but within those compounds the dominance of *del*.

Such persistence was not restricted to the West Riding, although it is most demonstrable there. In the Poll Tax for parts of Northumberland, although the absolute number of topographical bynames was much lower, most contained the preposition *del* and continued in syndetic form: *del Schele*; *del Byres*; *del Wode*; *del Haugh*; *del More* (four); *de le Low*; *del Grene* (two); *del Hay*; *del Mere*; *del Brig'*; *del Marche*; *del Par'*; *del Yle*; and *del Grave*. Moreover, *del* was associated still with some minor place-names: *del Lyndsay* and *del Newton*.[87] More extensive was the survival in Westmorland, where virtually all topographical bynames or surnames were constituted in the syndetic manner in the Poll Tax: almost fifty in a defective enumeration, including some minor place-names, comprising: *del Well*; *del Boll*; *de le Yate*; *del Bek*; *del Morland* (possibly a minor place-name); *del Wod* (two); *del Holm*; *del Garth*; *del Bernes*; *del Bowes*; *del Dale*; *del Fell*; *del Mosse*; *del Brekys*; *del Bank* (nine); *del Hull/Hill* (two); *del Park* (three – although this byname might be ambiguously occupational); *del More* (two); *del Hellergill* (minor place-name); *del Crage*; *del Yate* (three); *del Loge* (two); *del Rygge*; *del Myer*; *del Syle* (four – all at Tebay); *del Brygge*; *del Grene* and *del Kals'*.[88] Even within the city of Carlisle – the only Poll Tax return for Cumberland – syndetic topographical forms predominated and incorporated the preposition *del*: *del Parke* (ambiguously, as above); *del Birys*; *del Garth'*; *del Heuyd*; *del More*; *del Bek*; *del Kyrkgarth'*; *del Sandes*; *del Cow* and *del Strayte*.[89]

As prolific as in the West Riding was the persistence of syndetic forms of byname and surname combined with *dil* in Lancashire, where 134 different topographical features were combined with *dil* in bynames and surnames in the Poll Tax for the county, but additionally fifty-six different minor place-names retained the compound form with *dil*.[90] In total, almost four hundred contributors to the Poll Tax were identified by topographical bynames or surnames preceded by *dil*. To those taxpayers can be added almost eighty whose bynames or surnames derived from minor place-names containing the preposition *dil*.

Exceptionally, that situation did not obtain in the East Riding of Yorkshire, where the Poll Tax revealed that *del*, although persistent, did not retain the predominance exhibited elsewhere in the North.[91] Compared with forty-seven taxpayers with topographical bynames or surnames in asyndetic form and another forty-seven with such bynames or surnames retaining the syndetic form but preceded by *at*, only ten taxpayers bore topographical bynames or surnames with *del* and another five with *de*. In these aspects – the tendency to asyndetic form and the constancy of the preposition *at* in the late fourteenth century – the East Riding was affected by a different influence from the remainder of the North.

In this respect, as in several others, the East Riding exhibited an affinity with Lincolnshire, especially the northern Part of Lindsey. Most topographical bynames and surnames in Lindsey had by the Poll Tax been transformed into asyndetic form. Of the remaining syndetic forms, three assumed the preposition *atte*, one *in the*, five *del* and three *de*. Lindsey thus contained an admixture of West Riding and East Riding elements, but those were residual since there had been a greater movement to asyndetic forms. That process had advanced further in the southern Parts in Kesteven and Holland, where, furthermore, *atte* was almost the exclusive preposition.[92]

Further consideration can be devoted to this question by assessing characteristics on the periphery of the northernmost counties. In Derbyshire, the predominant feature was the persistence of syndetic topographical bynames and surnames and their continuation with the preposition *del*. Even in the county town of Derby, although the urban place exhibited few topographical names, those that existed were mostly combined with *del*: *del Crosse*; *del grene* (two); *del Wode*; *del Dale*; *del Ok*; *del Haye* (three); *del Begh'*; *del Wall'* and *del Nook*.[93] Even in the south of the county and in an urban place, therefore, the pattern was replicated. Accordingly, in the High Peak, the composition was even more pronounced, for here over forty contributors to the Poll Tax retained syndetic topographical bynames or surnames preceded by *del*. This dominance was interrupted only at and near Ashford where *in le* was consistently employed (*in le grene* – two; *in le dale* – six; and *in le dene* – three).[94]

Eponymous topographies

An equally important feature of topographical bynames in northern areas was the persistence of a relationship between the byname, the inhabitant and the topographical feature. That continuing association can be illustrated from the court rolls of the manor of Wakefield. In 1296, an entry fine of 1s. was exacted from Adam *del Scoles* for access to an acre of land in *Scoles* in Birton.[95] In that very same year the same amount was levied from Hugh *del Helme* to accede to a bovate of waste land at Helm.[96] Moving later, to 1349, John *de Boudrode* surrendered a messuage and twenty acres in Boothroyd to the use of his wife Isabella for her life with remainder to his son, William.[97] In the same year and on the same composite manor, Wakefield, William *de Thornes* was accused of the homicide of Robert *de Thornes* at Thornes.[98] The association is demonstrable when at Hyperum in 1315 Thomas *de Slaghwayt* offered 40d. to receive six acres in the *Bothes* from William *del Bothes* to hold during the life of Isabel *del Bothes* to whom they accrued as dower, she having alienated her life interest to William.[99] It was only at this point that the relationship between eponym and topographical feature was about to be disrupted. Later, in 1324, Robert *del Skoles* acquired a further acre in *le Skoles* in Alverthorpe.[100]

Voices of distinction

Above, some particular elements and simplex, uncompounded topographical bynames have been situated in their northern locations. As distinctly northern were some compounded topographical bynames which might, in some sense and in some cases, have existed as minor place-names. This feature of northern naming is exemplified by, for example, Hollingraike. Although not profuse, this surname became established in the late sixteenth century in Bingley – amongst other locations – where the children of Thomas – beginning with Robert in 1578 and comprehending at least seven others through to Mary in 1597 – were recorded as baptized in the parish church there. In 1585 and 1589, Helen and Stephen, offspring of John Hollingraike were christened in the same church. In 1600 daughters of Robert and Alexander Hollingraike received the same sacrament there.[101]

Of similar importance in northern husbandry was the rye croft, resulting in a distinctive – although not exclusive – development of an eponymous byname and surname throughout northern reaches. Anne, daughter of William Ricrofte, received baptism at Bingley parish church in 1592.[102] A generation earlier, Agnes Ricrofte had entered into married life in Snaith parish church.[103]

One topographical surname did not feature profusely in earlier centuries as a byname more generally through the north, yet became more visible on the western edge of the Pennines in the sixteenth century – *Moss(e)*. At Warcop the surname represented a number of kinship groups and developed as a focal surname there. Ten different male heads of household with this surname figured in the parish registers of Warcop between 1598 and 1612. Thomas Mosse of Warcop township had issue Dorothy, baptized in 1598, whilst in the same township James Mosse's daughter Elizabeth was christened in the same year when, too, Dorothy the daughter of Michael Mosse of Warcop received the same sacrament. Later in that township, Nicholas Mosse arranged the baptism of his daughter Ann in 1605 and Robert Morris organized the same for his daughter, Jenet. In the township of Blencarne within the parish, Katherine, child of Robert Mosse, was brought to the font in 1600, as also were the three sons of William Mosse of Blencarne in 1601, 1604 and 1607, and the daughter, Ann, of Humphrey Mosse of Blencarne in 1612. From Bank End in the parish, Thomas Mosse travelled with his daughter Ann in 1604 for her baptism.[104] Such a surname was particularly associated with the upland parts of the northern Pennines.

Distinctions of northern-ness inhered too in the surname Ewbank or Ubank. Although the byname and surname extended throughout the north, focal concentrations occurred in some parishes and townships, for example Morland and Brough in Westmorland. In Morland were registered the baptisms of Henry son of Thomas Ubancke in 1539, and Thomas's daughters Margaret and Jenet in 1540 and 1543, although Henry died in childbirth.[105] At nearby Brough, the baptisms were celebrated for Michael Ubank's children, Agnes (1560), Thomas and Richard (1563), Edward (1564), Michael (1567), and Isabel (1569). From 1561, the baptisms of children of Thomas Ubank were celebrated, commencing with Charles (1561), followed by Thomas (1563) and Roger (1567). In 1561 also the sacrament was conferred on Lancelot son of James Ubank. Some six years later, Rowland Ubank had issue James and in 1568 and 1570 further offspring, Thomas and Grace. Between those occasions, Anne daughter of Miles Ubank was baptized.[106] The impact of this surname on the parishioners, however, may perhaps be best estimated through the entries in the burial register. From the burial of John Ubanck in 1561, burials of Ubanks were certified in the register in 1561 (Agnes as well as John), 1562 (Christopher, Margaret and Brian), 1563, 1564, 1565, 1568 (Richard and Jeffrey), 1569 (Richard, Michael and Thomas), 1572, 1575, 1579 and 1581.[107] Frequent memorialization through burial ceremonies, as well as the celebrations of baptisms, made the surname highly visible to the parishioners.

Since *fell* represented upland topographies, its proliferation in the north was inevitable. This surname thus became a focal surname in some early-modern parishes, not least Aldingham (Lancashire). When the extant registers opened, the baptisms of James and Thomas Fell appeared early in the registration in 1562. Between 1563 and 1600, no fewer than fifty-seven christenings of Fells were recorded in this parish.[108] Numerous marriages were also, consequently, celebrated there, commencing at an earlier time in the registers since the extant registration of weddings opened in the 1540s, when William, Genet, Esota, Margaret I, Catherine, Margaret II, James, Alice I, Edward, Alice II and Thomas were all espoused.[109]

Tying up topographies

Topographical bynames and surnames contributed considerably to lived experience in northern areas through their onomastic particularity. Frequently encountered, they reflected back to inhabitants of the North the distinctive topographies which impacted upon their lives. Moreover, the topographical items in bynames and surnames consisted of a mélange of insular codes: Bretonnic, Scandinavian and Old English. Whilst the overall upland nature of the North – its characteristics of the Highland Zone – informed naming at a general level, the topographical variety of the northern zone again introduced localized differences. The detachment of parts of the East Riding constituted one such anomaly. Broad coherence was also instilled, however, by the predominance of the preposition *del* in formations of topographical bynames and the persistence of such syndetic forms later than in more southerly locations.

Notes

1   W. A. Hulton, ed., *The Coucher Book or Chartulary of Whalley Abbey* (4 volumes, Chetham Society 10–11, 16, 20, 1847–9), I, pp. 104, 110, 327 (38, 43, 105).

2   Hulton, *Whalley Coucher* I, p. 130 (64). For other charters witnessed by William *del Hakkyng*,

Whalley IV, p. 946 (x), 959 (xxii), 964 (xxix)1046 (cxxii), 1057 (cxxxvi), 1113. For those attested by his son, Bernard *del Hakkyng*, Hulton, *Whalley Coucher* III, p. 875 (lviii), IV, 976 (xliv), 987 (liii–liv), 1031 (ciii), 1041 (cxvi), 1060 (cxlii), 1066. All relate to Billington and it seems likely that this byname was developing into a hereditary surname in the first half of the fourteenth century.

3   Hulton, *Whalley Coucher* II, pp. 633, 635–6 (59–60, 62–3).

4   Hulton, *Whalley Coucher* III, pp. 700–2, 717, 723, 725 (74–6, 94, 97–8).

5   Hulton, *Whalley Coucher* III, pp. 680, 692, 699–700, 724 (52, 61, 63, 74–5, 95).

6   Hulton, *Whalley Coucher* II, pp. 517, 631 (31, 57). *Clogh* is omitted, apparently, from M. T. Lofvenberg, *Studies on Middle English Local Surnames* (Lund Studies in English XI, 1942), p. 39.

7   Hulton, *Whalley Coucher* I, pp. 290, 322, 329 (59, 90, 106).

8   *Lancashire Court Rolls*, pp. 6–15.

9   Lofvenberg, *Studies on Middle English Local Surnames*, p. xxi, for the usefulness of topographical bynames for dialect phonology.

10   Colonel Parker, 'Lay subsidy rolls 1 Edward III N. R. & City of York' in *Miscellanea II* (YASRS lxxiv, 1929), p. 123.

11   Parker, 'Lay subsidy rolls 1 Edward III N. R. & City of York', pp. 124, 129, 151, 159.

12   Parker, 'Lay subsidy rolls 1 Edward III N. R. & City of York', pp. 134, 140.

13   *Wakefield Court Rolls* I, p. 21.

14   *Wakefield Court Rolls* I, p. 31.

15   *Wakefield Court Rolls* I, pp. 37, 39.

16   *Wakefield Court Rolls* I, p. 50.

17   J. M. Todd, ed., *The Lanercost Cartulary* (Surtees Society 203, 1997), p. 263 (217).

18   R. L. Storey, ed., *The Register of John Kirkby, Bishop of Carlisle, 1332–1352, and the Register of John Ross, Bishop of Carlisle, 1325–1332* volume II (Canterbury and York Society lxxxi, 1995), p. 5.

19   See above n. 2.

20   Hulton, *Whalley Coucher* III, pp. 866–7 (xlvii, xlviii).

21   Hulton, *Whalley Coucher* III, pp. 875, IV, 1028, 1079 (lviii, xcix, xiii),

22   Hulton, *Whalley Coucher* IV, pp. 1116, 1125, 1118; see also Hulton, *Whalley Coucher* IV, pp. 946 (xi), 1045 (cxxi), 1051–2 (cxxx), 1078 (xii)1084 (xix)1106, 1131, 1135, for John's activities in the 1330s and 1340s.

23   Farrer, *Lancashire Inquests, Extents, and Feudal Aids* Part III, pp. 2, 4, 14, 25, and 57. For Hugh *del Hackyng* as a juror at Mitton, Foulridge and Preston in 1322–9: Farrer, *Lancashire Inquests, Extents, and Feudal Aids* Part II, pp. 45, 231–3.

24   Farrer, *Lancashire Inquests, Extents, and Feudal Aids* Part II, p. 12.

25   See n.23 for Hugh *del Hackyng*.

26   *Wakefield Court Rolls* I, pp. 47, 52 (1298).

27   *Wakefield Court Rolls* I, p. 54 (1306).

28   *Wakefield Court Rolls* III, p. 70 (1307).

29   *Wakefield Court Rolls* III, p. 113 (1316). It's possible that the etymology of *del Brighous* and variants has an occupational imputation, but it was consolidated as a minor place-name.

30   *Wakefield Court Rolls* I, pp. 59, 66; he was fined for an escape in 1316 at Sowerby: *Wakefield Court Rolls* III, p. 138.

31   *Wakefield Court Rolls* I, pp. 187–8 (1308).

32   *Wakefield Court Rolls* III, p. 141.

33   *Wakefield Court Rolls* III, p. 150.

34   *Wakefield Court Rolls* IV, pp. 83–5, 101.

35   *Wakefield Court Rolls* IV, p. 196; a heriot of 6d. had been exacted from William *del Hengandrode* on admission to his father's land in 1307: *Wakefield Court Rolls* III, p. 126 (1307).

36   *Wakefield Court Rolls* I, p. 218 (1309).
37   *Yorkshire 1301*, p. 59.
38   For *ad ripam*, *Yorkshire 1301*, p. 63.
39   S. Carlsson, *Studies on Middle English Local Bynames in East Anglia* (Lund, 1989), pp. 25–6.
40   Carlsson, *Studies on Middle English Local Bynames*, p. 67.
41   Carlsson, *Studies on Middle English Local Bynames*, p. 72.
42   Carlsson, *Studies on Middle English Local Bynames*, p. 93.
43   Carlsson, *Studies on Middle English Local Bynames*, p. 27.
44   Carlsson, *Studies on Middle English Local Bynames*, p. 28.
45   Carlsson, *Studies on Middle English Local Bynames*, p. 45.
46   Lofvenberg, *Studies on Middle English Local Surnames*, pp. 6, 17 omits *bank/bonk*.
47   Lofvenberg, *Studies on Middle English Local Surnames*, p. 39 omits *clogh*.
48   *Wakefield Court Rolls 1331–1333*.
49   *Wakefield Court Rolls 1338–1340*, passim.
50   M. Spray, 'Holly as fodder in England', *Agricultural History Review* 29 (1981), pp. 97–110.
51   *Wakefield Court Rolls* III, p. 129.
52   *Wakefield Court Rolls* III, p. 151.
53   'Derbyshire', p. 55; 'Staffordshire 1332', p. 115.
54   I. H. Jeayes, *Descriptive Catalogue of Derbyshire Charters* (London, 1906), p. 226 (1799).
55   Farrer, *Lancashire Inquests, Extents and Feudal Aids* Part III.
56   *Wakefield Court Rolls* I, p. 43.
57   Parker, 'Lay subsidy rolls 1 Edward III N. R. & City of York', p. 114.
58   *Northumberland Charters*, p. 340 (dcccxx).
59   G. Hughes, *A History of English Words* (Oxford, 2000), p. 75.
60   Hughes, *History of English Words*, p. 97.
61   *Wakefield Court Rolls* III, pp. 94–5. A Richard *del Ker* appeared in the court in 1298: *Wakefield Court Rolls* I, p. 44 (1298).
62   The term also survived in compounded form in what can only be presumed to be minor place-names, as illustrated by John *del Redykere* who fined for relief from the office of bailiff of Sowerby in 1316: *Wakefield Court Rolls* III, p. 112.
63   *Wakefield Court Rolls* III, p. 118. He was presented in 1316 for an escape: *Wakefield Court Rolls* III, p. 134.
64   *Wakefield Court Rolls* I, p. 189 (1308). This byname existed on the manor in 1298: *Wakefield Court Rolls* I, p. 40 (1298).
65   'Lancashire', pp. 61, 88; *Cumberland*, p. 39.
66   Fenwick, *Poll Taxes* II, p. 701.
67   Farrer, *Lancashire Inquests, Extents and Feudal Aids* Part II, p. 128.
68   T.N.A. (P.R.O.) E179/135/16, m. 2.
69   *Hertfordshire*.
70   Lofvenberg, *Studies on Middle English Local Surnames*, p. xxii.
71   These examples are extracted from *Cumberland*, pp. 3–10.
72   *Norris Deeds*, pp. 6–92.
73   J. Varley, ed., *A Middlewich Chartulary* (2 volumes, Chetham Society, 105, 108, 1941–4), II, pp. 267, 280–1, 283, 292, 292, 303, 376 (137g, 143f–g, 144d, 150c, 151d, 155b, 210i, 210k) (1316–1346).
74   *Cumberland*, pp. 50 52 for these two exceptions.
75   'Lancashire', pp. 14, 85.
76   *Northumberland*, pp. 64–6, 74, 136–7, 143, 151, 161, 175.
77   *Yorkshire 1301*.

78   *Wakefield Court Rolls 1331–1333*, pp. 3, 4, 6–7, 9, 14–15, 28, 30, 187.

79   *Wakefield Court Rolls 1338–1340*, pp. 10, 123, 202.

80   *Wakefield Court Rolls* III, p. 62 (1314).

81   *Wakefield Court Rolls* III, p. 61.

82   Carlsson, *Studies on Middle English Local Bynames*, pp. 147–9.

83   *Wakefield Court Rolls 1338–1340*, pp. 13, 22, 42, 58, 61; *Wakefield Court Rolls* III, p. 53.

84   Fenwick, *Poll Taxes* II, pp. 262–71.

85   *Cat. Ancient Deeds* III, p. 340 (C3201) (14 Ric. II).

86   A small number of other forms (*by-, in the-*) have not been counted as they are minimal.

87   Fenwick, *Poll Taxes* II, pp. 262–71, esp. 264 and 267 (for minor place-names).

88   Fenwick, *Poll Taxes* II, pp. 693–703.

89   Fenwick, *Poll Taxes* I, pp. 91–4.

90   Fenwick, *Poll Taxes* I, pp. 442–78.

91   'East Riding Poll Tax'.

92   Fenwick, *Poll Taxes* II, pp. 4–60.

93   Fenwick, *Poll Taxes* I, pp. 97–100.

94   Fenwick, *Poll Taxes* I, pp. 100–13 (*in le* clustered at pp. 110–11).

95   *Wakefield Court Rolls* I, p. 240.

96   *Wakefield Court Rolls* I, p. 245.

97   *Wakefield Court Rolls 1348–1350*, p. 156.

98   *Wakefield Court Rolls 1348–1350*, p. 159.

99   *Wakefield Court Rolls* III, p. 76.

100 *Wakefield Court Rolls* V, p. 21.

101 W. J. Stavert, ed., *The Parish Registers of Bingley* (Yorkshire P. R. Soc. 9, 1901), pp. 2, 4, 6, 9, 11, 13, 16, 22–4.

102 Stavert, *The Parish Registers of Bingley*, p. 15.

103 W. Brigg, ed., *The Parish Registers of Snaith* (Yorks. P. R. Soc. 57, 1917), p. 148 (1565).

104 J. Abercrombie, *The Registers of Warcop* (Cumberland and Westmorland P. R. Soc., 1914), pp. 1, 2, 3, 4, 5, 7, 58.

105 J. Anderson, *The Registers of Morland* Part 1 (Cumberland and Westmorland P. R. Soc., 1957), pp. 2, 3, 5, 183.

106 H. Brierley, ed., *The Registers of Brough under Stainmore* (Cumberland and Westmorland P. R. Soc., 1923), pp. 1, 2, 3, 5, 6.

107 Brierley, *Registers of Brough*, pp. 135, 136, 137, 138, 139, 141, 143, 146.

108 H. S. Cowper, ed., *The Registers of the Parish of Aldingham in Furness* (Lancs. P. R. Soc. 30, 1907), pp. 1–3, 5–10.

109 Cowper, *Registers of the Parish of Aldingham*, pp. 108–10.

8
NORTHERN NICKNAMES?[1]

In the Crown pleas in Cumberland in the middle of the thirteenth century, proceedings referred to Nicholas *Miriwistell,* Richard *Redmantel,* Robert *Broken-heuedknaue,* Robert *Bliscidblod,* Maurice *Strangthef,* Stephen *Upwythestreng,* and William *Cuttepurs,* the nickname bynames of some of whom were demonstrative of their character or criminality.[2] On the manor of Wakefield in 1313 William *Suerdsliper* was ordered to be attached for nightwalking with arms.[3] Descriptive nickname bynames of this ilk were associated in Crown Pleas elsewhere with some accused characters. In considering the distinctiveness of Northern naming, the question which must be addressed in this context is: were such epithets more frequent in a vernacular environment in the North than in other regions?[4]

Indeed, some of these particular nickname bynames must have been and remained extremely localized, not least *Blissedblod.*[5] Allusion above to Robert *Bliscidblod* in the Crown Pleas is complemented by later references to *Blissedblod* in Carlisle and its locality. Perhaps a century later, Adam *Blissedblode* was enumerated amongst those inhabitants of Carlisle who had recently been absolved from penance for preventing the bishop's servants from purchasing victuals.[6] Now, in the Poll Tax of 1377 for the City, Adam Blisidblode was assessed alongside John Blissidblode.[7]

Not only, however, is the question whether descriptive bynames continued to denote character, that is remained flexible, constructed compound bynames; it also demands whether bynames associated with the lower body – the sexual body – were deployed to discipline or to impute social criticism.[8] For example, in the middle of the fourteenth century, one of the pledges for the maintenance of houses and lands in Hundsworth in the West Riding was evoked as Roger *Gildanbollok'.*[9] Now a generation earlier, in the hamlet of Sowerby on the enormous manor of Wakefield, another Roger *Gildynballokes* had been amerced 3d. for escapes of animals.[10] Had such explicit bynames become residual to the North and if so, why?

Sexually-implicit nickname bynames

The replication of *Gildanbollok* in the West Riding in the fourteenth century reveals the continuation of salacious nickname bynames in the North of England. Whilst it is evident that such sexually-implicit nickname bynames had existed throughout

England at an earlier time, their persistence in the North apparently continued after their relative demise in the south. Whilst some of the bynames, such as *Gildanbollok*, are fairly precise in their imputations, others remained implicit or ironic, their content perhaps less demonstrative. The existence of the former, more direct nicknames, however, allows and informs the interpretation of the more concealed forms.[11]

In the understanding of other nickname bynames, then, it is necessary to invoke the implications of the more overt nicknames. When, in 1306, Adam *Luvelavedy* was amerced for collecting dry wood in Ossett, his nickname byname was open to interpretation. The strong possibility is that it reflected amorous inclinations, perhaps even harassment.[12] Behind the nickname byname of Peter *Strekelevedy*, who alienated land in Sandall in 1316, is the imputation of a fornicator.[13] The Lancashire Poll Tax contains other taxpayers in the late fourteenth century with this deuterotheme: Ledelady at Windle and Shakelady at Lathom.[14] Across the Pennines, *Ledelevedy* taxpayers to the lay subsidy were assessed at Harpham and in Sherburn.[15] This interpretation can be extended to *Tippeleuedy* in Kirkby in Cleveland and *Wakeleuedy* at Farndale in 1301 and to *Tipleuedy* at Hutton in 1327.[16] In the Poll Tax for Lancashire in 1379, this sexually-charged element persisted in the form of the taxpayer called Ledelady at Windle.[17]

Although formation with *-levedy* often indicated sexual content, the meaning of some sexually-imbued bynames remains more opaque to us, but was comprehended by medieval society.[18] In particular, *-rose* bynames in many cases were synonyms for *-levedy* formations, conveying a sense of action performed against maidens, young women. So, interestingly, a clerk appointed subdeacon and then ordained to the priesthood, in 1354 and 1356 respectively, responded to the name William Ryngrose.[19] *Ringrose* and *Ryngotherose* at Dacre in Cumberland and Ashton in Makerfield in Lancashire in the early fourteenth century may have the same implications – of sexually-implicit action against women.[20] Within this context, *Pullerose*, associated with a taxpayer to the lay subsidy at Stillingfleet in 1301, might be construed as metaphorically action against women.[21]

A recognised lexical element in the sexually-implicit nickname bynames was the deuterotheme *-tail*, strongly intimated in the taxpayers designated *Strektail* at Stainton in Yorkshire in 1301.[22] Sexual incontinence was imputed by the byname of Robert *Scrattayl* at Stainton in the North Riding in 1327.[23] Sexual parts of the body can be inferred in other nickname bynames, more usually male sexual organs. Conforming to this category was the taxpayer called *Scharpyntil* assessed at Wylam in Northumberland in 1296.[24] Amongst the lexicography of male sexual instruments, *pintil* furnished one euphemism for the penis, recurring in another Northumberland contributor to the lay subsidy, *Silverpintil'* at Wooperton.[25] Whether the uncompounded use of *Pyntel* or *Pintil* for taxpayers in the far north constituted sexual innuendo is less easily determined.[26]

More ambiguous in their intention were lexical elements for stick which might impute either aggressiveness and failure to control emotion – quick-tempered resort to weapons – or sexual proclivity, that is, as a metaphor for the penis. The latter construction might be inferred then for the *Shakeshaft* who was assessed in the early fourteenth century at Aughton in Lancashire.[27] The imputation resided too in *Schaktre*, contributing tax at Aislaby in 1301.[28] Given this context, *Waggestaffe* (*Waggestave*) might have imputed much the same sexual activity, attached to taxpayers at Dishforth and Colburn in 1301.[29]

Considering now the female pudenda, amongst the explicit bynames must be included *Silvercounte*, a byname which occurred once without a forename amongst the offences against the vert in Horbury on the manor of Wakefield in 1306.[30] Even more remarkable is the taxpayer's name *Clevecunt* at Old Malton in 1301.[31]

Sexual friskiness might have been imputed to Nicholas *Tuplamb*, a tenant of land in Catton in 1334.[32] Generic terms not associated with the body also informed the sexual vocabulary of nicknames. The byname *Playndamur* assigned to the John who was taxed 1s. 3d. at Ebberston imputes some lasciviousness.[33]

Somatic bynames

The predominance of bynames associated with the body was characteristic of Middle English (ME) bynames in many regions, but their profusion was especially pertinent in the North where reference to the body was poignant.[34] John *Crokebayn* was amerced at Hundsworth in 1328 for an offence in the lord's wood.[35] Now this exact bodily nickname byname recurred in Aspatria in Cumberland, where Richard *Crokebain* was a tenant in 1328x1332.[36] In Lonsdale Wapentake in Lancashire in the late fourteenth century a Crikbayn contributed to the Poll Tax.[37] Formations on *-bayn* were fairly distinctive of a northern zone, not merely because of the vowel change of a/o, but also for the lexical element (*-bayn*) itself. Remark on the stature of neighbours was fairly pervasive in northern counties. Reflection on the height of peers was also often described in terms of their 'bones'. Robert *Langebayn* was consequently listed amongst the tenants of Skerton in the early fourteenth century, contrasting with Richard *Schortbayn* assessed in Dishford in 1327.[38] Another Robert – *Stygbayn* – committed the theft of two lambs and a calf in 1316 in Wakefield.[39]

Pertinent for the body too was the moniker attributed to William Standhupryght who had held three acres of land in Ackley before 1358.[40] Gait and physical demeanour constituted easy targets, so that Richard *Smaltrot*, whose homicide was reported at Bolton (Lancs.) in 1292, might have been subjected to some ridicule for his pace.[41] Attitude might have been imputed in the byname of Robert *Cokespur*, engaged in a plea of debt on the manor of Wakefield in 1348.[42]

Presumably in these last and the formations with *-bayn* the perspective was the whole body – the silhouette. Inexplicably, *Crokebayn* – perhaps curvature of the spine – was adopted in a number of localities in the northern counties as an embodied nickname byname. If that byname had real connotations for John *Crokebayn*, taxed at Ebberston in 1327, he had not been impeded by disability, for his assessment was at the very respectable level of 3s. 3d.[43] At Middleton in the North Riding, John *Crocbayn* was itemised for 1s. of tax.[44] Above, mention has already been made to this byname at Hundsworth in 1328 and in taxation lists about that time for Cumberland (at Aspatria) and Lancashire (in Lonsdale Wapentake). To these taxpayers should be appended Alan *Crocbayne*, contributing merely 4d. at Dalton, in the assessment of Yorkshire in 1301.[45]

In the production of somatic bynames, however, principal questions to be resolved comprise: were these bynames more characteristic of the northern zone that elsewhere? and what was the respective attention directed to upper and lower body and, if the latter, did that represent a preoccupation with the lower body in the north? So what were the comparative etymologies of nickname bynames in this northern area and what focus of the gaze did they epitomize?

The face, of course, attracted much attention, encapsulated in nickname bynames. Fined 3d. for entering into a lease of three acres without licence in Holne in 1316, the byname of Henry *Bridmouth* has the implication of a small, birdlike mouth.[46] The murder of Peter at Pontefract was perpetrated in 1342 by John *Nikynose* son of Geoffrey *de Went*, the facial imperfection – perhaps a previous punishment – thus informing a nickname definitely attributed to the person.[47] A combination of speech and physiognomy perhaps contributed to the byname of Roger *Foulmouth* of Wakefield in 1286.[48]

In general, the head furnished numerous nickname bynames, not only in the North, but certainly with some profusion there, and, indeed, with considerable derogatory directness.[49] Thomas *Gretheued* attested a charter of 1334 relating to North and South Dighton.[50] Uncomplimentary too was the description applied in the byname of William *Cokheued*, tenant of land in Little Shap.[51] Other combinations for the head in the lay subsidies comprised *Bareheued* (Bootle, Lancs.), *Bereheud'* (Skeckling in Yorks.), *Blakhed* (Nether Darwin, Lancs., and Cotherstone, Yorks.), *Bradhewed* (Humbleton, Northumberland, and Masham and Sharlston, both Yorks.), *Brasseheude* (Rokeby, Yorks.), *Brokynheued* (Nicholforest, Cumberland, and Pickhill, Yorks.), *Bukenheued* (Stonegrave, Yorks.), *Chikehed* (West Cottingwith, Yorks.), *Clovenheued* (Great Salkeld, Cumberland), *Cobheuede* (Kirkby Hill, Yorks.), *Durheued* (code-mixed, Blencarn, Cumberland), *Greteheued* (Newton le Willows, Startforth and Stanwick, all Yorks.), *Feyrheud* (East Swinburn, Northumberland), *Herteheued* (Scotby, Cumberland), *Lethyheued* (Kirkandrews, Cumberland), *Popesheued* (Whitby Strand, Yorks.), *Redeheued* (Penrith, Blencogo, Dyrah, Dalston and Culgaith, all in Cumberland), *Rufheued* (Edlingham, Northumberland), *Strakehewed* (Hepscott, Northumberland), *Whitheued* (Nicholforest, Cumberland, Elwick and Hedresford, both in Northumblerand, and Birdforth, Wath and Kirkleatham, Yorks.).[52]

The presumption must be that the highly compounded *Haldebytheheued* at Thirlby in Yorkshire indicates rather action done by one person to another than being self-referential.[53] Furthermore, some of these compounds more readily reflect, perhaps, hair-colour rather than the full physiognomy. There remains, nevertheless, a significant corpus of bynames commenting on the head. In the late fourteenth century, these compounded bynames referring to the head persisted in Lancashire: Blakhede at Weeton; Griseheved at Chipping; and Whithed in Lonsdale Wapentake and at Scarisbrick.[54]

If the head occasioned no comment, then the hair might still attract attention, especially if associated with mannerism. So the quitclaim made by John to Lanercost Abbey in 1290x1326 described him as son of John *Scacloc* ('shake-hair').[55] At Grinton (Yorkshire) in 1301, another taxpayer suffered the same ignominious byname (*Schakelock'*).[56] The same habit informed the byname of taxpayers – *Scakelok* and

Shakelok – at Rockliffe in Cumberland in 1327 and at Chadderton in Lancashire five years later.[57] Richard Schackelok appeared as a substantial peasant tenant – holding a messuage and three bovates – in Allerton in 1372.[58]

Indeed, a preference for *lok* as the apposite noun in compounded bynames referring to the hair seems to have pervaded northern areas.[59] At Ayton in Cumberland, then, a taxpayer in 1327 was signified by *Blakelok*.[60] Hair condition was noticed in the byname of John *Schirlok*, a byname not unusual in any part of England, but at Wakefield attributed to a tenant who was amerced 2d. for escapes in Alverley in 1308.[61] The same attribution was made to a taxpayer at Skelton in Cumberland in 1327 – *Skirlok* – and at Carthorpe in Yorkshire in 1301 (*Shirelockes*).[62] Elsewhere in Yorkshire (at Croft, Harmby and Sand Hutton), taxpayers assessed in 1301 also received this byname in its Scandinavian-influenced form: *Skyrelock'*.[63]

At Stanley, on the large composite manor of Wakefield, Elizabeth *Langshank* fined for brewing, as did Alice *Longschank* a year later in 1327.[64] The lower body thus stimulated social comment in the North. Some nineteen years earlier – in 1308 – Richard *Longschank* had been involved in a case of battery in Stanley and in 1313 he was amerced 3d. there for an escape (as Richard *Longschankes*).[65] On the same manor, Thomas *Brounschanks* acted as a pledge in 1306 and defended a case of debt in 1316.[66] Accused of an offence against the vert, for which he was fined 2d., Henry *Cockeshank* inhabited Stanley in the 1320s.[67] Consequently, the recording of Blakleg as a surname in Liverpool in 1379 appears as an aberration.[68] *-schank* bynames had something of a presence in East Anglia too. In 1285, Nicholas *Gruelschanke* held land in Great Yarmouth.[69]

Feet were remarked upon in the same manner, epitomised by Thomas *Brodfot*, an offender against the vert in Wakefield in 1314.[70] The palor of feet was the attribute incorporated in the naming of Richard *Wytthefot*, defendant in debt in Wakefield.[71] With the alienation of three acres illicitly by Robert *Lyhtfote*, however, more contentious ground is reached, for the byname might impute swiftness or fleetness of foot (perhaps in equally notorious circumstances).[72] That same name (as Lyghfote) was conferred on a taxpayer in Little Crosby (Lancashire) in 1379.[73]

As significant amongst the bodily-derived nicknames in the far North was *Armstrang* or *Armstrong*, more frequent with the *a* substitution.[74] Taxpayers in the late thirteenth and early fourteenth century were identified by this byname (with the voicing of a second a instead of o) at Lucker in Northumberland and at Ousby and Great Corby in Cumberland.[75] The will of John *de Penreth*, vicar of Arthuret, in 1334 prescribed a legacy of a mare with foal from the tithe of John *Armstrang* senior.[76] Amongst the list of ordinations in the diocese of Carlisle in 1354, Adam Armestrang' was inducted to the status of acolyte.[77] Armstrong persisted in Lonsdale Wapentake in Lancashire in the late fourteenth century.[78]

Furnishing fewer *cognomina*, the hands were contained in some somatic nickname bynames, again with uncomplimentary intent. A contention of unmanliness probably inhered in the byname attributed to Robert *Wyithand* who had died by 1248x1256 and whose widow, Sigrith, made a benefaction to Lanercost Abbey.[79] The former unfree tenant of a bovate in Newton was simply described as *Kybbelhand* without a forename.[80]

As a demonstratively visible feature, clothing, of course, became an aspect of nickname bynames, especially in the North. Comment on clothing involved derogatory and ironic messages about fashion, style, impecuniousness, and habitual demeanour. In the middle of the thirteenth century, Adam suffered death in Robyr Forest at the hands of Adam *Sortkyrtell*.[81] Social comment on hose was as replete in the West Riding as anywhere, illustrated by Henry *Schorthose* who offered a payment of 6d. for licence to receive half an acre in 1286.[82] Presumably it was another Henry *Schorthose* who, with two accomplices, burgled two houses in 1316 purloining linen cloth and other goods from one and chattels valued at 40s. from the other.[83]

Within apparel, perhaps the item most familiarly represented in nickname bynames was the hood. Outlawed for robbery in 1219, Utting *Scutehod* had fled the vicinity.[84] A small amount of land in Alverthorpe was alienated by Richard *Wythud*.[85] Assessed at Darras Hall in Northumberland in 1296 was a taxpayer with the *cognomen Blachod*.[86] At Rockcliffe in Cumberland, a taxpayer responded to the byname *Redehode* in 1327, as did another at Penrith, and two others at Lee and Prudhoe in Northumberland in 1296.[87] Colour was less material than the texture in the byname of the taxpayer designated *Furhode* at Ayton in Yorkshire in 1301.[88] Shape also influenced naming, for reference was made to taxpayers at West Tanfield and Riccal in Yorkshire in 1301 as *Stepelhode* and *Straythode*.[89] Perhaps the most startling compound name of this description was that attached to the taxpayer in Lonsdale Wapentake in the late fourteenth century: Pernelhod – intimating the wearing of a striped hood associated with prostitutes.[90] Recognition through headgear, particularly the hood, thus constituted a frequent element in bynaming in northern territories.

Whilst numerous of the bearers of these nickname bynames are elusive, appearing infrequently in court rolls and other records, and thus perhaps reflecting their marginal status, the *Grenhod* kinship of the composite manor of Wakefield was prolific in its appearance in the court rolls. Established already between 1297 and 1306, when he was taxed and included in the tourn jury, William *Grenhod* maintained the early kinship.[91] Whilst Robert *Grenhod* was fined for an infringement of the vert, William *Grenehod* prosecuted four others for debt.[92] By 1308, William *Grenehod* was in a position to enter into the land market, procuring a *brodale* of meadow for a term of twenty years, for an entry fine of 6d.[93] In 1309 William *Grenehod* was involved in litigation in three hamlets of the composite manor, at Wakefield, Thornes (debt) and Alverthorpe where he was successful in a plea of detinue for a stone of wool.[94] By 1314, William *Grenhod* was of sufficient status to stand in the tourn jury.[95] In the same year, an essoin was presented by Thomas *Grenhod*.[96] William then entered the land market again, taking another *brodole* of meadow for a term of twenty years.[97] Subsequently, in the following year – 1315 – William *Grenhod* acquired in lease for six years an acre and a quarter in Thornes, but without the lord's licence, consequently incurring a fine of 1s.[98] He expanded his acquisitions further in 1316 by taking two and a half roods of land in lease, for which he offered an entry fine of 1s.[99] His expenditure was offset in that year by his recovery of 10s. in a plea of debt.[100] Continuing his acquisition of land William *Grenhod* expended another 2s. for an entry fine to accept two acres of land for twelve years in Alverthorpe in 1316.[101] As a new lessee of just over an acre for a term of twelve years, William *Grenhod* disbursed another 1s. as entry fine.[102] About that time, however, his fortunes might have temporarily collapsed somewhat, for he was accused of burgling a house and the theft of chattels valued at 40s.[103] By 1317, nevertheless, William *Grenehode* had returned to the land market, acquiring five acres in one transaction and another acre, half acre and two butts for a term of twelve years in others.[104] He was restored too to the tourn jury.[105] Not content with his acquisitions of land, he contracted to lease another two and a quarter acres for twenty years at a cost of another entry fine of 2s.[106]

The debt for which Adam *Grenhode* introduced a plea in the court extended to 70s., a significant amount, but he later compromised the action.[107] About that time, John *Grenhod* defaulted in another case of debt.[108] Another claim against him demanded 14s. for herring sold to him in Wakefield in 1341, the debt having been deferred over nine years.[109] William *Grenehod*'s son, Mr Robert *Grenhode*, was contemporaneously arraigned in the same court, once at the instigation of the 'community of the vill' of Horbury for trespasses.[110] The relationships of the kinship were illuminated in 1351, when John son of Richard *Grenehod* acknowledged that he held eleven and a half acres by hereditary right after the death of his uncles, Robert *Grenehod* and Adam *Grenehod*, but also referring to his other uncle, Oliver *Grenehod*.[111] Further clarification ensued when John son of Richard *Grenhod* quitclaimed his right in the great meadow *del Halkes* which John's uncle, Mr Robert *Grenhod*, whose heir John was, had taken for a term of twenty years from August 1350.[112] Intra-familial tension might have explained the arraignment of Annabel *Grenhode* by John son of Richard *Grenhod* in May 1350 for detinue of a cart, although John non-suited.[113] In May 1350, however, Annabel *Grenhod* acted in the manorial court as executrix of John *Grenhod, capellanus*.[114] Distinctive headware had thus become encapsulated in a hereditary family surname in the West Riding by the middle of the fourteenth century. Attention to headwear was almost universally expressed through *cognomina* of the *-hood* variety, but exceptionally and distinctively tax was levied in 1296 from a taxpayer known by the byname *Cornethat*.[115]

Other sartorial accoutrements worn distinctively also furnished nickname bynames, some of which, on the manor of Wakefield, might have tended towards accretion over generations. Involved in battery in 1307, Adam *Witebelt* (*Wytebelt*) then escaped judgement when Henry son of Gregory *de Walton'* non-suited against Adam, William *Witebelt* and Constance *Wytebelt* at the same session of the court.[116] Then William became embroiled in a suit of trespass with Thomas *de Burgh*.[117] Six years later William *Wytebelt* was involved again in inter-peasant litigation, now in a testamentary case.[118] Furthermore, impleaded in detinue for ten and a half quarters of rye, William *Wytbelt* admitted his culpability.[119] When, furthermore, Alice *Whitbelt* of Sandall, in 1317 pursued a debt in the manorial court, Adam *Whitbelt* furnished her pledge.[120] Through her litigation against John *Cokewald*, Alice *Whitbelt*'s status as a servant became visible, for she demanded wages for service from Whitsun 1310 to the following Michaelmas, seven years in arrears.[121] This colour was also associated with a nickname byname of clothing in Robert *Witkirtel*, plaintiff in debt in Holne in Wakefield in the early fourteenth century, and amerced for infraction of the vert in 1317.[122]

Utterances

Whilst it can cautiously be maintained that nickname bynames furnish one of the few non-rhetorical windows onto the language of medieval speech communities, one particular form of these nickname bynames illustrates utterances even more directly, if perfunctorily. It can be assumed that some nickname bynames were attributed because of habitual exclamations by some of the peasantry. With all written sources, of course, we encounter the potential interference and mediation of the *scriptor*, but the nickname bynames of utterances perhaps reveal a familiarity – if a low one – with different codes: some such bynames resolutely Middle English compounds, but others Anglo-Norman or French. To that extent, we can enquire how far the peasantry had acquired a limited Anglo-Norman or French vocabulary. Not exclusive to the northern area, Anglo-Norman or French lexis in northern nicknames of this type still has an importance. Here, where we might anticipate a stronger compound Middle English lexis, from all the evidence recited so far, the intrusion of this different code attests the impact of a cultural encounter in the late middle ages and throws some little light on attenuated second-language acquisition.

Within this adoption of code, *Jevousdy* – associated with a taxpayer at Yarm in 1301 – contains the compounded vocabulary illustrating an acquaintaince, however limited, with French lexis.[123] At Pickering, the byname of a taxpayer also in 1301 – *Par le Roy* – declaims the same circumscribed familiarity.[124] In considering the acquisition of language, indeed, some nickname bynames are particularly demonstrative rather than simply inferential. That Adam *Parlefrankays* inhabited Cumberland in the late thirteenth century promotes the idea of some of the local inhabitants acquiring something of a second language.[125]

Less certainly an exclamatory response – but likely to have been one – was *Fayrandgode*, a byname attached to taxpayers in 1301 in North Kilvington, Northallerton and Thornton le Street, in North Yorkshire.[126] Middle English exclamatory bynames thus complemented and developed alongside Anglo-Norman monikers. Within this ambiguous category too falls *Godynoghe* at Startforth in 1301.[127] It might more easily be expected that the byname *Godeday* derived from a propensity for salutation.[128] A similar habituation to valediction was imputed in Godspede, announcing a taxpayer in the Poll Tax for Lonsdale Wapentake in 1379.[129]

Within this category might be considered also not only the expletive words, but also the manner of their utterance. Whilst Jönsjö considered that *Greteword* signified a braggard, a wider interpretation might be invoked for that byname which was assigned to a taxpayer in 1296 at Framlingham in Northumberland and to another at Thirsk in 1301.[130] It would seem that the utterance was not necessarily self-referential, for the imputation of the term when employed (admittedly much later) in a controversy in Lapworth in Warwickshire in the late fifteenth century requires a different inference:

> ... he havyng grete wordes sayng on to me Symond Skynner he wold bryng me to London and so for dowt we selud the sayd wrytyng we not undurstondyng the contentes and maters in the said wrytyng comprisud.[131]

Seemingly, the imprecation in this complaint was that the 'grete words' were uttered in a portentous and dogmatic way. What the byname of a John *Greteword* of Hiperum in Wakefield evoked might thus be considered in the same light. Whilst he was merely fined 6d. for an offence against the vert in Hiperum in Wakefield, his byname invoked an idea of the self-important manner in which he made statements, perhaps induced by his selection for an inquest in 1315, not just that they were self-referential words.[132]

Animal metaphors and totemism

Disparagement inhered in numerous nickname bynames in which the metaphor was animal. Timidity was implied in the *cognomen* of Robert *Pusekat*, beaten up by Ilyf *le Messer* near Corbridge Bridge in the middle of the thirteenth century.[133] Nevertheless, nickname bynames of a totemic nature might also contain irony, a renowned example on the manor of Wakefield being William *Wodemous*. His activities included notoriously expelling Molle *de Mora* from her house, slaughtering her dog, carrying away ten ells of linen and a cloak. His counterplea invoked trespass against Molle in 1286.[134] Compounding that aggression, William *Wodemous* was presented for battery against his son, Thomas, in 1306, receiving a fine of 1s.[135] Implicated in further anti-social behaviour, William *Wodemous* admitted in 1307 that he was bound to Agnes *de la Grene* for her children's goods and chattels.[136] In similar vein, with such irony attached to his byname, John *Mous* was presented for battery against Matilda in 1324.[137] That same quality might be exhibited in the byname of a felon in the very early thirteenth century. Gilbert *Mus*, accused of the homicide of William *le Furmager* in Yorkshire, fled and was placed in outlawry, his chattels valued at 7s. 9d. – a considerable amount. Moreover, he was also appealed as an accessory to the murder of Henry Daget.[138]

Probably no irony was involved in the appellation of John *Styhog*, a designation which seems to emphasise his disreputable demeanour. Encountered at Sowerby in 1286 only, *Styhog* not only raised the hue unjustly against Richard *le Tynker* but also assaulted Hanne *le Walker*.[139] Not content with those offences, in the same year he was found responsible for the theft of two oxen and consequently despatched to York gaol.[140]

Indeed, quite profuse in the northern zone remained the byname *Cay* or *Kay*, which, although containing some ambiguity, is most appropriately considered in these contexts to have represented 'jackdaw'. Thus Beatrice *Cay* was listed amongst the cottagers (*les Cotiers*) at Allerton where she held a toft and croft.[141] At nearby Newton in 1345, Robert *Cay* was tenant of a messuage and three acres.[142] The wider distribution of the byname in the late-thirteenth to the late-fourteenth-century lay subsidies is illustrated in Figure 42.[143]

A peasant kinship disported this byname on the manor of Wakefield, where Hugh *Cay* assumed a lease of one acre in Sandall for twenty years and at the same time John *Cay* acted as a pledge and attorney for an essoin.[144] In 1309, John *Cay* entered into complicated litigation bringing a plea of pledge against John *Schirelock* for a stone and two pounds of wool at the value of 5s. per stone, which he recovered.[145] In 1314, John *Cay* became embroiled in cases of debt against seven other tenants, including Sir Ralph *de Emelay* whilst at the same time Hugh *Kai* acted as a mainpernor.[146] By 1314, John *Kay* had achieved the status of burgess of Wakefield.[147] Confusingly, despite his free status, he had acquired villein land in 1315 by which he became liable to act as grave (reeve).[148] By that time too, he had come into possession

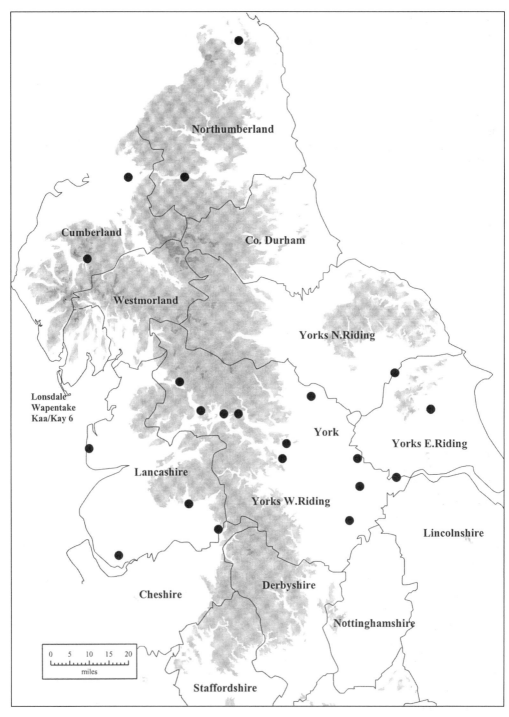

Figure 42 Kay/Cay, *late thirteenth and early fourteenth centuries*

of important other land. He held five acres of arable and half an acre of meadow of the *bordland*, for which he proffered 2s. 6d. as recognition to keep the land at a rent of 1s. per acre; for this tenure, he owed service of maintaining the mill pond in Wakefield and the chase of the park, although he was relieved from service as grave and from tallage.[149] On one of his first appearances in court in 1316, John *Cay* essoined by sending into court German *Cay*.[150] Shortly afterwards, John died, as reported in the record of his plea of debt against William *Nelot*; it was further noted that he had once been clerk to the lord's steward as well as a local tenant.[151] Soon afterwards, other *Cay* kin appeared in the manorial court, Agnes *Cay* for offences against the vert in Wakefield.[152] In the Poll Tax for Lonsdale Wapentake in 1379 six taxpayers were enumerated with the name Kay (one Kaa).[153]

More derogatory still was the attribution of the byname *Cockespore* ('cockspur') to one John who acted as a juror in an inquisition of 1307 in Stanley.[154] By 1323, however, John *Cockespore* was deceased.[155] Temperament as well as perhaps constitution received attention in the moniker *Wyldebore*, applied to William *Wyldebore*, a pledge in the court of the manor of Wakefield in 1314.[156] Essoins were proffered by William and Robert *Wildebor* in 1316.[157]

Malfeasance and emotions

As intimated above, some nickname bynames in the North were directed against delinquency, as a disciplinary measure, to humiliate and shame. Indubitably directed to this punishment by naming was John *Maufesour*, who, although dignified with a distinctive code (French), conformed to his moniker by burgling a grange and stealing one and a half bushels of oats and a horse in 1316, amongst other thefts.[158] Now in 1317, a Thomas *Maufesour* was arrested on suspicion of larceny because he was observed nightwalking and found in possession of two mares and other suspect items. Despite his plea of innocence, he was convicted on the accusation of Richard *Longschank*, the servant of the chaplain of Ardslow, of the theft of one of the mares, and hung.[159] In that same year, John *Maufesour* received his due as a thief and murderer.[160]

Also falling into this category was Alice *Brekhout*, amerced 2d. at Wakefield for collecting wood.[161] The expressive nature of some of these 'criminal' nickname bynames in the North is exemplified in the late thirteenth century by Alan *Ivelepeni* ('evil-penny'), a thief who was convicted and executed, his accumulated chattels accounted as 3s. 9d., and Geoffrey *Wolvesheved* who, seeking sanctuary in the church of Gunwarton, acknowledged his crime and abjured the realm – in other words, took the wolf's head as an outlawed and abjured criminal.[162] Overt criminality is contained within the surname Wolveshed amongst the taxpayers at Wigan and Aughton in 1379.[163] The wolf's head was adopted by those who had been outlawed or placed in *exigent* for felonies and were required to abjure the realm. Now to those two miscreants must be added one Henry, suspected of theft and consequently outlawed, whose chattels amounted to 4s. 2d., and who was summoned by the *cognomen Brendcheke*, indicating his punishment for previous offences.[164] Aggression against others seemingly inhered in the labelling of Robert *Bryghelbayn* who committed battery against Robert *Tyrsi* because *Tyrsi*'s sister had raised the hue against him.[165] Management of the emotions also informed the nickname byname of William *Dragespere* appealed by Adam *filius Alani* as accessory to the death of Jordan *nepos Johannis* in the early thirteenth century.[166]

At issue in these bynames was a failure to control or manage emotions, a contempt perhaps attributed to Nigel *Skakedag'* ('shake-dagger') who had the misfortune to be killed by a fallen oak in the early thirteenth century.[167] Now that same incapacity might have been attributed to Henry *Scakerdagg[er]*, a tenant of merely a toft and croft in the East Riding in the thirteenth century.[168] How far Serlo *le Skirmissur*, who brought an appeal against robbers, belonged in this category defies definition, for it is possible that he acted legitimately as a champion in the bilateral ordeal.[169]

Indolence was no doubt the subject of the stricture contained in the byname of John *Dolitel*, a free tenant in Tadcaster in the thirteenth century.[170] Nevertheless, the Walter *Dolitel* who was appealed for murder of her husband by Paveya widow of Arkell *de Breddal'* ultimately became more notorious for pernicious action rather than idleness.[171] Perhaps antisocial behaviour was also implied in the byname of Simon *Scortfrend* – that is, friendless – who alienated land in the West Riding in the thirteenth century.[172]

Gluttony seems more likely to have been inferred from the byname of the taxpayer at Hornsea Burton in 1297 assessed at 20d., whose byname was recorded as *Groyneporck* (French code: 'pig's snout').[173] As disparaging and perhaps with the same imputation was the byname of another taxpayer, assessed at 18d. in Lowthorpe, designated *Fathogge*.[174]

Of particular concern for medieval local societies, however – and a continuing social anxiety – was excessive drinking. Intimation of inebriation informed bynames on the social margins, not least in the stigmatization of the taxpayer called *Potfulofale* assessed at Pickering in 1301.[175] Excess in consumption was regarded as socially unacceptable as the brewing of poor ale, both activities criticized through bynames. Accordingly, the byname *Drinkale* – associated with a taxpayer at Ormesby (Yorkshire) in 1301 – implied frequency of imbibing and that moral dereliction might have been imputed also to Henry *Drinchale* of Newby in 1327.[176] Poll Tax payers in Lonsdale Wapentake in Lancashire received that name (Drinkal(e)) associated with excessive imbibing.[177] Equally, however, the resort to other liquids than ale might be perceived as deviant, marking out the taxpayer at Framlingham in Northumberland in 1296: *Drinckemilk'*.[178] Nonconformity to the local norms of consumption was an object of comment through bynames.

Although some degree of religious scepticism existed in late medieval England, its representation in bynames and surnames was tenuous. In the north, however, the attribution of irreligious behaviour was occasionally present, thus accounting for the Poll Tax payer in Lonsdale Wapentake called Godlese.[179]

Social associations

Without doubt, nickname bynames attached to peasants of all positions within the peasant hierarchy. On the other hand, an association also existed between unusual nickname bynames and marginal peasants, based on the supposition that infrequent appearance in manorial court rolls reflected a marginal status in local society. Thus we rarely encounter Henry *Stirthover*, fined for an escape in 1308, in the Wakefield manorial court rolls.[180] Sometimes the status associated with the byname has some ambiguity: when William *Wildbore* was amerced 12d. in 1308 for respite of suit, the court rolls had the qualification that the fine was limited to 12d. because he was poor. Now 1s. was actually quite a formidable fine for default of suit and the reference to 'poor' might simply explain that he was temporarily short of coin.[181]

More explicitly, Thomas *Sherewynd* – a man by imputation always in a hurry – was an unfree tenant at Allerton Maulever in 1338:

> Thomas Sherewynd naïf teint ij mees ij bouees de terre et rend xs. a mesmes les termes.
>
> [Thomas Sherewynd, unfree tenant, holds two messuages and two bovates of land and pays 10s. at the same terms].[182]

Amongst the small tenants of the bishop of Carlisle, Roger *Shaktrot'* held merely a cottage and a little land in Hawksdale, Mariota *Litilrede* a messuage and five roods in Aspatria, and Thomas *Pulgose* a messuage and four acres in the same place.[183] Rendering a tiny rent of 3d. in 1323, Agnes *Comelate* was tenant of only half a cottage in West Derby.[184] The unfree status of Adam *Hoppecogel* became apparent in the manorial court when his daughter was presented for marrying without the licence necessary as Adam had the status of a *nativus*.[185] In a similar manner it was divulged that Richard *Passemer* (French code) belonged to the status of a *nativus* when he illicitly bought a small amount of land by charter in 1316.[186]

Parsimony

Social comment on acquisitiveness as incorporated in *cognomina* was not confined to northern areas, but, although it existed in other locations, its incidence in the North appears to have a particular import. That lively stigmatization is represented in the taxpayer's byname *Yrenpurs* at Brompton in Yorkshire in 1301.[187] Vernacular expressions were directed against the acquisitive (or, possibly, tax-collectors), through such bynames as *Gederpeny*, assigned to a taxpayer at Hutton in Lancashire in 1332.[188] In this context, however, code-mixing was also evident, not only in the ubiquitous *Cachepol*, but in the less usual *Leuedime*, associated with a taxpayer at Edstone in Yorkshire in 1301.[189] Bynames of other taxpayers which connoted avarice or parsimony were reiterated in many other areas: *Penyfader* (taxpayer at Clifton, Northumberland, in 1296).[190]

Code-mixing

Code-mixing of nickname bynames existed in many regions, not least in the North. Moreover, in some cases, the code-mixed nickname bynames were developing into hereditary surnames in the early fourteenth century, if by implication rather than certain genealogical progression. The implication of inheritance of a code-mixed byname – *Briswod* – in the north-west existed in 1328x1332. In the rental of the bishop of Carlisle for Unthank, a messuage and a few acres had been held by William *Briswod*. At neighbouring Buckabank, in the same rental, two daughters of Ralph *Briswod*, Mariota and Joan, held small amounts of land, Mariota arrogating both messuages. Now, varying amounts of land were held contemporaneously in Buckabank by Richard *Briswod*, William son of Richard *Briswod*, Adam *Briswod*, Gilbert son of Gilbert *Briswod*, his daughter Joan, and John son of Richard *Briswod*. Their tenements extended from just over an acre to a messuage with ten acres and a little extra.[191] Firmly entrenched within the peasantry, then, this kinship disported a code-mixed nickname byname – consistently combining French prototheme and ME deuterotheme – which was becoming hereditary. We can thus refer to the association of code-mixed nickname bynames with peasant status, not a more exclusive social status, and to the uneven formation of hereditary surnames amongst the peasantry, some kinship groups acquiring heritability of surnames whilst the bynames of other peasant kinships remained unstable.

Colloquialisms and the *alias*

Although the nicknames discussed above reflected a perception of people and how they were regarded by others and also to some degree the presentation of the self in a local society, nickname bynames did not constitute the *only* manner of self-fashioning and perception by others.[192] The most direct form of colloquialism, largely concealed from the written record, was produced by a nickname other than a nickname byname, sometimes an *alias*, sometimes a formation on the forename, which might then be considered still to be the principal name within a local society. So, despite the obfuscation of the written record with its propensity for formalization of names, even the Poll Tax return for Haigh in Lancashire in 1379 referred to one contributor as *Joly Jac*.[193] Nor was he solitary, for at Atherton another taxpayer then was described as *Smale Atkyn*.[194] Now, although these sorts of nickname or *alias* pervaded the country and were occasionally introduced to written records elsewhere, the more liberal appearance of hypocorisms of forenames in northern written records might have allowed a higher incidence of these types of colloquialisms and *alias*es.

Survival and persistence

As might be expected, since they reflected highly personal traits, a proportion of nickname bynames became casualties and failed to persist. Nevertheless, some important survivals did continue the particular characteristics of northern nickname surnames.

In 1522, Christopher Pykavers subscribed to the forced loan at Pathorn and Rimington in Craven, complemented by John Pykhaver also at Rimington.[195] Previously, in 1510–11, Thomas Pykhaver of Bolton in Bowland and Christopher

Pykhaver of Rimington had been enlisted in a muster of 1510–11.[196] On the same occasion, Thomas Pykkehaver was enumerated at Wigglesworth.[197] Contributors to the subsidy imposed two years later comprehended William Pykhaver (Pychaver) at Newsham.[198] When another taxation was levied in 1543, those assessed included Nicholas Pikhaver at Stainton and Thomas and Christopher Pykhaver at Rimington, those two assessed again at Rimington in 1545 and 1547.[199] This particular byname and surname illustrated perfectly the phenomenology of naming, for it referred directly to the specific rural environment of those areas of the North where poorish soils demanded a virtual monoculture of oats (the element *-haver*).

Within this general location the survival of this surname was demonstrative, for it existed within the parish of Gisburne where Pichaver kinships inhabited the hamlets of Paythorne, Coptill and Evamhow.[200] When the extant burial register commenced, one of the earliest interments registered was for Helen Pichaver in 1558.[201] Within the space of a few years, sixteen burials of Pichavers were registered.[202] Between 1561 and 1579, numerous Pichaver children were baptised, the fathers comprising William, Stephen, Christopher, Thomas and Robert.[203]

This particular surname also existed across the Pennines in early-modern Aughton in Lancashire, for in 1550 Sir John Pykavaunce was buried there and Elizabeth Pikavaunce had been married in the parish in 1543.[204]

Amongst embodied surnames, especially distinctive survivals included Armestrong and Greathead. The persistence of Greathead as a vernacular form is noteworthy since the cognate *Grosseteste* was well attested in a different – perhaps higher – register. The universality of the vernacular form in the North and its endurance perhaps again testifies to a vital northern culture of directness in nickname bynames. In the 1327 lay subsidy for the North Riding, *Gretheued* encompassed the taxpayer William *Gretheued* at Sutton, where he was assessed at the very high level of 4s. 6d., but eschewed the opportunity to be fashioned in the French variant.[205] In contrast, only a 1s. was calculated against Nicholas *Gretheued* at Brompton on Swale in the same taxation.[206] Simultaneously, John *Gretheued* contributed 2s. at Caldwell.[207] At Marton, another John *Gretheued* paid an amount comparable with William, at 4s.[208] Two shillings were exacted from Robert *Gretheued* at Stainton with Thornton.[209] This bodily byname – in its Middle English guise – was thus encountered throughout the North Riding.

The nickname byname flourished too in the locality of Barforth in the West Riding, encountered initially, it seems, in written record in Robert *Gretheved* in 1257.[210] When Peter appeared, however, so did the conundrum of register and, perhaps, self-fashioning. In 1270, Peter's *cognomen* was inscribed in a charter as *Grosseteste*, but by 1280x 1294 the vernacular cognate was employed, *Gretheved*.[211] From then into the late fourteenth centuries, local charters referred to successive *Grethed* or *Greteheved* kin: John (1328–1340); Robert (1318); Hugh (1309x1317); and Thomas (1348–1369).[212] Perhaps it is not then surprising that it surfaced later as part of the experience of names in northern zones. At Winston in Northumberland, children of Laurence Greathead and Thomas Greathead were baptised in respectively 1593, and 1595 and 1597.[213]

Whilst Armestrong existed in many parishes in north-eastern areas in the sixteenth

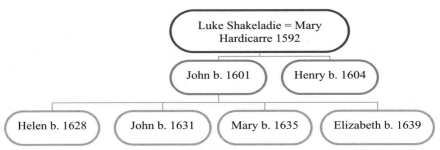

Figure 43 Genealogy of Shakeladie at Aughton, 1592–1639

and seventeenth centuries, its distribution can only here be illustrated by purposive examples. Inscribed in the registers of St Nicholas, Durham, in 1576, 1581, 1584, 1585 and 1608 were the marriages of Peter, Christopher, John, Thomas, and George Armestrong.[214] Baptisms at Corbridge in Northumberland recorded fathers as Charles and Alexander Armestronge between 1658 and 1665.[215]

Of particular interest is the survival of Langstaffe in northern zones, for two characteristics: first, the potential for sexual innuendo contained within the compounded surname, perhaps illustrative of northern connotations; and secondly because of the vowel substitution *a/o* discussed above. In 1570 Margaret Langstaffe was interred at Brough in the extreme North-west.[216] The lives of some Langstaffes were celebrated through baptisms at Winston in 1589–1615: Margery, Jane, Elizabeth, and Edward – but here the surname was corrupted by the interposition of *r*: Langstraffe.[217]

Another nickname surname with distinctively local significance in its distribution and survival was Brennand. After the marriage of Isabella Brennand celebrated at Gigglesick in Craven in 1559, the baptisms of William and Thomas Brennand were registered in 1563 and 1566 in that parish.[218] One William Breannande was buried in the parish churchyard in 1579, as was Agnes Brennand, widow, in 1602.[219] The surname became continuously inscribed in the registers in the seventeenth century.

From the corpus of sexually-implicit medieval bynames of the north survived Shackladye and its variants, especially at early-modern Aughton in Lancashire. Between 1550 and 1592, Margery, Anne, Edward, Alice and Luke celebrated their marriages in the parish, their surname variously inscribed as Shackladye, Sheickledye, Sheckledye and Shakeladie.[220] Burials there comprehended Margaret daughter of John Shackladye in 1571, Elizabeth wife of Thomas Shackladye in 1577, Anne wife of Edward Shackladye in 1584, John Shakeladie in 1587, and Alice Shakeladie in 1592.[221] During the late sixteenth century, then, the surname had become confirmed within the parish and it continued there into the seventeenth century. Between 1601 and 1625, numerous Shakelady burials were commemorated in Aughton, culminating with Jane Shakeladie and her bastard daughter.[222] Indeed at least six Shakeladies were interred there in the 1640s, reflecting the longevity of the surname in the parish as an established phenomenon.[223] One line of the surname can be illustrated genealogically.[224]

Conclusion about nicknames

Evidently, complicated Middle English nicknames did exist in other parts of England, illustrated, for example, by William *Fall' in Wolle* at Ludlow and Richard *Goby-theweye* at Staunton Lacey, both in Shropshire, and significantly both taxpayers assessed at low levels, respectively 6d. and 9d.[225] In Alstonfield in Staffordshire in 1332, John *Falleinthewall* (sic) was assessed highly at 7s. 4d.[226] Some of these inventive nicknames persisted into the late thirteenth century in the city of Norwich. In 1288, Laurence *le Cokysschanke* ('cock's legs') raised the hue and in that year too Ranulph *Saluz* committed battery at night against Roger *Ruchballok* ('red bollocks') as he came with corn around mid-night.[227] In the following year, an assize was infringed by Richard *Schepesheghee* ('sheep's eye').[228]

The impression remains, nevertheless, that although these inventive and sometimes salacious forms of nickname byname had existed in other locations, their survival and persistence characterized the north of England. Considerations of the reasons why that obtained inevitably venture into the realm of speculation. Linguistically, Middle English allowed greater latitude for compounded formations and northern Middle English might have been characteristically inviting to compounding.[229] Possibly the influence of Norse 'flyting' – the poetic insult – influenced northern social contacts and language use, intruding into nickname bynames.[230] It might, indeed, be merely that the persistence of these nickname bynames in northern areas attested to a continuing tradition of strong northern characteristics of speech, a directness and bluntness which valued irony and did not esteem dissimulation.

Notes

1   For general comments on nicknaming, J. Morgan, C. O'Neill & R. Harré, *Nicknames. Their Origins and Social Consequences* (London, 1979). A fuller and wider discussion is contained in D. Postles, *Talking* ballocs. *Nicknames and English Medieval Sociolinguistics* (Leicester, 2003).

2   H. Summerson, 'Crime and society in medieval Cumberland' *Transactions of the Cumberland and Westmorland Archaeological and Antiquarian Society* lxxxii (1982), p. 121.

3   *Wakefield Court Rolls* III, pp. 6, 16, 26; he was a defendant in a case of debt in 1316 in the borough court of Wakefield: *Wakefield Court Rolls* IV, p. 110. The etymology suggested by G. Fransson, *Middle English Surnames of Occupation, 1100–1350* (Lund, 1935), p. 154, as '?sword sharpener', seems highly unlikely. More probable seems 'sword brandisher'. For another instance of this unusual byname, *Chancery Miscellanea* VI (List & Index Society 81, 1972), p. 86: homicide of John Swerdslipere of Loughborough by John Bokelerplayer at Oakham (Rutland) in 1356.

4   Jönsjö, *Studies*, contains a list of nickname bynames from Northern lay subsidies and some other documents, with constrained etymologies, but refrains from too much interpretation.

5   Jönsjö, *Studies*, p. 59 furnishes an occurrence of this byname in Yorkshire in 1388; his explanation consists of OE *blissian* (happy, contented) and OE *blod* (temper, disposition), which does not seem to convey the real connotations. For comparison, see G. Hughes, *A History of English Words* (Oxford, 2000), p. 84: 'Rituals often have revealing roots. *Bless* has unexpectedly gruesome origins. A-S *bletsian* originally meaning "to sprinkle with blood", from the root *blot*, "a bloody sacrifice", reflecting a ritual of blood being sprinkled by the

pagan priest to confer magical powers on the faithful.' Perhaps we need to think less of a syncretic situation as a purely Christian environment of the Eucharist.

6   R. L. Storey, ed., *The Register of John Kirkby Bishop of Carlisle 1332–1352 and the Register of John Ross Bishop of Carlisle 1325–1332* vol II (Canterbury &York Society lxxxi, 1995).

7   Fenwick, *The Poll Taxes*, I, p. 91.

8   The discussion here is informed by the 'speech act' theory of Austin and Searle: J. L. Austin, 'Performative utterances' in his *Philosophical Papers* ed. I. O. Urmson & G. J. Warnock (3rd edn, Oxford, 1979), pp. 233–52 and J. Searle, *Mind, Language and Society. Philosophy in the Real World* (London, 1999), pp. 135–61.

9   Nottinghamshire Archives Office DDSR 1/18/1.

10   *Wakefield Court Rolls* III, p. 138.

11   As established by G. Fellows-Jensen, 'On the study of Middle English by-names', *Namn och Bygd* 68 (1980), pp. 107–9, P. McClure, 'The interpretation of Middle English nicknames', *Nomina* 5 (1981), pp. 95–104, esp. 98–9, and J. Insley, 'Recent trends into English bynames and surnames: some critical remarks', *Studia Neophilologica* 65 (1993), pp. 57–71.

12   *Wakefield Court Rolls* I, p. 60; see also III, p. 153 for his same offence in 1316; IV, p. 143.

13   *Wakefield Court Rolls* III, p. 140. For further alienation of land by him, IV, p. 49; for offence against the vert, IV, p. 71 (Sandall). Jönsö, *Studies*, p. 171.

14   Fenwick, *Poll Taxes* II, pp. 459, 471.

15   *Yorkshire 1297*, pp. 135, 140.

16   *Yorkshire 1301*, pp. 31, 48; Colonel Parker, 'Lay subsidy rolls 1 Edward III N. R. & City of York' in *Miscellanea II* (YASRS lxxiv, 1929), p. 144; Jönsjö, *Studies*, p. 177 ('fornicator').

17   Fenwick, *Poll Taxes* I, p. 459.

18   J. Coleman, 'The treatment of sexual vocabulary in Middle English dictionaries' in J. Fisiak, ed., *Middle English Miscellany. From Vocabulary to Linguistic Variation* (Poznai, 1996), pp. 183–206.

19   R. L. Storey, ed., *The Register of Gilbert Welton Bishop of Carlisle 1353–1362* (Canterbury & York Society lxxxviii, 1999), p. 115.

20   *Cumberland*, p. 6; 'Lancashire', p. 18.

21   *Yorkshire 1301*, p. 104. For the association of -*rose* with women's sexuality, S. Kay, 'Women's body of knowledge: epistemology and misogyny in the *Romance of the Rose*' in Kay & M. Rubin, eds, *Framing Medieval Bodies* (Manchester, 1994), pp. 211–35.

22   *Yorkshire 1301*, p. 40.

23   Parker, 'Lay subsidy rolls 1 Edward III N. R. & City of York', p. 148; Jönsjö, *Studies*, p. 157.

24   *Northumberland*, p. 106.

25   *Northumberland*, p. 177.

26   At West Chirton (Northumberland) and Rickcliffe (Cumberland): *Northumberland*, p. 102; *Cumberland*, p. 18.

27   'Lancashire', p. 7.

28   *Yorkshire 1301*, p. 63.

29   *Yorkshire 1301*, pp. 2, 101.

30   *Wakefield Court Rolls* I, p. 60.

31   *Yorkshire 1301*, p. 47.

32   M. T. Martin, ed., *The Percy Chartulary* (Surtees Society 117, 1921), p. 173 (dxxiv).

33   Parker, 'Lay subsidy rolls 1 Edward III N. R. & City of York', p. 111; Jönsjö, *Studies*, p. 143 ('philanderer').

34   How the body presents an immediate point of reference is described by A. Synnott, *The Body Social. Symbolism, Self and Society* (London, 1993), p. 3.

35   Nottinghamshire Archives Office DDSR 1/6/5: *pro bosco domini abcisso et asportato*; he also featured in a plea of covenant.

36 Storey, *Register of John Kirkby Bishop*, p. 21.

37 Fenwick, *Poll Taxes* I, p. 454.

38 W. Farrer, ed., *Lancashire Inquests, Extents and Feudal Aids* Part II (LCRS liv, 1907), p. 174; Parker, 'Lay subsidy rolls 1 Edward III N. R. & City of York', p. 138.

39 *Wakefield Court Rolls* IV, p. 146.

40 *Halmota Prioratus Dunelmensis*, p. 22. For a cognate byname, Henry Boltupryht (Avenham, Glos., 1376): *Cat. Ancient Deeds* I, p. 422 (B3610).

41 *Chancery Miscellanea* Part IV (List & Index Society 38, 1968), p. 259.

42 *Wakefield Court Rolls 1348–1350*, pp. 8, 21; Jönsjö, *Studies*, p. 72, suggests a strutting demeanour.

43 Parker, 'Lay subsidy rolls 1 Edward III N. R. & City of York', p. 111.

44 Parker, 'Lay subsidy rolls 1 Edward III N. R. & City of York', p. 135; Jönsjö, *Studies*, p. 77, however, infers 'crooked legs'.

45 *Yorkshire 1301*, p. 81.

46 *Wakefield Court Rolls* III, p. 151: *brid* represents metathesis of *bird*.

47 *Chancery Miscellanea* Part VIII (List & Index Society 105, 1974), p. 125.

48 *Wakefield Court Rolls* III, p. 160 (1286).

49 Extreme caution is required, however, since many topographical terms and minor place-names contained *-heved*, as, for example, in the byname of Henry *de Lupesheved* whose house in the manor of Wakefield was burgled in 1317: *Wakefield Court Rolls* IV, p. 185; Thomas *del Wodeheved* who broke the lord's fold: *Wakefield Court Rolls* V, p. 38 (1324).

50 Martin, *Percy Chartulary*, p. 210 (dcxxii).

51 Martin, *Percy Chartulary*, p. 77 (clxxxv).

52 'Lancashire', pp. 23, 82; *Northumberland*, pp. 21, 61, 87, 129, 133, 168; *Cumberland*, pp. 11, 12, 14, 23, 24, 36, 38, 63, 68, 69, 70; *Yorkshire 1297*, pp. 97, 120; *Yorkshire 1301*, pp. 2, 6, 7, 10, 17, 39, 47, 52, 88, 89, 94, 101, 104, 108,

53 *Yorkshire 1301*, p. 84.

54 Fenwick, *Poll Taxes* I, pp. 443, 448, 453–4, 461.

55 J. M. Todd, *The Lanercost Cartulary* (Surtees Society 203, 1997), p. 327 (277).

56 *Yorkshire 1301*, p. 92.

57 *Cumberland*, p. 18; 'Lancashire', p. 30.

58 York Minster Archives 1.5/39.

59 *Tatelok* at Aintree (Lancashire) in 1332 is probably toponymic (Tatlock): 'Lancashire', p. 27; *Scudlock* at Beverley in 1297 demands too much speculation, but probably pertains to hair: *Yorkshire 1297*, p. 156; *Scauelok* at Ainderby Steeple in 1301 imputes a 'number one' in hairstyle: *Yorkshire 1301*, p. 16.

60 *Cumberland*, p. 27.

61 *Wakefield Court Rolls* I, p. 177 (1308).

62 *Cumberland*, p. 9; *Yorkshire 1301*, p. 2.

63 *Yorkshire 1301*, pp. 16, 72, 96.

64 *Wakefield Court Rolls* V, pp. 90, 102.

65 *Wakefield Court Rolls* I, p. 162; also p. 108 (pledge in Thornes in 1307); p. 177 for escapes in Stanley in 1308; p. 182 offence against the vert in 1308; *Wakefield Court Rolls* III, pp. 71, 94; also IV, p. 60.

66 *Wakefield Court Rolls* I, p. 56; IV, p. 139.

67 *Wakefield Court Rolls* V, p. 13. As noted above, however, *-schank* bynames were not totally confined to northern regions; interestingly, lands in Henley (Warws.) were quitclaimed in the late thirteenth century by Ranulph *Folechanke*, replicating the *-schank* element in the West Midlands whilst also code-mixing in an unusual way (compare, for example, the

gentry family *Folejambe* in Nottinghamshire and Derbyshire): *Cat. Ancient Deeds* III, p. 82 (A4572).

68 Fenwick, *Poll Taxes* I, p. 458.
69 *Cat. Ancient Deeds* VI, p. 33 (C4040).
70 *Wakefield Court Rolls* III, p. 63.
71 *Wakefield Court Rolls* IV, p. 70.
72 *Wakefield Court Rolls* IV, p. 87.
73 Fenwick, *Poll Taxes* I, p. 478.
74 Jönsjö, *Studies*, p. 50, with the substitution of *a*.
75 *Northumberland*, p. 147; *Cumberland*, pp. 38, 66.
76 Storey, *Register of John Kirkby*, p. 5.
77 Storey, *Register of John Kirkby*, p. 112.
78 Fenwick, *Poll Taxes* I, p. 454.
79 Todd, *Lanercost Cartulary*, p. 116 (66).
80 Bodl. Fairfax MS 9, fo. 84r.
81 W. Page, ed., *Three Early Assize Rolls for the County of Northumberland Saec. XIII* (Surtees Society 88, 1891), p. 95.
82 *Wakefield Court Rolls* I, p. 215; he was involved in a plea of debt in 1298: *Wakefield Court Rolls* I, p. 47.
83 *Wakefield Court Rolls* III, pp. 116–17.
84 D. M. Stenton, ed., *Rolls of the Justices in Eyre … Yorkshire in 3 Henry III (1218–19)* (Selden Society 56, 1937), p. 281 (761).
85 *Wakefield Court Rolls* IV, p. 75.
86 *Northumberland*, p. 75.
87 *Cumberland*, pp. 18, 67; *Northumberland*, pp. 4, 12.
88 *Yorkshire 1301*, p. 35.
89 *Yorkshire 1301*, pp. 4, 50.
90 Fenwick, *Poll Taxes* I, p. 451; R. Karras, *Common Women. Prostitution and Sexuality in Medieval England* (Oxford, 1996), pp. 19, 21, 22; A. Brown, *Popular Piety in Late Medieval England. The Diocese of Salisbury 1250–1550* (Oxford, 1995), p. 15. In general, for the significance of striped clothing, M. Pastoureau, *The Devil's Cloth. A History of Stripes and Striped Fabric* trans. J. Gladding (New York, 2001).
91 *Wakefield Court Rolls* I, p. 56 (1306); *Yorkshire 1297*, p. 113.
92 *Wakefield Court Rolls* I, pp. 60, 65 (1306–7).
93 *Wakefield Court Rolls* I, p. 175 (1308).
94 *Wakefield Court Rolls* I, pp. 197, 198, 200.
95 *Wakefield Court Rolls* III, p. 51.
96 *Wakefield Court Rolls* III, p. 53.
97 *Wakefield Court Rolls* III, p. 54.
98 *Wakefield Court Rolls* III, p. 92.
99 *Wakefield Court Rolls* III, p. 113.
100 *Wakefield Court Rolls* III, p. 147.
101 *Wakefield Court Rolls* IV, p. 33.
102 *Wakefield Court Rolls* IV, p. 64.
103 *Wakefield Court Rolls* IV, p. 95.
104 *Wakefield Court Rolls* IV, pp. 172, 174.
105 *Wakefield Court Rolls* IV, p. 184.
106 *Wakefield Court Rolls* IV, p. 193.
107 *Wakefield Court Rolls 1348–1350*, pp. 1, 92.

108 *Wakefield Court Rolls 1348–1350* I, p. 47.
109 *Wakefield Court Rolls 1348–1350*, p. 94.
110 *Wakefield Court Rolls 1348–1350*, pp.75, 84.
111 *Wakefield Court Rolls 1348–1350*, pp. 167–8.
112 *Wakefield Court Rolls 1348–1350*, p. 189.
113 *Wakefield Court Rolls 1348–1350*, p. 179.
114 *Wakefield Court Rolls 1348–1350*, p. 229.
115 *Northumberland*, p. 127 (at Kimmerston).
116 *Wakefield Court Rolls* I, pp. 92, 94 (1307).
117 *Wakefield Court Rolls* I, p. 97 (1307).
118 *Wakefield Court Rolls* III, p. 1. He acted more decorously as a pledge in 1315: p. 69.
119 *Wakefield Court Rolls* IV, p. 99.
120 *Wakefield Court Rolls* IV, p. 166.
121 *Wakefield Court Rolls* IV, pp. 191–2.
122 *Wakefield Court Rolls* IV, pp. 19, 169.
123 *Yorkshire 1301*, p. 27.
124 *Yorkshire 1301*, p. 56.
125 *Cat. Ancient Deeds* IV, p. 334 (A8608).
126 *Yorkshire 1301*, pp. 65, 67, 69.
127 *Yorkshire 1301*, p. 10.
128 *Yorkshire 1301*, p. 92 (at Nappa).
129 Fenwick, *Poll Taxes* I, p. 452.
130 Jönsjö, *Studies*, p. 105; *Northumberland*, p. 160; *Yorkshire 1301*, p. 82.
131 *Cat. Ancient Deeds* V, p. 4 (A10451) (7 Edward IV).
132 *Wakefield Court Rolls* I, pp. 113, 187 (1307–8), III, p. 75.
133 Page, *Three Early Assize Rolls*, p. 76.
134 *Wakefield Court Rolls* I, p. 235. William *Wodemous* acted as a pledge for maintaining the peace in 1308: *Wakefield Court Rolls* I, p. 181;
135 *Wakefield Court Rolls* I, p. 56 (1306). In 1307, Henry *Wodemous* offered an entry fine of 3s. for three acres: *Wakefield Court Rolls* I, p. 102 (Holne).
136 *Wakefield Court Rolls* I, p. 91. He was also fined 3d. for collecting dry wood: p. 85 (1307). See also G. Redmonds, *Yorkshire, West Riding* (English Surnames Survey 1, 1973).
137 *Wakefield Court Rolls* V, p. 42.
138 Stenton, ed., *Rolls of the Justices in Eyre … Yorkshire in 3 Henry III (1218–19)*, pp. 317, 318.
139 *Wakefield Court Rolls* III, p. 158 (1286).
140 *Wakefield Court Rolls* III, p. 160 (1286).
141 York Minster Archives 1.5/37A.
142 York Minster Archives 1.5/38.
143 'Lancashire', pp. 33, 68; *Northumberland*, pp. 14, 152; *Cumberland*, pp. 4, 30; 'East Riding Poll Tax', pp. 348–9; 'West Riding Poll Tax', 5, p. 47; 6, pp. 16, 18, 19, 147, 167, 321; 7, pp. 12, 151, 159, 161, 170; Fenwick, *Poll Taxes* I, pp. 450–3, 463–4.
144 *Wakefield Court Rolls* I, pp. 169, 180–1 (1308).
145 *Wakefield Court Rolls* I, p. 214 (1309).
146 *Wakefield Court Rolls* III, pp. 55–6, 58.
147 *Wakefield Court Rolls* III, p. 66.
148 *Wakefield Court Rolls* III, p. 71.
149 *Wakefield Court Rolls* III, p. 89.
150 *Wakefield Court Rolls* III, p. 128. For John as attorney and plaintiff in trespass, *Wakefield Court Rolls* IV, pp. 1, 3.

151 *Wakefield Court Rolls* IV, pp. 52–3.

152 *Wakefield Court Rolls* IV, p. 31.

153 Fenwick, *Poll Taxes* I, pp. 450–3.

154 *Wakefield Court Rolls* I, p. 72 (1307).

155 *Wakefield Court Rolls* V, p. 15.

156 *Wakefield Court Rolls* III, p. 64.

157 *Wakefield Court Rolls* IV, p. 129.

158 *Wakefield Court Rolls* IV, p. 154.

159 *Wakefield Court Rolls* IV, p. 164.

160 *Wakefield Court Rolls* IV, p. 191.

161 *Wakefield Court Rolls* IV, p. 46. Jönsjö, *Studies*, p. 64, suggests 'fugitive'.

162 Page, *Three Early Assize Rolls*, pp. 341, 344.

163 Fenwick, *Poll Taxes* I, pp. 470, 473.

164 Page, *Three Early Assize Rolls*, p. 364. Jönsjö, *Studies*, p. 64 ('punishment').

165 *Wakefield Court Rolls* IV, p. 97; his wife had been accused of breaking palings in Alverthorpe and fined 3d.: IV, p. 72.

166 Stenton, *Pleas before the King or his Justices 1198–1212* III (Selden Society 83, 1967), p. 138 (930).

167 Stenton, *Rolls of the Justices in Eyre ... Yorkshire in 3 Henry III (1218–19)*, p. 275 (738).

168 BL Add MS 40008, fo. 176r.

169 Stenton, *Rolls of the Justices in Eyre ... Yorkshire in 3 Henry III (1218–19)*, p. 293 (806).

170 Martin, *Percy Cartulary*, p. 19 (xxiv).

171 Stenton, *Rolls of the Justices in Eyre ... Yorkshire in 3 Henry III (1218–19)*, p. 345 (945).

172 Martin, *Percy Cartulary*, pp. 112, 121 (cccxx, ccclxiii).

173 *Yorkshire 1297*, p. 126.

174 *Yorkshire1297*, p. 135.

175 *Yorkshire 1301*, p. 56.

176 *Yorkshire 1301*, p. 33; Parker, 'Lay subsidy rolls 1 Edward III N. R. & City of York', p. 148.

177 Fenwick, *Poll Taxes* I, pp. 453, 455.

178 *Northumberland*, p. 160.

179 Fenwick, *Poll Taxes* I, p. 453.

180 *Wakefield Court Rolls* I, p. 171.

181 *Wakefield Court Rolls* I, pp. 61, 66, 177 (1307–8).

182 York Minster Library 1.5/37A.

183 Storey, *Register of John Kirkby*, pp. 11, 20, 21.

184 Farrer, *Lancashire Inquests, Extents and Feudal Aids* Part II, p. 86.

185 *Wakefield Court Rolls* IV, p. 53.

186 *Wakefield Court Rolls* IV, p. 113.

187 *Yorkshire 1301*, p. 67.

188 'Lancashire', p. 45.

189 *Yorkshire 1301*, p. 49.

190 *Northumberland*, p. 58. An antonym is probably *Peniles* at Hayton in Cumberland in the assessment of 1327: *Cumberland*, p. 32 (although it is difficult to conceive of a contributor to the lay subsidy as *peniles* unless in the sense of experiencing a cash-flow problem or lacking coinage).

191 Storey, *Register of John Kirkby*, pp. 6–7.

192 For the origins of these terms about self-consciousness, E. Goffman, *Presentation of Self in Everyday Life* (London, 1969 edn) and S. Greenblatt, *Renaissance Self-Fashioning. From More to Shakespeare* (Chicago, 1980).

193 Fenwick, *Poll Taxes* I, p. 472.

194 Fenwick, *Poll Taxes* I, p. 458.

195 R. W. Hoyle, *Early Tudor Craven: Subsidies and Assessments 1510–1547* (YASRS 145, 1987), p. 10.

196 Hoyle, *Early Tudor Craven*, p. 119.

197 Hoyle, *Early Tudor Craven*, p. 5.

198 Hoyle, *Early Tudor Craven*, pp. 49, 60.

199 Hoyle, *Early Tudor Craven*, pp. 75, 83–4, 94, 101.

200 S. Simpson & J. Charlesworth, eds, *The Parish Register of Gisburne* I (Yorks. P. R. Soc. 114, 1943), pp. 239, 243, reveal, for example, the precise places of habitation.

201 Simpson & Charlesworth, *Parish Register of Gisburne*, p. 220.

202 Simpson & Charlesworth, *Parish Register of Gisburne*, pp. 220–6, 228–9.

203 Simpson & Charlesworth, *Parish Register of Gisburne*, pp. 1–4, 6–7, 9–11.

204 F. Taylor, ed., *The Parish Registers of Aughton* (Lancs. P. R. Soc. 81, 1942), pp. 1, 121.

205 Parker, 'Lay subsidy rolls 1 Edward III N. R. & City of York', p. 110.

206 Parker, 'Lay subsidy rolls 1 Edward III N. R. & City of York', p. 131.

207 Parker, 'Lay subsidy rolls 1 Edward III N. R. & City of York', p. 135.

208 Parker, 'Lay subsidy rolls 1 Edward III N. R. & City of York', p. 147.

209 Parker, 'Lay subsidy rolls 1 Edward III N. R. & City of York', p. 148.

210 *Pudsay Deeds*, p. 303.

211 *Pudsay Deeds*, pp. 302, 304

212 *Pudsay Deeds*, pp. 305, 326, 330, 332–3, 337, 340, 342, 345–6.

213 A. Edleston, *The Registers of Winston* (Durham & Northumberland P. R. Soc. xxxv, 1918), pp. 3, 4 5.

214 H. M. Wood., *The Registers of St Nicholas' Church* [Durham] (Durham & Northumberland P. R. Soc. xxxii, 1918), pp. 7, 8, 9 and 17.

215 H. M. Wood, *The Registers of Corbridge* (Durham & Northumberland P. R. Soc. xxiv, 1911), pp. 2, 3, 5.

216 H. Brierley, *The Registers of Brough under Stainmore* I (Cumberland and Westmorland P. R. Soc., 1923), p. 140.

217 A. Edleston, ed., *The Registers of Winston* (Durham and Northumberland P. R. Soc. xxxv, 1918), pp. 3–5, 7.

218 J. Foster, ed., *The Registers of the Antient Parish Church of Giggleswick-in-Craven* I (Settle, n.d.), pp. 3, 11, 17.

219 Foster, *Registers … of Giggleswick-in-Craven*, pp. 56, 111.

220 F. Taylor, *The Parish Registers of Aughton* (Lancs. P. R. Soc. 81, 1942), pp. 2–3, 5–8, 10.

221 Taylor, *Parish Registers of Aughton*, pp. 124, 126, 128–30.

222 Taylor, *Parish Registers of Aughton*, pp. 134, 136, 138, 140–1, 143–4.

223 Taylor, *Parish Registers of Aughton*, pp. 153–6.

224 Taylor, *Parish Registers of Aughton*, pp. 6, 54–5, 59, 61, 63–4.

225 'Shropshire', IV, pp. 291–2.

226 'Staffordshire 1332', p. 115.

227 W. Hudson, ed., *Leet Jurisdiction in the City of Norwich during the XIIIth and XIVth Centuries* (Selden Society 5, 1892), pp. 14, 17–18.

228 Hudson, *Leet Jurisdiction in the City of Norwich*, p. 34.

229 G. Hughes, *A History of English Words* (Oxford, 2000), p. 87.

230 Hughes, *History of English Words*, pp. 89–91.

9
Early-modern comparisons

Explored above in chapter 4 was how these northern counties were not only homogeneous at a higher level but also fragmented into a mosaic of discrete local areas. In that chapter, the categories of analysis were sociolinguistic: how the differences of the localities were expressed through speech, in dialect and lexis. There too discussion was confined to Middle English attributes. It is therefore perhaps also imperative to consider these localities as geographical entities, from the perspective of what English local historians have, borrowing one French expression, called *pays*, or perhaps more accurately what French regional geographers have – from a phenomenological approach – described as *l'espace vecu*.[1] Equally, there remains a compelling need to extend the analysis of these localities after the late middle ages, at least to assess the persistence of characteristics and, indeed, differences between localities. Such are the purposes of this chapter.

Two upland areas have been selected first for comparison as early-modern local societies: the moorlands of Westmorland and the uplands of the Craven area. Whilst both are, to different degrees, upland areas, pertaining to the 'Highland Zone', onomastic differences persisted into the early-modern experiences of their inhabitants.

First, attention can be directed to that delimiter of 'northern-ness', the intensity of patronymic or metronymic surnames. In the Craven area in the sixteenth century, patronymic and metronymic surnames with *-son* created a less intense impression than in the moorlands of the north-west. Although characteristic of Craven, these surnames did not insinuate so deeply into the lexis of surnames as in the north-western moorlands. In the first instalment of a lay subsidy exacted in 1524, 16.6 percent of taxpayers in Staincliffe Wapentake (comprehending Craven) disported patronyms and metronyms with the suffix *-son*.[2] In the second instalment, in 1525, the proportion comprised 17.4 percent.[3] Slightly higher in the lay subsidy of 1543, some 18.5 percent of taxpayers were registered with patronymic and metronymic surnames with *-son*.[4] Fairly conclusively, therefore, we might expect less than twenty percent of adult males here in the mid sixteenth century to have been identified by this form of surname, a significantly lower proportion than in the north-western moorlands.

Despite that comparative difference, however, *-son* surnames remained a distinctive characteristic of the Craven area, in the sense that they furnished fifteen of the surnames which proliferated so successfully here: Atkinson (twenty-eight of just over 2,300 taxpayers in 1543 – just over one percent); Dawson (ten), Diconson (fourteen); Edmundson (twelve); Harrison (seventeen); Lawson (twenty-three); Parkinson (twenty); Robinson (eighteen); Simson (ten); T(h)omson (twenty); Tillotson (twelve); Tomlinson (twelve); Watson (twelve); Wilkinson (thirty); and Wilson (thirty). To place these numbers more firmly into context, only fifty-four surnames accounted each for ten or more taxpayers in 1543.

In the uplands of Westmorland, by contrast, 27.8 percent of those who subscribed to the Protestation Oath in 1641–2 were identified by a patronymic or metronymic surname in -son – comprising 962 oath-takers out of a total of 3,432.[5] Altogether there existed in 1641–2 seventy-seven different patronymic and metronymic surnames. If those accounting each for one percent or more of the oath-takers are considered, the head of the ranking is revealed as: Atkinson (sixty-nine oath-takers); Robinson (sixty-seven); Richardson, Wilkinson and Wilson (each sixty-six); Harrison (sixty-two); Jackson (fifty); and Gibson and Thompson (each forty-three). Whilst a wide variety of these -son surnames had gained currency, nevertheless concentration was also characteristic. That concentration included, however, patronymic surnames constructed from both Adam and Gilbert and Atkinson was supplemented by twenty-four oath-takers designated Addison and another seven Adamsons. Whilst neither Adam nor Gilbert was a marginal name, their intrusion into the top echelon of patronymic surnames is singular.

The extent of patronymic and metronymic surnames can be observed through the descriptive statistics of their occurrence in the oath of 1641–2 (although no more than three surnames derived from metronyms).

Descending to the localized level – the existence of surnames with -son within each parish – patronyms and metronyms could have an even more significant impact. For example, at Crosby Ravensworth and Patterdale, respectively fifty-seven and fifty-six percent of the oath-takers in 1641 disported surnames with -son. In these two parishes, these surnames must have contributed immensely to local experience. Furthermore, accepting the mean of just under twenty-eight percent of oath-makers throughout Westmorland in 1641–2, in thirteen parishes that level was significantly exceeded: Crosby Ravensworth; Patterdale; Marton (forty-eight percent of oath-takers); Lowther (forty-six); Crosby Garrett (forty-five); Brougham (forty-one); Milburn (forty); Dufton, Kirkby Thore and Morland (each thirty-eight); Appleby (thirty-two); and Bampton and Ormshead (each thirty). In their quotidian experiences, therefore, parishioners in a number of Westmorland parishes would have recognised their neighbours by a patronymic or metronymic surname with the suffix -son.

Number of surnames	Mean	Trimmed mean	Standard deviation	Median	Min.	Max.	First quartile	Third quartile
77	12.49	10.00	18.41	5	1	69	2	13

Notes: in columns 2-3 and 5-9, the numbers related to oath-takers per surname.

Table 16 Descriptive statistics of patronymic and metronymic surnames in 1641–2 in Westmorland

Comparable material for county Durham reinforces the distinction between northern areas with moderate levels of patronymic and metronymic surnames in -*son* and those with intense density. Again, for Durham the Protestation Oath of 1641–2 provides a static count of all males over eighteen years. Within the county, just over 4,100 adult males were enumerated who were identified by -*son* surnames from within a listed population of just fewer than 16,000. Throughout the county on average, therefore, over one in four adult male inhabitants disported a -*son* surname, so that such monikers made an immense impression on quotidian existence and experience. The Durham material further confirms and defines, moreover, the increasing density of -son surnames further north.[6] The vocabulary or corpus of -*son*

Adamson 36	Hanson 4	Nickson/Nix(s)on 25
Addison 6	Harbeson 1	Parkinson 18
Alderson 4	Harrison 217	Patte(n)son 62
Allinson etc. 77	Hawkeson 1	Pearson/Peirson 98
Anderson 57	Hawson 2	Philipson 8
Annieson 2	Henderson 26	Polson 1
Atcheson/Atchinson 17	Hewetson/Huitson 21	Ranson 10
Atherson 1	Hewson 1	Renneson 11
Atkinson 117	Hickson/Hixon 31	Rennetson 5
Ayreson 5	Hidson 2	Renoldson/
Batmanson 3	Hindson* 3	Ranoldson 11
Benson 6	Hobson 17	Richardson 134
Betson 8	Hodgson/Hoghson 127	Richeson 5
Blaikson 1	Howson 5	Richinson 7
Branson 5	Hudson 17	Rickson 1
Burletson 2	Hugginson 3	Robinson 248
Burlinson 2	Hutchinson 114	Robson 100
Casson 1	Huxon 1	Rogerson 10
Clarkson/Clerkson* 13	Hyenson 1	Rowlandson 11
Co(u)lson 58	Isackson 1	Rowlinson 2
Collinson 2	Iveson 2	Sanderson 40
Cookson/Coxson* 9	Jackson 155	Sarrison 1
Cudbertson 3	Jameson 5	Selson 1
Cusson 4	Jefferson 40	Serientson* 1
Davison 73	Jenneson 3	Sheppson* (sic) 1
Dawson 44	Jobson 5	Shippardson* 12
Denison 8	Johnson 158	Simson 116
Dickinson 37	Judson 2	Sisson(s) 5
Dickson 98	Jurdinson 13	Sisterson* 2
Dirickson 2	Lambson* 3	Smythson* 5
Dobinson 21	Lawson 37	Stevenson 96
Dobson 55	Lockson 1	Stimson 1

* Indicates that the name possibly did not contain a personal name element.

Table 17 Surnames in -son: county Durham, 1641–2 (continued on the next page)

Dodgson 8

Donneson 5

Dowson 27

Ealeson 1

Ebison 1

Elgison 1

Elletson 1

Ellison 9

Emerson 116

Gelson 11

Gibson 94

Gillson 1

Gregson 4

Gurdison 1

Longson* 1

Lowson 8

Lumpson* 1

Maddison/Mattison/

Matheson 45

Madgson 1

Mawson 1

Megson 8

Mitcheson 7

Morrison 4

Murreson 2

Nelson 12

Neveson* 1

Nicholson 78

Swanson/

Swainston 15

T(h)om(p)son 234

Tailerson* 8

Tomlinson 4

Vinson 1

Waidson 4

Watson 173

Widdison* 4

Wilkinson 138

Williamson 32

Wilson 189

Wrightson/Ritson* 9

* Indicates that the name possibly did not contain a personal name element.

Table 17 Surnames in -son: *county Durham, 1641–2 (continued)*

Number of surnames	Mean	Trimmed mean	Standard deviation	Median	Min.	Max.	First quartile	Second quartile
137	30	22.15	51.44	6	1	248	2	31.5

Except for the standard deviation, figures represent the number of taxpayers per *–son* surname

Table 18 Descriptive statistics of -son *names: county Durham, 1641–2*

surnames in Durham exhibited an immense variety, but with the predictable concentration. The actual surnames occupy Table 17 and the statistics of their incidence Table 18.

Confirmed by both tables is the enormous variety of surnames derived from personal names with the suffix *-son* which existed in county Durham in the middle of the seventeenth century. Concentration at the core was consistent with the formation and persistence of an extensive range. Of course, the distribution in 1641–2 was influenced as much by the fortunes of kinship groups in later-medieval and early-modern local societies as by the original formations. Nevertheless, some interesting features appear. As elsewhere, the concentration of forms represented the common 'forenames' in general use throughout England: John; Richard; Robert; and William. In Durham, the persistence and survival of *-son* surnames from these four personal names had particular resonances. Formations from John continued in virtually equal numbers with both etymon (Johnson) and hypocorism (Jackson). In contrast, forms from William proliferated in their hypocoristic style (Wilson and Wilkinson). Hypocorisms accounted exclusively for forms from Robert, but more frequently with the Rob- hypocorism than Dob- or Hob-. By contrast, although the etymon (Richardson) appeared strongly, the hypocoristic elements slightly exceeded it, but most particularly the Dick- rather than the Hick- prototheme.

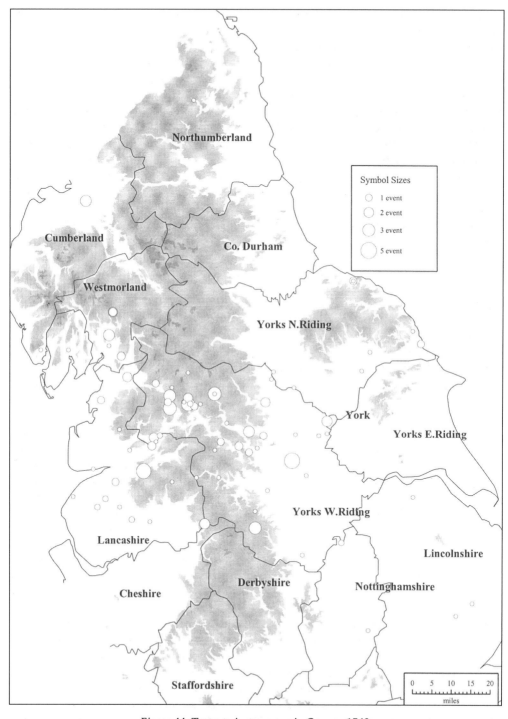

Figure 44 Toponymic surnames in Craven, 1543

Nonetheless, as distinctive of northern -*son* surnames was a second tier of quite profuse surnames. Forms from Roger attained high levels, especially Hodgson and its variant, more so than Dodgson or Rogerson. Equally, although like Roger not unusual forenames, Harrison and Tompson and variants persisted highly by comparison with the even more common forenames. Not exhibiting quite the same level of persistence, but contributing to the context of northern patronyms and metronyms were the numbers of Davison, Hutchinson, Allanson, Anderson, Atkinson, Emerson, Mattison (and variants), and Co(u)lson. Combined with the enormous numerical range of patronyms and metronyms with -*son*, this complex character of second and third tier of persistence imparted distinguishing characteristics to -*son* surnames in the far north.

Although successful internally within Craven, patronymic and metronymic surnames in -*son* did not have the density here of their distribution in the north-western moorlands of Westmorland. In another sense also the intensity of the distribution of all surnames had less density in Craven than in Westmorland. In Westmorland vills a high degree of isonymy pertained: that is, intense concentration of surnames. That isonymy was less evident in Craven. Only at Buckden is there some limited evidence of concentration through the surnames Loge (seven taxpayers) and Tenand (twenty taxpayers), but the wide distribution of other surnames there reduces the mean to 3.1 taxpayers per surname (trimmed mean 2.4; standard deviation 4.063). Moreover, the apparent concentration might be exaggerated by the composition of the upland parish, with dispersed settlement in about eight hamlets or settlement sites.[7]

Now, in discussing the levels of isonymy in the two areas, the argument is not directed to illustrating degree or extent of kinship relationships, but merely to indicating the repertoire of surnames in the locality. The two phenomena are entirely distinct and separate and not necessarily inter-related in any way.[8]

Characteristically, perhaps, the repertoire of toponymic surnames was entirely restricted in both locations. Distance from place-name of origin remained highly circumscribed through early-modern experience. Although that limited movement of toponymic surnames had a general application throughout pre-modern England, it has been demonstrated as a particular feature of upland areas, not least where there is a high degree of dispersed settlement. Both areas exhibited that circumscription of toponymic surnames, as illustrated in Figures 44 and 45. The distributions make allowances, as far as possible, for ambiguous place-names and the possible confusion about minor place-names and topographical features without settlements. For example, the toponymic surname Preston has been omitted from the figure for Craven, although it was borne by twenty-two taxpayers in 1543. Whilst it cannot be demonstrably proven to have originated from Preston in Craven, that is the likelihood. Its inclusion would enhance still further the circumscribed concentration of toponymic surnames.[9] The same problem obtains with Bolton; the same cautious approach is followed.[10] Moreover, Craven – the generic, 'regional' toponymic held by six taxpayers in 1543 – cannot be included on the map as a point.

Now, the extent of the concentration of surnames in Westmorland in 1641–2 had proceeded as far as, if not further than, in Craven. The degree can be represented by the mean number of oath-takers per surname in the Protestation Oath, as illustrated

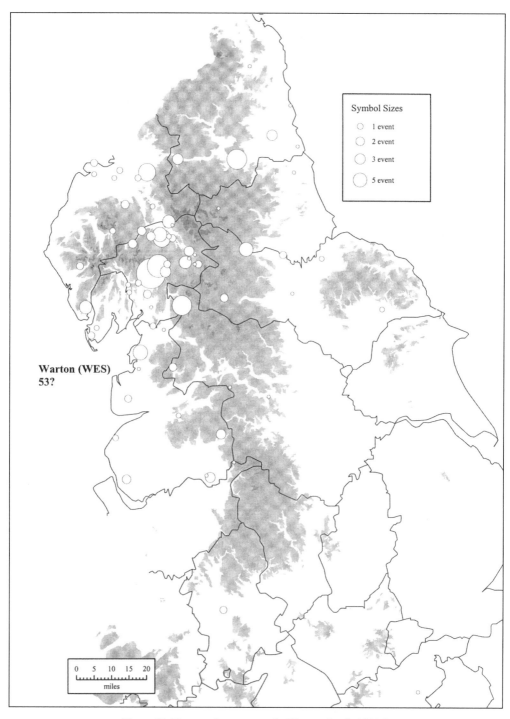

Figure 45 *Toponymic surnames in Westmorland, 1641–2*

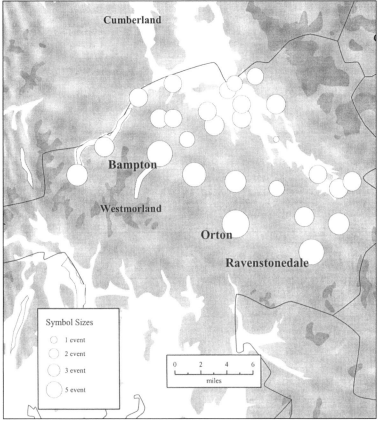

Figure 46 Surnames and oath-takers in Westmorland, 1641–2

both in Table 19 and in Figure 46. As well as divulging the generally high level of isonymy in these parishes, the numbers indicate an even greater intensity of concentration in particular settlements. Subjecting the two variables – number of oath-takers in relation to number of different surnames – to Spearman's rank correlation results in C= 0.918 with p= 0.000. As a consequence, it can be discounted that any particular size of population had a differential effect on the number of different surnames. Where there is a higher density of particular surnames, then, that proliferation is entirely contingent.

It is thus possible to isolate those parishes characterized by a high level of isonymy. The mean of association of oath-takers to surnames corresponded to 2.003 , but the trimmed mean produced a reduced figure of 1.932. To assess levels of more intense concentration, parishes with a mean level 2.00 or higher can then be separated: Appleby (2.0); Crosby Garrett (2.0); Kirkby Stephen (2.4); Ravenstonedale (3.3); Bampton (3.4); Crosby Ravensworth (2.4); Martindale (2.00); Morland (2.1); Orton (3.9); Patterdale (2.4); and Shap (2.9) (numbers are here rounded up to one decimal point). How that isonymy developed in part involved single repetitive surnames:

sixteen Harrisons in Appleby; sixteen each of Morland and Wharton and eighteen Wallers in Kirkby Stephen; twenty Shawes, twenty-two Fothergills and thirty-nine Fawcetts in Ravenstonedale; fifteen Wilkinsons and twenty-one Baxters in Bampton; and fifteen Howes in Shap. In Crosby Garrett, ten Skaifes and ten Richardsons influenced the level of concentration, for both constituted more than ten percent of

Parish	Total number of oath-takers	Total of different surnames	Mean of oath-takers per surname
Appleby	294	144	2.04
Asby	49	39	1.26
Brough	146	76	1.92
Crosby Garrett	92	46	2.00
Dufton	92	45	2.04
Kirkby Stephen	332	139	2.39
Kirkby Thore	73	44	1.66
Marton	75	42	1.78
Milburn	40	26	1.54
Musgrave	41	22	1.86
Newbiggin	44	35	1.25
Ormshead	56	31	1.81
Orton	329	84	3.92
Ravenstonedale	261	80	3.26
Temple Sowerby	33	22	1.5
Warcop	99	59	1.67
Askham	71	39	1.82
Bampton	196	57	3.44
Barton	87	49	1.80
Bolton	57	30	1.90
Brougham	54	41	1.32
Cliburn	42	24	1.75
Clifton	44	28	1.57
Crosby Ravensworth	145	61	2.37
Lowther	48	28	1.71
Martindale	37	19	1.95
Morland	150	71	2.11
Patterdale	40	17	2.35
Thrimby	29	23	1.26
Shap	243	85	2.86

Table 19 Oath-takers per surname in Westmorland, 1641-2

Total number of surnames	Mean number of taxpayers per surname	Standard deviation	Trimmed mean of taxpayers per surname	Median number of taxpayers per surname	Maximum number of taxpayers for a surname	First quartile: number of taxpayers per surname	Third quartile: number of taxpayers per surname
602	3.9	5.189	3.2	2	61	1	5

Table 20 Descriptive statistics of the distribution of surnames in Craven in 1543

Parish	Number of taxpayers			Number of surnames			Surnames surviving from 1379 to 1543
	1379	1524	1543	1379	1524	1543	
Addingham	29	3	23	25	3	19	3
Airton	21	2	20	17	1	10	2
Appletreewick	47	4	38	40	4	20	3
Arncliffe	36	5	16	33	4	12	3
Bracewell	26	8	16	24	7	14	2
Burnsall	32	6	27	26	6	18	0
Calton	20	5	28	18	5	21	1
Coniston	35	6	18	31	5	14	2
Cowling	25	3	26	19	3	15	2
Cracoe	18	6	19	15	4	13	0
Easington	13	5	34	13	5	2	1
Eshton	17	3	21	17	3	15	1
Gargrave	42	5	53	38	5	40	6
Giggleswick	52	13	42	38	12	28	7
Glusburn	23	2	19	19	2	18	0
Grindleton	27	5	34	27	3	26	4
Hanlith	4	4	16	4	3	12	0
Hartlington	7	?	16	7	?	12	0
Hebden	23	4	20	15	4	13	0
Hellifield	46	8	30	34	8	24	3
Keighley	60	6	112	46			6

Table 21 Craven: (dis)continuity of surnames at parish level, 1379–1543[14] (continued opposite)

Kettlewell	46	5	57	42	5	39	5
Litton	36	?	27	31	?	18	2
Malham	44	9	60	39	9	38	5
Middop	18		8	16		7	0
Mitton	24	?	32	20	?	22	0
Newsome	24	10	15	20	9	12	0
Otterburn	16	5	11	12	4	8	0
Pathorn	19	15	24	14	6	13	1
Rathmell	34	7	27	30	5	16	2
Rimmington	61	5	50	47	4	39	4
Settle	52	9	49	48	8	34	3
Silsden	40	6	51	31	6	32	3-5
Skipton	72	12	95	65	11	61	2
Slaidburn	50	5	50	42	4	42	2
Steeton	61	4	21	51	3	13	2
Swinden	20	3	13	14	2	11	0
Threshfield	23	7	38	16	7	32	2
Waddington	18	9	35	15	7	20	1
Wigglesworth	26	13	36	25	12	25	1

Table 21 Craven: (dis)continuity of surnames at parish level, 1379–1543[14] (continued)

the local oath-takers. At the extreme, the level of concentration evolving from these iterative surnames attained great intensity, as at Orton, habitation of seventeen Whartons, twenty-six Birkbecks, twenty-seven Whiteheads, and a similar number (twenty-eight) of Whiteheads. To a considerable degree, then, isonymy was generated by the frequency of a select group of repeated surnames.

Returning to toponymic surnames, one measure of the extent of localization is the continued concentration of place-name surnames around their location of origin. That phenomenon obtained for place-name surnames in very many regions, but the intensity was emphatic in northern areas. The density of concentration can be estimated through the distribution of origin of surnames which feature in parish registers of burials in the sixteenth and seventeenth centuries. Addressing the eastern side of the Pennines initially, the origins of place-name surnames in Croston between 1538 and 1550 was highly concentrated, even omitting the incidence of place-names of the numerous dispersed settlements within the parish.[11] Surprisingly, the distribution for Warcop (Figure 47) contained wider dispersal for the later decades of 1597 to 1636.[12]

Upland areas, still partially isolate, remained susceptible to this extreme con-

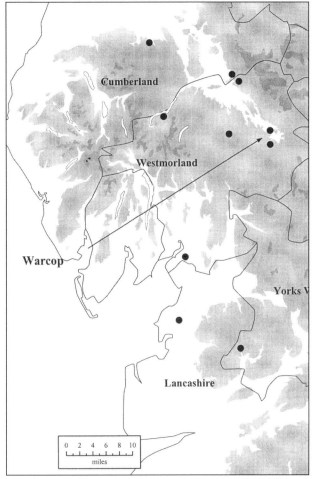

Figure 47 Toponymic surnames in Warcop, 1597–1636

centration of surnames. In northern zones, this early-modern isonymy was represented through the density of surnames with the suffix -*son* and the even more locally circumscribed corpus of toponymic surnames. Although during the later middle ages a radical disruption of surnames occurred at the level of the parish, so that only a small group of surnames survived in exactly the same settlement through the later middle ages, those very surnames remained circumscribed in the region and their localized retention informed the character of the region.

Localization and persistence should, however, be tempered by the recognition that in the late middle ages surnames were severely disrupted at one level. Whilst over the wider area there was indeed continuity of surnames, at parish level dislocation occurred on a massive scale. The prospect suggested therefore is of rapid and wholesale turnover of surnames in parishes over the late middle ages, but the localized nature of the migration of surnames contributing to their persistence in the area as a whole.[13]

Those two levels of existence can be best illustrated by reference to the Craven area, since the Poll Tax returns of 1379 and the lay subsidy of 1543 provide largely complete data, in the sense of legibility and survival. Of course, questions remain about the level of capture of lay subsidies, particularly a later one like 1543. Nevertheless, what the data reveal is the suspect nature of the lay subsidy of 1543 rather than inefficiency in 1543.

What is apparent is that in each parish only a very small proportion of surnames of 1379 persisted into the middle of the sixteenth century in that parish. All the surnames continued to exist in the Craven area as a whole, but disappeared from the parish. During the later middle ages then each parish exhibited a fundamental turnover of surnames. That transformation might not have been completely associated with the disappearance of kinship groups from the parish since continuity of families might have been assured through the female line. Surnames are only indicative of the male lineage. Considering the immense level of the disruption of surnames, however, it is not untenable to suggest that kinship groups were mobilized as well as surnames.

Moreover, those surnames which extended from 1379 into the sixteenth century did not necessarily (and probably did not) represent continuity of kinship groups in each of the parishes. First, of course, numerous of these surnames were common ones not attached to any particular kinship and not unique or distinctive. It would be stretching the bounds of credulity to pretend that the *Smyth* in Airton in 1543 was conclusively related by descent to the *Smyth'* in 1379. Secondly, residual Latin forms in 1379 compound our difficulties: for example, what vernacular form did the *filius Roberti* of Addingham in 1379 later assume – the *Robertson* in Addingham in 1379 or the *Robynson* there in 1543? The figures in the table for survival of surnames thus exaggerate the actual extent of persistence. It is emphatic therefore that a only very small number and proportion of surnames of 1379 continued in the same parish into the sixteenth century.

Appreciation of the diversity of the north, as well as its unifying characteristics, however, demands a comparison with other localities. In view of the plenitude of information, Acomb presents an appropriate illustration. Moreover, its location importantly contrasts with the upland regimes above, for Acomb was situated within the Vale of York, adjacent to the provincial capital, York. As might be expected, although there was some continuity of surnames, there was equally a significant turnover in early-modern Acomb. From the suit rolls intermittently listed in the court rolls of Acomb, the surnames of tenants of land can be compared over a secular trend. Nevertheless, the suit rolls indicate quite clearly that some tenants were non-resident, inhabitants of York. In 1570, the tenants collectively held thirty-five different surnames; by 1601 that number had proliferated to forty-eight; but they had diminished again to thirty-eight in 1683. It might therefore be adduced that the profusion in 1601 was associated with a temporary influx in times of extreme hardship. Over this period of a hundred years, six surnames only were continuous, one of which, Newarke, was associated with gentry status. The other five – Burdeux, Hill, Scadlocke, Metcalfe and Coates – although persistent over the whole period, had fluctuating fortunes. The vicissitudes were most obvious for two surnames which in 1570 had dominated the parish: Gill (four tenants) and Skadlock (six). By 1683, Gill had disappeared and Scadlock had declined to a smaller representation. Continuous surnames did not therefore consistently represent dominant families. In this sense, a distinction is made between core – in the sense of continuous – surnames and dominant kinships. Still, the persistence of these surnames – even if in diminished number – provided some cultural continuity.[15]

Acomb then was influenced by its proximity to York. It might be anticipated that the environment of large urban places was distinctly different from rural parishes. Of course, in many senses was that so. On the other hand, the cultural and sensed environment of distinctively urban places – in the north – still shared some characteristics with rural locations. Northern urban centres exhibited a high level of patronymic and metronymic surnames in -*son* which provided one cultural conduit between rural and urban. In the muster for Newcastle-upon-Tyne in 1539, about twenty percent of the 'fencible' men (200 of a total muster of 1,097) were identified by -*son* surnames, so that urban and rural surnames were at this time complementary in kind rather than differentiated.[16] Amongst those patronyms which distinguished a northern nature, Patenson and Atcheson were well represented in the muster in Newcastle.[17] Four Armstrongs furnished a further linkage between urban and rural environments.[18]

That complementary nature was enhanced by the expansion of the surname Blithman in the borough. In 1539, Davy Blythman was audited for military duty alongside William Blythman, a butcher, his servant Piers Blythman, another butcher, William Blythman with his servant, Roger Blythman, Jarret Blythman and Nicholas Blythman. Indeed, the surname had existed in Newcastle for some time and had become well established by the early sixteenth century. The chamberlains of the borough repetitively paid William Blithman, mason, for his services between 1508 and 1511.[19] Contemporaneously, another mason, John Blithman, supplied tallow for plumbing work and other services, remunerated also by the chamberlains.[20] Indeed, that surname existed in another urban context, in the parish of St Nicholas, Durham, where George Blythman was married in 1546, William Blythman in 1584, and Richard Blithman, butcher, in 1607, this surname thus here too linking urban and rural through surnames in the early-modern cultural context.[21]

That affinity of surnames was replicated also in the existence in Newcastle of the surname Todd. Repeatedly the chamberlains incurred expenses to John Tod for his days of work for the 'pawer' (poor) in 1510.[22] The same official compensated James Todd for four and a half days of assisting the plumber in1510.[23] The surname recurred in the 1539 musters for the borough.[24]

Whilst, consequently, the *cognomina* of the medieval borough might have differentiated it culturally from the surrounding rural hinterland – principally through the divergence in the proportion of toponymic and occupational bynames – the naming environment of the early-modern northern borough was less distinguished from its rural environs.

Concluding early-modern surnames

After the instability of surnames in villages through the fifteenth century, stability was restored towards the middle of the sixteenth century. Thenceforth, it was possible in many – although not all – villages for the persistence of a core of surnames to represent the continuity of some focal kinships in local society. In the late seventeenth and early eighteenth centuries, there might have been a consciousness of continuous inhabitants which successfully allowed some stability. Perhaps the incumbent of Long Houghton in Northumberland was reflecting a wider understanding and not simply his own predilections when he annotated the burial register of his parish between 1696 and 1738.[25] He eschewed a purely hierarchical description of his local society – whether in local or national categories – in favour of a prescriptive division into the 'honest' (embellished further sometimes as 'serious' and 'good') against the marginal element in his categorization, the 'ignorant' (and in one case, 'bruitish ignorant'), 'wicked' and 'careless'.[26] His perceptions concerned integrity and character (as well as church attendance), situating 'honesty' with 'age', but allowing for the 'poor but honest'.[27] His comments, however, extended further, to identify those kinships which were defined by longevity as well as precedence amongst the farming 'community'. When he recorded successive Taite burials, his epitaphs concluded 'antient farmer' (1697), 'one of the antient farmers' (of Lionel Taite senior in 1698), 'one of the ancient farmers' and, importantly, when William Taite was buried in 1728 'of a very ancient race of farmers'.[28] What that last commendation implies is that his remarks about 'antient' were directed towards the longevity of the kinship; indeed, for individuals, he normally employed the word 'old'. So, when the widow of Lionel Taite died in 1710, he referred to Lionel as 'one [of the] antient tenants' and, in glossing William Taite in 1726 and 1727, 'an ancient race of farmers'.[29]

That last epithet was similarly accorded to other farming kinships, and thus he remarked of Henry Nisbet in 1728: 'born of an ancient stock of Longhoton farmers'.[30] He had previously, in 1711, dignified Mr Robert Burrel as 'of an ancient race of Burrels and farmers.'[31] In the same vein, the Adams kinship was complimented in 1726 as 'an ancient race of Longhoughton farmers'.[32] When, therefore, he commended Margaret, widow of Thomas Andrews, against the entry of her burial in 1699, as 'one of the antient and principal farmers', what he intended to convey was a respect for the lineage of the kinship which had provided stability; that attribute was also directed to Rainoldson in 1701, 'one of the antient farmers'.[33]

It is doubtful, however, that the longevity – memorialized as it was by the incumbent in the register – extended back beyond the early sixteenth century. Before then, widespread dislocation was evidenced in most places in the rapid turnover of surnames, only a very small core surviving through the later middle ages. The early-modern restoration of stability allowed the persistence of a wider corpus of surnames to indicate to inhabitants of villages the genealogical continuity of core or focal families. Within those local societies, those persistent surnames had a rhetorical ring, memorializing the recent past, and instilling the experience of present and future.[34] Between the injunction of 1597 and the canons of 1604, the entries in parish registers – all of baptisms, marriages and burials – were read out on Sundays after morning or evening prayer. Whilst the declaring of baptisms and marriages might have been appropriated for matters of entitlement to parish resources and humiliation of parents of bastards, the repetition of surnames in burials memorialized local families.[35]

Notes

1   P. Claval, *An Introduction to Regional Geography* trans. I. Thompson (Oxford, 1998), pp. 45–6, 126–30.

2   R. W. Hoyle, ed., *Early Tudor Craven. Subsidies and Assessments 1510–1547* (YASRS cxlv, 1987 for 1985), pp. 48–55.

3   Hoyle, *Early Tudor Craven*, pp. 56–63.

4   Hoyle, *Early Tudor Craven*, pp. 64–90.

5   M. A. Faraday, ed., *The Westmorland Protestation Returns 1641/2* (Kendal, 1971), the numbers of oath-takers is provided at pp. xi–xii: 2,157 in the East Ward and 1,275 in the West Ward.

6   H. M. Wood, ed., *Durham Protestations, or the Returns made to the House of Commons in 1641–2* (Surtees Society 135, 1922); the listed population has been independently tallied by myself.

7   Hoyle, *Early Tudor Craven*, pp. 86–7.

8   For recent discussions of surnames and core or focal families, reciting the literature, D. Hey, 'Stable families in Tudor and Stuart England' and S. & D. Postles, 'Surnames and stability: a detailed case study' both in D. Hooke and D. Postles, eds, *Names, Time and Place* (Oxford, 2003), pp. 165–80 and 193–207. For an alternative methodology, P. Spufford, 'The comparative mobility and immobility of Lollard descendants in early modern England' in M. Spufford, ed., *The World of Rural Dissenters 1520–1725* (Cambridge, 1995), pp. 309–31.

9   Hoyle, *Early Tudor Craven*, pp. 72–3.

10 Hoyle, *Early Tudor Craven*, p. 73.

11 H. Fishwick, ed., *The Registers of the Parish Church of Croston* I (Lancs. P. R. Soc. 6, 1900), pp. 161–72.

12 J. Abercrombie, ed., *The Registers of Warcop* (Cumberland and Westmorland P. R. Soc., 1914).

13 For the demographic conditions, R. M. Smith, 'Human resources' in G. Astill & A. Grant, eds, *The Countryside of Medieval England* (Oxford, 1988); for the association of families and land – and the potential for dislocation – Z. Razi, 'The erosion of the family-land bond in the fourteenth and fifteenth centuries: a methodological note' and C. Dyer, 'Changes in the link between families and land in the west midlands in the fourteenth and fifteenth centuries' in R. M. Smith, ed., *Land, Kinship and Life-cycle* (Cambridge, 1984), pp. 295–312.

14 Where the 1543 return is illegible or defective, that for 1545 has been employed.

15 H. Richardson, ed., *Court Rolls of the Manor of Acomb* I (YASRS 131, 1969), passim.

16 G. B. Richardson, 'A muster of the fencible inhabitants of Newcastle-upon-Tyne in the year 1539…' *Archaeologia Aeliana* IV (1855), pp. 119–40. For the total number mustered, p. 135.

17 Richardson, 'A muster', pp. 125, 126, 134, 135 (Atcheson); pp. 126, 127, 129, 130, 132, 135, (Patenson).

18 Richardson, 'A muster', pp. 131, 132.

19 C. M. Fraser, ed., *The Accounts of the Chamberlains of Newcastle upon Tyne 1508–1511* (Society of Antiquaries of Newcastle upon Tyne, Record Series 3, 1987), pp. 9, 37,41, 181, 183, 232.

20 Fraser, *Accounts of the Chamberlains*, pp. 197, 201, 232.

21 H. M. Wood, *The Registers of St Nicholas' Church* [Durham] (Durham & Northumberland P. R. Soc. xxxii, 1918), pp. 2, 9, 16.

22 Fraser, *Accounts of the Chamberlains*, pp. 159, 161, 163, 166, 168, 170, 172, 174, 177, 179, 180; he had also received a payment for another service in 1508: p. 7.

23 Fraser, *Accounts of the Chamberlains*, p. 181.

24   Richardson, 'A muster', pp. 127, 129 (*bis*).

25   H. M. Wood, *The Registers of Long Houghton* (Durham & Northumberland P. R. Soc. xxxvi, 1926), pp. 118–38.

26   For this context, H. French, 'Social status, localism and the "middle sort of people" in England, 1620–1750', *Past and Present* 166 (2000), pp. 66–99.

27   Wood, *Registers of Long Houghton*, pp. 120 ('a very honest but poor day labourer', 1699), 121 ('a very honest hinde', 'a very honest poor taylor'), 122 (describing a collier as 'an old good man' and a hinde as 'an old very good man' in 1703); for an example of his antipathy, p. 122 (a shepherd denounced as 'a gratly ignorant and wicked man', 1703).

28   Wood, *Registers of Long Houghton*, pp. 119, 133, 134, 135 for comments on the Tait(es).

29   Wood, *Registers of Long Houghton*, pp. 125, 133, 134.

30   Wood, *Registers of Long Houghton*, p. 135.

31   Wood, *Registers of Long Houghton*, p. 126.

32   Wood, *Registers of Long Houghton*, p. 133.

33   Wood, *Registers of Long Houghton*, pp. 120, 121.

34   See now B. Misztal, *Theories of Social Remembering* (Buckingham, 2003), for the performative and active process involved in collective remembering, reflecting on historical processes delineated by Connerton and by Wickham and Fentress.

35   P. Marshall, *Beliefs and the Dead in Reformation England* (Oxford, 2002), pp. 290–4, esp. p. 293.

10

CONCLUSION

'...looking at Rother'am, yer know, if ye' di'n't live 'ere and know it, ye'd think it wo' a really nice place. Yer just can't see what it's like to live 'ere.'[1]

The 'North' of England and northern-ness are elusive concepts, both academically and in popular perception. What contribution the isonymy of surnames has made to a sense of regional identities is equally complicated.[2] In any case, perhaps a notion of northern cultural identities constructed around a consciousness of place demands more than can be delivered through an onomastic study. Whichever geographical conception is taken of a medieval 'North', it contained a *mélange* of diverse influences.[3] In the twelfth-century 'North', in particular, there was an agglomeration of residual, oppositional and conformist cultures. In later (and, indeed, our own contemporary) expositions, differences between south and north have been rhetorical. Equally, they have been imprecise, implying zones rather than delineating a precise boundary.

Perhaps two implications can be elicited about how surnames have informed our understanding of a northern zone. First, surnames might be constituted a sort of 'cultural capital' that defined the lived experience.[4] What, secondly, the repetition and concentration of surnames may bring into vision at one level is a 'thin cultural coherence' of northern-ness.[5] Patronymic and metronymic bynames and surnames in the vernacular form with the suffix *-son* existed as a homologous cultural item over the whole area which might, under any geographical conception, be considered northern. Although a unifying element, this cultural item provided only a thin veneer of cultural coherence. Indeed, the intensity of concentration of this form of surname varied within this broad northern entity. Accordingly, some localities within the broad northern expanse might be expressed as more 'northern' than others. The differentiation might seem to conform to notions of a higher/upper and a lower north.[6] Nevertheless, the southerly persistence of this form of surname – if at reduced levels – suggests that what happened down here consisted of a spilling outside the 'North'. That suspicion is confirmed by the existence of these bynames in East Anglia. How the dissemination of this form of byname and surname might then be construed is as a characteristic, but not a criterion, of northern-ness. Where there existed a really dense concentration of patronymic and metronymic names with the Middle English vernacular suffix *-son*, we encounter an attribute of northern-ness.

Below that more expansive construal of northern-ness, nonetheless, other lexical and phonemic items contained within surnames intimate a mosaic of localities – a varying pattern – with their particular speech traditions. These intimate speech communities are revealed through the localized use of very specialized items.

To some extent the mosaic pattern of these lexical and phonemic items conforms to the patterning of northern 'cultural provinces' suggested by Phythian-Adams: Cumberland and Westmorland having an association with Solway; Lancashire and Cheshire constituting a seaboard of the 'Irish' sea; Northumberland and Durham collectively a seaboard region of the North ('Scandinavian') sea; and the ridings of Yorkshire focused on the Ouse basin – with, incidentally, below them two expanses directed respectively to the Trent (Staffordshire, Derbyshire and Nottinghamshire) and Witham (Lincolnshire) systems.[7] Items in surnames certainly express a difference between east and west of the Pennines. Similarly they demonstrate a difference between north and south of the Ribble on the western side of the Pennines. Some items correspond to a difference between the far north on the eastern side of the mountains and Yorkshire.

To recapitulate some of these distinctions, the voicing of a/o separates, on the eastern side of the Pennines, south and north of the Ribble. *Punder* and *Pinder* distinguish upper and lower North on the eastern side. The conformity, however, is not absolute, since some localities transected those 'provinces'. The voicing of a/o actually delineates the area south of the Ribble as an extension of (North-west) West Midlands dialect into most of Lancashire, differentiating that area from the whole of the remainder of the North. In that respect, the far north-west had a common currency with the land mass west of the Pennines. *Tod* extended across the whole of a far north, so that this item in Cumberland, Westmorland, Northumberland and Durham coalesced across the Pennines.

Another nonconformity is the spilling out of the North into lower reaches. For example, the occupational byname and surname Walker extended out of the north into the east and, more particularly, west midlands. Similarly Thacker comprehended a southerly area, more especially the east midlands. Perhaps we should describe these bynames and surnames as northerly rather than northern or of the North. Nevertheless, their density was more intense in the northern-most reaches so that they can be construed as characterizing the north if not exclusively northern.

In some cases, the smaller localities of the mosaic extended outside the 'traditional' northern counties. Most particularly is that the case with the topographical byname constructed with the suffix -by, which belonged to a southern, peripheral zone of the North. The distribution of that form of byname constitutes an area consisting of the northern and southern reaches of Humberside, comprising the southern East Riding and Holderness and the northern part of the Parts of Lindsey.[8]

Inherent in that particular conglomeration is the immense problem of separating northern-ness and Scandinavian influence. Although the extent of Scandinavian linguistic impact remains an intractable problem, it afforded that 'thin coherence' between northern England and the east midlands (and some correspondence with East Anglia too).

Indeed, language codes seem critical to the elucidation of northern-ness, for much of the difference of the north seems to originate in a particular usage of Middle English not only in the speech community, but in written records. The lexis of Middle English naming, of course, also varied between northern and southern. That divergence explains the thin broad differentiation of area with patronymic and metronymic surnames with -*son* in contrast to those geographies of the appositional patronym/metronym or the inflection of the genitival -*s*. Whilst bynames and surnames with suffixes of relationship (-*son*, -*daughter*, -*wif*) were not confined exclusively to the north, they were intermittent, sporadic and less usual in more southerly areas. In the case of -*wif* and -*daughter*, their appearance elsewhere was extraordinary, whilst not non-existent. When the portmoot rolls of the borough of Colchester alluded to John *Batewyf*, a defendant in trespass in 1334, the paradox of its occurrence is revealed not only by the solitariness of this form of naming there, but by its evidently hereditary progression.[9] The inclusion of Philippa *Anneysedouhter* in a case of battery in 1346 is unique for this form.[10] Whilst, therefore, these forms had a scattered existence in southern zones, this dispersal was insignificant in comparison with northern usage.

Finally, how does the language of personal names assist the representation of dissonance between north and south? Some inferences can be deduced from the persistence of insular personal names and the character of northern nickname bynames. The longer continuity of insular personal names in the north implies a cultural dissonance with the south – perhaps in terms of a residual culture, but equally perhaps in terms of a resistant or oppositional culture. Since (what others might assume to be) insalubrious nickname bynames continued later in the north than in more southerly environments, northern speech through names could be represented as (by northerners) direct and (by southerners) uncivil and rude.[11]

Another characteristic of Northern naming was the persistent flexibility of bynames and surnames, in addition to the bynames of relationship mentioned above. It is important not to accept an unremitting and reductive geographical diffusion of the principle of heritability of family names. A proportion of northern bynames, nonetheless, including occupational forms, seem to have retained their flexibility until later than in more southerly reaches – taking a very general perspective.

At this point, it is appropriate to return to 'The Reeve's Tale' and the insinuation of some direct speech purporting to be northern. One assumption about the language imputed to the two northern scholars is that their tongue was intelligible to all the audience, regardless of its members' origins. It has, however, been indicated that accretions of northern speech have been inserted in the text by redactors. The amount of northern dialect is, moreover, limited in quantity and circumscribed in character. The vowel substitution of *a* for *o*, which constitutes much of the phonemic difference in the scholars' speech, is not a serious adjustment. The amount of lexical variation is restricted. Although the scholars resort to symbols of northern-ness – 'by Seint Cuthberd' – there is not an extreme linguistic corpus for the audience to comprehend. Furthermore, cognizance must be taken of who the actors were: scholars in Oxford. Now, although scholars no doubt engaged in a precarious life-style, they can also easily be represented as an ideal. Their language use – as projected by Chaucer and his redactors – might therefore only weakly imitate the language of the north and, especially, its lexical content.[12] Which was more significant: their scholarly profession or their northern-ness?

That question is significant because when we consider the contribution of naming to a consciousness of northern-ness, our main approach is a phenomenological one: how people experienced their life-world within a North and its constituent mosaic. Naming belonged to the lived experience and the environment was assumed from within the life-world: from topographical features, from place-names, from working the landscape. Moreover, the life-world was constantly informed by those namings, through the constancy, persistence and repetition of them in early-modern local societies.[13] On the other hand, the names deduced from the life-world also offered information which could and was appropriated – and exaggerated – in outsiders' representation of northern-ness. In that dialogic moment, naming in the North influenced the perception of the North, from both the inside and outside.[14]

Let's conclude by returning again to Chaucer. When he – or his redactors – intended to signify the northern-ness of the two scholars in 'The Reeve's Tale', the symbol deployed was a name – the name of a saint: 'Now,' Symond,' seyde John, 'by Seint Cuthberd.'[15] Although described as from the pseudonymous 'Strother', that exclamation located the two clerks' origin as the north-east. In early-modern north-eastern society, Cuthbert continued as a not insignificant forename as well as surname.[16]

Notes

1   S. Charlesworth, *A Phenomenology of Working Class Experience* (Cambridge, 2000), p. 95 (response of an unemployed man) – Charlesworth elucidates an understanding of this life-world experience.

2   The term 'isonymy' is borrowed from bio-anthropologists without their clear precision of the notion; all that is intended here is concentration of names, in this case surnames.

3   As exhibited in C. Phythian-Adams, *Land of the Cumbrians. A Study in British Provincial Origins, A.D. 400–1120* (Aldershot, 1996).

4   P. Bourdieu, *The Logic of Practice* trans. R. Nice (Cambridge, 1992), pp. 52–65, esp. p. 56; see also, Bourdieu, *Outline of a Theory of Practice* trans. R. Nice (Cambridge, 1977); Bourdieu uses the idea in a different way; my intention here is in particular to avoid notions of the restrictions imposed by structuration on agency.

5   W. Sewell, 'The Concept(s) of Culture' in V. E. Bonnell & L. Hunt, eds, *Beyond the Cultural Turn* (Berkeley & Los Angeles, 1999), pp. 35–61.

6   As proposed by H. M. Jewell, *The North-South Divide. The Origins of Northern Consciousness in England* (Manchester, 1994).

7   C. Phythian-Adams, ed., *Societies, Cultures and Kinship, 1580–1850. Cultural Provinces and English Local History* (London, 1993), Figure 1.2 [p. xviii].

8   Consider too Kristensson's suggestion that Lindsey had a closer association with southern Yorkshire than with the rest of Lincolnshire: G. Kristensson, *Studies on the Early Fourteenth Century Population of Lindsey* (Lund, 1976–7).

9   I. H. Jeayes, ed., *Court Rolls of the Borough of Colchester* volume 1 *(1310–1352)* (Colchester, 1921), p. 135.

10   Jeayes, *Court Rolls ... of Colchester*, pp. 212, 215.

11   For further explanation, D. Postles, *Talking* ballocs. *Nicknames and Medieval English Sociolinguistics* (Leicester, 2003).

12   D. Crystal, *The Stories of English* (London, 2004), pp. 161–68 (quotation at p. 168); but compare D. Howard, *The Idea of the Canterbury Tales* (Berkeley, 1976), pp. 106–9. Some contend that Chaucer only intended to give a flavour of northern speech: N. F. Blake, *Non-standard Language in English Literature* (London, 1981), p. 33; S. Horobin, 'J. R. R. Tolkien as a philologist: a reconsideration of the northernisms in Chaucer's *Reeve's Tale*', *English Studies* 82 (2001), pp. 97–105, esp. p. 99 and the reference there to J. J. Smith, 'The great vowel shift in the North of England and some forms in Chaucer's *Reeve's Tale*', *Neuphilologische Mitteilungen* 95 (1995).

13   In this respect (only), then, is visible a recursiveness and recursion of naming which might be construed as structuration or *habitus* in the sociology of Giddens or Bourdieu: R. Peet, *Modern Geographical Thought* (Oxford, 1998), pp. 153–4, 161–2.

14   Although this final elucidation owes much to a general reading of Peet, *Modern Geographical Thought*, it is crystallized by R. Shields, *Places on the Margin. Alternative Geographies of Modernity* (London, 1991), pp. 29–70, although I am more circumspect about the efficacy of binary divides and favour more the complexity of dialogic interactions.

15   *The Riverside Chaucer* (3rd edn, Oxford, 1987), p. 81 ('The Reeve's Tale', l. 4127).

16   D. Postles, 'The poetics and politics of naming in early-modern northern England' (unpublished paper).